Critical Praise for
Investor's Guide to the Net

"Encyclopedic in scope . . . a must read for any Internet investor's library."

—David Brown
Chairman & CEO, Telescan, Inc.

"Paul Farrell has written the TV Guide of Financial Cyberspace with a vision of how financial markets will operate in the future."

—Ivy Schmerken, Editor-in-Chief
Wall Street & Technology

"From institutions to individuals, access to the Financial Markets is undergoing rapid transformation. This is your invaluable roadmap to that changing landscape. Don't navigate without it!"

—William Adiletta, President & CEO
Market Vision Corp.

"Believe the hype: The Internet has the potential to transform business, culture, and economics in profound and fundamental ways. This book provides a provocative and comprehensive guide to bountiful opportunities scattered all across cyberspace."

—Gordon Anderson, Editor
Individual Investor

"Paul Farrell has rendered what is clearly the definitive work on the important and timely subject of investing on the Internet."

—Jay Kemp Smith, Chairman
Leading Market Technologies, Inc.

"I believe that anyone who has interests in the financial world will definitely find this book to be a valuable asset."

—William Eng, author
Technical Analysis of Stocks, Options & Futures

"This book is a must for any investor, beginner to expert, trying to navigate in our new information age, the investor's Megatrends."

—Stephen C. Wendel, President
StockPro Technologies

"Dr. Farrell has brought a perspective to the computer aided investment process that is unique, refreshing, and enlightening."

—Del Blake
American Association of Individual Investors,
Computer Investor Group

The Investor's Guide to the Net

Making Money Online

Paul B. Farrell, J.D., Ph.D.

John Wiley & Sons, Inc.

NEW YORK • CHICHESTER • BRISBANE • TORONTO • SINGAPORE

Library of Congress Cataloging-in-Publication Data:
Farrell, Paul B.
   Investor's Guide to the Net: Making Money Online / Paul B. Farrell,
     p.   cm.
   Includes index.
   ISBN 0-471-14444-4 (pbk.)
   1. Investments—Data processing. 2. Investments—United States—
Data processing. 3. Internet (Computer network). 4. World Wide Web
(Information retrieval system). I. Title.
HG4515.5.F37 1996
025.06'3326—dc20   95-47510

Printed in the United States of America
10 9 8 7 6 5 4 3 2 1

INVESTING ON THE NET . . . YOU HAVE THE POWER

The new source of power is not money in the hands of a few, but knowledge in the hands of many. . . .

The great unifying theme at the conclusion of the 20th century is the triumph of the individual. . . . It is the individual who creates a work of art, embraces a political philosophy, bets a life savings on a new business, inspires a colleague or family member to succeed, emigrates to a new country, has a transcendent spiritual experience.

—John Naisbitt, *Megatrends* and *Megatrends 2000* with Patricia Aburdene

Develop a trust in your intuitive inner voices. . . . If you feel a strong inner inclination to . . . try a particular investment, then place more trust in that hunch. This is your divine guidance encouraging you to take a risk, to ignore the ways of the herd, to be the unique individual that you are.

—Wayne W. Dyer, *Real Magic*

Without going beyond his own nature, one can achieve ultimate wisdom.

—Lao Tsu in Bennett W. Goodspeed, *The Tao Jones Averages*

The great events of the world are, at bottom, profoundly unimportant. In the last analysis, the essential thing is the life of the individual, here alone do the great transformations take place, and the whole future, the whole history of the world, ultimately springs as a gigantic summation from these hidden resources in individuals.

—Carl G. Jung, *Modern Man in Search of a Soul*

Success in trading is a worthy goal, but it will be worthless if it is not accompanied by success in life.

—Jack Schwager, *The New Market Wizards*

Acknowledgments

Cyberspace is the *new frontier* for a new breed of investor—successful men and women driven by a powerful inner voice that says *take charge of your own destiny.*

Financial independence—and the personal freedom that goes with it—is the number one priority of the cyberspace investor. In unprecedented numbers, these new investors are going online and on the Net to take charge of their own investment portfolios—doing their own research, their own analyses, selecting securities, acting as their own broker—*taking total responsibility and control of their future.*

In cyberspace they are discovering an endless supply of *do-it-yourself* resources, plus a strong spirit of individualism and adventure. This is the perfect place for the new *take-charge* investors; here they can create their own economic freedom.

The Investor's Guide to the Net is dedicated to this powerful inner spirit, a drive for personal freedom and financial independence.

In cyberspace, this spirit will achieve its goal.

Special acknowledgment and thanks are due to so many wonderful people who made this book possible, especially:

❑ My friend, Stephen C. Wendel, president of StockPro Technologies, for being there every step of the way, and Jay Kemp Smith, chairman of Leading Market Technologies, and William F. Adiletta, president of Market Vision, for sharing their visions of the future of Wall Street cyberspace investing.

❑ Colleagues in the press and media: Bill Griffeth, CNBC anchor; Sunny Harris, publisher of the *Traders Catalog and Resource Guide;* and Ivy Schmerken, editor-in-chief of *Wall Street & Technology,* for her insights into the information revolution on Wall Street.

- A truly supportive editorial team at John Wiley & Sons, especially Myles Thompson, executive editor; Jacqueline Urinyi, editor; and Jennifer Pincott, editorial assistant, all of whom brought out the best in me while making this book a real joy to write.

- Technical experts Glee Cady of Netcom Communications for her early encouragement and Mike Brown at Inset Systems for his help with the screen capture software. And a special thanks to Netcom for their excellent Web browser.

- Countless marketing professionals and tech support staff who provided us with tons of research information and software.

- The many financial newsletter editors and publishers who have entrusted me with their confidence in recent years.

- All my friends in the program, especially Carmela and Sandy, for planting the seeds at the right time, and nurturing them through all seasons.

- My friend and wife, Dorothy Boyce, for her love, her prayers, and her constant encouragement.

- And to my Higher Power, a loving God, for a life filled with so many wonderful adventures and gifts, especially writing this book.

Contents

Preface   xvii
Introduction   xxiii

1. Emerging Superpowers of Online and Internet Investing

Commercial Online Services for Investors   1
   New Competition: The Internet, Sun, and Microsoft Network   1
   CompuServe: The Merrill Lynch of Online Services   3
   America Online: Your Friendly Neighborhood Shopping Mall   6
   Prodigy: The Wal-Mart of Commercial Online Services   7
   Delphi, Interchange, and GEnie: Struggling Giants   9
The Power Players Creating Wall Street Cyber$pace   11
   Wall Street Cyber$pace: No Longer an Exclusive Club   12
   Dow Jones: The *Real* "America Online" in Cyberspace   14
   Reuters: Cyber$pace's Largest Financial "Exchange"   17
   Knight-Ridder: Cyber$pace Giant in Commodity Futures   19
   Bloomberg: Wall Street Cyber$pace's Newest Powerhouse   21
   Battle Lines: Big Institutions Versus Individual Investors   24
Basic Starter Kit for the New Cyber$pace Investor   27
   Investor's War Room: Go First Class, Buy Ahead of the Curve   28
   The Wall Street Cyber$pace Connection for Investors   30
   High-Powered Software and Tons of Data at Discount Prices   30
   The Internet's Fabulous New Web Browsers   32
   A New Generation of Browsers on the Horizon   36

New Browsers from Grad Students and High-Tech Quants   37
A Basic Wall Street Cyber$pace Library   39

2.   The Internet: Investor's Global Resource Library

Internet Meta-Lists: Links to the World of Investing   41
Meta-Lists: Yellow Pages and Road Maps for the Internet   42
Yahoo: One of the New Baby Bells of Meta-Lists   42
Yahoo: Two Grad Students Having Fun on the Net   44
Yellow Pages and Instant Direct Dialing at No Extra Cost   45
The Internet . . . Breeding Ground for the Next Bill Gates   46
FINWeb: A Texas-Sized Meta-List on Financial Economics   46
Financial Economics for the Serious Investor   48
The Top Investor Meta-Lists at Universities   49
New Commercial Meta-Lists: Investor's Yellow Pages   52
Meta-List from a Computer Users' Group: InvestSIG   52
American Association of Individual Investors' Meta-List   54
Personal Finance at the Global Network Navigator   55
Investment News Online: Brokerage Firm's Meta-List   56
Innovation: European Investment Firm's Meta-List   56
The Wall Street Directory and Your "Money Mentor"   57
Wall-Street-News: Internet Broadcasting Superstation   58
Bookmark! Create Your Own Personal Meta-List   61

3.   News Online: Financial Markets, Money, and Investing

Financial Newspapers: Electronic Publishing Is Here, Today   65
MediaInfo Interactive: "All the News That's Fit to Print"   67
London's *Financial Times:* Setting the Pace on the Web   69
Investor's Business Daily: Delivery on America Online   70
The *Wall Street Journal*'s Personal Journal   71
Market Monitor: Dow Jones Expanding in Cyberspace   74
New York Times' Business Pages on America Online   75
Los Angeles TimesLink: Hotline to Hollywood and Washington   76
San Jose Mercury News: Silicon Valley in a Shrinking World!   77
Dow Jones News/Retrieval and Other Multidatabase Searches   78
Executive News Services: Digests and Clipping Services   81
Executive News Service: ENS at CompuServe   81
Prodigy's "Heads Up" Executive News Service   82
NewsNet: Comprehensive Industry Sector Coverage   82
NewsPage on the World Wide Web   85
Profound: Online for News, Quotes, Searches, and More   85

InfoManager's InfoExpress: Staying Connected Anywhere 86
Farcast News Digest Service: When E-Mail Is Easiest 88
Free Internet News Services: Yahoo and the Newsroom 89
Executive News Services: Luxury or Basic Utility? 90

Newswire Services for Finance, Business, and Investing 95
Associated Press and United Press International 95
Dow Jones Newswire Services 96
Knight-Ridder: Commodities, Options, and Futures 98
Reuters Newswire Services: World News Leader 100
Bloomberg Business News: The Next Generation 101
ClariNet and AP: The Net Investor's "Free" Newswires 102
Foreign Newswires Online and on Internet Meta-Lists 103

Search and Research Tools: Accessing Large Databases 106
Knight-Ridder's Dialog: Searching the Ultimate Database 106
Lexis-Nexis: A Superpowered Database in Cyberspace 108
Commercial Online Keyword Searches 109
Keyword Searching on the Internet 110
Internet Searches: New Superpower Search Engines 112
ProSearch: Sample Search Tool for Stock Market Selections 117
Bottom Line: No One Search Engine Can Do It All 118

Cyberspace Magazines on Finance and Investments 119
The Electronic Newsstand (E-News) 120
NETworth's Investor's Newsstand on the Web 122
Time Warner's Pathfinder: Publisher's Own Newsstand 122
Online Services: The New Electronic Magazine Newsstands 125
Reuters, Dow, and Nexis: Will They Replace Barnes & Noble? 126
Internet Magazines for Professionals and Technicians 128
Internet Magazines Covering Technology and Computers 129
The Future of Magazines Is in Cyberspace 130

Investment Advisory Newsletters on the Net 133
Technical Analysis of Stocks and Commodities 133
Prodigy Online Newsletters: Wall Street Edge 134
AOL's Top Advisors' Corner for Investment Newsletters 135
CompuServe's Financial Advisory Newsletters 137
Financial Newsletters: Start with the Net's Meta-Lists 138
Internet Newsletters: Hot Stocks or Hot Air? 141
Internet Newsletters: Where Is Rukeyser's Wall Street? 142
Wall-Street-News Forecasts 143
Newsletters: By Mail, Broadcast Fax, and 900-Number Hotlines 144
Financial Newsletters: Are They Worth the Price? 146

The Hot New Cyberspace Investment Clubs 147
Special Usenet Newsgroups for Investors Only 148

Online Forums and Discussion Groups for Investors	149
Club Rules: Read the FAQs and Observe Proper Netiquette	150
The Commercialization of the Web's Usenet Newsgroups	152

4. Accessing Major Financial Market Data

United States and Global Securities Exchanges	157
The Chicago Mercantile Exchange	157
American (AMEX) and Philadelphia Stock Exchanges	159
The Other Major U.S. Securities Exchanges	159
Major International Securities Exchanges	161
Securities Exchanges Versus Free Quotes on the Internet	165
Stock Quotes and Market Index Reports: Basic Data	168
Internet: MIT's Experimental Stock Market Data	170
Internet: Ohio State University's Financial Data Finder	171
QuoteCom and Other Quote Sources on the New Web	172
PC Quote: Leading Data Provider to Individuals and Institutions	174
PAWWS: More than Just a Few Free Quotes	174
NETworth: The Website for Mutual Funds Quotes	176
Holt's Stock Market Reports on the Internet	177
InfoManager: Central Data Manager for the Net	178
Internet's Interquote: A Cost Comparison for Quotes	179
Quotes from the Big-Three Commercial Online Services	180
Competition Is Driving Down the Price of Quotes . . . to Zero	184
Bottom Line: Raw Data Versus Analytics and Instincts	185

5. Investment Research and Analysis

Government Economic and Monetary Statistics	189
U.S. Census Bureau's Monthly Economic Indicators	189
University of Michigan's Economic Bulletin Board	191
STAT-USA: Commerce Department's Economic Bulletin Board	194
Business Cycle Indicators: Software from Media Logic	195
Industry Sector and Company Analysis: Fundamentals	198
Hoover's Reports: Profiles of Companies and Industries	198
Dun & Bradstreet's Corporate and Industry Research	202
The Disclosure Database of Public Companies	203
Value Line's Electronic Publishing: Value/Screen	204
Standard & Poor's: The Financial Industry's Standard	205
Fundamental Research with Dow Jones News/Retrieval	206
CompuServe's Company and Industry Sector Analyses	208
Securities Filings: EDGAR, Disclosure, and the SEC	213
The EDGAR Project at New York University	213

The Disclosure Organization Develops EdgarPlus 215
Lexis-Nexis and Required SEC Electronic Filings 216
Dow Jones' Federal Filings Newswire 216

6. Alternative Securities for Online Investors

Mutual Funds: Research, Analysis, and Selection 219
Morningstar Mutual Funds Research Services 220
NETworth's Website: Almost Everything on Mutual Funds 223
MIT's Artificial Intelligence Lab for Mutual Fund Data 224
NYU/Stern School's EDGAR Project and Mutual Funds 225
CompuServe's Online Mutual Funds Services 226
America Online's Mutual Funds Services 227
The Calvert Group: Socially Responsible Mutual Funds 228
Reuters and DJN/R: Competing for the Mutual Fund Investor 229
Reuters Money Network: Mutual Funds and Much More 230
Dow Jones News/Retrieval: The Traditional Leader 232
Fixed-Income Securities: Treasury, Muni, and Corporate 238
America Online: Bond Mutual Funds 240
CompuServe's Bond Market Research Services 242
The Web and the Bond Market: Limited Free Information 243
Professional Bond Traders Need High-Powered Data 246
Commodity Futures, Options, and Precious Metals 248
World Wide Web: A Bright New Face for the Exchanges 251
The Web: A World Market for the New Brokerage Firms 254
Usenet Newsgroups for Commodities and Futures Trading 256
Commodities on the Commercial Online Services 258
Cyberspace Is Old Hat to Professional Traders 260
Knight-Ridder Financial: Cyberspace Leader in Commodities 263
FutureSource: Total Packages for Commodities Trading 265
FutureLink and Futures World News for Traders 266
Bottom Line: Futures and Options = Risk and Stress! 267

7. New Software for Real-Time Trading Systems

New Total-Service Packages for Cyberspace Investors 271
Competition: The Investor's Search for a Total Package 272
Real-Time Data Delivery Systems for Individual Investors 276
Dow Jones News/Retrieval and Reuters Money Network 278
S&P Comstock: The Leaders Rely on Standard & Poor's 279
Data Broadcasting Corporation: Signal and QuoTrek 280
BMI: Bonneville Market Information—First Class 282
DTN Wall Street: "No Computer Needed!" 283

StockQuoter 2: Discount Competition for DBC and DTN 284
Tradeline Electronic Stock Guide 284
Telemet America: A Leader in Radio Technology 285
Dial/Data: Reliable Real-Time Data Delivery to Investors 286
CD-ROM Technology: Historical Data and Telechart 2000 287
Equis' DownLoader for Data Management 289
New Software for Technical Analysis and Trading Systems 291
Telescan Analyzer: Cyberspace Analytical Powerhouse 294
Equis Research: MetaStock, Downloader, and The Technician 296
Omega: Wall Street Analyst, SuperCharts, and TradeStation 298
Windows on WallStreet from MarketArts 301
Aspen Research Group: Software for the Global Investor 302
Specialty Software Systems for Very Special Investors 303
The Lowly Spreadsheet: Are We Going Back to Basics? 305
New Software Battles: Spreadsheets, Chartists, and Quants 307
Individual Investors: Profiting from the New Technologies 310
Bottom Line with Investment Software: Go First Class 312

8. New Electronic Brokers and Portfolio Management

Electronic Trading and Do-It-Yourself Brokerage 315
PCFN: Investment Banker Turns Discount Broker 317
Charles Schwab: Discount Broker Is Full Service Online 318
Fidelity On-line Xpress: FOX Chasing Mutual Funds and Stocks 321
Quick & Reilly: A New Breed of Broker 322
E*TRADE Securities: Global Coverage from Silicon Valley 323
AccuTrade Is Cruising the Financial Superhighway 324
WealthWEB: Aufhauser's Winning Website 325
Lombard's LIST: Unlike Any Online System You've Seen 327
Lind-Waldock: The Nation's Largest Futures Discounter 328
Bottom Line: Will AT&T, Sprint, and MCI Be Your Next Broker? 329
Portfolio Management and Personal Finance Software 330
Home-Banking Revolution: Big Banks, Quicken, and Competition 331
Home-Banking Competition: Computer Associates and Microsoft 332
WealthBuilder from Reuters Money Network 333
TechServe's CAPTOOL: The Professional Choice 335
Bottom Line on Portfolio Management Software 336

9. Alternative Information Systems for Cyberspace Investors

Financial Television and Radio Broadcasting 339
CNBC: National Television for Cyberspace Investors 340
Regional Television: KWHY-TV in Los Angeles 342

Television Networks Moving into Cyberspace   345
Radio Also Delivers Investment News   346
Bottom Line: Local Television Going Worldwide   347
Bulletin Board Systems for Investors   348
American Association of Individual Investors   349
FinComm and the Free Financial Network   350
The BBS of the Future: Strategic Demands and Alternatives   352
Creating a Marketing and Tech-Support BBS for Your Business   353
Bottom Line: Federal Policies Are Commercializing BBSs   354

10. Other Resources for Investors

The New Mental Game: Cyberspace Psychological Coaching   358
The Winning Edge: Investment Games and Simulations   359
Marketing Yourself: Successful Selling in Cyberspace   363
Transactions: E-Cash, Firewalls, Hackers, and Scams   366
Cyberspace Dictionaries of Investment Terms   370
Catalogs, Books, Periodicals, and Software   373

Epilogue   375
Index   379

Preface

The Revolution Bringing Wall Street Online

Alvin Toffler and Marshall McLuhan warned us of an information revolution years ago. Now it's here in full force. Today, from every corner of our world, we're constantly bombarded by data, facts, information. We are overwhelmed by gigabytes coming at lightning speed.

The new billion-dollar high-tech industries of the past decade tell a powerful story: cable television, fax machines, microchips, cellular phones, bulletin board systems, laptops, commercial online services, interactive media, Windows 95, the Internet, electronic brokerage, home banking, E-cash, the Web.

Information revolution, yes . . . and Wall Street is at ground zero.

In the brief period since Vice President Al Gore began promoting the information superhighway, the revolution has moved into high gear, a hot topic with endless coverage in the major business and financial magazines: in *Forbes, Business Week,* and *Fortune,* as well as technical journals, *Technical Analysis of Stock & Commodities, Futures, Individual Investor, Information Week,* and *Wall Street & Technology.*

New technologies are unpredictable. Information, the capital asset of the new economy, appears suddenly in massive doses on microchips, from the minds of minimoguls. Whole new industries arrive virtually overnight. *Forbes* calls it the new gold rush.

Transforming Wall Street for Online Investing

This brings us to a central theme of this book. Wall Street is at the center of the revolution. Last year *Business Week* published a special issue on the "Information Revolution." The headline of a *Forbes* cover story warned that "The Cyberspace Revolution Is Getting Serious." An earlier cover story in *Wall Street & Technology* magazine dubbed it the "Quiet Revolution."

Well, it's quiet no more. Wall Street is now information- and technology-driven, not capital-driven. Nobody really knows who will emerge as the next superpowers of cyberspace, who will be the next Microsoft, the next Mosaic, the next Netscape. Fortunately, we can see a few hints filtering through all the noise and confusion. Here's an overview of the new power structure, with details unfolding later.

New and Expanding Online Services

There is no doubt that CompuServe, America Online, and Prodigy are already powerhouses in cyberspace. All three now have their subscribers hooked onto the Internet's Web. Their customer base is still relatively small, less than 10 million, about 5 percent of the total PC market. Next comes the wild card, Microsoft Network. They could double the existing market, quickly capturing 10 million for themselves. Even that is quite small compared to projections of 100 million hookups to the Internet by 2000. The upside potential is enormous.

The very term *online service* is now being redefined: by home-banking hookups, by magazine publishers offering stock quotes at their Websites, by newswires, and by cable networks. There is a big, hungry, untapped market out there. The estimates are far too conservative. Expect 200 million on the Internet by 2000, using online services.

New Rules for the Cyberspace Investors Club

Wall Street cyberspace is no longer a private club reserved for the big institutional investors. The doors are now open to every individual investor with a computer and a modem. All 52 million stockholders, all 10 million online subscribers, all 175,000 members of the American Association of Individual Investors are now members of this new Cyberspace Investors Club. Membership is now open to every investor on the globe, from Seattle to Singapore, Buenos Aires to Beijing, Madras to Moscow.

New Electronic Publishing and Paperless Newspapers

The print publications and publishers are also prospecting in cyberspace, including major publishers such as the *Investor's Business Daily*, McGraw-Hill's *Business Week*, Dow Jones' *Wall Street Journal*, Time Warner's *Money* and *Fortune* magazines, many with circulations around two million. These traditional-print publishers are pioneers in this new media, and doing a great job. Newswire services and television broadcasters are also delivering more information online.

Newly Involved Regulatory Agencies and Exchanges

Paradoxically, as the central government has backed out of sponsoring the Internet, individual departments and independent agencies are getting more directly into the action. The Securities and Exchange Commission has become one of the leading forces moving investors, traders, and money managers into cyberspace. Soon we'll have a totally paperless market. Electronic filings are required. Paper stock certificates will be optional. And electronic brokers are providing investors with direct links to the exchanges.

Similarly, the exchanges are playing a crucial role here, going online, creating an ever expanding global market. The whole business of trading futures, options, and derivatives has grown exponentially in just a couple decades, made possible by a new level of sophisticated computer software for data delivery and analytics.

New Electronic Banking and Discount Brokerage

Electronic money—paperless bytes on your hard disk or encoded on a microchip or embedded in a plastic credit card that you can transmit directly to and from your PC through a modem or from a public payphone—provides new links to your bank and your electronic broker.

Commercial banks, worried that computer software and telephone companies will end-run the banking system, are jumping into E-cash and E-money with great force to maintain control of all financial transactions. Quicken and its competitions are arming the banking industry with the software necessary for both cyberspace banking and discount trading.

New Technologies for Financial Decision Making

Online investing requires a steady stream of new analytic software, rapid access to massive databases, and real-time information—and gets it, thanks to the constant development of new technologies from computer systems developers. In addition, the big telecommunications firms are accelerating the process with fiber optics, integrated digital networks, and interactive audio-video. Wireless technologies, voice recognition, and superpowered laptops create new freedoms.

Renewed Offline Information Technologies

Many earlier technologies are also discovering new life in cyberspace. Basic satellite, radio, and cable television are competing with online services for the delivery of information to home-based investors in remote areas. Broadcast fax and 900-number hotlines continue their popularity. CD-ROMs can deliver huge databases, helping cyberspace investors avoid long download times. As cyberspace investing becomes more demanding, these offline alternatives are becoming more crucial.

New Private Networks Competing with the Internet

New technologies are encouraging wider use of private, special-purpose networks—IntraNets—separate from the Internet. Reuters' Instinet is one of many such Wall Street cyberspace networks, a privately run global stock market. These networks operate internally, within large organizations, and externally, circling the globe with financial information. Eventually, these new private networks may dwarf the Internet in cyberspace, providing all investors, institutional and individual, with greater access to the most powerful asset in the new world economy: information technology.

Newly Empowered Individual Investors

Armed with all these new resources, empowered by the force of these trends, and driven by a strong sense of self-determination, a new breed of individual investor is emerging. For them, cyberspace investing *is* the new frontier, the new gold rush, the freedom to be yourself, with the opportunity to become financially independent while working at home.

The demographics of the new individual investor have been substantially altered. According to *Wall Street & Technology*, in one brief generation the average age of a market trader has dropped from a 40-year-old in a midlife crisis to a socially-conscious, energetic 26-year-old Generation X entrepreneur.

This new generation is educated, computer literate, financially savvy, and a fiercely independent risk taker with both feet on the ground. They prefer do-it-yourself online tools. Investment- and savings-driven, they understand the shortcomings of 1960s freedoms and the welfare state. They are naturally entrepreneurial, taking responsibility for their future.

The Future of Wall Street Is Online Investing

The number of computers linked to the Internet, especially the Web, is increasing exponentially, from a few million in the late 1980s to 30 million in the mid-1990s to 100 million by the year 2000. The competition for a piece of the action will be fierce.

There are more than 52 million stock owners and over 25,000 publicly traded companies. Mutual funds are growing faster than the number of public companies, with $2.5 trillion invested and over 40 million shareholders. And the fascination with futures, options, and derivatives trading has grown enormously in recent years. Meanwhile, individual and institutional investors alike are demanding more and more information, supported by real-time software systems loaded with user-friendly analytic tools for decision making, portfolio management, and trading.

How will this new world of online investing look in the next five years? If the last five years is any indication, the future of Wall Street cyberspace will push our world way *beyond anything we can imagine:* loaded with investment opportunities and surprises, unpredictable, a superhighway with sudden twists and turns, more like the Indy 500 than the Interstate—an exciting ride for all investors.

On Wall Street cyberspace every investor is on equal footing. Today's investor may be wearing a three-piece suit, managing billions from a New York skyscraper, or wearing khakis on a Montana ranch, making investments from their 4×4, a laptop, and a cellular phone. The Net is leveling their playing field. Today every online investor has a seat on this new global exchange, Wall Street cyberspace.

TEN FORCES SHAPING THE NEW WALL STREET CYBER$PACE

❏ New and expanding online services
❏ New rules for the cyberspace investors club
❏ New electronic publishing and paperless newspapers
❏ Newly involved regulatory agencies and exchanges
❏ New technologies for financial decision making
❏ Renewed offline information technologies
❏ New electronic banking and discount brokerage
❏ New private networks competing with the Internet
❏ New levels of information unpredictability
❏ Newly empowered individual investors

Introduction

Wall Street cyberspace is bigger than the Internet, much bigger. It includes many private networks, databases, online brokers, off-line analytics, software systems, exchanges, publishers, newswires, data vendors, satellite broadcasters, and much more. They are definitely not linked into a single monolithic network, as the Internet and information superhighway mythmakers suggest, and may never be.

The emerging Wall Street cyberspace does include the new technologies and marketing opportunities of the Internet, but in fact this new Wall Street Net is vastly more complex and comprehensive. And as this brave new world of online investing expands further, it is destined to become even more diverse, with many parallel and crisscrossing networks.

Hopefully, with the launching of the Microsoft Network and Netscape's IPO, the high-pitched media hysteria surrounding the Internet has reached its peak. Now we can go about the tough business at hand—developing and integrating the subsystems emerging from this Wall Street cyberspace revolution.

This book is designed to reflect the new structure emerging from the impact of the information revolution on Wall Street. *This revolution is creating a paradigm shift for investors worldwide, a new way of investing.* As a result, we are experiencing a powerful global transformation into the new Wall Street cyberspace.

THE POWER PLAYERS IN A HIGH-STAKES GAME

In Chapter 1 we examine the battle now surfacing between two adversaries that we previously thought were playing on two totally different fields. On one end are the commercial online services aligned with the individual investor.

At the other end, we have the real power players, the institutional investors who created their own private Wall Street cyberspace a few decades ago, *before most individual investors even had computers.* Until recently each side played in different stadiums and different ballparks. But now the game is changing. The rules are blurring. The leagues are overlapping.

The big three online services—CompuServe, America Online, and Prodigy—have been primarily tools to help the individual investor, such as the 175,000 members of the American Association of Individual Investors, and the bulk of the nearly 50 million shareholders on Main Street America.

While all of America has been focused on how the Microsoft Network and Windows 95 would reshape the balance of power in the commercial online arena, the real power players in Wall Street cyberspace continue grinding away in their own "quiet revolution," out of view from the popular press.

In the opening chapter we outline the awesome power of Reuters Instinet, Dow Jones Telerate, Knight-Ridder Financial, and Bloomberg, the "fearsome foursome." These information pioneers and revolutionaries have been in cyberspace for a long time, operating in the background with the usual discreet silence of the Wall Street investment banking world, yet controlling vast wealth, huge fortunes. They have already worn some deep ruts into the information superhighway while digging the foundations for their own information delivery systems.

In a very real sense, the fearsome foursome controls not only Wall Street cyberspace, but the entire information superhighway—everything—beyond the big three, beyond the Internet, beyond even Microsoft. The annual revenues of the fearsome foursome are only $10 billion, less than Microsoft's total, yet in their trading activities they sit at the controls of trillions of dollars every day. They *are* Mission Control, the central command for Wall Street cyberspace. In fact, their 500,000 terminals may control more money in a day than all of AAII's 175,000 members control in a year.

Chapter 1 concludes with a down-to-earth outline of some basic tools necessary to get into the game, the computers, software, modems, printers, browsers, and so forth. This section also includes a list of the five key publications you'll need to stay on top of this rapidly changing field. In a real sense, however, the rest of the book is an amplification of the arsenal necessary to become a successful investor in today's Wall Street cyberspace.

THE NEW COMMERCIAL INTERNET

As we will explore in Chapter 2, the Internet, like the Microsoft Network, is a wild card in the Wall Street cyberspace equation. After 25 years of providing seed capital, the federal government is bailing out, withdrawing its funding . . . and commercialism is taking over like wildfire. At present, the Internet is primarily a lightweight tool for the individual investor, the investor to whom "five free quotes" (a common Internet teaser) might appeal. But that's changing very fast. The heavyweights are arriving.

Some of the best investor-related Internet meta-lists are identified. These electronic road maps function as cyberspace yellow pages, helping you manage the enormous information overload and the chaos inherent in the exploding number of new Websites.

We'll identify both the investor-related meta-lists that evolved at American universities in the recent past as well as the new Internet meta-lists emerging from commercial organizations storming the Internet. The former are disappearing, while the latter are growing exponentially.

THE NEW ELECTRONIC PUBLISHERS: MONEY TALKS

The world of publishing has been upended by cyberspace, and publishers are moving in for the kill. In Chapter 3 you'll see a detailed map of the new world of electronic publishing. The publishing industry obviously loves cyberspace. As the print publishers go electronic and hit the Net, they may soon be replacing the beleaguered television networks as the dominant means of broadcasting.

We know that the financial newswires of the fearsome foursome have been around a while. Along with the Associated Press business and financial coverage, they have been delivering the news in cyberspace for some time. However, what's different is that today a local newspaper such as the *San Jose Mercury News* is being read in China and Russia, thanks to its electronic publication on the Internet's World Wide Web.

We'll also examine several new search tools that are helping the cyberspace investor dig through millions of documents on the Internet and billions of documents that already exist in several private cyberspace databases, vaults, and archives.

The publishing industry has jumped into cyberspace with a passion rivaling the early days of television. Newspapers, newswires, magazines, and financial newsletters are all creating electronic editions . . . because the cyberspace investor wants it this way, as an alternative news delivery system. The investing public is obviously ripe for electronic publishing.

Another major new element of this transformation of the financial-news business is the emergence of new cyberspace investment clubs. These online and Internet forums, newsgroups, conferences, bulletin boards, and chat groups specifically cater to individual investors. Here, news travels quickly through cyberspace from person to person and in small groups bound only by their common interests in finance and investing, totally independent of their physical location on the planet.

NEW GLOBAL EXCHANGES AND MARKET QUOTE SYSTEMS

Wall Street cyberspace is measured in nanoseconds. As we'll see in Chapter 4, the power players want information when it's happening, if not in advance. At a minimum, the power players demand real-time data. Information on a 15-minute delay spells death or the loss of substantial capital—at a minimum, a missed opportunity.

These demands for real-time information are not really new. But what is new is the fact that the exchanges themselves and their oversight agencies are now being forced to play by the rules in this new electronic ball game. As a result we now have electronic filings and settlements, support for electronic trading by modem with minimum broker contact, paperless stock certificates, a de facto abandonment of the Glass-Steagall Act, and so much more. Wall Street truly does exist in cyberspace today.

Recently the press has been gaga over the first round of Internet quote services, with their amusing teasers offering "five free quotes." Now we're already into the next phase, as the discount brokers offer not only quotes, but many other services that come close to resembling what the traditional retail brokers once called full service. Forget free quotes. Today, if you're a big enough player, a broker will give you a Bloomberg free so you can really enjoy the Wall Street cyberspace game.

Next in this paradigm shift the exchanges themselves are likely to begin dealing more directly with the cyberspace investor, sidestepping the brokerage industry. Certainly their new Websites are bringing exchanges around the world right into the individual investor's home.

Simultaneously, the brokerage industry may also sidestep the exchanges by creating more of their own private exchanges, mini-Reuters Instinets, if you will. Of course the fund switching that already exists *within* families of mutual funds is right in line with this concept of the private exchange.

FUNDAMENTAL SECURITIES ANALYSIS IN CYBERSPACE

In Chapter 5 we see the traditional database companies that supply Wall Street with information are rapidly tooling up for the new electronic era, much like the print publishers and news-delivery services. And while this move is not news as far as their internal operations, it is definitely a quantum leap forward from a marketing perspective, as vast new audiences are opening to them both online and on the Internet.

Their databases have been computerized for a long time, in a sense waiting for the cyberspace revolution to open new markets for them. To put it another way,

Standard & Poor's, Hoover's, Dun & Bradstreet, Moody's, Value Line, Disclosure, Lexis-Nexis, Dialog, and other large financial databases have also been hot-wired into cyberspace for years, serving institutional investors. They've had a transaction-based technology in place for some time; now the Internet will increase their marketing and sales reach.

The withdrawal of government support also impacts the availability of free government statistics. Until recently you could get free economic, monetary, financial, and investment data on a number of university-based Internet sites. Now the SEC, the Department of Commerce, and the Bureau of Census, for example, are all pulling back from the universities as information intermediaries. Instead, they are offering the information either directly or through established commercial information companies who are wholesaling and retailing this information for a profit, while the government gets its cut.

MUTUAL FUNDS, FIXED INCOMES, AND DERIVATIVES

Cyberspace Wall Street is having an equally dramatic impact on other sectors of the securities industry, as well as on stocks and equities. For example, in Chapter 6 we see mutual funds now so powerful that Fidelity alone accounts for almost 10 percent of the trading on the NYSE. Also, their shareholders trade and exchange funds internally, keeping it all in the family.

Morningstar, the leader in electronic data on mutual funds, is already out there. In addition to the mutual funds, the major discount brokers are racing into cyberspace, online and on the Internet, trying to capture this new cyberspace investor. Websites are cropping up specifically to serve mutual fund investors. Discount brokers are even making available free real-time information on bonds and mutuals as well as equities.

And certainly one of the more interesting aspects of this revolution is the head-to-head competition for the individual investor client by the institutional side. Reuters and Dow Jones, previously information vendors to the institutional investor and businesses, are now competing for the small investor's business. Both of them are now running ads touting themselves as online services.

Reuters Money Network and the DJN/R Private Investor Edition are aimed at the AAII/CompuServe crowd, and probably getting a share. This is clearly a subtle but powerful shift in the Wall Street cyberspace paradigm, a fundamental blending of two markets previously at opposite poles in the spectrum.

Meanwhile, with the exception of Microsoft, the commercial online services appear to have topped out with the number of content providers they can add. And the content providers are stampeding to create their own private storefronts on the Web, which is a global marketplace much larger than all of the online services put together.

POWERFUL NEW REAL-TIME ANALYTIC SOFTWARE

In Chapter 7 we'll look at the competition among financial data vendors. This competition is intense, and it will become even more so as Wall Street shifts more and more of its trading action onto the information superhighway—to dial-up and online services, to the Web, the Net, and through private trading networks and exchanges. On the electronic street, talk is cheap, and quotes are even cheaper (usually free).

Nevertheless, there are strong reasons for buying market quotes, company statistics and news, and other financial information from an established data vendor, and you'll see just who some of the key players are here. And why the CD-ROM is becoming a time-saving solution to the rapid handling of large databases.

Then there are the new supercharged analytical software systems. With these systems, the individual cyberspace investor now has enormous firepower at his or her fingertips. While hardly duplicating the systems available to the institutional investor, this new firepower gives the individual investor the necessary tools for technical and fundamental analysis of securities, tools that show strong signs of leveling the playing field in Wall Street cyberspace.

Another key element is the trend toward one-stop total packages—the bundling together of newswires, quote data, analytics, trading accounts, and portfolio management is a single system, creating something that in rudimentary form resembles a trader's workstation at one of the major institutional investors. Mutual funds, online services, discount brokers, and software developers are all competing here, targeting the same individual cyberspace Investor with packages such as StreetSmart and Telescan.

Right now the institutional investor still has the more high-powered software available, for analytics, news, and trading, usually costing in excess of ten times the expense of an individual investor's workstation. Key to this firepower is some unique software that interfaces with and integrates multiple real-time applications at a single workstation. While most of the institutions work with computer operating systems other than DOS and Windows, their technology is beginning to filter into the PC world, to individual investors. And the new Microsoft Windows 95 is bound to accelerate this trend, as will the pressure among these software developers to uncover new markets for their supertechnologies.

ELECTRONIC BROKERS AND PORTFOLIO MANAGEMENT

Chapter 8 explores the paradigm shift in the brokerage business, an example of the rising power of the individual investor on Wall Street cyberspace. PC Financial Network, Schwab, Fidelity, E*Trade, Lind-Waldock, and Quick & Reilly are just a few names of the new electronic discount brokers. In addition, the commercial banks are creating bold new partnerships with software developers like Intuit and Microsoft to capitalize on the home banking revolution, further eroding the positions of the retail brokers, and perhaps even the discount brokers themselves as the new cyberspace investor shift into the do-it-yourself brokerage era.

Meanwhile, the traditional retail brokers and investment bankers remain noticeably silent, pausing and digesting the dramatic impact electronic brokerage is having on their business. Hopefully they are restructuring, developing new strategies to deal with the paradigm shift. Meanwhile, the individual investor becomes more and more self-sufficient, competing with the institutional investor.

THE NEW POWER OF FINANCIAL TELEVISION NETWORKS

At present there is only one major national television station, CNBC-TV, feeding financial and business information to the investment community. As we see in Chapter 9, that will change soon, thanks to the Internet. Technology is being developed to carry television, video, sound, and music across the Internet. Then local business and financial stations will be able to reach an international as well as national audience.

Financial television is definitely emerging as a very important resource for the cyberspace investor, all in just one decade. These television broadcasters do a remarkable job of pulling together the best of the financial newswires, newspaper commentaries, press releases, and interviews, while adding solid editorial analysis. For many investors, financial television is their primary resource in the emerging new Wall Street cyberspace.

MENTAL GAMES, SIMULATIONS, E-CASH, AND MARKETING

Chapter 10 covers some miscellaneous loose ends floating around in Wall Street cyberspace, items tied to the rest of the revolution, yet in our peripheral vision at the moment.

The relentless thrust of information racing at lightning speed at the individual players—both the individual investor *and* the institutional trader—is having a major psychological impact: rattled nerves, frustrations, stress. As a result, many traders now find it necessary to work periodically with specialized coaches to create a balanced psyche and restore the mental edge necessary for successful trading.

Investment games and simulations have become surprisingly popular in the Internet culture, similar to the five-free-quotes teasers. Virtual trading with virtual money. In fact, these simulations are an excellent educational tool, a way of honing investment skills, and there are many new opportunities popping up to play these games with hypothetical portfolios.

Marketing is also included. It is a major subject with many who see the Internet as a golden opportunity for new business. Cyberspace is definitely a major lure for many investors with an entrepreneurial drive and some special information to sell. This section also covers various resources currently available and necessary in order to launch a cyberspace business.

We'll also examine the issues surrounding the problems of creating secure commercial transactions on the Internet and in cyberspace, and discuss electronic money and E-cash, the home banking revolution, cyberscams, and problems tied to the privacy and security of personal data—all as they tie into the emerging new Wall Street cyberspace.

CHAPTER 1

Emerging Superpowers of Online and Internet Investing

COMMERCIAL ONLINE SERVICES FOR INVESTORS

The monopoly enjoyed by the three major commercial online services—CompuServe, Prodigy, and America Online—may be fading fast, and not just for the obvious reasons. The Internet's Web, Microsoft Network, and other information vendors (for example, Dow Jones, McGraw-Hill), as well as cable networks, telephone companies, telecommunications giants, magazine publishers, and so many other businesses are offering the big three some serious competition for the cyberspace investor's dollar. Indeed, technological forces appear to be conspiring against much further growth of the existing online services.

All three are in the same vulnerable spot . . . much like the regional shopping malls when a Wal-Mart or a bigger superregional center positions itself in a superior location, with bigger selection, and more fun things to do.

New Competition: The Internet, Sun and Microsoft Network

Microsoft Network is just one example of this trend. Consider the enormous cyberspace purchasing power opening to American business, with less than 10 million subscribers online now. Suddenly . . . up comes Microsoft Network with marketing access to 70 million Microsoft Windows users. Plus, the Internet is *doubling every few months* (that's right, *doubling*) and is estimated to reach 100 million computer terminals by 2000. Some experts say that estimate is entirely too conservative. And with 50 million shareholders in America, the big three are in the same position as were U.S. auto manufacturers when Honda and Toyota invaded American markets.

THE EMERGING NEW CYBER$PACE MARKET

7,500,000 commercial online subscribers
75,000,000 Windows users for the Microsoft Network
Forecast of 100,000,000 computers on the Internet by 2000
52,000,000 shareholders of public companies in America

But don't expect the big three to roll over and die. In fact, they are getting more competitive, offering Internet connections and upgrading their services. America Online is fighting aggressively like a cornered tiger. And CompuServe, for example, already has over 3,000 content providers, compared to perhaps 300 with Microsoft Network when Windows 95 opened for business. So when it comes to serving the specific needs of the investor, the online services are becoming extremely competitive . . . thanks to the Internet, Microsoft, and now Sun Microsystems' new Hot Java software.

INVESTORS' SERVICES ON THE NEW MICROSOFT NETWORK

BestQuote Agency Inc.	Individual Investor Magazine
CNBC-TV	Interactive Data
Cowles Business Media	Knight-Ridder Information
DataTimes	Lexis-Nexis Research
Decision Point	NewsPage
Dun & Bradstreet	TRW Business Information

Plus another 200 initially . . . then they'll probably draw to TMN thousands of the other content providers already on the other commercial online services.

This book will refer to specific services the big three offer for the investor, along with services of every other competitor in cyberspace. But first, let's get an overview of what the big three (CompuServe, America Online, and Prodigy) offer.

Keep an open mind, because if you're not a professional trader or broker, one of the big three may well be perfect for your particular investment needs, while also providing many other services for your family and your noninvestment needs. Whether you're just starting out, or already online with one of the big three, check out what's offered on the others; you may just decide to switch. They'll usually give you a trial period to check them out. Take advantage of it.

CompuServe: The Merrill Lynch of Online Services

Of the three major online services, CompuServe is clearly the premiere service for the serious investor and business executive, starting in 1969. If you join, you'll be in good company. One study showed that 24 percent of CompuServe's subscribers were senior executives with average household incomes in excess of $90,000 annually.

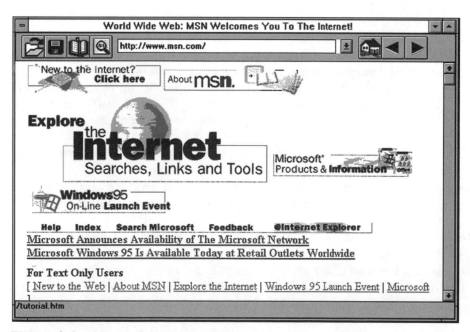

Figure 1.1   Microsoft Network: the newest major online service.

COMPUSERVE'S MASSIVE ONLINE DATABASE

Business News: CompuServe has a clipping service, Executive News Service, to save you time by preselecting only news you want from the newswires, AP, UPI, Dow Jones, Reuters, and other national and world news services.

Expert Opinions: The database includes content from over 500 industry newsletters, 100 regional business publications, as well as reports of more than 100 brokerage and investment research firms. They cover over 8,000 U.S. publicly held companies and 2,000 foreign companies, all the important ones.

Financial Quotes: As you might expect, you can look up ticker symbols and check out quotes for your favorite stocks, commodities, and indexes. Stock quotes are on a 15-minute delay. You can access the 600 market indexes, the DJIA, S&P 500, Nikkei, and whatever else suits you. Ask for and you'll get a host of statistical input, volume, a/d lines, put/call ratios, and more.

Mutual Funds: The *Money* magazine FundWatch is designed to help you screen and analyze over 2,000 mutual funds. Check out the FundWatch "Top Performing Funds."

Historical Database: CompuServe's MicroQuote database is loaded with 12 years of history on more than 125,000 financial instruments: stocks, bonds, mutuals, options, and more, updated daily. There are United States, Canada, and OTC exchanges and foreign currencies. These charts are updated daily to prior day's closing data. Start your day by looking at the previous day's activity, by major markets, including most actives.

Global Companies: From databases such as D&B and various foreign databases, including the *Financial Times* Analysis Reports Europe.

Fundamental Analysis: There are over 10,000 companies in the database, with the usual selection criteria: historical growth, financial ratios, book and market valuation, cash flow, sales, income, etc. Try the CANSLIM formula of Bill O'Neil, *Investor's Business Daily*'s publisher, and other methods to screen your portfolio.

Technical Analysis: If you're interested, you'll need additional software for timing turning points in the market and for particular stocks.

Trading Online: Through CompuServe you can set up an account with E*Trade, Quick & Reilly, or other brokers, and make online portfolio trades at a discount.

Investors' Games: Want to test your skill at managing a portfolio? E*Trade will give you $100,000 in game money and a couple of games.

Discussion Forums: CompuServe has a variety of chat groups for investors.

Nonfinancial Resources: All the other services on CompuServe, such as travel, entertainment, sports, health, cooking, etc., are outlined in detail in such books as L. O'Loughlin's *Free Stuff from CompuServe* (Coriolis Publishing).

For the demanding cyberspace investor, CompuServe is one stop shopping at its online best, with over 3,000 content providers and 3 million customers to prove it. Your family may want to subscribe to Prodigy or America Online for family and fun stuff, but *you* can rely on CompuServe for most of your investment needs. Besides, they do have a lot of noninvestment services that give balance to their subscribers.

CompuServe has a huge database, thanks to their parent company, H&R Block, the tax preparation giant for whom CompuServe generates annual revenues of over $500 million. It's easy to get lost in CompuServe because there's so much information. So be careful: you pay for just about every bit of data you click on or download.

There are a few classic horror stories about CompuServe subscribers getting stuck with charges of $1,000. However, if you take the time to read their complex billing schedule and watch how you select services, using the offline planning where possible, you'll probably coast by with a modest $20 to $40 monthly bill. And you can help yourself by using the CompuServe File Finder CD to search files *offline first;* then you'll minimize online

Figure 1.2 CompuServe's hot new Website.

time by going directly to the required material . . . zip and you're on and off in minutes. So don't let any fears about hidden costs make you take something less than you really need for successful investing.

Bottom line: CompuServe is a five-star winner. They are a one-stop shopping center for most investors. You may want to add a separate Internet connection to save a few bucks on E-mail and Web surfing. You will also need more sophisticated software for technical analysis. And you may want to upgrade to a real-time service later. For most investors, though, CompuServe is an excellent choice. Start by visiting CompuServe's Website, and call for their promotional materials.

America Online: Your Friendly Neighborhood Shopping Mall

America Online (AOL) expanded rapidly with a great marketing program . . . giving away free software in just about every magazine ever published (or so it seemed). We must have collected about 20 free disks. As a result, in about a year AOL's circulation jumped substantially to rival CompuServe. They have user-friendly and eye-catching graphics. When it comes to investment services, AOL may not be in the same class as CompuServe, but they've got more than the basics, and they're improving all the time.

AOL has an excellent Personal Finance section. Check out CompuServe at the same time. You'll either need its extra power, or you will discover that AOL is just fine for now. What AOL has may very well suit your purposes, and the price is reasonable. Here's the good news about America Online (lots of good news).

America Online actually has few faults. It's like a great big regional mall, serving your whole family's needs. It's excellent if you're looking for one service to satisfy everyone. AOL isn't in the same league as CompuServe or Dow Jones when it comes to pure investor-oriented services, but they're not trying to compete with them.

Bottom line: AOL is a *must-try.* They are very likely to serve the needs of a majority of America's investors. But first, do a little comparison shopping for a month. Explore CompuServe, Dow Jones News/Retrieval, and the other services discussed later, such as Telescan, Reuters Money Network, or StreetSmart. In this rapidly changing cyberworld, you *must* explore all new opportunities. Just don't be surprised if you wind up ordering more than one.

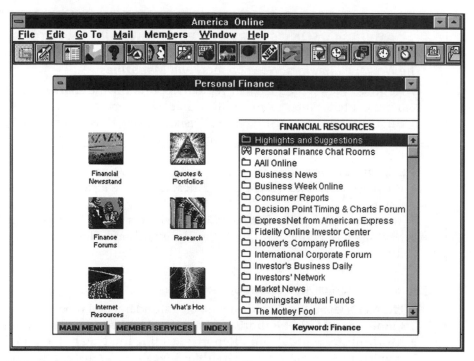

Figure 1.3 America Online's Personal Finance menu.

Prodigy: The Wal-Mart of Commercial Online Services

Maybe Prodigy isn't quite in the same league as CompuServe, Dow Jones, and even America Online when it comes to financial services, but they do serve a basic meat-and-potatoes menu that may well suit many investors just fine.

Prodigy certainly doesn't make any pretense about who they are. They are a family-oriented online service, with solid news, sports, entertainment, and shopping options. Backed by Sears and IBM, Prodigy has a clear picture of their target audience, and they go after them with a user-friendly system that's color-coded to make it easy for anyone in the family to identify Prodigy's major sections. That way you quickly know whether you're in the financial section or the sports pages.

When it comes to financial information for investors, it may be more than adequate for most families. Prodigy Business/Finance section has been highly rated by *Individual Investor* magazine. Their upgraded Investment Center offers solid investor services: business and financial news,

AMERICA ONLINE'S SERVICES FOR INDIVIDUAL INVESTORS

The News: Newswires, Newspapers, and Magazines

- ❏ **Reuters:** Newswires feed in regular reports on the markets, stocks, bonds, interest rates, commodities, gold, the economy—you name it.
- ❏ **Business Newspapers:** *Investor's Business Daily.* Plus you get the business sections of the *Chicago Tribune* and the *New York Times.* Excellent news.
- ❏ **Nightly Business Report:** Analysis of business/financial news.
- ❏ *Business Week* and *Worth* **magazines:** Extensive articles from current issues.
- ❏ **Top Advisers Corner:** Summary of newsletters from 15 market experts.
- ❏ **Mutual Funds:** Includes both the Vanguard and Fidelity families of funds.

Analysis: Market and Company Research

- ❏ **Hoover's Company Profiles:** First-class fundamental reports.
- ❏ **Quotes and Market Reports:** On specific stocks, funds, and indexes.
- ❏ **Morningstar Mutual Fund Reports:** Leading fund analyst, top flight.
- ❏ **American Association of Individual Investors:** A must for the investor.
- ❏ *Inc. Magazine's* **E-Zone:** For the new entrepreneurial spirit.

Forums and Discussion Groups

- ❏ **Motley Fool:** A very popular section. Users love its witty approach. A strange cross between a Dan Dorfman segment, Louis Rukeyser's talk show, and a Tony Robbins infomercial. Or an Irish pub. There's a real online portfolio with trades announced the prior day, stock tips, helpful investors forums, beginner courses, no-nonsense library, and more.
- ❏ **Technical Analysis:** The Wall Street SOS forum uses Telescan as their primary analytical process. You can also learn all about Telescan yourself. Read David Brown's book, *Cyber-Investing.* He's the president of Telescan. SOS has some excellent materials, top stocks, top funds, Bull/Bear index, etc.; the ads obscure the good stuff.

stock and fund quotes, most active stocks, company fundamentals, stock selection techniques, national and global market data, closing prices, online trading, technical analysis, and a lot of forums. Finance may not be Prodigy's main focus; nevertheless, Prodigy offers a great basic menu, complete with such features as Kiplinger's online, Stock Hunter, Strategic Investor, and an excellent financial newsletter service, Wall Street Edge.

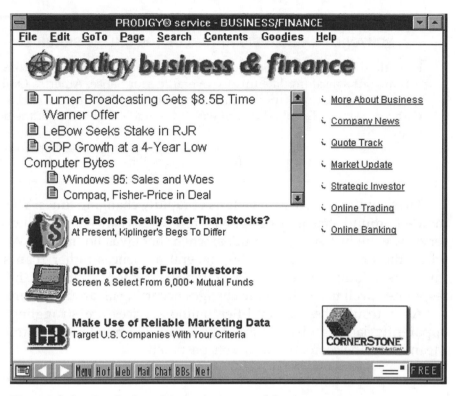

Figure 1.4   Prodigy's solid new Investment Center.

Bottom line: Prodigy is a good place to experiment with an online service. A sophisticated investor is likely to want more. But if you have a family, you may need Prodigy to help them take their first steps into the superworld of cyberspace.

Delphi, Interchange, and GEnie: Struggling Giants

If you're serious about investing, you'll quickly see that the other online services aren't quite in the same league as the big three today, which is partially reflected in the differences in their subscriber bases. For example, the big three each claim 2 to 3 million paid subscribers, while the next three have less than 10 percent of that.

You would think that with the powerful backing of Murdoch's News Corporation (Delphi), General Electric (GEnie), and AT&T/Ziff-Davis (Interchange), success would be guaranteed. But so far the dream has not been realized with this second tier. And the competition is pulling away, which is quite unfortunate for the public.

PC WORLD MAGAZINE'S RATING OF THE ONLINE SERVICES

How do the computer experts rate the online services? Well, in mid-1995 it came out something like this for overall performance. America Online got an A– while CompuServe came up with a B+. Prodigy squeaked by with a passing C. Delphi did well with a C– grade. GEnie was at the bottom with a D.

(SOURCE: Judy Heim, "Best Online Services," *PC World,* June 1995.)

These online services are victims of rapidly changing times. They were molded around strategies designed a few short years ago . . . when online services were just overgrown BBSs, when there was no Internet Web, and when the onlines were targeting general audiences rather than serious investors (CompuServe and Dow Jones excepted). But they have not responded well to the dramatic changes occurring all around them.

As a result, these second-tier online services are struggling today, apparently lacking visions, identities, and a commitment of resources. Meanwhile, the competition rockets past them.

PRESENT AND FUTURE SUBSCRIBERS OF ONLINE SERVICES

	Estimates in millions		
	1995	*1997*	*2000*
Microsoft	0.7	2.4	2.1
America Online	2.2	2.8	1.7
CompuServe	2.2	2.3	1.4
Prodigy	1.4	1.3	0.9
All Others	0.7	0.8	0.6
Total	7.2	9.6	6.7

(SOURCE: Forrester Research, Cambridge, quoted in *Inc. Technology* magazine, August 1995.) These are only forecasts. Remember, Microsoft has 65 million Windows users.

Bottom line: At least get their literature and check them out. Cyberspace is so dynamic you can't write anyone off. Keep an open mind. One of them is bound to surprise us, big time . . . the most likely being Delphi. Why? With the new joint venture between Delphi's parent, Rupert Murdoch's News Corporation, MCI, the giant telephone company, and the licensing of the Netscape browser, we can expect this new venture to give AOL and the competition, including Microsoft Network, a run for the money . . . or they may all soon go the way of the Studebaker and Edsel.

More important, with MCI and AT&T actively involved, we can anticipate the entry of other aggressive telecommunications companies in this competition. Given their enormous technological and capital resources, there is a reasonably high probability these giants will take over the role of the commercial online services. That, plus the incredible success of the World Wide Web, may soon make the online services quaint relics in the rapidly unfolding history of telecommunications.

THE POWER PLAYERS CREATING WALL STREET CYBER$PACE

For the past couple of years the public has been inundated with stories about the new information superhighway, cyberspace, and the information revolution. In early 1994, Vice President Al Gore popularized the phenomenon, giving this new industry a massive shot in the arm. Since then, the Internet and its related tools have acquired the status of a never ending premiere for a Spielberg film. Hardly a day goes by without yet another article touting the entertainment, if not commercial, opportunities on this new media. The public can't get enough . . . as the number of online subscribers and Internet connections *doubles every few months.*

The power players: everybody's heard of Dow Jones, and probably Reuters and Knight-Ridder, right? But Bloomberg, who the heck's

---

WILL THE INTERNET KNOCK THE ONLINE SERVICES OFFLINE?

Pioneers don't always win. CompuServe, Prodigy, and America Online may be crowded out in the battle for cyberspace.

(SOURCE: Nikhil Hutheesing, "Who Needs The Middleman?," *Forbes*, August 28, 1995.)

Microsoft is launching MSN when content providers are swarming to the Internet's World Wide Web . . . Microsoft is playing yesterday's game.

(SOURCE: Kathy Rebello and Paul M. Eng, "Microsoft's Online Timing May Be Off," *Business Week*, July 10, 1995.)

Bloomberg? Well, the big-time professional investors know, even if the public has only a vague inkling of what any of these powerhouses are doing in cyberspace.

These high-powered information services companies exist primarily because institutional investors such as Merrill Lynch and the J. P. Morgan bank, for example, each spend almost $1 *billion* annually on information. *That nearly equals the total revenues of all the online companies.* And that's only two institutions, and only 5 percent of their revenues. The big players spend huge sums on information.

However . . . the fact that most of the new online public doesn't even consider Dow Jones and Reuters as online services (like America Online or Prodigy) and, more important, the fact that Bloomberg is virtually anonymous to these online customers brings up a major issue in the emerging competition to supply information to the emerging new cyberspace investor.

Wall Street Cyber$pace: No Longer an Exclusive Club

The *real* big players supplying high-powered information to high-stakes investors are often ignored by today's popular press. That's understandable for two reasons. In the first place, *the institutions have been in cyberspace for decades,* quietly creating their own *private* "third market" in cyberspace, trading billions of dollars daily, way ahead of the online services. Dow Jones has been an electronic publisher for decades, since the time of the Apollo missions. The commercial online services are babies when it comes to the real leaders in Wall Street cyberspace.

SUPERPOWERS IN THE CYBERSPACE INFORMATION GAME

	Reuters	Knight-Ridder	Dow Jones	Bloomberg
Revenues*	$3.5 billion	$2.5 billion	$2.2 billion	$1.0 billion
Terminals	300,000	45,000	100,000	50,000
Employees	13,500	20,000	10,000	2,300
Editorial	1,650	4,500	1,000	400
News Bureaus	120	105	50	55

*AOL's annual revenues for 1996 have been estimated to be $1.2 billion; and the CompuServe division of H&R Block contributes over $500 million in annual revenues to the parent company.

Second, these information vendors may not appear to have as many subscribers or "terminals" as the popular commercial services, and don't even seem to be interested in the same markets. But then, they don't need as many subscribers to turn a profit. Their services can cost $1,000 to $2,500 a month, versus $10 to $20 a month for one of the commercial online services. Thus, even Bloomberg's 50,000 terminals are generating more revenue than the 3 million subscribers on America Online (which isn't very profitable). And the big players don't offer much stuff for the family, kids, and Net surfers.

Obviously this ballpark is for the serious, sophisticated investor, the day-trader, brokerage firms, and money managers playing with millions and billions. But surprisingly they are beginning to offer limited services for the smaller investor who wants to go first class on a budget, with the option of trading up later. Let's take a closer look at these Wall Street cyberspace leaders.

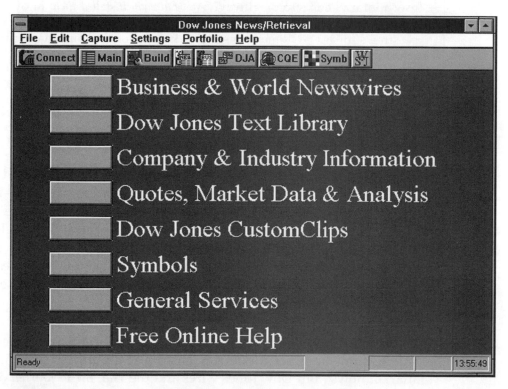

Figure 1.5   Dow Jones News/Retrieval's online services.

Dow Jones: The *Real* "America Online" in Cyberspace

The Dow Jones information services are so vast it is unfair to call them an "online" service (although they are delivered online), and certainly unfair to compare them to the online competition, except perhaps CompuServe. Their database and their analytical tools are so vast that the commercial online services just can't compete when it comes to investor services. Dow is truly the leader when it comes to coverage of the global financial markets.

THE ORIGINAL CYBER$PACE EXPLORERS AND ADVENTURERS

Dow Jones Telerate and the other major power players in the information services business—Reuters, Knight-Ridder, and Bloomberg—virtually created cyberspace many years before the PC was a household utility and a basic tool of the individual investor. They had created their own private cyberspace. And Telerate's ads attest to this claim: "Looking for tomorrow's information superhighway? *We've already installed them* in over 30 countries."

In a similar way Reuters Instinet is known for the third market they created for investors and traders with their global electronic network. Only CompuServe's history and performance is modestly competitive. Today these superpowers of information are all expanding to provide information services to the individual investor.

(SOURCE: *Wall Street & Technology's 1995 Buyer's Guide.*)

Their markets are also different. Dow Jones is niche-marketed to the big business and financial community, while the online services—in particular Prodigy, America Online, and Microsoft Network—are mass-market-oriented, targeting the needs of the whole family. And while Dow Jones probably leans more toward large institutional investors, professional brokers, and full-time traders, they still publish the *Wall Street Journal* electronically at a modest price and offer other lower-priced services. Here's a sketch of their major services:

❑ *Wall Street Journal's* **Personal Journal.** An entirely new electronic publication designed to deliver customized business and financial market news from Dow Jones wires and the *Wall Street Journal* directly into a subscriber's personal computer. Includes *Journal's* quotes, sports, weather, and entertainment as well financial news. A high-value-added bargain.

❏ **Dow Jones News/Retrieval.** Here's the Tiffany of the information business. This is the one service in the world that delivers the full text of *Wall Street Journal,* the *New York Times,* London's *Financial Times,* and the *Nikkei Telecom Japan News,* along with 1,500 other publications. You get the *Los Angeles Times, Washington Post,* along with smaller newspapers and magazines such as *Time, Business Week, Forbes, Fortune, The Economist,* etc. You get the electronic editions long before the print deliveries, and you can use their CustomClip service to scan and send you selected articles. For the active trader, Dow Jones' Tradeline service keeps you on top of information about 25,000 actively traded issues and another 25,000 on foreign exchanges.

❏ **Dow Jones Market Monitor.** Designed specifically for the active private investor: securities and funds data, corporate reports, earnings estimates, market quotes, historical pricing, and performance analysis for trading, plus market-making news, research reports, national and international articles and columns. All this plus built-in screening techniques to help isolate investment opportunities; includes discounts on the Dow Jones technical analysis and portfolio management software packages. Market Monitor is a flat-fee ($30), online service that's competitive with CompuServe. If you can live with an off-peak-hours service, this will work for you. Also referred to as DJN/R Private Investor Edition.

❏ **DowVision.** Dow Jones experts will tailor news-delivery systems from their vast database to an internal network within a large corporation, in real time and customized to each separate workstation and department. Subscribers can tap into all Dow newswires, press release services, the *Journal,* and other resources.

❏ **Dow Jones Telerate.** One of the largest suppliers of real-time information to market professionals in 85 countries. In fact 60 percent of their income comes from foreign operations. Their Trading Room Systems and workstations provide sophisticated analytical and decision-making tools linked through worldwide networks. Telerate covers all major exchanges, markets, and securities—all 150,000 securities.

❏ **Dow Jones News Services.** The nation's premiere supplier of business and financial news to brokerage firms, banks, investment firms, and businesses. This division has five newswires, including Federal Filings and the Capital Market's Report.

❑ **Dow Jones Investor Network.**   A video business-news service delivered direct to customer terminals; exclusive interviews with business leaders, corporate events, etc.

❑ **Dow Jones Newspapers, Magazines, and Radio.**   Print publications of the *Wall Street Journal* with 1.8 million subscribers, plus European and Asian editions, the prestigious *Barron's* newspaper, and *Smart Money* magazine; also, syndicated radio. Dow Jones even has a group of general-interest daily community newspapers with a circulation of about 550,000.

❑ **Dow Jones Software Products.**   Not the kind you're going to buy off the shelf at your local software discounter, but some high-powered tools for major corporations.

Because the *Wall Street Journal* and *Barron's* are print publications, Dow Jones' public image is one of a traditional print publisher. They may look stodgy and conservative, but in fact Dow Jones has been a leader in cyberspace for a long time. Before NASA put men on the moon, Dow Jones

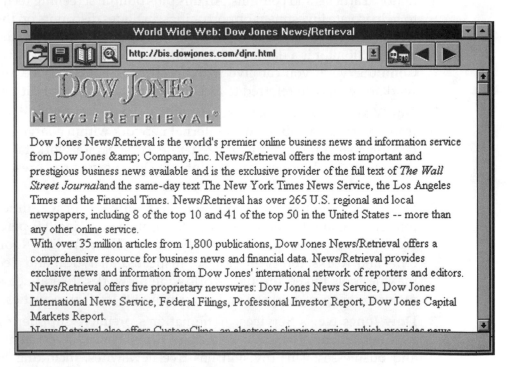

Figure 1.6   Dow Jones News/Retrieval Website.

was pioneering cyberspace, with its international newswires and elaborate network of reporters and client workstations throughout the world, now linked by satellite, with an Indiana Jones spirit. Today, *Smart Money*'s slick look better illustrates the Dow spirit than the staid appearance of the newspapers. Investors: keep tabs of Dow's next moves in cyberspace; you will learn something.

Bottom line: Dow Jones is first-class financial information of all kinds. Get their detailed brochures, and bookmark their Websites for future updates.

Reuters: Cyber$pace's Largest Financial "Exchange"

British-based Reuters is the single largest information service in the world, and perhaps the oldest, with an esteemed heritage dating back to 1851. And what a history. In the early years their reporters covered Lincoln's murder and Napoleon's speeches. Reuters' annual revenues exceed $3.5 billion.

THE QUIET REVOLUTION . . . BILLIONS TRADING PRIVATELY

The birth of passive matching systems like . . . Instinet Corp.'s The Crossing Network are finally giving money managers what they want—anonymous matching, low transaction costs, and no market impact. Executions are bypassing the block trading desks. Could the NYSE floor become a museum devoted to vintage technology?

(SOURCE: Ivy Schmerken, Editor-in-Chief, "Wall Street Revolution," *Wall Street & Technology*, June 1992.)

* * * * * * *

Reuters Instinet is one big private cyberspace trading network, complete with opportunities to make new connections . . . big connections for billions in trading. Nobody outside knows for sure, but with Fidelity trading $1.5 billion a day, and $1 trillion traded on the Chicago Mercantile Exchange each day, private networks or mini-exchanges like Instinet could well be trading at least $1 billion daily, all quietly and privately outside the public eyes, out there in cyberspace.

The Wall Street *private club mystique* is changing, however, with the rising power of the individual investor. Today, individual investors can tap into this private network through *discount brokers* such as Aufhauser & Company. You can explore this new opportunity through their Wealth Web site at http://www.aufhauser.com.

Today they have 300,000 terminals linked to the Reuters' electronic network in 149 countries, operated by 13,500 employees. Their stated mission: to "inform the world instantly by the latest electronic means [and] help our customers to analyze the facts and trade on them." Reuters has three principal product areas:

❐ **Media Services.** Reuters delivers the news on politics, economics, business, finance, arts, sports, science, and general interest to newspapers, television, radio, governments, and private institutions everywhere. Reuters delivers text, photos, and graphics by newswires, directly and through national news organizations.

❐ **Information Services.** Real-time information, historical databases, and analytical software technology covering 217 international exchanges and OTC markets with 1,630 reporters, including foreign exchange, money, commodities, securities, bonds, energy, and shipping markets. The news is delivered in 18 different languages. Seventy percent of Reuters' holdings come from this area.

❐ **Instinet Transaction Services.** Reuters also creates a private market for traders hooked into their international Crossing Network. Their Globex joint venture includes the Chicago Merc and Chicago Board of Trade as partners, to match futures and options trades outside of normal hours. Their Instinet subsidiary operates as an information exchange and trading system for global equity transactions, providing market data, and matching buy-and-sell orders. Instinet has affiliate members on every major stock exchange in the world.

Reuters should be a familiar name to online subscribers, as it serves investors on the commercial online services, America Online, and Prodigy, although rather quietly reserved, in true British tradition. In its annual report, Reuters lists Bloomberg, Dow Jones Telerate, and Knight-Ridder as their principal competitors in the area of information products. There is no mention of CompuServe, AOL, and Prodigy as competitors, so apparently their attorneys saw no legal reason to conclude that the online services were serious competition . . . yet.

Bottom line: Get Reuters' brochures, especially on Reuters Money Network, find out what services they're offering individual investors. Even though Reuters' Instinet is not in the same online league as the so-called big three, you can buy a reasonably priced basic package of news and

Figure 1.7   Reuters: world's largest financial information network.

quotes from Reuters Money Network, which is certainly competitive with the Dow Jones News/Retrieval and CompuServe's basic package. They have the biggest global news service because they help their customers make money. And Reuters can probably help you, too.

Knight-Ridder: Cyber$pace Giant in Commodity Futures

Knight-Ridder Financial is part of the Knight-Ridder organization, the $2.5 billion publishers of the *Philadelphia Inquirer, Miami Herald, Detroit Free Press, San Jose Mercury News,* and 22 other newspapers. Their reporters have won over 60 Pulitzer Prizes.

Knight-Ridder Financial's reputation is built on supplying data and analytical tools to active traders and institutional investors rather than to the average investor with stocks, bonds, and mutual funds. KRF provides these clients with news services, along with real-time and historical prices, market data, and analytical services. KRF covers money markets, government and corporate debt, foreign currencies, commodities, futures, options, and derivatives. They also specialize in the Asian equities markets. Some key products and services of KRF include:

❏ **MoneyCenter.**   Real-time workstation for news, quotes, and charts.

❏ **ProfitCenter.**   Options analysis, test alternatives/risk management.

❏ **TradeCenter.**   High-powered technical analysis in real time.

❏ **DataKit.**   The basic end-of-day package with a year of quotes in 40 markets, Supercharts or MegaTech Chart software, KR-Quote communications software, KRF news services, and DataDisk with 10 years of futures data on 40 markets.

❏ **SmartNews.**   Timely reporting plus expert analysis and commentary.

When it comes to world commodities and financial information, KRF has no equal. They have one of the most complete coverage of "future prices, cash quotes, spot news and analysis—from Midwest grains to Mideast oil, Australian copper to Argentinean soybeans . . . the impact of a frost on the Florida orange crop, or the outlook for freight costs after strikes in French ports."

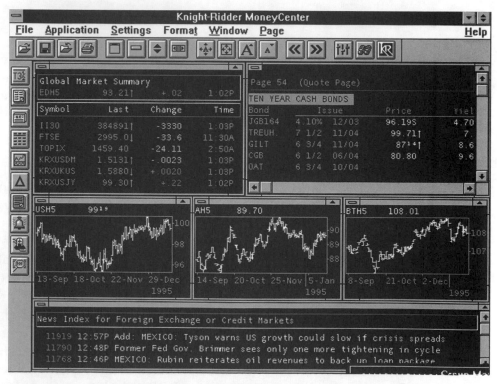

Figure 1.8   Knight-Ridder Financial: KRF Money Center.

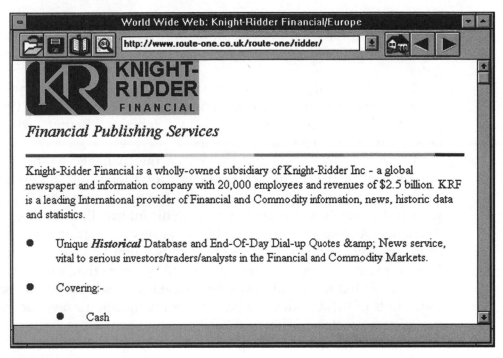

Figure 1.9   Knight-Ridder Financial Publishing.

Knight-Ridder also has other valuable products to serve the investment community. They recently purchased Dialog, one of the world's two largest document search systems with over 330 million documents in 450 databases. They also own the prestigious Commodities Research Bureau, 14 newspapers, including the *Philadelphia Inquirer* and the *Detroit Free Press,* and much more operating under the Knight-Ridder Financial organization.

Bottom line: If you're interested in the commodities, options, futures, and derivatives, Knight-Ridder Financial is your window to the world. Definitely get more information; KRF delivers.

Bloomberg: Wall Street Cyber$pace's Newest Powerhouse

According to a *Forbes* magazine article, after Michael Bloomberg got fired from the Salomon investment banking (for telling his boss that he could "run the goddam company better"), Bloomberg jumped into the hot new field of providing computerized information to securities traders . . . to Wall Street cyberspace. Bloomberg knew well what Dow Jones and other data vendors had to offer and he knew he could beat them at their own game.

This brash young banker/computer genius had to face overwhelming odds against such formidable and entrenched adversaries as the venerable patriarchs of business information as Dow Jones and Reuters, which have been around for over a hundred years.

Bloomberg welcomed and thrived on the challenge, "Whenever you see a business that's done the same way for a long time, a new guy can come in and do it better. I guarantee it." Sounds like another Ted Turner, who at the time was also tooling up with his information empire.

So in 1982 Bloomberg started his news service, putting up $10 million of his money (a retirement package from Salomon) plus $30 million from Merrill Lynch. Before long he was providing more than just raw market data. He added news and developed some highly sophisticated analytical tools. Lots of them. Today the Bloomberg organization's revenues are estimated at more than a billion dollars, and climbing.

Bloomberg's strategy is to give their customers all the information they need in one centralized format and then work directly with them, helping them utilize it to make money.

The core of Bloomberg's business is The Bloomberg, a "real-time financial information network." That's right, they call it *The Bloomberg*. Customers use his proprietary terminals, 50,000 terminals used by more than 150,000 investment decision makers, in over 60 countries worldwide.

Bloomberg covers all major global securities markets, including equities, money markets, currencies, municipal, corporate and Eurobonds, mortgage-backed securities, commodities, derivatives, and government issues. They have a huge database filled with information from insiders as well as superior tools for analysis: "Bloomberg users have the ability to consider alternatives and evaluate scenarios through The Bloomberg's unique analytical capabilities."

In addition, Bloomberg's rapidly expanding empire also offers a major broadcasting network for the sophisticated investor:

❐ **Bloomberg Business News.** For round-the-clock coverage of global news about governmental, corporate, business, and financial markets: 250 reporters in 45 bureaus instantly alerting customers of developments that can impact their decisions.

❑ **Bloomberg Information Network.** Information is also released through syndicated television programming, direct television, their radio station in New York City, newsletters, and magazines—1,500 news stories daily, including sports and entertainment news coverage. Bloomberg also supports an executive interview forum, a unique service to help customers reach institutional investors.

BLOOMBERG'S SUPERANALYTICS: NEW GUYS DOING IT BETTER

Forbes magazine wrote, "Bloomberg knew that every second a trader loses looking up information can cost thousands of dollars. So he packed all the basics into easy reference form. More important, he jammed the machine full of complex calculations that enable traders to determine the relative values of securities . . . users will tell you they love it. . . . A single screen on a corporate bond, for example, might contain 40 separate nuggets of information arrayed around a central chart of up-to-the-minute prices for that bond—everything a harried trader or portfolio manager needs for a snap decision. . . . If a broker calls with a hot stock tip, with three or four keystrokes on the Bloomberg a customer can summon up any one of at least 63 screens full of information on that stock . . . each screen opens new possibilities."

(SOURCE: Richard Stern and Jason Zweig, "A New Guy Can Do It Better," *Forbes*, November 25, 1991.)

Bottom line: If you're serious about making some money in the stock markets and confident of your abilities, call Bloomberg and get the full presentation of what they have to offer. You'll be amazed at their energy, depth, and coverage. If you don't explore this road along the information superhighway, you may be automatically limiting your upside potential by choosing a less sophisticated system.

Yes, you need a higher breakeven point to justify Bloomberg's services. But you'll be in the big leagues, where the big money is played and made, armed with better tools for winning. Bloomberg may soon be bigger than Dow Jones, Reuters, and Knight-Ridder because their product may be more sophisticated.

Finally, given the dynamic nature of the evolving new Wall Street cyberspace, it's very probable that Bloomberg may soon be offering a wider selection of lower-cost services for the smaller investor, as do Reuters and Dow Jones, to better capitalize on the powerful analytical tools

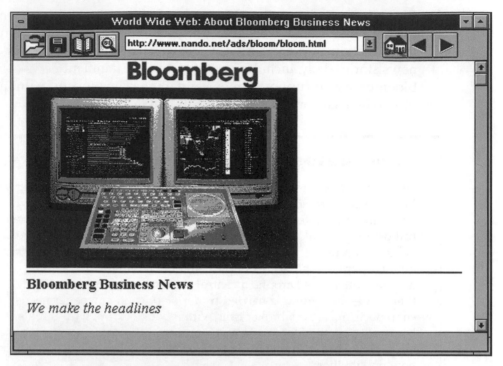

Figure 1.10   Bloomberg Business News: new Wall Street leader.

and database they control. A hint of this comes in their radio and television efforts as well as Bloomberg's joint venture with Applix, the developer of some excellent quantitative analytics and graphics software for real-time trading systems. Eventually, as Bloomberg's technology broadens and the market as a whole becomes more sophisticated, you can expect them to target the individual investor market more aggressively.

Battle Lines: Big Institutions Versus Individual Investors

As you read about how Dow Jones, Reuters, Knight-Ridder, and Bloomberg target the larger institutional and corporate clients, keep in mind that the smaller investors are becoming a larger share of the information market. Today, even these giants are starting to take the individual investor more seriously, and may eventually be a bigger threat to the big three commercial online services than Microsoft Network.

There is a huge information-buying market out there, and you'll see why we expect that the big information suppliers will soon be offering more services to the investor who is now on America Online for $9.95 a month and a $49 a year member of American Association of Individual Investors.

While it is very easy for an individual investor to dismiss Dow Jones and the other giants on price alone, don't make that mistake. Of course many of the services offered by these heavy hitters are designed more for the big corporations and institutional money managers, but they are beginning to develop effective lower-priced alternatives.

For example, the AOL/AAII customer is not their typical large institutional client, but the information demands of this consumer market are expanding rapidly. And Reuters, in a bold, aggressive move, has already accelerated this exciting new trend with their Reuters Money Network. It's virtually guaranteed that they will become even more aggressive, forcing their competitors to make similar bold moves.

THE DYNAMICS OF CHANGE ON WALL STREET CYBER$PACE

❑ **Fact** . . . that the Internet will triple in the next several years, while Microsoft is creating the most powerful online network in the world.

❑ **Fact** . . . the markets for PCs, faxes, and cellular phones went from being high-priced luxuries to discounted necessities in less than a decade.

❑ **Fact** . . . IBM missed out to Microsoft, and the online services were recently shocked by the increasing competition from the Internet.

❑ **Fact** . . . Dow Jones' electronic *Personal Journal* costs less than the print edition, plus it updates throughout the day, with current quotes on your portfolio.

❑ **Fact** . . . Reuters, Knight-Ridder, and Dow Jones are already going after the individual investor market, and the competition will increase.

❑ **Fact** . . . about two-thirds of all big-time money managers and an even larger percentage of the newsletter writers fail to match the market indexes.

The individual investor needs to keep an open mind, and you will learn something while watching the institutional investor in action. Get to know what the giants play with. Ask for information about the smaller, affordable packages that could give you just the edge you need to enter the big leagues. After all, the introduction to the *Wall Street Journal*'s Personal Journal is another clear indication of this news trend toward services designed for the consumer markets, which are growing rapidly.

Getting familiar with what these giants do will also inspire you, and give you something to aim for down the road as your portfolio grows. Someday you may want the whole package, perhaps even your own Bloomberg, and you'll know where to get it and what it does.

Keeping an open mind may also show you how you can beat the giants at their own game today, without all their firepower, and give you the self-confidence to "just do it."

After all, if the majority of the institutional investors can't even beat the major indexes, why not jump into the contest with total confidence that you can be a winner against the giants?

Maybe all you really do need to be a successful investor is a membership in the American Association of Individual Investors, some software from Reuters' Money Network, a subscription to the Microsoft Network, and a copy of the *Beardstown Ladies' Common-Sense Investment Guide*. Later, after building a solid track record and self-confidence, you can graduate to Telescan and Metastock, or Telerate, Instinet and The Bloomberg.

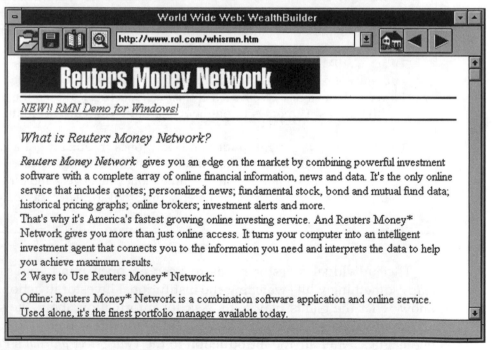

Figure 1.11   Reuters Money Network: for the new cyberspace investors.

BASIC STARTER KIT FOR THE NEW CYBER$PACE INVESTOR

Last year the *New York Times* ran a story about Chase Manhattan Bank's new foreign currency trading room, complete with photos of the managing director's workstation, which looks like the NASA control center. The boss had six monitors, several real-time data feeds, global newswires, telephones, and video equipment. Plus all kinds of electronic gadgets. It looked like they raided Sharper Image.

THE NEW INTRANETS: WILL GLOBAL "PRIVATE NETWORKS" REPLACE THE INTERNET?

New Internet tools from major vendors are helping to accelerate the growth of corporate networks based on the World Wide Web, allowing the companies to develop their own private "Intranets" for enterprise applications and communications, both inside and outside the corporate firewall. . . . The development of private Intranets provides opportunities for companies to use the Web as an alternative—or complement—to groupware products. . . . Nearly a quarter of companies already have implemented or plan to implement a Web server as an internal groupware platform or Intranet. An additional 20% are studying the use of Web servers inside the corporation.

(SOURCE: Clinton Wilder et al., "Top Story, Internet Tools," *Information Week,* November 6, 1995.)

* * * * * * *

For the Internet, the lack of central planning (centralization, bureaucracy, ownership, and censorship) has made it what it is today—the most democratic and fastest growing form of mass media in history. Now, governments and multinational corporations around the world are planning to build their own global network. . . .

The Information Superhighway is not and never will be anything like the democratic Internet. The difference between the Internet and the Information Superhighway is a matter of ownership and content. The Information Superhighway has not yet arrived. . . .

The Information Superhighway will be built, owned, and controlled by a consortium of entertainment, telecommunications, and cable corporations—all networked together.

(SOURCE: Michael Strangelove, "The Information Superhighway," *Online Access,* September 1995.)

What a dramatic change in the 20 years since I started with Morgan Stanley. I worked with a handheld Texas Instruments calculator. And that was it.

How can anyone possibly compete against the massive firepower of a Chase Manhattan, other than a Smith Barney, Merrill Lynch, or Goldman Sachs? Does the individual investor and trader have a ghost of a chance against these big guns?

Yes, it happens all the time. The small investor is often the big winner. Burton Malkiel, author of *A Random Walk Down Wall Street,* observed that the majority of mutual fund and pension fund managers can't even beat the street indexes.

Malkiel states that long-term performance studies show that 65 to 70 percent of these high-priced managers—who control the bulk of America's wealth—fall below the market averages. And of course there's the famous Beardstown Ladies' Investment Club that beat the street with returns of over 20 percent. Don't be intimidated.

Investor's War Room: Go First Class, Buy Ahead of the Curve

First you need the right computer hardware and peripherals. Fortunately, you may already have the right hardware. Let's see what's necessary.

Even if you decide to jump in with both feet and start trading pork bellies and index futures on the Chicago Board of Trade, you can do it from your den in Seattle or Tucson with at least a 486 coprocessor operating at 66 MHz, 8MB of RAM, and a 500MB hard drive. Of course you'll need a monitor (preferably 17-inch), a laser printer, and a high-speed modem (at least 14.4, preferably 28.8). We also strongly recommend that you get a computer with a CD-ROM system. You will need it for historical data. It will pay for itself quickly. And presto, you're ready for business.

Here's the good news. Even if you completely replace your existing equipment, you don't have to spend much more than $2,000 to $3,000 for this hardware upgrade in today's highly competitive computer market. This system is hot enough for the day-trader watching the markets full-time for a living. It's right in line with the "Sample Trading System" recommended in *Futures* magazine's annual *Guide to Computerized Trading.*

Whatever you do, don't skimp on the hardware.

Go first class, buy ahead of the curve. Hardware technology is changing so rapidly. And the hardware is relatively inexpensive compared to your time and the risks to your portfolio. For example, a *Business Week*

FUTURES MAGAZINE: SAMPLE TRADING SYSTEM AND WORKSTATION

Here are the estimated costs for a trader who wishes to trade markets at the Chicago Mercantile Exchange, Chicago Board of Trade, New York Mercantile Exchange, and the London International Financial Futures Exchange. Variations in price will result from user's location and choice of vendor. The prices listed below are representative of a trader living relatively close to a medium or large metropolitan area, needing a mid- to upper-level-quality system. The more remote the location, the more communication costs generally increase.

1. **Personal computer** with a 486 processor, monitor, and printer; $2,600.
2. **Real-time price quotes and news**
   a. Communications fee
      Vendor fee $250/month
      Dedicated phone line: $450/month
   b. Exchange fees $200/month total (four exchanges)
      Note: Vendors normally access a one-time installation fee for setting up the communication link (approximately $1,000)
3. **Charting and analysis software** with over 100 technical studies and charting options, historical price information, and trading system design and testing capabilities: $600.

Total one-time charges: $4,200
Total monthly charges: $900

(SOURCE: *Futures 1994 Guide to Computerized Trading.*)

Alternatively, you can start with a less ambitious investment program by jumping into the Reuters Money Network system discussed in the Mutual Funds section below ... for a $50 setup fee and $25 a month. Or a similar package from Dow Jones News/Retrieval or CompuServe.

magazine story on technology noted that a computer costs over ten times the initial investment during its useful life.

In 1992 we went from a 286 processor with a 40MB hard drive to a 486×66 with 530MB hard drive and 8MB RAM ... and we quickly filled *half* the new hard drive, while also experiencing longer wait times. *Bottom line: Today's individual investor will soon need a Pentium6 chip with at least a gigabyte (1,000MB) hard drive and 16MB of RAM memory.*

With today's intense competition, computer prices continue falling rapidly. Meanwhile, new software demands more capacity and faster speeds. So take this warning to heart and go first class. Buy much more capacity than you think you need. Lots more. The hardware will ultimately pay for itself in reduced frustration and time saved.

DANGER ZONE—PROTECT YOUR COMPUTER SYSTEM

Install a tape backup system. And use it on a regular basis, preferably daily. In addition, make sure the manufacturer provides first-class technical support, not just a discount price. And pay for the extended warranty. You may need it before you know it. One expert once remarked, "It isn't *whether* you'll have a hard-disk crash, but *when* . . . and that you cannot predict." He learned the hard way.

The Wall Street Cyber$pace Connection for Investors

Wall Street is no longer physically located in Manhattan. It's not in New York State. And it's light-years past Manhattan, Kansas. It's not even in the United States. It has no fixed location for investors. It's an instantaneous global market. And it no longer belongs to the big institutions. It's an electronic state of mind. Anyone, anywhere in the world, can trade on this new *Wall Street cyberspace.*

You can, too. All you need to do is connect your computer to cyberspace through your modem. More than likely you'll be using a telephone line (although we'll look at other competing types of cyberspace delivery systems such as cellular phones, FM radio, cable television, and satellite disks).

Next, you'll need a dedicated telephone line. Otherwise, your computer connections may interfere with voice and fax communications. In fact, the growing demand for online connections and fax machines is the big reason U.S. telephone companies are outgrowing area codes and telephone lines so fast.

A word to the wise: Look for Internet and online services that have local access numbers. If you have to make long-distance calls (as is often the case with regional BBSs), your connection charges will eat you alive.

High-Powered Software and Tons of Data at Discount Prices

Now that you've got the hardware, that's the easy part. That's just for openers if you want to bet at the biggest casino in the universe, Wall Street cyberspace. The cost of your hardware could disappear on the first deal at the tables.

Next you'll need many other basic resources to make your computer hardware function as a tool for investment decision making.

You'll need data on stocks and the various indexes, and other market information. You'll want the news from providers such as Dow Jones, Reuters, or the *Investor's Business Daily.* And you'll need some sophisticated software to help you analyze, pick, manage, buy, and sell your portfolio. If you also want real-time data, you'll have to pay exchange fees. And other costs are guaranteed to pop up. It all depends on how much investing and trading you intend to do. For example, consider the following types:

❒ **Passive investor.**   You're just a buy 'n' hold investor with most of your money tied up long term in mutual funds.

❒ **Active investor trader.**   A businessperson who loves following the market and may spend eight to ten hours a week.

❒ **Day-trader.**   A full-time day-trader making your living in the futures market.

❒ **Institutional investors.**   Brokers, money managers, investment advisors, research analysts, or other professionals serving clients 60 hours a week.

Whether you're making a $1,000 bet on your first mutual fund or trading $10 million a day in financial derivatives, you need some basic computer hardware to process all the data and analytical tools necessary to make your investment decisions.

THE INFORMATION REVOLUTION

Like any powerful technology, the computer leaves little room for sentiment. It has spawned an Information Revolution that promises even more profound changes than we have witnessed already. There can be little doubt that these changes, like those of the Industrial Revolution, will, on balance, provide great benefits.

(SOURCE: Stephen Shepard, Editor-in-chief, "The Information Revolution," Special Bonus Issue of *Business Week,* July 12, 1994.)

So what's this big gamble going to cost you, aside from your portfolio risks? Surprisingly, it's quite reasonable.

New Investors.   If you're just starting out, go slowly. Take it easy. While you're checking out the Internet's Websites, subscribe to one of the commercial online services, testing the waters before making any investments using cyberspace. You could try America Online or CompuServe until you gain confidence.

By going this conservative route, you can get by with a one-time setup charge under $30 and monthly fees of around $25 (if you're careful about the amount of time you spend online). And you'll be pleasantly surprised about the vast amount of information available to you online for nominal costs.

The Pros.   Even if you decide to go full blast as a day-trader and individual investor with the best real-time data feeds and the best analytical software, you can do it with a one-time initial investment of $4,000 to $4,500 for hardware and software. In addition, your ongoing charges will probably run under $1,000 monthly.

Of course, you now have to make that much just to play the game and break even, before you add any profits to your portfolio. And, of course, the capital and operating costs of the professional money manager or trader working at an institutional trading desk will be quite a bit higher.

And that's one of the things the rest of this book is about . . . discovering the wide range of alternatives available to fit any cyberspace investor's needs, today and in the future.

The Internet's Fabulous New Web Browsers

By now you've heard that you need a *browser,* a special graphical interface to *see* all the beautiful stuff on the Internet's World Wide Web. In fact, all the commercial Internet services now offer their own browsers.

You can also go direct to the Web without using your commercial online service. In fact, it will likely be cheaper to have both a commercial service *and* a separate Web connection. Many of the new Web connections offer as much as 40 hours of *prime-time* connections and unlimited off-hours usage as part of a nominal basic fee of 20 bucks. A real bargain.

Here are a couple of the many commercial options available to you:

Netscape's Navigator.   A major improvement over the original government-issue NCSA Web browser, Mosaic, probably because Netscape was designed by the same man. Today it's the main browser used in about two-thirds of the 10 to 12 million Web browsers in operation.

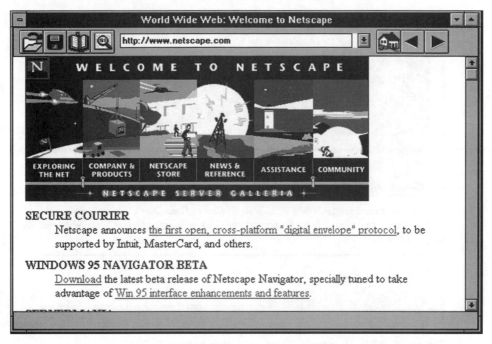

Figure 1.12   Netscape's World Wide Web browser in action.

Netscape is a first-class browser, easy to use for a first-time Web surfer. Many features make it a solid choice: easy bookmarking, downloading, and even a convenient View History, a road map to keep track of where you've been in your current trip around the world.

Another big advantage for Netscape is that you can use this browser on any Internet server you choose, anywhere. In fact, the latest retail version has features that help newcomers and old-timers alike select, find, and change Internet servers.

Netcom's NetCruiser.   This Web browser can be used only if you have an account on their system. But their Internet access charges are so low that you can't go wrong with Netcom. They are also building a major network of local access numbers, so you can hook into Net-com on a local call from anywhere in the nation. Since telephone charges may be a higher cost than the Internet server connection charges, don't be penny-wise and pound-foolish.

For a while Netcom was running ads in the *Wall Street Journal* and other publications, comparing the cost of using Netcom for 40

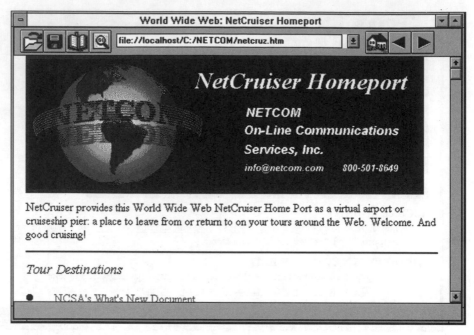

Figure 1.13   Netcom's Netcruiser Web browser.

hours ($20) versus using either AOL or CompuServe for $100 to $200 for the same 40 hours of usage. Obviously, this is a strong argument for maintaining separate online and Internet connections.

The Netcom service includes unlimited E-mail, which can also become very costly on other services that charge you by the message. With Netcom, E-mail comes with the basic 40-hour fee. Let's face it, a Netcom or EarthLink Internet service provider is like a second car in a busy family . . . a necessity!

Big Three Online Services.   Of course, you can always use the Web browser that now comes as part of your basic commercial online service. Prodigy was the first of the big three back in early 1995. AOL scored a victory in buying the Web browser programming of Booklink Technology and incorporating it into America Online's service. What's great about it is the seamless integration between the Web browser links and the other AOL services, something missing in Prodigy's system.

CompuServe acquired Spry, Incorporated, developers of Spry Mosaic and the ever popular Internet-in-a-Box product line. And with the CompuServe system you can also use any other browser, Netscape, NCSA's Mosaic, Cello, or any other if you don't like the Spry connection.

One of the main drawbacks with each of the big three is that you have to pay their high hourly fees while on the Web. That may not be all that bad if you're an infrequent Web surfer. However, if you're a heavy user, you may want a backup account with some Internet provider such as Netcom that gives you 40 hours of prime-time use and unlimited off-peak usage every month for about $20. And that *includes* E-mail usage. Compare this alternative (plus the inconvenience of logging on/off) to your online service's cost of buying a block of 20 to 30 hours of Web access before making your decision.

Bottom line: Whatever you do, go first class. Of course you can download the latest free version of the NCSA's Mosaic, but it's not likely to have all the bells and whistles and tech support as the newer commercial products. So, with all the improvements to the newer commercial browsers, we

Figure 1.14   AOL's Booklink browser Website.

strongly recommend that every investor go first class and use one of the more advanced commercial systems. You have too much at stake. In the long run you'll save a lot of time and money.

These browsers aren't the only ones, but they're some of the best. You'll see other products advertised in the popular press, like NetManage's Internet Chameleon and Spry's AirMosaic. Get something. Just do it. It's time for action. Do some comparison shopping . . . but get on the Web and find out what this element of the information revolution is all about.

Just remember, your Internet Web connection is only one small part of Wall Street cyberspace. Eventually, you'll need software for off-line analytics and portfolio management, online banking and brokerage services, dial-up and commercial online services, CD-ROMs for historical databases, wireless transmission equipment, investor and computer user support groups, reference books, and much more if you want to keep up with the exploding technology and function in cyberspace.

A New Generation of Browsers on the Horizon

The World Wide Web's basic browser, Mosaic, has often been called a "killer app" (application), presumably referring to its advanced state of the art within Internet technology. After decades of drab, clunky, text-based messages on the Internet, the graphics that the Web browsers produced was a quantum leap equivalent to the addition of sound to motion pictures.

CORPORATE WEBS, RESIDENTIAL WEBS . . . AND *THE* WEB

Despite the buzz it has created on the Internet, Netscape makes most of its money selling browsers and servers to companies that create internal Webs as a way of sharing information. At Sun, for example, employees use more than 500 Web servers, including many with Netscape software, to pass along things like engineering plans and organizational charts. Using Navigator, any employee can read such documents and click on key sections to related articles. . . . As more and more homes get connected to cable and telephone lines with greater bandwidth, a good front end that allows them to navigate between text, video, graphics, and sound to be delivered will be in high demand—software that's a lot like Netscape Navigator.

(SOURCE: Alison Sprout, "The Rise of Netscape," *Fortune,* July 10, 1995.)

Suddenly, the Internet was commercially viable to a generation weaned on television visuals.

Then the Netscape company—a partnership between a high-powered team that included the primary designer of the Mosaic browser and the former head of the Silicon Graphics—developed their own advanced browser, and in the space of a year a brand new company captured 65 to 70 percent of the total market for browsers. So Netscape is the new killer app. In fact, Netscape has already released a 32-bit version that specifically supports Windows 95 as an alternative to Microsoft's own Internet browser, the Explorer. But how long before some new technology replaces it?

Technology and the interests of the online consumer are changing more rapidly than fads in the fashion industry, so don't count on anything being too permanent here. Microsoft's Windows 95, with its flexible architecture, and the new graphical integrators being used by the institutional investors will open many new opportunities for interactive graphics, sound, music, video, and telephone transmissions. Plus the advent of secured Internet transactions, online trading, E-cash, and the home-banking revolution will make cyberspace commerce easier and invite a whole new level of competition for all these graphical data integrators.

New Browsers from Grad Students and High-Tech Quants

Moreover, rumor has it that some grad students are now designing the next generation of advanced killer-app browsers as part of a thesis project, and, as with Mosaic, they'll be giving it away free.

Meanwhile, there's a new group of Wall Street software designers—Leading Market Technologies, Applix, Market Vision, Open Market, A-T Financial, and others—who have already designed some very expensive "mother of all killer app" programs, thousands of which are now very much in use in firms like Morgan Stanley and Smith Barney. Eventually they'll see the enormous profit potentials in the individual investor market.

In simplest form, these supersophisticated *graphical users interfaces* (GUIs) are really just souped-up versions of other Web browsers, such as Mosaic and Netscape. Of course, the Wall Street versions aren't called *browsers*, they aren't used on the Web, they cost 100 times more, and they do 1,000 times more. Conceptually though, they're similar.

They are called *interfaces, integrators,* and *navigators* because that's what they do. They provide ease of interface with multiple data feeds; they integrate what would otherwise be information overload coming in from too

WILL HOT JAVA REPLACE MOSAIC AND NETSCAPE?

According to Sun Microsystems, Wall Street has to look no further than their new Java object-oriented programming environment. . . . All of the major securities firms and brokerage houses are evaluating it. . . .

Hot Java, a Web browser based on the Java language, features CD-ROM-like multimedia and can receive. For instance, traders can use Hot Java to access a window on their terminals that might provide a television feed from CNN, or they can receive live feeds of stock quotes. With portfolio management tools and live feeds, traders can see updated portfolios by accessing the Internet.

(SOURCE: Dean Tomasula, *Wall Street & Technology,* October 1995.)

many data sources; they navigate through many different applications. Platforms like Sun Microsystems' new Hot Java browser may eventually replace existing Web browsers with technology that lets you access programs in cyberspace, as well as send data.

Bottom line: Browser technology—including everything for the new investor learning to surf the Web, to the active trader using Telescan, Reuters Money Network or Signal, on up to the big-ticket trader with a major institutional investor using a Market Vision or Leading Market Technology platform—is about to change again, dramatically.

COMING SOON: THE WIRELESS GLOBAL INTERNET

The day is dawning when, through wireless communications, we will be able to access cyberspace from the beach of a remote village in central Africa. . . . Today, with little effort, you can log on to the Net from practically any major city in the United States. All you need is a cellular-ready modem and a cellular phone.

(SOURCE: Ira Brodsky, "Wireless World," *Internet World,* July 1995.)

Expect another quantum jump. Two short years from now, the Netscape browser—which didn't even exist a couple years ago—may be an artifact of Web history, as curiously dated as silent films. And it is the next generation that will give the cyberspace investor true global power and freedom and make this game even more exciting.

A Basic Wall Street Cyber$pace Library

Rather than include a bibliography at the end—after the fact, so to speak—in this case you're getting the information up front, now, before you get too far out there in cyberspace. No one source can possibly answer all the questions you have as a cyberspace investor. Not this book. Not any other one. So, *before* you spend $500 to $2,000 next month on outdated software, another $750 on seminars describing how to use the software, plus $10,000 of your valuable time trading with your software, and risk $100,000 of your hard-earned portfolio . . . please, invest another couple hundred bucks on

---

HOW THE CYBER$PACE INVESTOR STAYS AHEAD OF THE CURVE

Here are five key publications that will keep you current with the advancing technology related to finance and investing.

AAII's Guide to Computerized Investing (800-428-2244)
> This American Association of Individual Investors guide is a basic catalog of available financial data and software resources. Also, join AAII and receive their monthly newsletter.

Futures Magazine's Annual Guide to Computerized Trading (800-635-3931)
> Published annually by *Futures* magazine. Although the information is written primarily by the vendors, it'll help identify the big players.

Technical Analysis of Stocks & Commodities, Annual Bonus Issue (800-832-4642)
> Includes a Software Comparison Table for quick review, plus the results of a poll of readers' choices of the top investor software.

Traders' Catalog & Resource Guide (619-930-1050)
> The original yellow pages for the individual trader of stocks, options, futures, plus a full catalog of software, books, newsletters, and magazines.

Wall Street & Technology's Buyer's Guide (800-227-4675)
> *Wall Street & Technology*'s directory is the yellow pages for institutional investors, and many resources are equally applicable to individual investors. The *Buyer's Guide* includes a CD-ROM with demos and additional data.

The technology is changing so rapidly, we recommend you also subscribe to their monthlies, along with *Information Week* magazine.

this basic cyberspace resource library, the only kind that makes any sense in this dramatically changing technological environment.

That's right, you should buy *and use* several other books and periodicals. Get out your credit card, pick up the phone, call and order these books for express delivery if you can't find them at your local bookstore.

THIS REVOLUTION IS NOT A "SUPERHIGHWAY"
IT'S A GLOBAL "MARKETPLACE" WITH GLOBAL EXCHANGES

We stand at the brink of another revolution. This one will involve unprecedentedly inexpensive communication: all the computers will join together to communicate with us and for us. Interconnected globally, they will form a network, which is being called the information superhighway. A direct precursor is the present Internet, which is a group of computers joined and exchanging information using current technology.

The revolution in communications is just beginning. It will take place over several decades. . . .

The highway metaphor isn't quite right, though. The phrase suggests landscape and geography, a distance between points, and embodies the implications that you have to travel to get from one place to another. In fact, one of the most remarkable aspects of this new technology is that it will eliminate distance.

A different metaphor that I think comes closer to describing a lot of the activities that take place is that of the ultimate market. Markets from trading floors to malls are fundamental to human society, and I believe this one will eventually be the world's central department store. It will be where we social animals will sell, trade, invest, haggle, pick up stuff, argue, meet new people, and hang out. Think of the hustle and bustle of the New York Stock Exchange. . . .

(SOURCE: *The Road Ahead*, Bill Gates, Viking, 1995.)

The anchor stores on this global cyber-mall will be the IntraNets, private global networks like Telerate, Instinet, and Bloomberg. These power-players believe they have an edge over the masses. Will they share this secret with the individual investor—the online subscriber surfing the Internet? Hardly. Securities markets thrive on competition. Most likely, the private networks will continue competing with the emerging global cyber-exchange.

CHAPTER 2

The Internet: Investor's Global Resource Library

INTERNET META-LISTS: LINKS TO THE WORLD OF INVESTING

If you're not on the Internet, if you don't have a Web browser, you're missing the information revolution. What's more, you're also missing the global paradigm shift, a shift to the new world order and the transformation of life as we know it on this planet:

❏ Being *on the Net* is rapidly becoming as essential as owning a computer, and probably as easy, with all the new online services.

❏ If you're already hooked into the Internet, then you need access to *the Web*. The Internet's World Wide Web, that is.

❏ And if you're on the Web, you *start with the Web's meta-lists*, large directories with links to other Websites, cyberspace shopping malls.

Why? The Internet is growing so rapidly it's hard to find things. The Web has been described as chaotic and anarchistic. To a newcomer on the Net, it often feels more like you're at a wild demolition derby than on the great American interstate highway system. Maybe that's why it's called *surfing* the Net, rather than *traveling* it. If you're not careful, you're liable to drown in this sea of information.

And there is absolutely no centralized government controlling the Internet. None. It is a pure democracy, bordering on anarchy. The inmates are running this institution.

Fortunately, the inmates are doing a reasonably good job, and they're improving all the time. Especially the emerging new meta-lists. They are creating order where there was chaos, structure out of insanity. Our job here is simply to help you identify several sites that will give you direct access to a lot of valuable historic and real-time information that can help you manage your investment portfolio.

Meta-Lists: Yellow Pages and Road Maps for the Internet

Meta-lists is a buzzword for the Internet yellow pages. Meta-lists are directories that will help you cut through gridlock and detours on the Internet. Thank God for these meta-lists.

Meta-lists were originally developed by dedicated professors and students with an Indiana Jones spirit. They accepted a challenge to boldly go into the new frontier, and they did it for the fun of it—a novel concept reflecting a time (only a few years ago) when the Internet was solely a communication vehicle for universities and the government. Meta-lists were not intended for commercial use.

One of the best *printed* guides to the Internet's Web is printed periodically by the magazine, *PC/Computing*, on a single 25- by 38-inch sheet. It even looks and folds like the map you have in the glove compartment of your car. This great foldout chart called the *Road Map to the World Wide Web* is a masterpiece rivaling the best of Rand McNally—your road map into the new frontier of cyberspace. Call them and get it for your library; it's a great overview perspective.

Yahoo: One of the New Baby Bells of Meta-Lists

Yahoo is a perfect example of how rapidly the Web has evolved, from an academic exploration into a commercial business.

Please don't let the name fool you. Yahoo isn't some football cheer or secret college password. When I first heard of it I thought it might have had something to do with my alma mater, the University of Virginia, also known as the Yahoos. Wrong. It's an amusing tongue-in-cheek acronym for Yet Another Hierarchical Officious Oracle: Yahoo.

REVOLUTION? PARADIGM SHIFT? OPPORTUNITIES? OR HYPE?

In mid-1995 the *Individual Investor* magazine ran a cover story on "Internet Investing." In it they quoted Gregory Curhan, an analyst with the Wall Street firm of Volpe, Welty: "The Internet is experiencing explosive growth that is creating new business and investment opportunities at an incredible pace."

The author notes that "the industry is evolving with startling speed . . . there is a palpable feeling that the world is on the precipice of some technological breakthrough. And anyone might get rich off of it."

Recently, the online commercial services doubled in a little over a year.

As impressive as the expansion of the commercial services may be, the growth of the Internet itself could soon be even more prodigious. Total revenues from Internet-related products and services came to $350 million in 1994, according to Forrester research, a Cambridge, Mass.-based market research firm. That should more than double in 1996. From there, Internet-related industries "will grow to a $10 billion juggernaut by the end of the century," says Forrester's Jay Batson.

In another industry, projections such as these might be dismissed as mere hype . . . but the emergence of on-line communications has been profound in just the last year. So it's tempting to think that estimates like Forrester's are conservative, if anything.

Already an estimated 30 million people worldwide use the Internet in some way. By the turn of the century, that number is projected to have grown tenfold [and] what's more, the Internet isn't the only game in town.

(SOURCE: Gordon Anderson, ed., "Internet Investing," *Individual Investor,* August 1995.)

This list is a must for investors. Bookmark it. That is, add it to your list of favorite sites on your Web browser, so you can easily point, click, and return to it without typing in its full cyberspace address every time you're exploring the Internet.

Better yet, bookmark Yahoo's subsection on business and finance. It's excellent and it already has over 80,000 Websites listed. This is an excellent yellow-pages directory to a wealth of research material aimed at the new cyberspace investor.

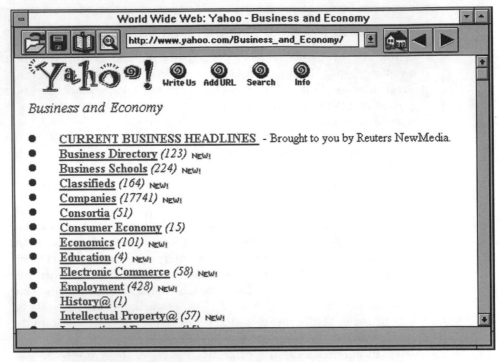

Figure 2.1   Yahoo meta-list: business and financial yellow pages.

Yahoo: Two Grad Students Having Fun on the Net

Yahoo's growth is a mirror of the short-term explosive growth of the World Wide Web and a sign of who's "ahead of the curve" in the race to capitalize on the explosive commercial opportunities on the Internet.

Back in the Web's infancy, that is, way back in 1994, two bright young Stanford University grad students in their mid-20s, David Filo and Jerry Yang, started amassing a list of their personal favorite sites. The Web was this "real cool" new cutting-edge frontier for adventurous spirits. What a way to learn. It sure beat dull classes.

David and Jerry's classmates got caught up in the game, and a massive list emerged. In less than two years there were over 36,000 sites on this meta-list. And every day 200,000 computers were checking out this list. That's right folks, 200,000 curious cyberspace travelers logged in daily in mid-1995! Not just from New York and New Mexico, but Mexico, Russia, Thailand, Canada, Japan, South Africa, Costa Rica, Romania, China, Ireland—all over the globe. That's what the Internet is all about. And all these potential customers are looking for information from content providers. What a great advertising vehicle.

Yellow Pages and Instant Direct Dialing at No Extra Cost

Not only did they get directions, but they got *immediate* connections (links) to the hot spots on the Internet's World Wide Web . . . anywhere on the entire planet. That's what's so great about meta-lists.

Yahoo and its competitors are *better* than yellow pages because you get instant automatic call-dialing. Find an interesting Web site on the directory. Then bingo! Point 'n' click and you're rocketed directly to that location, anywhere in the world. No stamps. No long distance costs. No inane recorded messages. No waiting. Just results.

Meta-lists are becoming essential tools in navigating the Internet. And with the Web doubling every few months, there's always new stuff to discover. Cyberspace is the interactive magic dreamed of in *Star Trek*. From this new frontier you'll discover a constant flow of new commercial and financial opportunities unfolding right before your eyes, on your computer monitor.

HOW THE INTERNET ALSO CAUGHT BILL GATES BY SURPRISE

In a major *Fortune* magazine article, "As the Internet Sizzles, Online Services Battle for Stakes" (May 1995), David Kirkpatrick succinctly captured the uncertainties of the information revolution and the weaknesses of almost any battle strategy in this dynamic environment:

> Microsoft and AT&T thought they knew how to upstage the leaders in the online services. Then the Internet exploded. From this chaos could emerge a radically new consumer market . . . the Net is turning out to have such strong appeal for consumers and marketers that it is forcing the players in the online industry to rethink the way they do business . . . the Web opens cyberspace to anyone who wants to publish information or set up shop, from AT&T to the lowliest entrepreneur, with no need to go through existing online services. That promise of a direct link to the customer has attracted marketers in droves.

Not only Bill Gates, but the other commercial superpowers were thrown off by the Internet. Billion-dollar giants such as GE, Ziff-Davis, and Murdoch's News Corporation all floundered with their online services, Delphi, GEnie, and the Interchange.

APPLYING MOORE'S LAW TO GROWTH ON THE INTERNET

In a *Forbes* interview with Gordon Moore, the founder of Intel, he said that the Internet "supplies less than 1% of the information to the world now. It is just one large step toward the global electronic library. The Library of Congress is nowhere near computerized yet. So the opportunities are immense."

(SOURCE: Robert Lenzer, "Whither Moore's Law?," *Forbes*, September 11, 1995.)

The Internet . . . Breeding Ground for the Next Bill Gates

What about Dave and Jerry, the two grad students doing this for fun and for free? Well, no more. They built a great Website in a year. Then it became so big that America Online, Prodigy, and other commercial online services offered to buy them out. They decided to maintain the integrity of their dream.

Yahoo got so big, Dave and Jerry were working full-time on the List. No time for classes. They had to move off the free computer servers at Stanford University. They installed some bigger, expensive equipment. It's paid off. Today they have a venture capitalist backing their dream—a new partner the *Los Angeles Times* says put in a cool million to help young Dave and Jerry convert this hobby into a successful commercial moneymaker.

That should tell you how fast this new frontier is growing. Faster than fax machines, fiber optics, and cellular phones. Get in on the leading edge.

FINWeb: A Texas-Sized Meta-List on Financial Economics

FINWeb was another one of the early university-based meta-lists on the Internet. FINWeb is physically located at the University of Texas. Of course, its physical locale doesn't matter in cyberspace, but you have to give those Texans credit for doing it up right in the early days of the Internet.

FINWeb was one of the first Internet Websites, or yellow pages, focusing on investments, finance, and economics, beginning back in 1994. Why at a university? Remember, the Internet was originally designed in the 1960s at the height of the Cold War to serve as a decentralized government communications system in case of a nuclear attack. This computer network linking the government with the research and academic community accomplished this task. That was the original cyberspace.

This vast network became the primary communication medium between college professors and government. It was a loose, nonprofit federation funded by the U.S. government for the first 25 years, until 1994. So, obviously, this cyberspace was not originally intended as a business venture for commercial profits, which explains why there was so little commercial information on how to make a buck. Any talk about profits was frowned on by the academicians. Civil defense and research integrity had to be maintained.

FINWeb's opening banner reminds me of a commercial for a "bold new" soap or a used car dealer: the word *profits* jumps off the screen against a colorful backdrop of a hundred-dollar bill with a jazzy uptrend suggesting a rising stock market.

You can't help but admire this kind of boldness, especially when you realize that this emphasis on profits was not traditionally accepted in the nonprofit, academic world that built and maintained much of the Internet. Before we even examine the content of FINWeb, it is important to recognize its historical significance during the transition of the Internet from its nonprofit academic roots to a dominantly commercial communication vehicle.

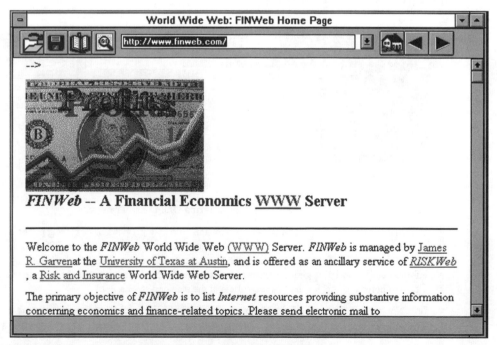

Figure 2.2 The University of Texas FINWeb meta-list.

Financial Economics for the Serious Investor

FINWeb is another of the *must-bookmark* Websites for every investor building a database on the Internet. At first its orientation seems designed more for the pipe-smoking college professor than floor traders frantically waving signals on the floor of the Chicago Mercantile Exchange. Not true, this is one very valuable set of *yellow pages*.

And don't let the term *financial economics* fool you. While many of their links do point to the more esoteric academic perspective, there are many others that would fit on the stock pages of *Barron's* or a script for today's CNBC-TV "Closing Bell Report."

FINWeb is linked to a Texas-sized database, so full of information you could easily spend well over an hour using FINWeb as a jumping-off point in your quest for investor resources on the Internet. Remember to bookmark the Websites you find appealing as you link to sites from FINWeb.

Powerful stuff. And there's much more. If this doesn't stir your desire for FINWeb's Profits, nothing will. You are strongly encouraged to survey the FINWeb (and other meta-lists) before you continue running up those expensive connect charges at CompuServe and America Online. You might just find what you want for free.

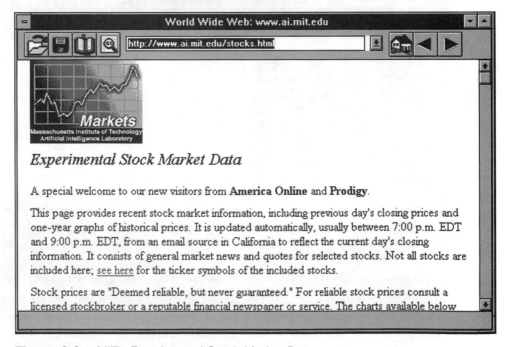

Figure 2.3   MIT's Experimental Stock Market Data.

The Top Investor Meta-Lists at Universities

We have already mentioned a couple key university-based meta-lists focused on financial, business, and market information. In addition, you should be aware of the other key university-based Websites. Since they are all part of the same vast network, you'll likely find them cross-linked to each other through one of the meta-lists already mentioned in this chapter:

❐ **Ohio State University.** Probably the single most comprehensive meta-list of this kind, with links to almost every other key resource for cyberspace investors.

❐ **Massachusetts Institute of Technology.** MIT's Artificial Intelligence Laboratory manages a Website for experimental stock market data.

❐ **Carnegie Mellon University.** The Lycos search system is the Internet's most complete database for Web searches.

❐ **University of Virginia.** Check UVA's site for SIC classifications.

❐ **Cornell Law School.** Copyright, UCC, and Supreme Court rulings.

❐ **New York University.** Stern School maintains the EDGAR database of SEC and other legal and public filings.

❐ **University of Michigan.** Economic data from U.S. Department of Commerce.

Each of these has some value for the investors. When the Internet was originally created as a joint venture between the government and academia, each of the university-based sites was funded primarily by the federal government. Today, as the privatization of the Internet progresses and federal funding is withdrawn, the universities are developing alliances with commercial organizations. Carnegie Mellon is licensing its Lycos search engine to Microsoft. NYU's EDGAR project is now taking on advertisers such as R.R. Donnelley and Zacks Investments. And Stanford University's Website is now privately backed by venture capitalists.

Bottom line: There are a number of great university-based meta-lists mentioned here. The Ohio State University Website is certainly one of the most extensive from the practical cyberspace investor's needs, and may well be the number one in its class. Texas leans a bit more toward the academic brains. MIT is solid data. Michigan is basic government economic statistics. Check all of them out at least once. Bookmark the ones that best serve you and stop back regularly.

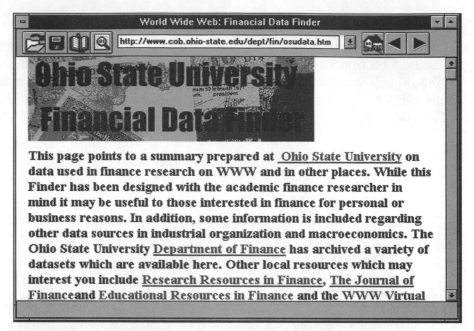

Figure 2.4   Ohio State University: Financial Datafinder.

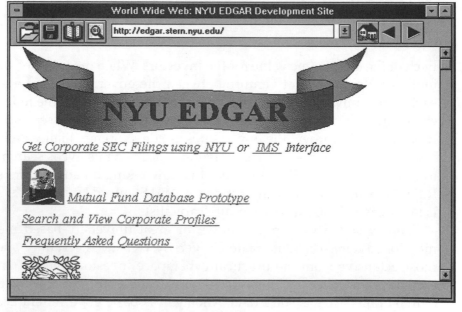

Figure 2.5   NYU's Sloan Business School Website.

FINWEB'S LINKS TO FINANCIAL CYBERSPACE

Market and Company Information

Holt's Stock Market Reports (daily updates)
Quotecom's stock quotes
The Chicago Mercantile Exchange's Website
NETworth mutual funds database
The FDIC's gopher research

University Databases on Finance and Economics

Experimental Stocks Data (MIT)
Ohio State University's Financial Data Summary
The EDGAR/SEC filings at New York University
U.S. Department of Commerce (University of Michigan)

Journals and Working Papers on Financial Economics

National Bureau of Economic Research
Journal of Financial Abstracts
Cambridge Journal of Economics
Journal of Business and Economics
Financial Executives Journal
Journal of Applied Econometrics
American Financial Association's Journal
ECONbase: index/database to specific articles on forecasting, accounting,
　monetary policy, etc.
Indexes to 17,000 articles of finance and economics

Links to Other Websites for Investors

RAND Corporation's *Journal of Economics*, etc.
FEN: Financial Economics Network, journals on economics, corporate
　finance, derivatives, banking, capital markets.
Money Center Banks: J.P. Morgan, Chase, etc.
RISKWeb: Insurance & Risk Management
Federal Reserve Bank of Philadelphia, with current economic reports.
Directory of Business Schools
Electronic Commerce on the Internet, including business and shopping
　malls
Directory of federal, state, city, and foreign governments, including the
　FBI, Congress, and the White House.
Even a list of Nobel Prize winners in Economics

NEW COMMERCIAL META-LISTS: INVESTOR'S YELLOW PAGES

When the U.S. government's funding of the Internet began drying up in 1994, private businesses jumped on this golden opportunity and the general public became mesmerized by the Web. The Yahoo meta-list is a perfect example of this rapid shift from a nonprofit academic status to hard-nosed commercialism.

As a result of this new commercialism, the Internet will be entering a new phase of development during the next few years. All the important new Websites will be developed by private businesses and profit-making ventures. Here are a couple of these new Websites targeted at the investing public.

Meta-List from a Computer Users' Group: InvestSIG

One of the best meta-lists for serious investors is InvestSIG, a special interest group of the Capital PC User Group, a nonprofit organization. CPCUG is located in Rockville, Maryland, serving a total membership of 5,200 in the D.C. metro area. InvestSIG is a small subgroup of CPCUG that serves computer users in many areas other than investing.

InvestSIG's Website appears to be the work of a sophisticated investment club, complete with mention of their monthly seminars (on subjects such as investments in the Pacific Rim, Gold Future Roll Forward Strategies, and seminars on Telescan and Reuters Money Network). This is one of the best meta-lists, with a solid collection of links classified under the following headings:

- Current news and prices
- Intraday charts
- Daily bar or line charts
- Daily candlestick charts
- Data sources—current
- Data sources—historical
- Mutual funds
- Investment books
- Investment journals, articles, and newsletters

❐ New groups and FAQs

❐ Other links to investment, financial, and economic information

Bottom line: If you're in Singapore or Zurich and can't get to the Washington Metropolitan meetings of InvestSIG, you certainly can make use of their excellent meta-list. The list is very professional. Bookmark it!

And by the way, if you prefer a *live* support group or investment club, you have three avenues. First, join a real investment club located in your geographic area. Second, you can also find one of the computer user groups (e.g., InvestSIG) in your area that specializes in computerized investing. The National Association of PC User Groups can help you locate one in your area. And third, you can contact the American Association of Individual Investors for their list of about 50 AAII Computer Special Interest Groups in U.S. metropolitan areas. It's listed in the back of the *AAII Guide to Computerized Investing.*

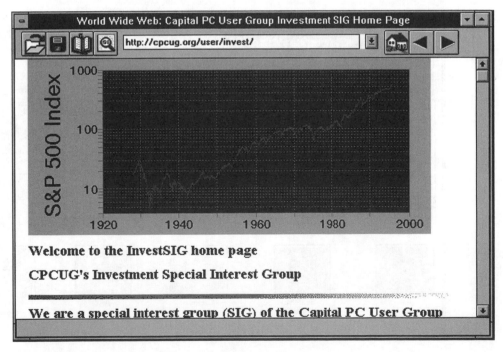

Figure 2.6   InvestSIG: computer user's support group.

American Association of Individual Investors' Meta-List

Another of the new-style meta-lists is the Website under development by the American Association of Individual Investors, the world's largest investment club with about 200,000 members. AAII is one of the primary resources for investors, other than the institutional investors—the pension and mutual fund managers, banks, and brokerage firms. The needs are different for these two classes of investors, and AAII focuses on the individual investor.

AAII's history and experience in cyberspace is important. They saw the potentials of this new medium early and created a bulletin board system to serve individual investors back in 1983. Then in 1994, with the growth of the online systems, they located on America Online, and phased out the BBS in 1995. Then, as the popularity of the Internet's Web grew, AAII again shifted gears and decided to create a Webpage which should be available in 1996.

AAII's enormous database of financial data systems and analytical software, their online library of articles, reports, books, and newsletters, their access to forums, directories, conferences, seminars, local chapters,

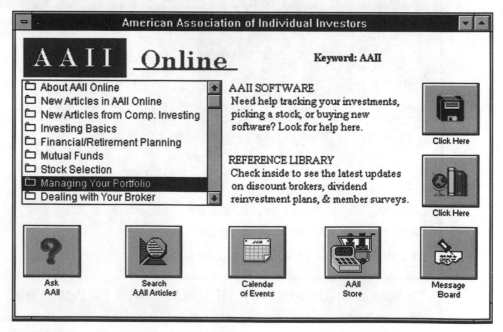

Figure 2.7 American Association of Individual Investors.

and tech support, makes for an awesome resource for investors. Hopefully the AAII's Website plans will materialize on schedule. If the AAII Website is even close to the AOL version, it'll be a winner.

Personal Finance at the Global Network Navigator

The Internet has gone from being a joint venture of the U.S. government and academic worlds prior to 1993 into an incredible communication tool with unlimited commercial opportunities. One of the early leaders in this expansion was O'Reilly & Associates, publishers of many books on the emerging computer technology and the new Internet since 1978. Recently the Global Network Navigator was sold to AOL, so we expect even greater contributions by this pioneer.

The GNN Website has a special Personal Finance section that offers the cyberspace investor a number of interesting features:

❏ **Personal Finance mailing list.** Subscribe and stay current with all the new financial and business resources on the Internet.

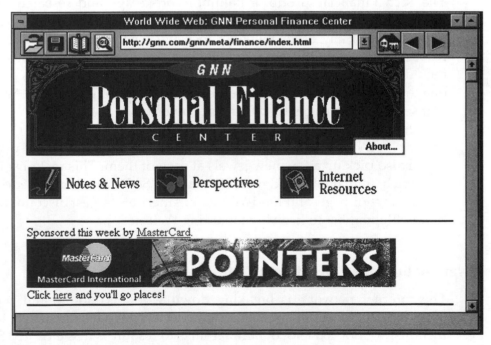

Figure 2.8 Global Network Navigator on Personal Finance.

❏ **Personal Finance archives.** Very helpful, using search links.

❏ **GNN's "What's New: Investment & Personal Finance."** Helps you quickly link to new financial and business Websites on the Internet.

Anyone surfing the Internet knows that NCSA, the original U.S. center for the Internet, has a What's New site with postings of *all* new Websites updated each and every week. With the Net growing so rapidly, however, there are so many sites each week that it's a hassle to bother wading through all of them if you are just interested in business and financial sites. It's overwhelming; it's time-consuming. That makes the GNN meta-list special. They pull out all the new listings that apply to only business and finance.

Bottom line: GNN's site has some very special features. Bookmark it; get on the mailing list for important updates from GNN's Personal Finance page; and regularly check GNN's What's New section.

Investment News Online: Brokerage Firm's Meta-List

The Rich Financial Group, a Baltimore brokerage and research firm, is developing an excellent meta-list. Their meta-list has many of the links you'll find on any other meta-list focusing on financial and investment resources, but with these unique features. For example, the Rich Website includes an excellent directory of financial advisory newsletters and also one for global stock and futures exchanges, among other listings. An excellent set of yellow pages for cyberspace investors.

This is a common pattern with the better meta-lists. As you surf the Internet you'll see many of the same Websites referred to over and over, but you'll also pick up a few new jewels at each of them. This meta-list is specially rich, with quotes and market data from S&P ComStock, *Futures* magazine's anchor page, and Lind-Waldock, America's largest discount futures broker. Remember to keep bookmarking Websites.

Innovation: European Investment Firm's Meta-List

The Internet network is breaking down world economic and political boundaries. Here's an excellent example. When we first linked to this meta-list we noticed a lot of familiar links to resources in the United States. But there was a lot more. The Webmaster, Innovation Information, is a

Figure 2.9 Investment News Online's Super Website.

group of consultants physically located in the Netherlands with a directory that is structured similar to our domestic meta-lists, but with new resources from the continent.

Check it out. You'll see some helpful subdirectories cross-referenced, such as, Cyberspace Roadmaps, Business Sites, Technology & Business, Banking, Major Companies, Web Mall Directories, Research, and so on. It has a definitely European slant to the financial world. Worth bookmarking.

The Wall Street Directory and Your "Money Mentor"

The *Traders' Catalog & Resource Guide* publishes an excellent *print* directory of resources for investors, brokers, and securities traders. After years of printing a large bulky print version of their *Catalog* plus the *Wall Street Software Digest* with their partners, they discovered the World Wide Web. They immediately saw the commercial advantages of electronic publishing on the Net, and have now created two separate Websites: Money Mentor and Wall Street Directory.

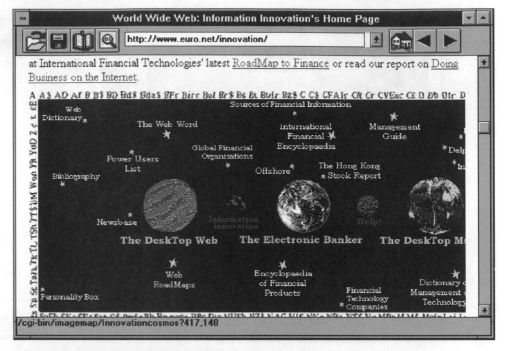

Figure 2.10   European financial meta-list: Innovation.

More important, as successful software designers, they also saw the Web as a powerful new medium for marketing and the delivery of software to investors and traders. If you know the software you want, you can even download working demos before purchasing the latest version of the more popular new software for investors. *Try before you buy.*

You can bet there'll be many other excellent financial meta-lists coming to you in cyberspace soon, with news and quotes, selling discount software, downloading demos, offering electronic publications. Start here and bookmark both.

Wall-Street-News: Internet Broadcasting Superstation

In late 1993, Al Gore's support of the information superhighway inspired a lot of entrepreneurs to discover the commercial potential of the Internet. We were publishing a financial advisory newsletter that was suited to electronic publishing. At first we focused on the BBS as a vehicle. Bulletin board systems were quite popular.

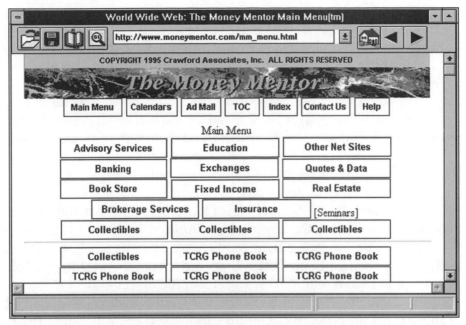

Figure 2.11 *Traders' Catalog & Resource Guide*'s Website.

Figure 2.12 The Wall Street Directory.

Then a close business associate spent some time with NASA and discovered the World Wide Web. He convinced us that the Web—which at the time was still in its infancy—would quickly outstrip all other Internet tools for commercial purposes. And he was right. The Web is to electronic publishing what the Guttenberg press was to the printed word.

We knew that *electronic* publishing would become the wave of the future. Some years ago I was head of the Financial News Network, the cable channel that's now CNBC-TV and, before that, an associate editor of the *Los Angeles Herald Examiner* newspaper. Rising costs of postage, paper, and advertising were making electronic publishing a highly competitive alternative to the printed word.

We called the Wall-Street-News Website a "broadcasting superstation" to reflect this trend. Communicating information on the Web more closely resembles broadcasting than publishing. The image of broadcasting studios just seemed to fit better than the image of printing an "electronic newspaper" and selling it on an "electronic newsstand."

In fact, the Wall-Street-News/Forecasts mailing list quickly became the largest on Netcom Communications servers, a national Internet ser-

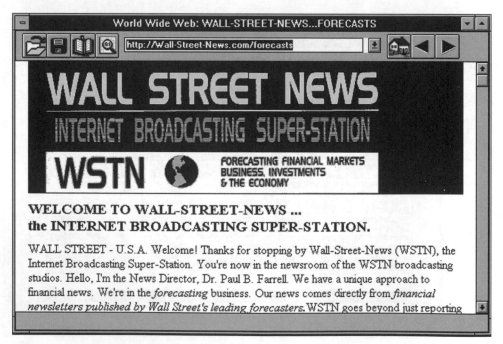

Figure 2.13   Wall-Street-News: Internet broadcasting superstation.

vice provider. Then *Business Week* magazine discovered Wall-Street-News early in 1995 and favorably recommended it to investors. Each broadcast includes:

❏ **Bull/Bear sentiment** index and forecasts

❏ **Hotspots,** or turning points, and key reversal dates

❏ **Soundbytes** or quotes from leading forecasters

❏ **Editorial** analysis and commentaries

One of the main features at this broadcasting superstation is the Global Research Library. From this library you can quickly link to key cyberspace resources for investors. Our forecasts are also "broadcast" to thousands by Internet mailing lists and the Usenet groups.

Also included on our Website is an article on the psychological pressures of today's dynamic financial markets, focusing on the impact of the stresses created by the information revolution on the individual investor, as well as general market instability and volatility. Bookmark this Website and check out the mailing list.

Bookmark! Create Your Own Personal Meta-List

Bookmark hot sites that appeal to you. All Web browsers have a bookmarking function built in. By bookmarking you create your very own personal meta-list. Then, in the future, just point 'n' click and you'll automatically return to that favorite Website.

Think of bookmarking as adding a new telephone number to your Rolodex directory of important people. Don't even second-guess yourself; bookmark everything that looks remotely interesting! Get in the habit. This is very important. Every single interesting Website you log on to, bookmark it. You can easily delete it later if you decide it isn't much help.

You don't want to find yourself a week later trying to remember where *out there* in that vast cyberspace jungle you saw a certain reference or special resource . . . *just where was it?* Believe me, it'll sure save you a lot of frustrations trying to remember and reconstruct "the one that got away." Bookmarking will also save you time retyping those dumb "http://" addresses that are often so irritating. Besides, bookmarking doesn't really cost you anything, so start doing it. Remember, you are building your very own meta-list of profitable cyberspace money centers.

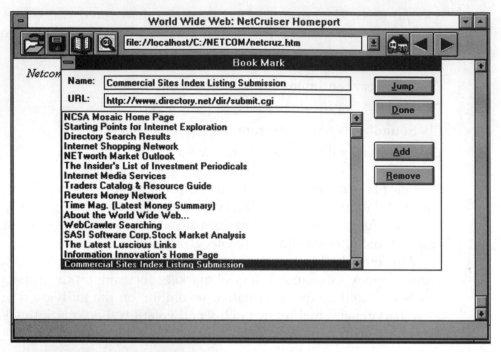

Figure 2.14   Web Bookmark menu on Netcom's NetCruiser.

If you link into several of these key meta-lists, then go back and browse through them occasionally. You'll probably be able to stay ahead of the curve, as these Websites are constantly being updated with new materials, exchanging linkages with other key Websites, and occasionally disappearing. Cyberspace is actually quite cooperative and mutually supportive in this regard. As a result, you can discover a steady stream of new resources coming up for cyberspace investors.

INTERNET YELLOW PAGES ON CD-ROM! . . . FROM MA BELL?!

They're coming soon; some are already being tested. They are the new version of the meta-lists.

The bookstores already have print versions of yellow page directories of Internet addresses. And CD-ROM versions are also surfacing for Website addresses. Only they're not from the real telephone companies, and at this stage of development, not very helpful.

So this is just the tip of a huge iceberg, the leading edge of an avalanche. Soon every single business in the world with a telephone number will also have an Internet mailing address *and a Website address!* It will be a business necessity, just like having a working telephone.

Then the telephone companies and their telephone book publishers will move in and suddenly you'll have both print and CD-ROM versions of Internet yellow page directories delivered free to your home and business.

Think of it, on a couple CD-ROM disks you could have easy access to every computer with E-mail in the world, plus a convenient, organized directory for *direct dialing* to all of these wonderful commercial Website resources in cyberspace, right from your modem onto the Web.

Of course, the dark side of all this is that the direct-mail marketers will also have this information and will start applying their mass-mailing skills to cyberspace. Then your E-mail box will begin filling up with junk E-mail, unless we can find a way to block access of unwanted material while still staying open to all the exciting opportunities.

NETWORKS AND THE INTERNET ARE CREATING A NEW KIND OF COMPUTER

If you're a bit skeptical about the future of all this new technology, you're in good company. Take comfort in knowing that the major computer industry leaders agree with you about the promise of the Internet and networking. This division was evident in the speeches at last year's giant Comdex trade show in Las Vegas, where industry leaders parade current products and forecast the future of the computer world.

"What will the PC of the next millennium look like? This momentous question has come to the fore largely because of the incredible growth of the Internet, that global confederation of information-laden computers. The Internet, and the possibilities it holds, is shaping every assumption about the PC business."

(*Los Angeles Times*.)

"Few end users, particularly consumers, care where the processing, storage and data movement and all that stuff takes place—whether it happens inside their tin box or somewhere on the network—just so long as what happens in front of the screen is compelling, simple to use and is the least expensive solution available."

(IBM Chairman, Louis V. Gerstner Jr.)

"The computer does three things. It displays information, it processes it and it stores it. The debate is about *where* it happens—whether it's on your desktop or somewhere *out there*. There is a fundamental flaw in the logic that everything—your databases and even your word processor—will be stored on the Internet: When you have data elsewhere, someone's going to charge you for it."

(SOURCE: "A Change of Direction?" Julie Pitta, *Los Angeles Times*, November 15, 1995.)

* * * * * * * * * *

From the perspective of the new cyberspace investor, this may all be of little relevance. In either scenario, the individual investor will continue to grow more powerful. Whether the action takes place on the Net or at your desktop, the major trends are leveling the playing field in Wall Street cyberspace.

CHAPTER 3

News Online: Financial Markets, Money, and Investing

FINANCIAL NEWSPAPERS: ELECTRONIC PUBLISHING IS HERE, TODAY

Every major newspaper publisher in the world is being *forced* into cyberspace—and not just because of the rising costs of paper, delivery costs, and environmental issues such as the vanishing rain forests and global warming:

Competition and consumers are forcing them. Cyberspace is where the new readers are . . . staring into their monitors! And every other newspaper is chasing after the vast new global audience opening up in cyberspace. Newspapers can't afford to miss this opportunity.

For many of these newspapers, the first step was a piggyback ride on one of the commercial online services, such as the business section of the *New York Times* and *Investor's Business Daily,* both of which appeared on AOL early. Conversely, the onlines needed content to lure new customers. So it was a two-way street, with the newspapers and the online services in a marriage of convenience, both hunting for new subscribers, trying to figure out what all this cybermania meant, while testing their electronic publishing skills.

NATIONAL NEWSPAPERS' ONLINE BUSINESS SECTIONS

The transition to electronic publishing is going quite well when you see all the newspapers already being delivered by commercial online services:

CompuServe

Associated Press Newswire
United Press International
Washington Post
USA Today
Detroit Free Press
The London Guardian
U.K. News/Sports
Deutsche Presse-Agentur
Reuters Newswire
125 Regional Business Publications
Reports from 50 Broker/Investment Firms
500 Industry Newsletters

America Online

New York Times
Investor's Business Daily
Reuters Newswire
Knight-Ridder/Tribune—Business
PBS's Nightly Business Report
San Jose Mercury—Business
Orlando Sentinel—Business
Business Week Online
Worth Magazine Online

Prodigy

L.A. Times/TimeLink
News Day
Richmond Times-Dispatch
Atlanta Journal Constitution
Tampa Bay Tribune
and over 20 other newspapers

Electronic newspapers are here now, and soon they'll all be on the Web!

But that was all before the Net's Web and Microsoft Network came along. Now watch things change, fast and furiously.

Belonging to a single online service with only 2 to 3 million subscribers is dwarfed by the opportunities on today's cyberspace horizon: The Internet's Web is projected to include 100 million hookups within a few short years. And Microsoft Network's tie-in to 65 million Windows users will trigger even more exponential growth in cyberspace.

So why should a newspaper stay limited to AOL's subscriber base, for example? Why not put the *New York Times, San Jose Mercury News,* and *Rhode Island Horizon* on a Webpage so anyone, anywhere in the world, can see and read your electronic edition in cyberspace? After all, isn't the Internet itself just one big newsstand? Well, that's exactly what's happening today on the information superhighway.

MediaInfo Interactive: "All the News That's Fit to Print"

Electronic publishing is sweeping through the newspaper publishing industry like a forest fire on a dry summer day. And electronic publishing

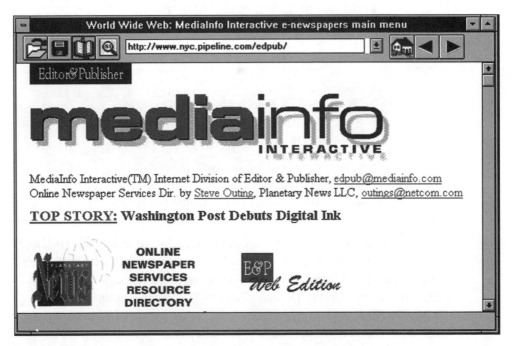

Figure 3.1   MediaInfo's master list of newspapers worldwide.

may do more to save trees than the Rainforest Foundation. If you want to discover everything you ever wanted to know about what's happening in cyberspace with electronic newspapers, access the Website for MediaInfo Interactive.

We first linked to MediaInfo through the Mercury Center Website reviewed below. Of course, you can directly link to the MediaInfo Interactive Webpage. This Website is not only a superb example of the great resources emerging in cyberspace, it is also a study of the dynamic paradigm shift dominating the new world of publishing. With the support of *Editor & Publisher* magazine, this Website is a truly comprehensive resource, helping you find newspapers at all the major cyberspace locations all over the globe.

MEDIAINFO INTERACTIVES' GLOBAL NEWSPAPERS

❏ Commercial online services
❏ Free newspaper services
❏ Modem/dial-up services
❏ Links to Internet Websites with more than 200 newspapers
    worldwide in these geographic areas:
    –Africa
    –Asia
    –Australia and New Zealand
    –Canada
    –Europe
    –Latin and South America
    –Middle East
    –U.S. dailies and weeklies
❏ Electronic publishers
❏ Publications in development
❏ Newspaper consultants
❏ Research on the future of electronic publishing

MediaInfo's Asian sites section includes direct links to the *Singapore Business Times*, *Madras Hindu*, and *Kyodo News*, plus links to Africa, Australia, Europe, Canada, Middle East with newspapers such as *Die Welt*, *Moscow News*, *Irish Times*, *Gazeta Wyborcza*, *Sydney Morning Herald*, *Jerusalem Post*, and the *Halifax Daily News*. And, of course, you'll find the U.S. dailies, weeklies, and even collegiate newspapers. This is another great Website, bookmark it.

London's *Financial Times:* Setting the Pace on the Web

In the spring of 1995 the United Kingdom's highly regarded *Financial Times* became one of the first major financial/business newspapers with a Website. For that, they deserve a round of applause. They moved ahead of the curve, a step ahead of the competition, and ahead of most American newspapers in reaching the global cyberspace market. This kind of competitive pressure is guaranteed to nudge American newspapers onto the Web and further out into the cyberspace.

The *Financial Times* offers an excellent menu of free news. News briefs include the day's current headlines with several lines of coverage. As an ex-television newsman, I immediately thought of the teleprompters used by television anchors as I scanned through the *Financial Times* newsbytes. They read much like the nightly television news. Headlines are brief and to the point. No padding. If this trend continues and enough newspapers hit the global Internet "channel," network television may have a lot more than cable TV competition to worry about.

Not only was their coverage timely, the *Financial Times* also had the major international market indexes—London's FT-SE, Germany's DAX,

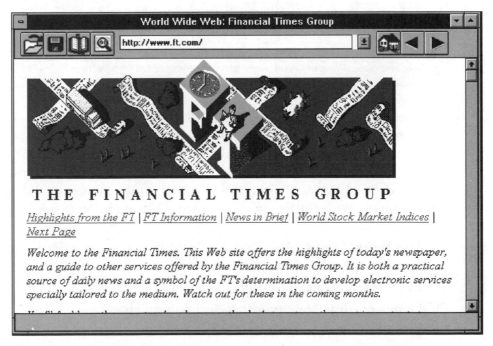

Figure 3.2 London *Financial Times:* free news delivery on the Web.

Japan's Nikkei, the DJIA, and others. Definitely worth bookmarking! If you want the full text, you can dial up and download it through several sources.

Investor's Business Daily: Delivery on America Online

What a deal! The America Online subscription price is worth it just to get *Investor's Business Daily.* IBD is a great business newspaper. In subscriber base, it's only one-tenth the size of the *Wall Street Journal.* But it has a dedicated audience of highly successful investors, and a dedicated publisher who's covered major operating deficits to live his commitment and vision of creating a great newspaper. And it's happening.

THE "CANSLIM" FORMULA OF *INVESTOR'S BUSINESS DAILY*

C = Current quarterly earnings
A = Annual earnings increase
N = New: products, management, highs
S = Shares outstanding; common stock
L = Leader/laggard in industry sector
I = Industry/underwriter sponsorship
M = Market trend and direction

(SOURCE: William O'Neil, *How to Make Money in Stocks,* McGraw-Hill, 1988.)

The publisher, William O'Neil, is also a highly successful investor and the author of the best-seller, *How to Make Money in Stocks.* O'Neil is the originator of the popular "CANSLIM" formula for picking winning stocks. *Investor's Business Daily* is one of the early electronic publications online, delivered on America Online. And O'Neil really delivers a lot of high-quality news to his readers in cyberspace. Their menu includes:

- ❐ **The Week Ahead:** A schedule of upcoming economic indicators, new issues, political and business events.
- ❐ **Executive Update:** Headline stories.
- ❐ **New America:** New products, technology, etc.
- ❐ **The Economy:** National and international stories.
- ❐ **Markets & Investing:** Stocks, bonds, everything.

- ❐ **Archives:** For the prior ten weeks.
- ❐ **Message & Bulletin Boards:** On special topics.
- ❐ **Quick Search:** On keywords.
- ❐ **Learn to Invest:** The IBD short course for winners.
- ❐ **CANSLIM Training:** And a contest to test your skills.

Bottom line: Very impressive, a definite five-star performance. The *Investor's Business Daily* is an exceptional electronic newspaper that is the pacesetter for all other electronic business publications tied into an online service. Next, we expect to see *Investor's Business Daily* with their own visually distinctive Web-based Personal Journal competing with Dow Jones.

The *Wall Street Journal*'s Personal Journal

In mid-1995 Dow Jones came out with a handsome electronic version of the *Wall Street Journal,* downloaded from a local access number by dial-up modem service. Not only do you get the news from the whole *Journal* for less than the cost of the street version, you also get to customize it. As their

Figure 3.3   *Investor's Business Daily* for first-class financial news.

ad says, it's "published for a circulation of one," the perfect newspaper for the busy professional. Here's what you get to save you time:

❐ **Customized news.** Essentially you've got an automatic clipping service that responds to your needs. Personal Journal starts you off with a quick read, giving you the key front-page stories and letting you preprogram other areas of interest from the 35 regular columns, editorials, special reports, and so forth.

❐ **Breaking news.** The Personal Journal is actually more than an electronic newspaper, with one edition per day. This is what's great about electronic publishing; stories are updated continually. Any time of the day or night you can dial in and get the latest-breaking stories, without waiting for the next delivery. In other words, Personal Journal is really more analogous to a newswire, videotext, or television broadcast than a print publication.

❐ **Portfolio monitoring.** You can also track your personal portfolio easily. This is heck of a time-saver you'll really appreciate. Just plug in the

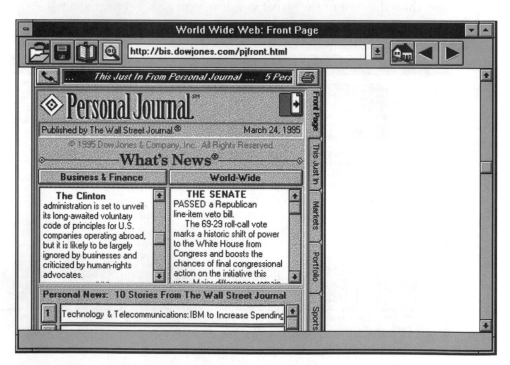

Figure 3.4   Dow Jones Personal Journal: front page.

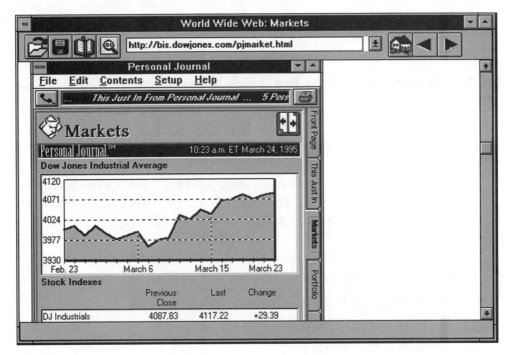

Figure 3.5   Dow Jones Personal Journal: markets page.

stocks and funds you own and you'll get a daily summary of your portfolio's performance.

☐ **Global market reports.**   You name the market, stock, index, etc., and
it's right there for you: quotes, historical trends, patterns, and much
more.

What's missing on Personal Journal? Advertisements are screened out.
Some readers may be glad to see them go, while other readers, like myself,
actually read the ads because they often contain important information
(introductions to new services and contacts, hints to new technologies,
etc.). Some illustrations are also screened out, although certain simple
financial graphics and charts do remain.

Bottom line: Personal Journal is the wave of the future in cyberspace.
And you can bet you'll soon see similar news products coming online and
on the Internet very soon. Interested in current history? You can get an
entire year of the Journal on a single CD-ROM for about $70, complete with
all company and market data. You can search it, graph it, print it, and
export the data to other applications. This is another fine example of how

important the CD-ROM technology is becoming for the Wall Street cyber-space investor.

Market Monitor: Dow Jones Expanding in Cyberspace

If Personal Journal, the electronic version of the *Wall Street Journal* isn't enough firepower for you (and you think their real-time Dow Jones News/Retrieval service will be too much), well then, just move over to Dow Jones' Private Investor Edition service for $30 a month. This service is designed primarily for the buy-and-hold investor interested mainly in fundamental analysis and end-of-day quotes. The DJN/R Private Investor Edition delivers news, quotes, analysis, and forecasts:

❐ Five Dow Jones newswires with market-moving news
❐ News articles from the *Journal* and hundreds other publications
❐ Weekly stock quotes back the prior two years
❐ Mutual fund quotes back two years
❐ International news
❐ Abstracts from securities analysts' research reports

You can also add on the DJN/R-Technical Analysis service for another $40 a month. One of its main features is Tradeline, one of the largest historical and performance sources available, with over 20 years of daily price data on over 200,000 securities, plus screening capabilities to identify investment opportunities. The Market Monitor services also include access to:

❐ Futures and index quotes on 80 major contracts
❐ Zacks corporate earnings estimator
❐ Insider trading at 8,000 public companies
❐ Innovest technical analysis reports on 4,500 stocks
❐ Wall $treet Week online, transcripts from PBS
❐ S&P online database of 4,700 companies
❐ Media general financial services, 6,200 companies in 180 industries

Bottom line: Before taking the easy way out and just grabbing one of the commercial online services for a newspaper, go the next step and check out the full range of Dow Jones news services, from Personal Journal to Private

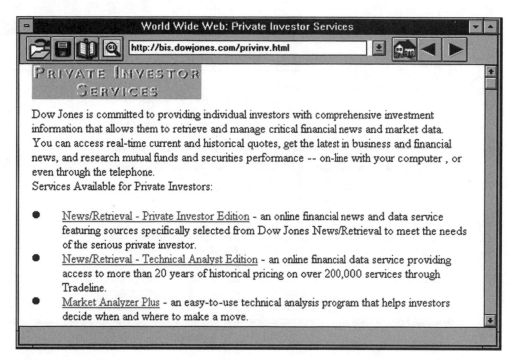

Figure 3.6 Dow Jones Private Investor Services.

Investor Edition (also called Market Monitor) to the full Dow Jones News/Retrieval service. These services have a lot to offer, and could have exactly what you need. Moreover, they will likely become much more competitive in supplying news services to the average investor as the competition heats up in cyberspace generally.

New York Times' Business Pages on America Online

If you want "all the news that's fit to print," here's another excellent online business section for you, from the *New York Times*. Actually, there are a number of ways to get the *New York Times'* electronic version, in addition to the online commercial services such as AOL. America Online has an electronic version of the *New York Times,* with their excellent business pages. The *Times* selection includes 20 excellent stories:

❑ Release dates for economic reports
❑ Corporate dividend meetings

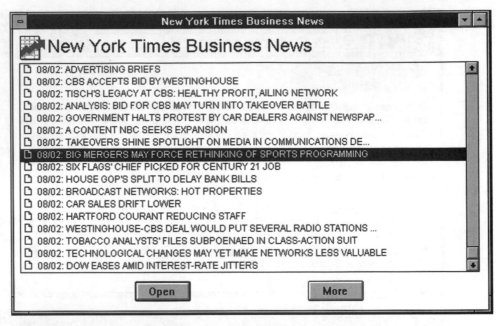

Figure 3.7 *New York Times* Business News online.

❐ Schedule of upcoming equity issues

❐ Calendar of new bonds

❐ Other key information

You'll also find a full-text version of the *Times* on Dow Jones News/ Retrieval and the larger database services, such as Dialog and Lexis/Nexis. Next step? Bet on the venerable *New York Times* soon following the lead of the *Wall Street Journal*, *Financial Times*, Knight-Ridder's *San Jose Mercury News* and other great newspapers . . . soon they'll all be on the Internet, as well as the online services and other sections of the cyberspace universe. These are truly exciting times.

Los Angeles TimesLink: Hotline to Hollywood and Washington

TimesLink has all the latest business news, personal financial tips, stock quotes, and breaking newswire stories on the news scene for southern California. Plus you'll get the latest scoop from Hollywood and Las Vegas. Leave it to the TimesLink connection to add some pizzazz to their version of an electronic newspaper. This is one jazzy online newspaper, definitely reflecting the southern California lifestyle (all that's missing is an interactive Baywatch!).

TimesLink is actually much more than an electronic newspaper. The *Times* has created its own online service, accessed through the Prodigy service, complete with live chat forums, special-interest bulletin boards, sports, weather, dialogs with your favorite columnists . . . and even an access to the Internet.

The *Los Angeles Times* is known for its Washington news bureau and political coverage. Perhaps that's why the Dow Jones News/Retrieval service features it as one of their major news services. And where else are you going to get the inside stories about southern California's top 100 companies? TimesLink is both a local and a great national news resource.

San Jose Mercury News: Silicon Valley in a Shrinking World!

Do you have a special interest in hot news on Silicon Valley's computer giants? Tap into Mercury Center, located in the center of the Valley's action.

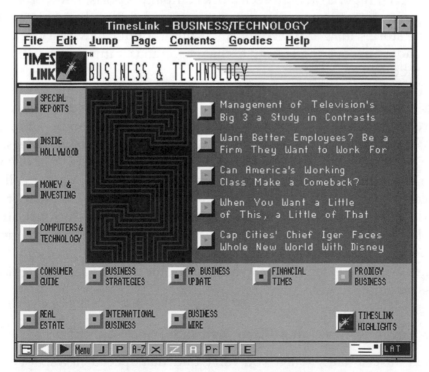

Figure 3.8 *Los Angeles Times'* TimesLink: Hollywood and the world.

The Mercury Center, as the electronic edition is known, is a trendsetter in the electronic publishing business, reflecting their position in the center of the dynamic computer industry.

Here's one of the great newspaper sites in cyberspace, 1995 winner of the *Interactive Age* magazine's award for the best business site on the Web. Mercury Center is the electronic edition of the *San Jose Mercury News* newspaper, and a subsidiary of the Knight-Ridder news chain. Actually, Mercury is much more than an electronic newspaper; they are going beyond just publishing.

This industry leader already has big plans to aggressively move into the interactive communication fields on the Internet as well as with the commercial online services. In fact, they are close to becoming a quasi-commercial online service, acting much like Time Warner's Pathfinder Website discussed below. Mercury Center is a perfect example of these new cyberspace newspapers. Look closely at their outstanding work.

Mercury Center is also on America Online with a very hot site packed with quality news and more. Their Business and Technology subdirectory has special reports on high-tech stock company reports, news on the economy, investments, technological advances, and personal finance. They also report stories in *MicroTimes* and the Knight-Ridder news services, one of the leaders in covering foreign exchange, options, futures, derivatives, and commodities.

Plus there's the general news, entertainment, sports, and a library that is a gateway to Dialog and Viewtext, two Knight-Ridder-owned news search and research services. In the Mercury Center Library subdirectory you can even access the newspaper archives from the past ten years.

So, whether you're in Singapore, San Moritz, or South Africa, you can get the *San Jose Mercury News* news if you want it . . . and find out all about Silicon Valley, just like the local neighbors. Soon, every newspaper in the world will be at your fingertips (or rather desktop), following the lead of the *San Jose Mercury News*. They'll have to follow suit in order to be competitive.

Bottom line: Bookmark it. Knight-Ridder's Mercury Center is an award-winning example of the new electronic newspaper business. Don't miss this one.

Dow Jones News/Retrieval and Other Multidatabase Searches

When all else fails, when you can't find that special newspaper you're looking for on its own Website or located at your commercial online service

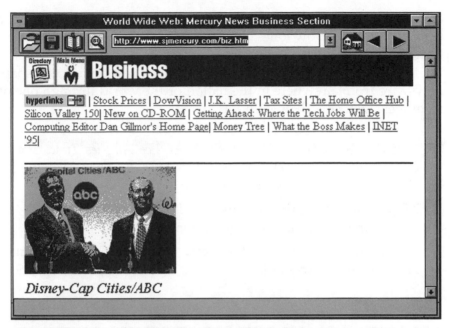

Figure 3.9 *San Jose Mercury News:* Silicon Valley and the world.

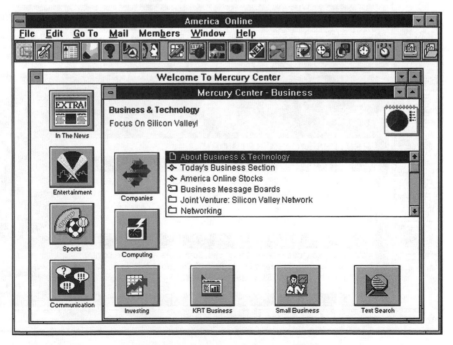

Figure 3.10 Knight-Ridder's Mercury Center on AOL.

or your local newsstand, you'll probably find the full text at a reasonable price through the Dow Jones News/Retrieval (DJN/R), Lexis-Nexis, or the Dialog search services.

You can download copies of just about any respectable newspaper and newswire from anywhere in the nation or the world through one of these resources. DJN/R will give you:

❐ **Major U.S. papers.** *New York Times, Los Angeles Times* Washington edition, *San Francisco Examiner, Dallas Morning News, Washington Times, Denver Post, USA Today,* and 40 more.

❐ **Major business publications.** *Wall Street Journal, Barron's, Business Week, Forbes, Fortune, The Economist,* and many, many more.

❐ **Other first-class national papers.** *Hartford Courant, Buffalo News, Sacramento Bee, Rocky Mountain News, Arizona Republic,* and more.

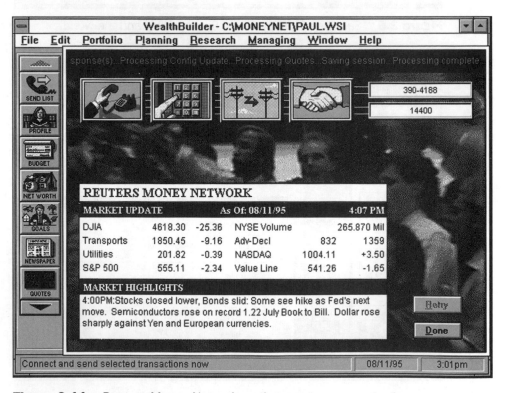

Figure 3.11   Reuters Money Network market news.

❏ **Key international papers.** *Wall Street Journal*'s editions covering Asia, Europe, and the Americas, plus London's *Financial Times, Nikkei Japan News*, and most major international newspapers.

The image of the young boy or girl on a bicycle delivering the morning newspaper before going to grade school has been replaced by satellites that download real-time data into your desktop computer workstation without you knowing it's happening. Newspapers throughout the world are now networked in cyberspace. Tomorrow morning you can get your favorite newspaper before the kid next door even gets up.

EXECUTIVE NEWS SERVICES: DIGESTS AND CLIPPING SERVICES

One of the biggest headaches for travelers on the information superhighway is caused by information overload; there's just too darn much stuff to absorb. And everybody in cyberspace feels it. Well, that's the problem. And the executive news services are one of the main solutions:

❏ They are designed to help you wade through large databases and weed out the junk while helping you target exactly on what you're looking for.
❏ They'll also save you valuable time, money, and reduce frustrations.

In short, these executive news services (ENS) will keep you on top of any market sector or specialty you choose to focus on.

Executive News Service: ENS at CompuServe

CompuServe subscribers have the option of storing incoming news articles in a clippings folder based on *keywords.* They are filed separately from your E-mail so that you don't have to wade through a ton of news articles to get to your E-mail messages. From these clippings folders you can print or save to the articles to your hard drive.

There are some drawbacks to CompuServe ENS service, however. Aside from the added expense of this service, the files can be a pain in the butt to manage. For example, each incoming article must be separately deleted.

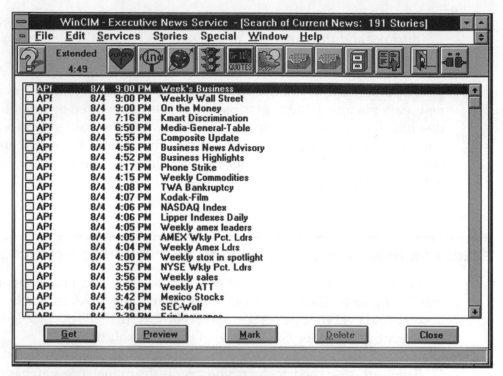

Figure 3.12   CompuServe's Executive News Service.

Prodigy's "Heads Up" Executive News Service

Prodigy is set up to take orders for Individual Inc.'s Heads Up executive news service, a timesaving search tool. Once your account is opened, you get morning delivery by E-mail to your Prodigy account (or another E-mail account for that matter) or by fax directly from the Heads Up organization.

For the investor interested in specialized information on industry sectors such as telecommunications and information services, this digest service might provide just the right bit of additional information to give you the edge on a move in the market sector that you're following. Do some comparative shopping before making your decision to spend $30 a month for this or any other ENS service.

NewsNet: Comprehensive Industry Sector Coverage

NewsNet is another excellent source of timely news that is customized or preselected by you, the subscriber. NewsNet maintains a first-class data-

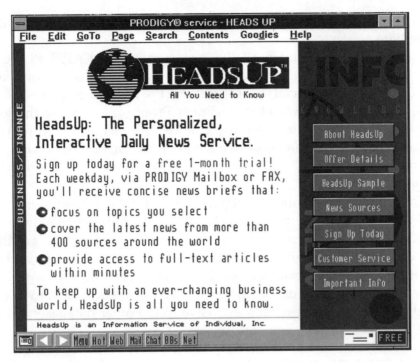

Figure 3.13   Prodigy's Heads Up executive news service.

base that puts hundreds of "vital business information sources at your fingertips." Every day over 17,500 news items are sent to the NewsNet database from 700 news sources. This includes hundreds of business journals and newsletters in all industrial categories, plus real-time access to more than 20 worldwide newswires. You get full-text stories on companies and industries you track, 24 hours a day, including:

❏ Hot news stories on your company and its industrial sector

❏ The competition's latest strategies and actions

❏ Industry trends, mergers, acquisitions, and other developments

❏ Business opportunities and breaking international events

❏ Quotes on stocks, bonds, commodities, indexes, etc.

With NewsNet you get important information ahead of the crowd. Their NewsFlash option is a basic clipping service, screening through their huge network of news resources. In effect, NewsFlash is constantly monitoring the incoming news, searching for topics critical to your selected profile. This information is then downloaded directly into your computer for immediate action.

NewsNet also includes all the major newswires: AP, UPI, Business Wire, PR Newswire, Reuters, Knight-Ridder, Federal News Service, Xinhua Beijing, UK Financial Times; plus S&P's Emerging & Special Situations, Dun & Bradstreet, TRW Business Profiles, as well as the leading newsletters and journals in all major industrial sectors, including periodicals such as *Airline Financial News, Derivative Engineering & Technology, Managed Care Outlook,* and reports from *Investext* and the *Investment Analyst.*

Even if you're on another database you should check out this competitor. Why? Because many of NewsNet's reports are unavailable on other databases, probably as many as 25 percent of the total numbers of titles in their database; for example, many in such key sectors as energy and transportation, including *Aviation Litigation Reporter, Hazardous Waste Litigation Reporter,* and 200 more titles. Similarly, if you're already on NewsNet, you should also investigate what's exclusive to the other databases; you may want to switch, or add their service, too.

Bottom line: A must. Check out the NewsNet list of 800 sources. You'll be amazed at the depth of their database. As with any of these large databases (e.g., Dialog and Nexis-Lexis), you just might feel like a kid in a

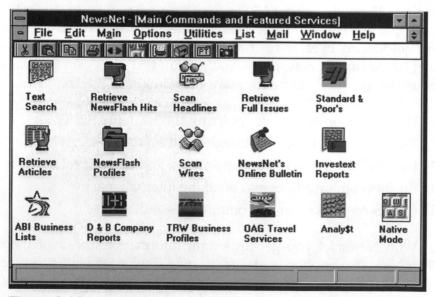

Figure 3.14   NewsNet's comprehensive news database.

candy store looking at all these wonderful, exciting, unusual publications available in cyberspace.

ARE YOU STILL GETTING YOUR NEWS FROM DEAD TREES?

Now there's a better way to get your news. Just surf to our hot new Website. NewsPage filters over 15,000 stories from over 500 news sources every night, and categorizes them by topic. Bookmark topics you like, and NewsPage goes to work. Every day by 8:00 A.M. you'll receive news that matches your interests. Scan concise briefs, then drill down to get the whole story. It's the fast, easy way to keep up with rapidly changing technologies and other critical information. Explore free NewsPage briefs today. NewsPage briefs are free, while full-text articles are available for a modest subscription fee. Check it out. You'll never get your news the same old way again.

(SOURCE: Individual, Incorporated, ad copy for NewsPage, in *Internet World*.)

NewsPage on the World Wide Web

If you're on the Web, you should also check in on NewsAgent from Individual, Incorporated. The day we checked in there were quite a number of current articles from several major newspapers and news agencies: the *Toronto Star, Knight-Ridder/Tribune-Business, Journal of Commerce, Vancouver Sun, Agence France Presse, Reuters,* and *Xinhua*. NewsPage searches through 15,000 stories in 500 news sources every night and categorizes them by topic. You preselect the categories you want. They're delivered to your desktop. Scan the digests and, if you want, pull down the full text of the story.

The NewsPage's NewsAgent covers a variety of national and international news. Their news ranges over many areas of business, economics, finance, and politics. Their Website was under development but they're definitely on the right track. Access was free in the early months, once you registered. Today you can still get the headline news free, while detailed, full-text articles are billed to subscribers on a monthly fee basis.

Profound: Online for News, Quotes, Searches, and More

Profound is an "online service that pinpoints what you need to know in a matter of seconds." The core of the Profound system is a proprietary search

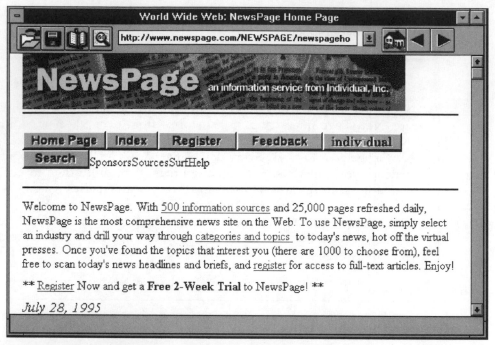

Figure 3.15   NewsPage focuses on key industry topics.

software program that allows you to scan large databases quickly. Profound's system will access company and industry research (Disclosure's database, S&P's 4,600 companies, D&B's 4 million worldwide, etc.); 40,000 market research reports securities quotes (including stocks, commodities, etc., from all major global exchanges); news from Reuters, AP, Knight-Ridder, and other newswires; research from investment banks; and forecasts from leading international economists.

The exciting aspect about new search systems such as Profound is not so much that it may be the particular system for you, but rather, as such systems come on the market, it shows an awareness among software entrepreneurs that information overload and database searching are major problems. And companies such as Profound are searching for solutions. Check out this quality service.

InfoManager's InfoExpress: Staying Connected Anywhere

InfoManager is a special executive news service that's specifically designed for the busy, on-the-go professional who needs access to infor-

Figure 3.16   Profound's NewsNow special delivery.

mation while moving between several locations during the day. InfoManager quickly updates information into your computer, so you can work offline to fit your schedule. InfoExpress' main features are:

❏ **Custom News & Retrievals:** Includes Reuters, S&P ComStock, Business Wire, NewsBytes, and the PR Newswire.

❏ **Stocks & Mutual Funds:** Automatic daily updates to stocks and mutual funds, tracking fundamentals, historical charts for your portfolio (high/low/close).

❏ **E-mail Messaging:** Plus Internet and Web applications.

InfoManager's design creates an easy interface with Netscape, Mosaic, and other Internet applications. This product was created especially to take the frustration out of the hectic schedule of a professional who must stay in touch with several resources, clients, news, investment services, and such. InfoManager is available on a trial basis. Definitely check it out.

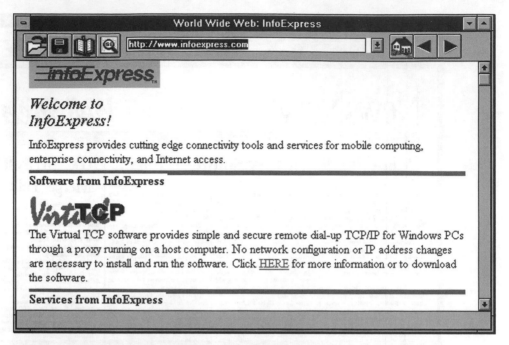

Figure 3.17   InfoManager's InfoExpress on the Web.

Farcast News Digest Service: When E-Mail Is Easiest

Farcast is an Internet news and information service designed for the investor still operating solely with E-mail connections. For less than a dollar a day you have access to an extensive range of services. You can search their database or have Farcast clip the news to match your selected profile, thus creating your own personalized newspaper. Their package includes:

❏ Unlimited stock quotes on 15-minute delay from NYSE, AMEX, NAS-DAQ, indexes, mutual funds, and more.

❏ Headline news from AP, UPI, Businesswire, and PR Newswire before they appear as articles in the newspapers.

❏ Company reports from Hoover's database of 1,000 companies.

You get round-the-clock access to Farcast service by E-mail across the Internet. Since there are an estimated 20 times as many Internet users with E-mail service as with Web access, Farcast E-mail delivery makes a lot of sense for now. But the Web access is growing rapidly, so we expect to see a

Farcast Website in the near future. In any event, you can try the Farcast service free for ten days, a no-risk opportunity to see if it's easier than logging on to a Website.

Free Internet News Services: Yahoo and the Newsroom

If you don't have an online commercial service to feed you news, there are many high-quality resources on the Internet that you can access for free to get a sampling of major news events impacting the world of investing. The Yahoo meta-list has a large News subdirectory. Especially review The Newsroom, which will help you access many financial, business, and general-news sites, including Reuters, ABC News, CNN Newsroom, *Time*, *Mercury Center*, *San Francisco Chronicle*, *New York Times*, and *USA Today*. In addition, we have accumulated a list of at least 15 Websites providing free business and financial news.

Take time to review these sites. See which ones fit your special needs. Then bookmark them for future reference. Each of these resources will pro-

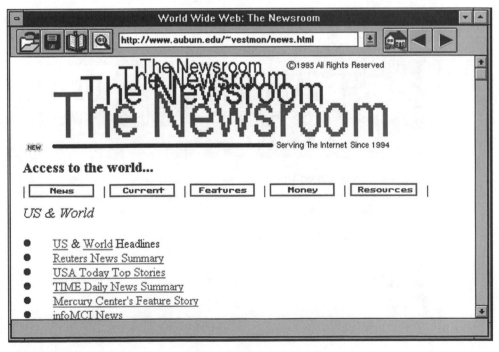

Figure 3.18 The Newsroom: great global news links.

vide you with free news analysis and commentary. And as you travel the Internet you'll surely pick up more (and lose a few as they convert to subscriber services).

Executive News Services: Luxury or Basic Utility?

As you look through these ENS options, you'll probably get a strong sense that *all* electronic newspapers will come with some kind of ENS tools in the near future, that is, some kind of subroutines designed to help you search, clip, and/or digest only the news you want . . . anything to help you cope with the tremendous information overload we are facing. Some ENS services will be more efficient than others, but the advantage of one over the other will probably boil down to the scope of the database included—or rather, databases.

In fact, as this area of cyberspace develops, you can expect that more and more ENS services will be designed to *simultaneously* search, clip, and/or digest *several* newspapers and other electronic publications at the same time. If an ENS service is truly customer focused, it will be subject

Figure 3.19   *Wall Street Journal*'s Update on the Web.

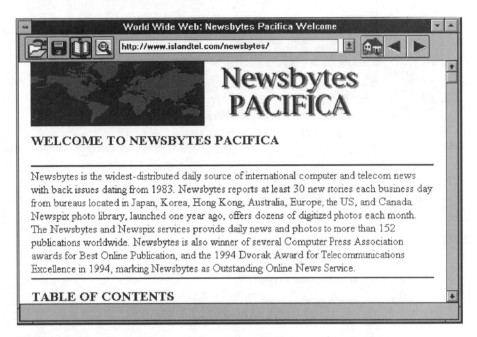

Figure 3.20 *Newsbytes* on telecommunications and computers.

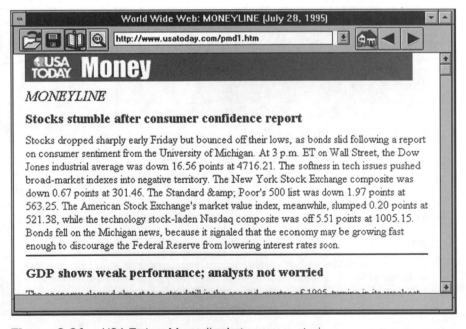

Figure 3.21 *USA Today:* Moneyline's top news stories.

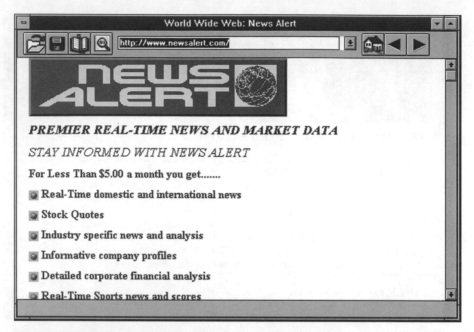

Figure 3.22   NewsAlert: stock quotes and market news.

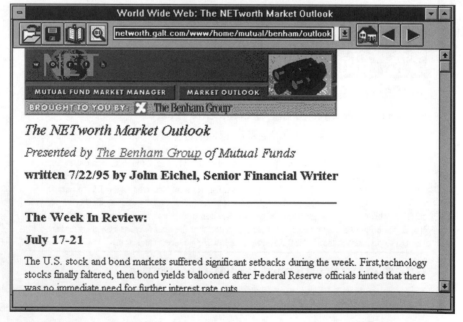

Figure 3.23   NETworth's Market Outlook from The Benham Group.

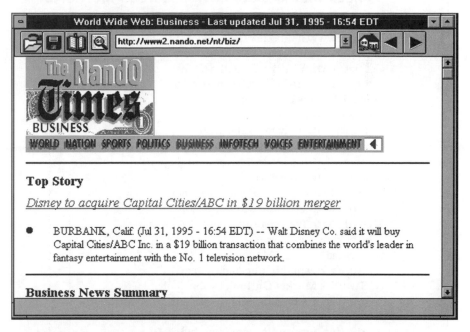

Figure 3.24 *News & Observer:* Business Times section.

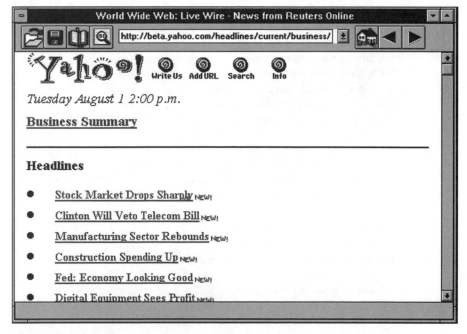

Figure 3.25 Yahoo's Business News Summary from Reuters.

FREE FINANCIAL AND BUSINESS NEWS ON THE NET

❏ **Bloomberg Business News,** financial markets.
   http://www.nando.net/newsroom/nt/stocks.html
❏ **ClariNet** newswires on the Usenet newsgroups.
❏ **Cowles/SIMBA,** news about the media.
   http://www.mecklerweb.com/simba
❏ **Financial Times** of London.
   http://www.ft.com
❏ **Holt's Report,** daily market statistics
   http://turnpike.net/metro/holt
❏ **Hoover**'s Top Ten Business Stories of the Week.
   http://www.hoovers.com
❏ **Mercury Center**'s headline business news.
   http://www.sjmercury.com/biz.htm
❏ **Merrill Lynch News;** midday and closing markets.
   http://www.ml.com
❏ **Money** magazines's Money Daily.
   http://www.pathfinder.com/money
❏ **NETworth's Market Outlook** by the Benham Group.
   http://networth.galt.com/www/home/networth.html
❏ **Newsbytes** daily news headlines
   http://www.islandtel.com/newsbytes
❏ **NewsPage**'s headlines of today's top stories.
   http://www.newspage.com
❏ **The Newsroom,** Business & World News.
   http://www.auburn.edu/~vestmon/news.html
❏ **PAWWS Financial Markets Outlook.**
   http://www.pawws.com
❏ **PR Newswire** for full-text corporate news.
   http://www.prnewswire.com
❏ **Reuters Business News** Summary.
   http://www.fyionline.com/infoMCI/update/BUSINESS-MCI.html
❏ **Time** magazine's business and financial pages.
   http://www.pathfinder.com/time
❏ **Trade Plans Newsletter,** Futures & Options Trades.
   http://www.teleport.com/~futures
❏ **USA Moneyline & USA Money.**
   http://www.usatoday.com
❏ **Wall Street Journal**'s Update.
   http://update.wsj.com
❏ **Wall Street Net** for new issues and their bankers.
   http://www.netresource.com
❏ **Yahoo Business News Summary.**
   http://www.yahoo.com/headlines
❏ Check MediaInfo's directory of news links.
   http://www.mediainfo.com
❏ Expect many other free news sites to be added regularly.

focused rather than tied to just one publication. Certainly that's the approach of the larger services such as Dialog.

Your choices are increasing daily. If you want to clip stories from just the *Wall Street Journal,* for example, that's your choice: Get their Personal Journal. If you want more, then you'll want to subscribe to their Market Monitor or the Dow Jones News/Retrieval. Or try one of the multidatabase search outfits discussed below, such as Dialog, a Knight-Ridder news organization. In cyberspace, you have an almost unlimited number of choices to serve the esoteric needs of every investor, with new technologies emerging almost daily to help you minimize the frustrations.

NEWSWIRE SERVICES FOR FINANCE, BUSINESS, AND INVESTING

All major newswire services have special financial and business newswires. Moreover, they are readily available to the small investor as well as the major institutions, investment and commercial banks, money managers, and stock brokerage firms. For example, Reuters is on CompuServe as well as America Online's Personal Finance section, the Associated Press is on Dialog, and AP also has a joint venture with Dow Jones News, and of course there's the Dow Jones News/Retrieval service that is served by the worldwide network of Dow Jones reporters, bureaus, and newswires.

Associated Press and United Press International

The Associated Press and UPI are networks of newspapers and other newswires linked throughout the world. Both newswires have been around for decades. Their staff reporters blanket the world. Their member newspapers cooperate by exchanging information as well as reporting breaking stories for their network. Many newspapers or cyberspace news services will carry stories with an AP or UPI byline. Most of the time you'll get their information secondhand, as part of some other publication.

Moreover, the individual investor can also access these big-time newswires at a reasonable price by going directly through CompuServe, Dialog, and other cyberspace services. Fees are usually based on the size of the customer. When I was associate editor of the *Los Angeles Herald Examiner* in the 1980s, our paper had a circulation of 250,000, and we paid over $13,000 weekly for the Associated Press newswires. Today, an individual investor can get substantially the same on their commercial online service

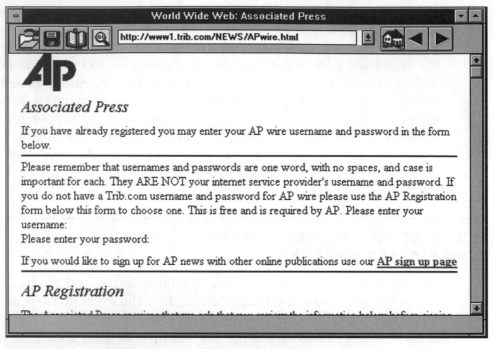

Figure 3.26   Associated Press (AP) newswire service.

or from the ClariNet AP newswire included as part of their basic Internet access provider's services.

Dow Jones Newswire Services

Dow Jones News has five newswires, each providing different information and each serving a different market. These wires feed information primarily to major institutions, banks, stock brokers, and money managers. However, an individual investor can also get the Dow Jones newswires through vendors of market quote information, such as S&P Comstock, PC Quote, Data Broadcasting's Signal, and Quotron.

❑ **Dow Jones News Services.**   Real-time news for the equities investor. Corporate, economic, market, and political news that shapes investment decisions. Hot stocks, economic indicators, world events, stock splits, mergers and acquisitions, bond market action, and political events.

❏ **Dow Jones Professional Investor Report.** This newswire operates like a hunter, tracking down the unexplained anomalies in the market, reporting special situations fast so you're first with info on new opportunities, while monitoring your portfolio. Covers stocks delayed or halted, unusual trading patterns, earnings alerts over or under analysts' expectations, index futures, most active, best and worst performers, and more.

❏ **Dow Jones International News Services.** This wire provides timely news and statistics coupled with analysis and expert commentary to explain the impact of world events on financial markets, as well as your investments and business sectors. Included in this group are special newswires on the global exchanges, banking, foreign currencies, European companies, petroleum, and world equities.

❏ **Capital Markets Report.** Street intelligence for investors and traders in fixed-income securities and financial futures, specifically focused on the flow of funds around the globe every 24 hours. Interest rates,

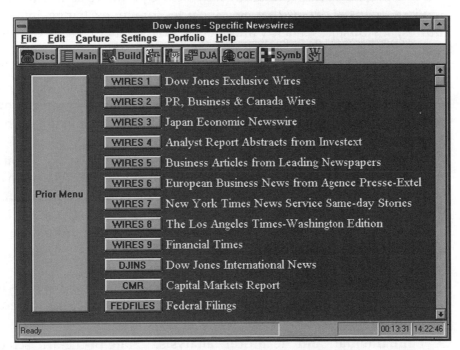

Figure 3.27 Dow Jones News: Specific Newswires.

yields, central bank actions, government securities offerings, index futures, options, and expert street talk.

❏ **Federal Filings.**   Monitors and reports on all SEC and other federal agency and court filings and proceedings that can impact investment decision making.

Dow Jones is one of the world's leading providers of financial, business, and investment news covering domestic and international markets. Their print publications—*Barron's, Smart Money,* and the *Wall Street Journal*—are respected throughout the world. Their newswires, though less well known publicly, are the core of their business and are available to serious investors and traders.

Knight-Ridder: Commodities, Options, and Futures

If commodities are your game, Knight-Ridder Financial (KRF) News is one of your leading sources of information. KRF began serving the commodities exchanges in 1953, and today may be the premiere source of information in a financial drama that now includes foreign exchange, interest rate futures, agribusiness, energy and metals, OTC derivatives, as well as pork bellies, soybeans, and cocoa.

KRF is not for the casual investor or the fainthearted. Many of their clients (such as businesses hedging crop prices or foreign trade contracts) *need* to trade here. Others in KRF are money managers because they love the action, and they see high-profit margins in trading foreign currencies. It's a rough-and-tumble, high-pressure business.

There are over 50,000 financial instruments actively traded throughout the world. The data is enormous. What's more, these markets are in action 24 hours a day, with trading moving around the clock and around the globe, from European exchanges, through the Americas, to the Far East.

Fortunately, the KRF store of data is tuned in, open around the clock, supplying you with all the hot information:

❏ **Real-time and historic data feeds.**   The most extensive quotes covering all major futures, options, and derivative instruments traded in 75 markets worldwide.

❏ **Fundamental and technical analysis.** State-of-the-art screening, monitoring, and decision-making tools using your favorite indicators.

❏ **Market vane's bullish consensus.** Tap into the best thinking of more than 100 top experts following all these markets.

❏ **Global News Coverage.** KRF has an award-winning global news network structured to ensure that you get the news first, political events, crops estimates, weather patterns, interest rate changes, you name it.

Plus, you can select only the information you need to fit your area of speciality. This is very useful because many traders concentrate on only a few areas (say, soybeans, corn, and wheat, because they're agribusiness executives), while others, such as money center bankers, are focused on yen, marks, and dollars. As with buying groceries, you pay for only what you order from the vast KRF database.

Bottom line: Definitely check it out. The KRF services are extremely comprehensive. Yes, you'll pay more than your subscription price on Prodigy or America Online, a lot more ($649 for the introductory Super-Charts offer, with a year of analytics, data, quotes, and news). But it's well worth it if you want to trade in this arena. In fact, you won't be able to trade

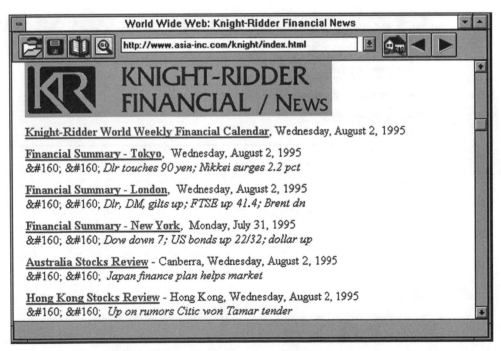

Figure 3.28 Knight-Ridder Financial News on the Web.

without KRF's SuperCharts or something comparable. You need the right equipment to play the game.

Contact Knight-Ridder and get samples of their printed reports as well as the demo disk. They will even send you a fabulous free wall chart of your favorite commodity covering the past ten years.

Reuters Newswire Services: World News Leader

Dow Jones' SEC filing concedes that the British-based Reuters news services is probably the only news service bigger than Dow Jones in the area of financial news. Reuters is a giant, with 13,500 employees in 120 news bureaus worldwide. Fortunately, you can see Reuters news regularly on CompuServe, AOL, and even Dow Jones News/Retrieval.

An investor with an AOL account, for example, is likely to log on early in the morning and catch the opening Reuters news stories over a cup of coffee, along with *Investor's Business Daily.* That'll get your financial day off to a good start. On AOL, you can select Reuters along with a large menu of other news services to fit your particular tastes.

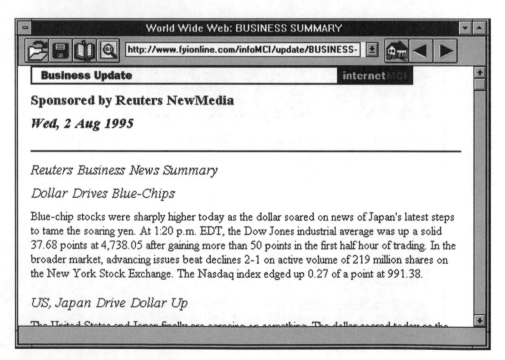

Figure 3.29   Reuters Business News on InternetMCI.

Bloomberg Business News: The Next Generation

Most individual investors might conclude that the Bloomberg Business News services are out of their reach. After all, it can easily cost you a couple thousand a month to have The Bloomberg terminal installed in your office or den. But before you dismiss them, please remember that the Bloomberg News group now has 250 reporters in 42 bureaus throughout the world, transmitting 1,500 stories a day through 62 leading newspapers, plus television and radio stations. So, if you don't get the real-time service directly from Bloomberg, you can still get it indirectly.

Moreover, Bloomberg even has their own all-news radio station operating in New York City. Bloomberg is a welcomed news maverick in a competitive arena dominated by some giants. Today you'll see Bloomberg's stories on a regular basis in papers such as *Dallas Morning News* and *Singapore Straits Times,* and quoted on television programs on CNBC and the USA channels.

More important, you can bet on seeing much more of Bloomberg Business News in the future, as supplier of news and other services to smaller individual investors and in the popular press.

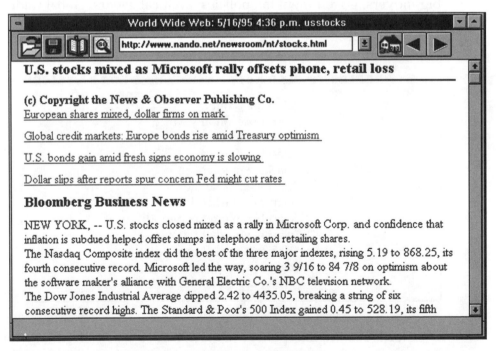

Figure 3.30   Bloomberg Business News on the Web.

ClariNet and AP: The Net Investor's "Free" Newswires

ClariNet is the original newswire service that's available on the Internet. They're a for-profit subgroup of the Usenet system on the Internet. Your Internet service provider must pay a fee before you can read the ClariNet newswires. However, this service can be one of those great hidden benefits of an Internet connection service such as Netcom. Along with your basic fee of $20 a month, you also get ClariNet, which includes the Associated Press newswires.

All you do is click on the Usenet button, locate the Business and Finance subdirectory, and you'll see the ClariNet newsgroups. Bookmark the ones you want. See our selection of a dozen or so key newswires for investors from the ClariNet organization.

There are many other business groups that might be of interest to investors, and many more on general news topics. Moreover, the selection will vary depending on what your particular Internet provider makes available. But once you have the connection, you'll find a steady stream of news information on the usual subjects . . . newsbriefs, company reports, gold prices, insider trading, interest rates, mutual funds, index averages, big movers, government tax policies, political events, global trade, and so forth.

SELECTED CLARINET/AP NEWSWIRES FOR INVESTORS

clari.biz.economy
clari.biz.economy.world
clari.biz.invest
clari.biz.finance
clari.biz.mergers
clari.biz.market.news
clari.biz.market.dow
clari.biz.market.commodities
clari.biz.market.report.usa
clari.biz.market.report.usa.nyse
clari.biz.market.misc (bonds)
clari.biz.news.europe

ClariNet's original policy was to consider articles from any reputable news agency. Today, most of the stories appear to be from the newswires of

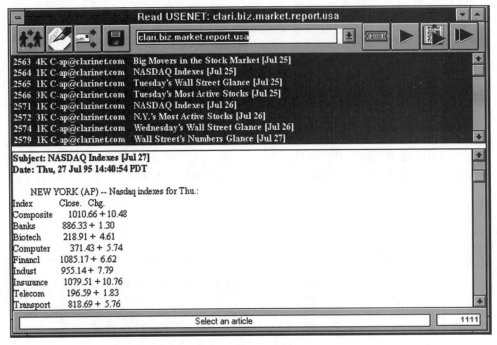

Figure 3.31 ClariNet: market newswire on Netcom.

the Associated Press, which is the most comprehensive, serving all newspapers worldwide, so it's a great service as is. You are guaranteed to find a wealth of information here.

The ClariNet newswire on Netcom's server made me recall my days at the *Los Angeles Herald Examiner*, with hot news coming across the wires day and night, usually too much to absorb unedited—which is why the fierce competition now coming from clipping, digest, and executive news services is likely to force the ClariNet organization to upgrade its service with some kind of screening or search provisions, as Dow Jones has done with Personal Journal, for example.

Bottom line: Most likely, your Internet server will also have the ClariNet newswires. The price is right and the AP always has quality information, so you can't go wrong . . . check it out.

Foreign Newswires Online and on the Internet Meta-Lists

An astute cyberspace investor will also periodically check the key Internet meta-lists for new additions, as well as their online subscription service.

Investors News Online, Yahoo, Wall Street Directory, NETworth, and the others are continually adding new links to newswires and newspaper resources.

For example, on CompuServe you'll find the Citibank Global Report; Dow Jones has the Kyoto News Service. And while surfing the Net you'll find little gems such as the Asia News. You'll soon discover that the opportunities for cyberspace news are endless. And as the Internet quadruples in the next five years to 100 million computer connections, the competition will also intensify. In this environment, the investor will come out the winner, with more news, faster, and at lower prices.

STANDARD & POOR'S MARKETSCOPE NEWS SERVICE

- ❏ Market Commentary; all major exchanges
- ❏ Stocks in the news; with corporate analyzed
- ❏ Street Analysts Commentary
- ❏ Stock of the Week; analyzed in detail
- ❏ Today's Headline news; in politics and business
- ❏ Touted on Television; NBR, Wall Street Week, etc.
- ❏ Touted in The Media
- ❏ Today's Perspective
- ❏ Stock Splits upcoming
- ❏ Technical Market Indicators with analysis
- ❏ New Issues Calendar, with underwriters
- ❏ New Issues; performance tracking
- ❏ C Talk by specific company and date
- ❏ Stock Allocation Model; stocks versus T-bills, etc.
- ❏ Investment Strategies
- ❏ Economic Calendar & Forecasts
- ❏ Monthly Watch Indicators
- ❏ MoneyScope; monetary issues, currencies
- ❏ Current Interest & Exchange Rates
- ❏ Treasury Market Commentary
- ❏ New EPS/Earnings Estimates
- ❏ STAR; Stock Appreciation Rating System

MarketScope is available through various sources: Dow Jones, CompuServe, Telescan, QuoteCom, etc.

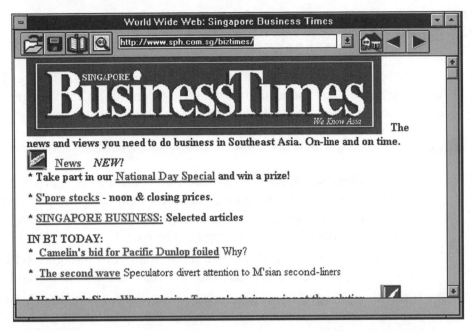

Figure 3.32 Singapore BusinessTimes: news from Southeast Asia.

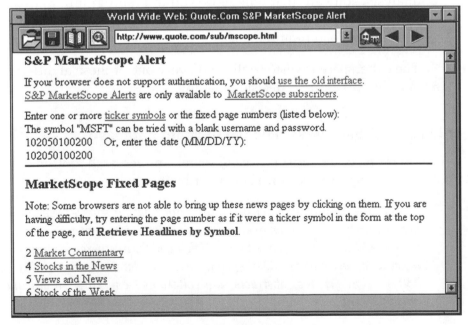

Figure 3.33 S&P MarketScope: QuoteCom's Website.

SEARCH AND RESEARCH TOOLS: ACCESSING LARGE DATABASES

Search tools are common to most database management software. They'll help you screen out the junk, laser on the essential, and save time as you jump directly to your target. In this section you'll see a few key examples of these search tools in practice. There are now many excellent services to help you:

☐ **Multidatabases.**   Cull through hundreds of millions of articles buried in archives of current and back issues, of specialized and popular news periodicals covering every conceivable industry sector and every company ever traded on any exchange in the world.

☐ **Online services.**   There are search commands to navigate within the commercial online services to save valuable time when logged on.

☐ **Internet surfing.**   Special search engines that are constantly burrowing through the massive buildup of documents on the Internet, cataloging them for future reference.

☐ **Stock screening.**   There are search features attached to most stock's analysis, software that will allow you to preprogram multiple investment selection criteria and then pick out the few winners that fit your special portfolio requirements.

The cyberspace investor will need every one of these at different times in his or her investment decision making.

Knight-Ridder's Dialog: Searching the Ultimate Database

Dialog is one of the most powerful search and research tools in the arsenal of any cyberspace investor. They describe themselves as

> *the world's most comprehensive online information source. Whether you need a quick fact from today's news or an exhaustive survey of the world's published literature on your topic, Dialog has the answers—online, all the time, wherever you are. Dialog comprises 450 databases containing over 330 million articles, abstracts, and citations—covering an unequaled variety of subjects.*

No wonder the Knight-Ridder organization acquired the Dialog organization.

DIALOG'S MASSIVE DATABASE RESEARCH

☐ **Newspapers:** Complete text of over 60 leading U.S. and international newspapers, including, *UK Financial Times, Commerce Business Daily, USA Today, St. Louis Post-Dispatch, San Francisco Chronicle, Cleveland Plain Dealer,* etc.

☐ **Newswires:** Wire services stories from AP News, UPI, Reuters, Knight-Ridder/Tribune, Business Wire, the Japan Economic Newswire and the PR Newswire, Agence France Presse, etc.

☐ **Corporate Financials:** Profiles and background materials on more than 12 million domestic and 1 million international companies; also, Moody's Corporate Profiles, D&B Directories, TRW Business Credit Profiles, Disclosure Database, etc.

☐ **Research Articles:** Complete texts from over 2,500 journals, magazines, and newsletters, including *Jane's Defense & Aerospace News/Analysis, Merck Index, Microcomputer Software Guide,* etc.

☐ **Professional Journals:** Reference and abstracts of articles from more than 100,000 national and international publications, including the *Harvard Business Review, Economic Literature Index, Electric Power Database, Chemical Business Newsbase, World Textiles, Consumer Reports,* etc.

☐ **Patents:** Details on 15 million patents in 56 world agencies.

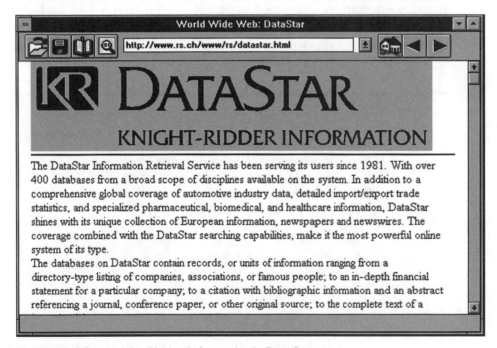

Figure 3.34 Knight-Ridder Information's DataStar.

Dialog operates through a flexible search language that networks all these databases into a single database. As such, you can access all relevant material on your topic through a single research function—easy access through dial-up modem. And keep your eyes open for the Knight-Ridder organization's many subsidiaries on the Web. For example, this $2.5 billion giant also owns DataStar, their European database version similar to Dialog, Knight-Ridder News, tops in global commodity futures, plus a chain of newspapers, including the *San Jose Mercury News* with its leading-edge electronic publication and Website located in the heart of Silicon Valley.

Lexis-Nexis: A Superpowered Database in Cyberspace

The Lexis-Nexis system has expanded way beyond the legal research service I knew when I practiced law years ago. Today Lexis-Nexis includes extensive news and other general-subject research. The Nexis news service was added in 1979. Together they have over 400 million documents in their databases, with 5,800 in the news and business categories and 4,300 in legal. Almost 2 million new documents are added *every week*. Check the Lexis-Nexis Website for an introduction to this service.

Like Dialog, the Lexis-Nexis network of databases is huge, and while lawyers are some of their major clientele, today that's only part of this vast database. It is loaded with many other resources for the serious investor, with most recent reports in a full-text format. Their resource bases are so numerous (the list is nearly 80 pages) that we can only touch on the general

---

LEXIS-NEXIS BUSINESS AND FINANCIAL CATEGORIES

❏ Quotes on Stocks, Indexes, everything
❏ Corporate Annual Reports: Fundamentals
❏ Investment Banking & Research Reports
❏ SEC filings
❏ Newsmakers & Executive Profiles
❏ Mergers & Acquisitions
❏ News Reports: Current & Historic
❏ Periodicals: Financial, Business, General
❏ Television Program Transcripts
❏ Patents & Other Legal Research
❏ Legislation & Pending Bills
❏ And much more research

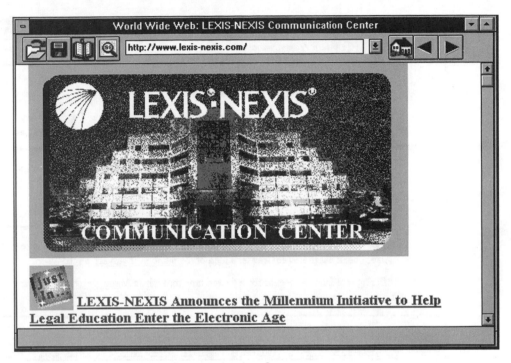

Figure 3.35   Lexis-Nexis Communication Center.

categories. We strongly suggest you link to their Internet Website for more information.

Lexis-Nexis has a solid research database with search tools. They serve over 700,000 customers in 60 countries. With over 4,000 employees, their telephone service alone responds to 5,000 calls a day. Like the Dialog service, you can get the full-text versions of 2,400 news sources, including the *New York Times, Washington Post, Business Week,* and *Fortune.*

Bottom line: Research organizations such as Lexis-Nexis and Dialog are perfect tools for cyberspace investors. They offer in-depth research capabilities—diverse libraries plus sophisticated search processes. These are the kind of resources that will give a cyberspace investor that special edge in the new global electronic marketplace.

Commercial Online Keyword Searches

Today all the major commercial online services have some keyword search techniques that allow you to quickly access their databases. This allows

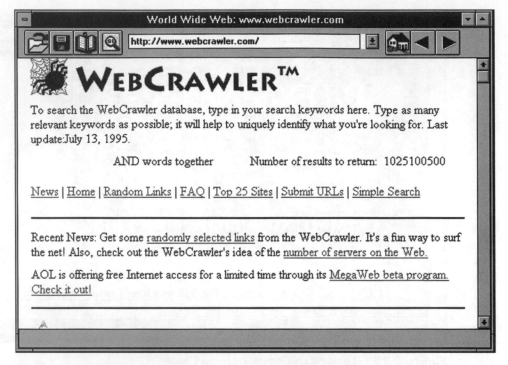

Figure 3.36   WebCrawler searches on the World Wide Web.

you to quickly discover and jump to your topic of special interest, often without having to plow slowly through a bunch of menus.

For example, from AOL's opening menu you simply click on **go to.** Then from the pull-down menu, click on **keyword.** Now try typing in **AAII** or **American Association for Individual Investors . . .** and bingo, you jump immediately to the AAII menu. CompuServe, Prodigy, and Microsoft Network all have similar commands. You won't be able to search outside your online service's particular database, but it sure can save a lot of time getting around *within* their systems.

Keyword Searching on the Internet

Searching databases is a simple process for the user. Simply type in your keyword or words. Different Web browsers have different commands, but they all have some kind of internal and/or external search processes. You may have to try different words and explore several search engines to get results. And you are likely to draw a frustrating blank all too often. A particular search engine may be limited to Internet addresses only, or the database may be limited, or the choice of keywords may corrupt your efforts. The Internet search technology is admittedly still in its infancy.

INTERNET SEARCH LINKS LISTED ON FINANCENET'S WEBSITE

- ❏ Lycos at Carnegie Mellon University
- ❏ Yahoo at Stanford University
- ❏ Usenet Searches at DejaNews
- ❏ Internet Search at NASA
- ❏ Harvest Search
- ❏ WWW Worm Search at CU
- ❏ Search at PrimeNet
- ❏ Wide Area Search at FSU
- ❏ WebCrawler
- ❏ Galaxy Search at EINET
- ❏ Internet Search at W&L
- ❏ WWW and Gopher Search Tools, NSF
- ❏ Search Internet at NovaLinks
- ❏ Search the Internet, Univ.Ottawa
- ❏ SearchCUI W3 Catalog
- ❏ WWW Robots, UK Nexor
- ❏ People Finder
- ❏ Internet Search Tools via Gopher
- ❏ QuickGopher Search
- ❏ Quick Jughead Search W&L
- ❏ Archie Search (FTP Sites)

(SOURCE: http://www.FinanceNet.gov/wwwgen3.htm.)

For example, one Web search of the keyword phrase "Wall Street" turned up a bunch of oddball references to the construction methods for walls and streets. Fortunately, another search also turned up the Wall Street Directory Website, which could lead you to some great bargains in new software for investors.

Keep experimenting with these search tools. You'll improve, and they are definitely improving. In the next year you can expect considerable advances in this technology, progress that could substantially improve your investment decisions. Since new developments are being added to this technology all the time, you should stay on top of these Internet search tools.

Internet Searches: New Superpower Search Engines

The Internet is a network of networks, a database that ties together all databases in cyberspace, bigger than the biggest. Unfortunately, there's no central high command running the show. As a result, the search mechanisms are still in their early development stages. Simply browsing the meta-lists themselves may also help you in your search. However, be forewarned, you cannot expect as reliable or complete results as you would with Dialog, Lexis-Nexis, CompuServe, or Dow Jones when it comes to investment and financial research.

If you're on the Web, start with the Yahoo Website. At the top of their opening menu you'll find the Yahoo search button, which will open a menu with several links to the other major Internet search programs:

❐ **WebCrawler.** Recently acquired by AOL as a part of their expansion into the Webworld, WebCrawler is a major search tool still available free to the public. They may have access to over a million Web docu-

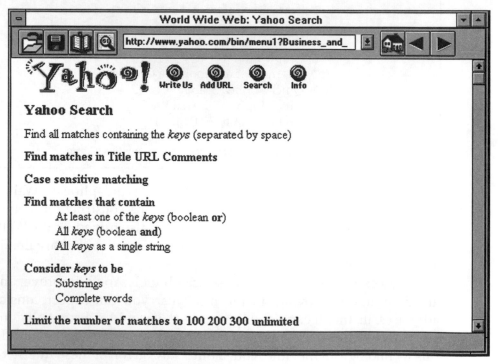

Figure 3.37 Yahoo's general search engine menu.

ments occupying more than 100MB of storage. Check out their list of the Top 25 Websites for an introduction to the beginner's mind on the Web: the favorite new sites include several well-known high-tech companies (Sun, Novell, Microsoft, and Silicon Graphics), NASA, world and weather maps, some beginners' HTML instructions, and the White House.

❑ **Lycos.** Developed and located at Carnegie Mellon University, Lycos has already cataloged 75 percent of the more than 4 million Websites. CMU has seven computers humming away with over 2 million inquiries or *hits* every month. The Microsoft Network was impressed enough with Lycos' power that they license this jewel for MSN customers.

Lycos searches the Internet's major databases (text-only gopher and ftp files as well as the Websites) on an ongoing basis, adding new information to its database. When Lycos finds a new or changed Website, it builds an abstract consisting of title, headings, the 100 most significant

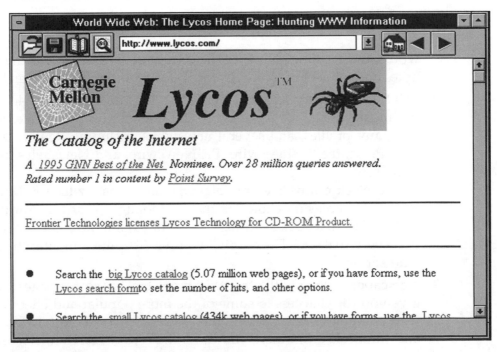

Figure 3.38 Lycos Web searcher from Carnegie Mellon.

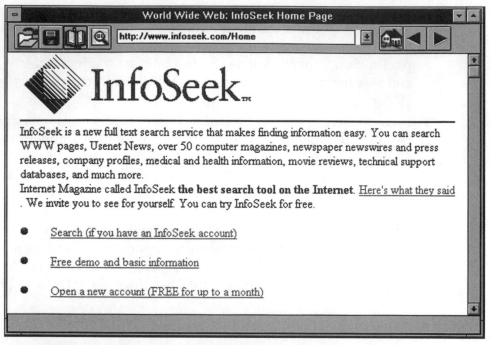

Figure 3.39   InfoSeek text searcher: bigger than Lycos.

words and the first 20 lines of the document. Plus it records the size in bytes and number of words. Lycos is clearly one of the best search tools.

❏ **InfoSeek.**   Databases for searches that include an index of 400,000 of the most popular Web pages, 10,000 Usenet groups, Hoover's 7,000 company profiles, and several newswires, including Reuters, Associated Press, the Businesswire, PR Newswire, and Newsbytes. Sounds impressive.

　　InfoSeek claims they're "bigger than Lycos," which is Microsoft Network's licensing choice as they're tooling up for the World Wide Web. With InfoSeek's strong sense of confidence, they definitely deserve a trial use. They'll give you ten free hits a month; then it's a paid service.

❏ **Netscape.**   Along with other Web browsers, has search pages that will give you direct access to some of the more popular and effective Web search engines. Netscape will link you directly to WebCrawler, Lycos, and InfoSeek. From there you can initiate your search for Websites of interest.

THE WINNERS AMONG THE WEB SEARCH ENGINES

The World Wide Web was developed to make it easier to find information on the Internet, whether it's hidden at an FTP site or a newsgroup, [but] so many people have put documents, files, pictures, and programs on the Web, it's becoming harder to find what you want. But don't despair . . .

"If you have a Web browser like Netscape, the easiest way to get going is to click on the Directory menu and go to Netscape's search page, which gives you access to three of the most popular Web searchers: Info-Seek (which has a free search area and a more thorough area for a fee); the Lycos search program; and WebCrawler. All of these search tools will search the keywords tied to a given Web page's title, some search a catalog of Web pages they maintain, while others actually search within Web pages for test strings.

(SOURCE: Elizabeth Crowe, "Searching the Web," *Computer Currents*, August 13, 1995.)

You'll also see a number of other search engines, as they're called, on the Yahoo Website and its competitors: names such as the World Wide Web Worm, Aliweb, EINet, and others. And if you jump to any of these sites, they will also offer links to yet other sites as you zip around the World

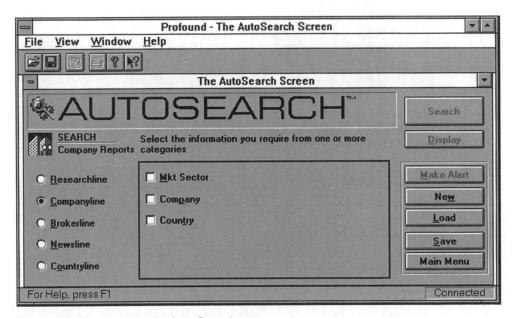

Figure 3.40   Profound's AutoSearch menu.

Wide Web. This level of cooperation reflects the strong supportive spirit that currently exists throughout the Internet community.

CERN, the original Swiss university center for the Internet, provides a list of the "Best Search Engines in the World," with lists of servers, software, publications, news, and people to contact. In addition, the FinanceNet, an information center for government assets, also has a terrific list of search engines. Between these sources, FinanceNet, Netscape, and the Yahoo site, you will be able to identify the best search tools available in cyberspace.

BULLSEYE! ARCHITEXT'S HOT NEW TOOL FOR INFO OVERLOAD

"Six brainy Stanford University seniors who liked to poke around the Internet's World Wide Web decided to start a company" because they saw "lots of neat stuff" on the Web. So, the venture capital firm of Kleiner Perkins Caulfield & Byers invested $750,000 of the $1.5 million they raised for their start-up.

> The Architext "handle" is a superpower search engine that scans millions of documents on the Internet—or any network—to help users find the information they need. Most search software works by looking for key words. . . . What makes Architext revolutionary is that it will find relevant documents even if the name doesn't appear anywhere in the article. . . . Architext allows you to search by concept . . . that makes Architext a news junkie's dream come true.

> Their first product: a scaled-down version of the software for companies that have their own Websites. Called On-Target, the program is designed to help visitors to those sites find what they're looking for. Architext is also planning to sell products that will help employees at large companies track down information on internal corporate networks.

(SOURCE: Jennifer Reese, "Information Searching," *Fortune,* July 10, 1995.)

Of course, that still leaves a lot to be desired, partly because it's not as focused as most investors and traders need. The search engine technology and databases are definitely in their infancy. Even if you use several of these tools you may come up with a less-than-adequate answer to your research question . . . and may prefer using some of the commercial online and dial-up databases specifically designed for the investment community.

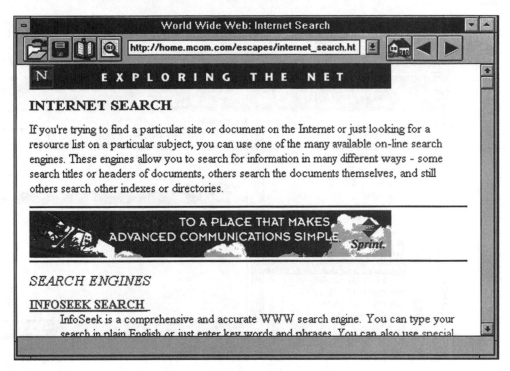

Figure 3.41 Netscape's Internet Search page.

ProSearch: Sample Search Tool for Stock Market Selections

The search engines discussed above are more generally oriented toward news research. Searches oriented to the selection of securities for your portfolio require more specialized search engines, ones usually built right into the analytical software discussed in later chapters. Telescan's ProSearch is one example.

Telescan claims that ProSearch is "the most advanced stock market search program on the market today . . . a must for the serious investor. In seconds, it allows you to customize your own searches using 207 important technical, fundamental, and forecasting indicators."

Telescan's system is a best-seller among cyberspace investors, and we'll discuss it in detail below. Right now, we just want you to be aware that there are many search systems available in cyberspace . . . for many different purposes. No one search engine will allow you to search and access everything you need all the time from a single database. *The real key is that each database is likely to have its own special search tools to help you burrow*

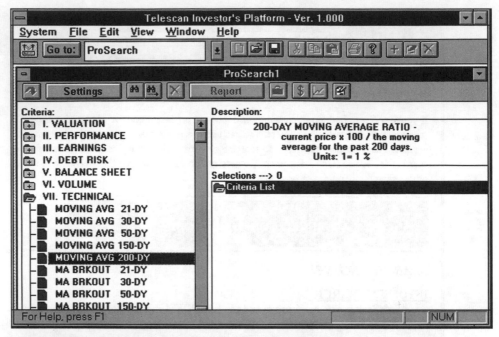

Figure 3.42   Telescan's ProSearch for securities searches.

through their specific database material. The Internet database is different from the Lexis-Nexis, and the CompuServe database is different from Telescan's.

Bottom Line: No One Search Engine Can Do It All

Let's face it, there's an enormous amount of new information being generated in cyberspace every second from somewhere in the world, and the Internet is just one small sector of this cyberspace information explosion. In addition, cyberspace Wall Street also generates its own unique explosion of new data.

New information is coming at the cyberspace investor all the time, tons of it, at lightning speed. We are locked in a tense, minute-to-minute, real-time trading machine that rattles on endlessly, creating new data from over 100,000 securities on more than 100 financial exchanges scattered throughout the world every day.... It is constantly generating new information. As a result, one of the most important functions of any investment program will be the tools for *searching* for the right information, in the right location, at the right time.

With Telescan's ProSearch, and other similar programs, you can do customized searches from their database of 14,000 issues traded on NYSE, AMEX, NASDAQ, and Canadian exchanges. Maybe you won't get all the exchanges and all the securities in the known world, but you'll get the more important ones. And ProSearch then lets you pick 40 of their 207 search criteria for screening securities. And in seconds you'll have a list of stocks that fit your portfolio requirements, ranked by the strongest companies within your set of criteria.

Telescan says, "no other program does all this." At least you won't find anything close to it on the Internet. But what you will find in just about every other investor software program covered in this book is a set of unique search features, *each designed specifically for a different database and separate set of functions.*

CYBERSPACE MAGAZINES ON FINANCE AND INVESTMENTS

Extra! Extra! Read all about it! The publishing world loves cyberspace. That goes for the magazines as well as newspapers. They're jumping into this challenge with the same spirit and enthusiasm the American people felt when Kennedy inspired us to put a man on the moon.

This is an exciting moment in history for newspeople, writers, and publishers everywhere. They're watching their profession change from within, while at the same time actually using this powerful new technology in reporting on a dramatically changing world around them. Let's look at some of these changes in the world of electronic magazines or *cyberzines.*

FORBES DISCOVERS INFO-SPIDERS CRAWLING ON THE WEB

[The Internet] library has no call numbers, no card catalog, no shelving by subject . . . so-called spiders, software really, comb the Web for new sites and for updated information on old ones. They bring back the data to their lairs, index it and then search the index on command . . . spiders can track down millions of cross-references that crisscross the Web, saving you precious minutes—or hours—of trips down dead ends to Web sites that have nothing to do with your search. . . . It's fair to bet that by the turn of the century the Web will be patrolled by more numerous, more powerful and very different beasts. But today's lowly spider will be their ancestor.

(SOURCE: Philip Ross and Nikhil Hutheesing, "Along Came the Spiders," *Forbes* October 23, 1995.)

Cyberzines or just *zines* are some of those cool nicknames Net surfers slapped on electronic magazine publications. They refer to magazines published in electronic form, and there are many out there. Delivery is instantaneous. You simply download it into your computer and read it on the monitor. You can even print a hard copy if you want. That's the new cyberspace publishing. Fast, efficient, cheap, and environmentally safe. Let's see a few examples of how well and how rapidly this field is developing.

The Electronic Newsstand (E-News)

The electronic newsstand. Its very name captures the essence of the new cyberspace publishing revolution. Back in 1993 the publisher of the *New Republic* magazine saw the coming revolution in the publishing business and created a cyberspace newsstand for himself and some of his fellow publishers. As the lead character in the movie *Field of Dreams* says, "If you build it, they will come."

That's exactly what happened—in droves they came. Today he has over 300 top magazines lining the racks of the electronic newsstand. E-news is a hot property, with 50,000 visitors a day, enough to fill most sports stadiums. So they're doing something right.

PUBLISHERS NOW BYPASSING THE ELECTRONIC NEWSSTANDS

Content providers (i.e., information vendors like magazines, newspapers, game makers, etc.) are now bypassing on-line services and posting their editorial goods up on the Web themselves. For example, Hearst announced the Multimedia Newsstand, an interactive shopping and entertainment service located on the Web. It allows users to subscribe to about 250 magazines, buy compact disks, and videos.

(SOURCE: David Geraciotti, "America Online is Tops—and Spinning," *Individual Investor*, August 12, 1995.)

Today, they're running into a lot of competition as major publishers are beginning to create Websites or newsstands for their own magazines. But E-news still has many important magazines. You can even read many articles or summaries from magazines such as *Business Week, Financial World, Individual Investor, Artificial Intelligence in Finance,* and *The Economist.*

By way of comparison, the *Business Week* material on America Online has more content and is visually more appealing, but then, of course, you'll need an account with AOL. So just wait a few months; you'll probably see *Business Week* on the Internet's Web as McGraw-Hill completes its Website (and eventually, I suspect, every other magazine on the electronic newsstand will follow suit).

While business and financial publications are not a major item at E-news, they are expanding into many new areas that may interest you—automobile sales, games, sports information, you name it—so they may discover some neat ways to help you spend all your profits you're making elsewhere.

Personally, we still prefer walking around Barnes & Noble and their Starbucks coffee shop, but when you're in a hurry at 2 A.M., cyberstores are a perfect way to get information fast. One final note: While you're browsing the racks of E-news, thank these electronic pioneers for leading the way.

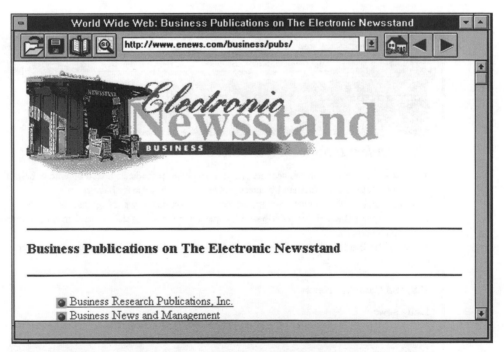

Figure 3.43 E-news: Electronic Newsstand's business page.

NETworth's Investor's Newsstand on the Web

NETworth, now a Quicken subsidiary, is an Internet leader in mutual fund information with major tie-ins to the Morningstar Mutual Funds service. When you visit their Website section, see their special Insider's Guide to Investment Periodicals. You'll find a number of specialized publications covering business and finance matters in countries such as Ireland, Canada, Britain, Hong Kong, and other Asian countries.

In addition, you can link to the Websites for a number of leading magazines, including *The Economist, Financial World, Worth, Money, Individual Investor,* and a number of mutual fund publications. More are planning to join NETworth in the coming months, including Louis Rukeyser's *Wall Street* and many other important publications. Bookmark this site and return to it frequently for the updates.

Time Warner's Pathfinder: Publisher's Own Newsstand

Time Warner's new Website, Pathfinder, is one very high quality newsstand, fitting their classy publications. The people who brought you Bat-

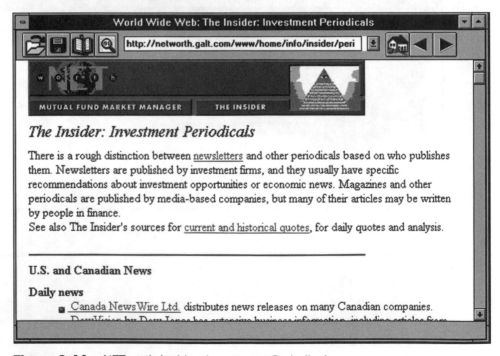

Figure 3.44 NETworth Insider: Investment Periodicals.

man and more first-class entertainment really delivered the goods here, setting a high standard for every other electronic publisher on the Net. Although this one will be hard to beat.

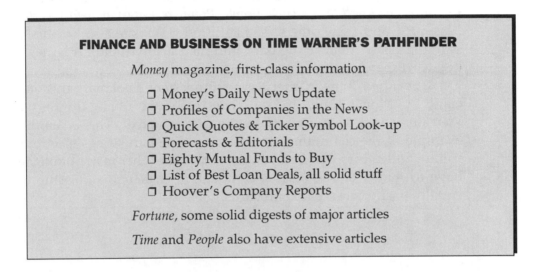

FINANCE AND BUSINESS ON TIME WARNER'S PATHFINDER

Money magazine, first-class information

- ❏ Money's Daily News Update
- ❏ Profiles of Companies in the News
- ❏ Quick Quotes & Ticker Symbol Look-up
- ❏ Forecasts & Editorials
- ❏ Eighty Mutual Funds to Buy
- ❏ List of Best Loan Deals, all solid stuff
- ❏ Hoover's Company Reports

Fortune, some solid digests of major articles

Time and *People* also have extensive articles

Figure 3.45   Time Warner's Pathfinder Web newsstand.

The graphics are so well done you feel like you're standing in your favorite corner newsstand looking at the actual covers. Plus the content is surprisingly substantial. Browse all you want. Read a few articles in the business magazines and relax with the rest of them. Pathfinder's selection includes *Fortune, Money, Time, People, Premiere, Entertainment Weekly, Sports Illustrated,* and a few others. The Pathfinder Website also has an excellent search process. You can dig back into their archives of past issues using a keyword search tool.

Bottom line: Time Warner has a winner here. Bookmark this one, especially the Money Daily update. They really did a bang-up job with this Website; it cost them a pretty penny, and it's great. This is another clear example of the commitment of the magazine industry to electronic publishing and cyberspace. You just know that the other major publishers will have to match or one-up this competitive challenge and come up with equally flashy cyberspace billboards!

Figure 3.46 Pathfinder: news, quotes, and company data.

MAGAZINE NEWSSTANDS ON THE BIG THREE ONLINE SERVICES

CompuServe

☐ The largest database of the three onlines, with full-text magazine articles from 125 key business and financial magazines—obviously the most comprehensive, with six ways to do targeted information searches.

America Online

☐ *Business Week*, great—many articles in full-text.
☐ *Time* magazine's business subsection with schedules on equity issues, dividend meetings, bond calendar, release of economic reports, etc.
☐ Plus *Worth* magazine and several newspapers with investor information: Investor's Business Daily, N.Y. Times Business, Chicago Tribune, and ABC News, the Nightly Business Report.

Prodigy

☐ Kiplinger's *Personal Finance* magazine and Brendan Boyd's *Investment Digest*.

Online Services: The New Electronic Magazine Newsstands

All the commercial online services have magazines available. Investors can get abbreviated versions of most major newsmagazines (along with the newswires and newspapers) covering Wall Street online . . . from any one of the big-three commercial online services. This is another example of the competitive forces pushing the publishing industry into cyberspace. If you look at the magazines offered on each of the big-three online services, you'll see their unique approaches.

CompuServe and America Online have taken quite different approaches. CompuServe is obviously more comprehensive by far, with a huge menu of resources, perfect for the investor who knows what information they want and isn't interested in graphics. CompuServe was obviously designed *specifically* for the serious business executive and investor who is using the information during the workday.

America Online, on the other hand, is more glitzy (visually appealing) and spoon-feeds the viewer. AOL is targeted more for today's rapid-fire television viewers, giving them a limited menu of (hopefully) high-quality information. These viewers have generally had a hard day and want every-

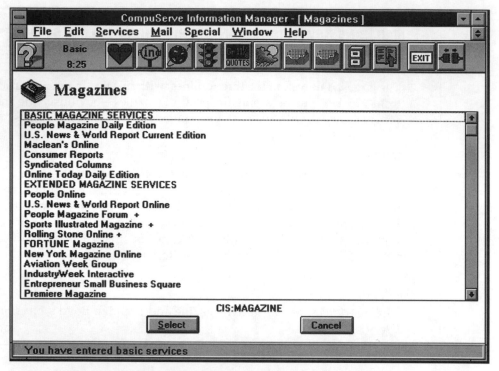

Figure 3.47   CompuServe's magazine newsstand.

thing packaged neatly for them on the eight o'clock news. In time, CompuServe will become more graphic, as AOL is becoming more comprehensive. And the Microsoft Network may well outdo all the online competition when they get the bugs worked out.

Reuters, Dow, and Nexis: Will They Replace Barnes & Noble?

Remember walking into a big metropolitan library and seeing shelves and shelves of magazines? Or browsing your favorite international newsstand, with racks and racks of magazines from all over on everything imaginable? Or the new megastores being built by Barnes & Noble? Well, that's what we have here . . . only it's on digital tape. Here you can browse with the speed of light, using a few keywords.

The databases controlled by these organizations are so huge, so gargantuan, that the question is not what's *in* them, but rather . . . *what's not in them!* And the answer is—they have it all, everything. This galaxy of cyberspace is truly awesome:

❑ **Knight-Ridder's Dialog** service claims to have over 350 million documents in their databases, which tap into 2,500 periodicals.

❑ **Lexis-Nexis** service says they have access to 417 million documents with full-text availability from 2,400 sources.

❑ **Dow Jones News/Retrieval** simply notes that their database is linked to 1,500 periodicals.

It's awesome . . . three and four *hundred million* documents, and 1,500 to 2,500 periodicals. Obviously, if a magazine is published and you need a copy, one of these superdatabases can locate it for you and will print you a copy with a snap of the fingers.

So why, you ask, would anyone ever fool around with a (comparatively) dinky resource like AOL? The answer is very simply that life is too overwhelming in this age of information overload. Most people want to KISS ("keep it simple, stupid"). And AOL does just that. As Sergeant Friday would say in Dragnet, "Just give me the facts." And hopefully AOL and the others will deliver the goods with a little glitz and pizzazz to take the edge off the dull facts.

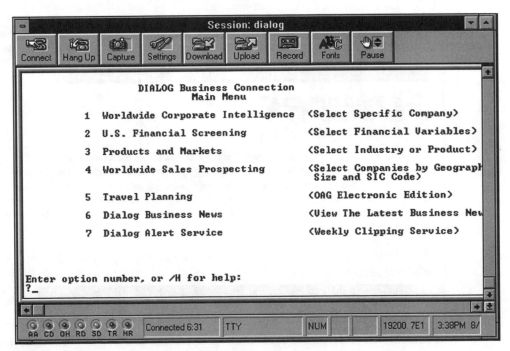

Figure 3.48 Knight-Ridder's Dialog database menu.

Internet Magazines for Professionals and Technicians

There are some excellent magazines for investors who trade the market frequently and use technical analysis, charting, and computer technology. And remember, the *advertisements* in these magazines are often as valuable as investor resources as the *articles* in keeping you abreast of advances in the field. Every one of them deserves the highest recommendation to the serious investor:

❏ *American Association of Individual Investors Journal*

❏ *Futures* magazine

❏ *Individual Investor*

❏ *Information Week*

❏ *Technical Analysis of Stocks & Commodities*

❏ *Traders' Catalog & Resource Guide*

❏ *Traders' World*

❏ *Wall Street & Technology*

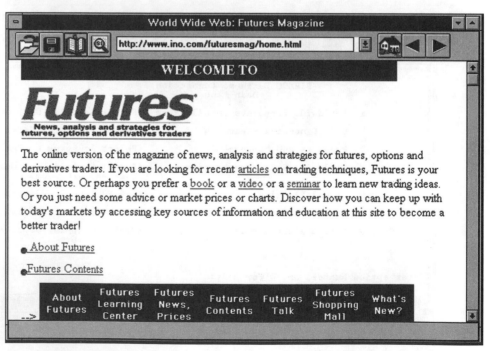

Figure 3.49 *Futures* magazine: finance on the Web.

If you've missed any of these on your newsstands recently, check them out. At least call and get a trial issue along with their Web location. The *Traders' Catalog* has a great meta-list already discussed above. *Futures* magazine is part of the Rich Financial Group's Investment News Online (I-NO) Website discussed previously, along with S&P ComStock and Lind-Waldock, the nation's largest futures discount broker. AAII and *Technical Analysis of Stocks & Commodities* are completing their Websites. And *Individual Investor* magazine is located on the Microsoft Network servers. Bookmark these Websites as they are evolving into major sources of information.

Internet Magazines Covering Technology and Computers

There are a few magazines that focus specifically on cyberspace business that you should be aware of. There are a few published magazines that, while not just resources for investors, deserve the attention of anyone interested in business happenings in cyberspace. Topics for investors are often

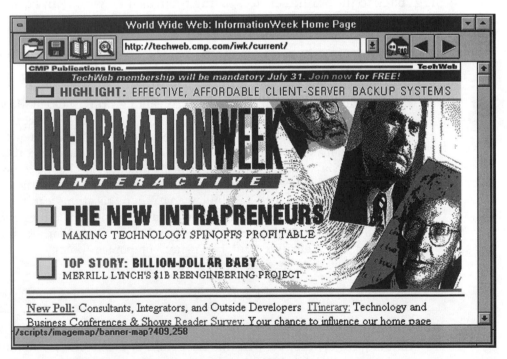

Figure 3.50 *InformationWeek* interactive Website.

included, and hopefully more will be added in order to make them more competitive.

A couple of these magazines are the *Internet Business Journal* and the *Electronic Journal of Finance*, which is available by E-mail at listserv@vm. temple.edu. Another one, the *Internet Business Advantage* recently changed ownership and is going through a transition at a time when the number of new general-interest Internet magazines is on the rise.

New general-interest cyberzines are *NetGuide*, *Internet World*, *Online Access*, *Net*, *Infobahn*, *Wired*, and *Boardwatch*, to name a few. You should get a sample issue of each and review current developments in cyberspace business, financial, and money matters in general.

The Future of Magazines Is in Cyberspace

In the next phase of electronic magazine publishing, the publishers themselves will be venturing more and more into cyberspace. Up to the present, the aggressive publishers used the online services as a way to "dip their toes into the water," so to speak. Traditional publishers have been riding piggyback to the online services, using them as they would any other retail bookstore or magazine newsstand that sells their material.

BROWSERS CHARGING FOR BROWSING? BACK TO BRENTANOS!

Time Warner is paying [the Cambridge consulting firm of] Open Market $1 million to help it start charging people who visit Pathfinder Website to read magazine articles online [and] Open Market uses sophisticated data encryption to make sure no one else runs up a bill in your name. [Open Market is also in] a deal with Ohio's BancOne that could change the way large publishers sell books and periodicals to libraries. Under the new system, librarians, who order $2 billion a year in publications, can bypass book sales reps. Instead, they'll choose from electronic catalogues available on the Web, and point-and-click their orders . . . Open Market's main competitor [is] Netscape . . . of the many companies looking to get a foothold on the Web, these are two to watch.

(SOURCE: Michelle Slatalla, "Open Market," *Fortune*, July 10, 1995.)

Next stop in cyberspace? In this new field of electronic publishing, it's almost guaranteed that you'll see many more publishers bypassing the

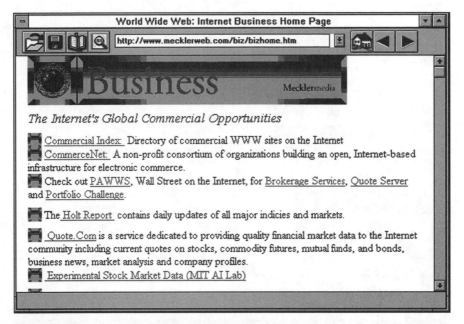

Figure 3.51 MecklerMedia Publisher's Website.

Figure 3.52 BusinessWeek at America Online.

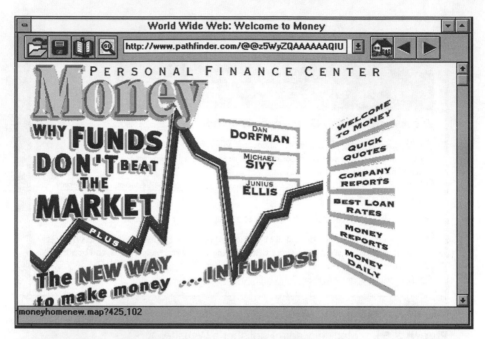

Figure 3.53   *Money* magazine at pathfinder Website.

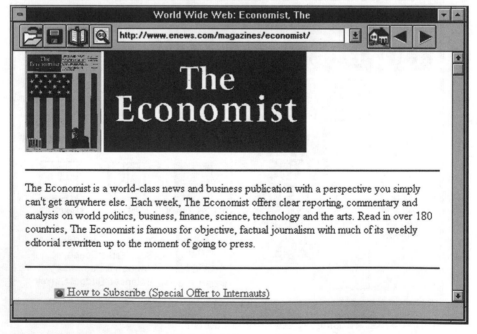

Figure 3.54   *The Economist* for world news.

intermediary (the distributors and newsstands). And like Time Warner's Pathfinder, the next generation will be developing and operating their own Websites for marketing and delivery. That way they'll reach everybody in cyberspace, anywhere in the known world. And that is enormously exciting to this new breed of electronic publishers.

INVESTMENT ADVISORY NEWSLETTERS ON THE NET

The dramatic shift to electronic publishing and marketing is changing the nature of the investment newsletter business in a big way. This fact was brought home very forcefully in a 1995 article in *Technical Analysis of Stocks & Commodities* magazine titled "The Trader and the Internet."

Technical Analysis of Stocks and Commodities

After discussing the new wave of resources on cyberspace investing—through online data retrieval, analytical tools, brokerage, trading, networking, and E-mail—the author concluded, "The financial advisory newsletter as we know it may be dead . . . a relic as curious to contemporary society as Stonehenge. The compelling immediacy of online communications may make dinosaurs of newsletter writers who stay with the print medium." Although perhaps a bit overstated, we do know that today's newsletter writers are facing fierce competition from several alternative information sources already in high-tech, high-speed cyberspace:

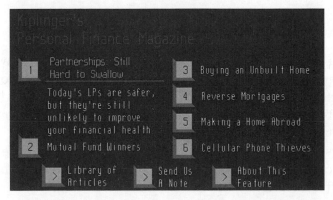

Figure 3.55   Prodigy: *Kiplinger's Personal Finance.*

- ❏ **Major news sources** such as Knight-Ridder and Dow Jones are going after the smaller investor and trader with their huge databases.

- ❏ **Software developers** such as Telescan and MetaStock have developed sophisticated tools that arm investors with new firepower to make superior decisions.

- ❏ **Discount brokerage firms** such as Charles Schwab, Aufhauser, and Quick & Reilly are already leaders in providing new kinds of advisory services to cyberspace investors.

- ❏ **Mutual fund advisory services** such as NETworth and the Benham Group have substantial backing to provide free news and advisory reports.

- ❏ **Other new competition** includes online forums and chat groups where sharp investors exchange tips, support organizations like AAII, and so many more advisory resources.

Bottom line: The newsletter writers' customers, today's investors, are better trained, better informed, and better equipped to make their own investment decisions, now armed with a huge arsenal of alternatives available at their desktop, online, and on the Net. This is putting considerable pressure on newsletter writers to meet the electronic publishing challenge.

Some advisory newsletter publishers are on the leading edge of this new communications technology, ready to make some major advances. They see the Internet as an ideal advertising vehicle, with E-mail a fast, inexpensive delivery tool for timely information. And many of these publishers are teaming up with existing cyberspace marketing experts (e.g., Prodigy's Wall Street Edge and the Microsoft Network). Let's see where to look for this new wave of cyber-advice.

Prodigy Online Newsletters: Wall Street Edge

The Market Data Corporation has managed Prodigy's online newsletter service, Wall Street Edge, since 1993. Wall Street Edge digests about 150 financial newsletters, hotline numbers, and 900-number dial-up advisory services. Subscribers get an average of five or more digests each day, assuming monthly publications.

Prodigy offers this digest service for a relatively modest extra fee, considering the typical cost of these types of newsletters. For example, at an average cost of at least $100 a year for the print versions (and many cost much more), you're getting over $150,000 of advice. Plus you get it digested into the essential points.

Market Data does a respectable job here. They have assembled some well-respected newsletter publishers.

The major categories of the Wall Street Edge service are varied. They cover market overviews, best-bet stocks, best-bet options, low-priced stocks (NASDAQ stocks under five bucks), new issues, mutual funds, and guest commentaries. The Edge even adds street rumors under a Whispers section. A day's download might run 10 pages, so you could wind up with more than 200 pages a month—not bad for 20 bucks. But does a dollar a day keep the investor really informed? Or will it just confuse you with too much potentially contradictory and diverse information. Will the bulls off-set the bears? Decide for yourself.

NEWSLETTERS ON PRODIGY'S WALL STREET EDGE

- ❏ **The Addison Report**
- ❏ **California Technology Stock Letter**
- ❏ **Chartist Mutual Fund Timer**
- ❏ **Dines Letter**
- ❏ **Donoghue's Moneyletter**
- ❏ **Jerry Favor's Analysis**
- ❏ **Global Market Strategist**
- ❏ **Sy Harding's Hotline**
- ❏ **Investment Quality Trends**
- ❏ **The Leibovit Line**
- ❏ **Vanguard Advisor**
- ❏ Plus 140 more

Bottom line: Wall Street Edge is actually quite well done compared to the other options in this changing field. It is well worth exploring if the rest of Prodigy line fits your requirements. And please keep an open mind with these kinds of services. Prodigy might well suit the needs of your family, and the Wall Street Edge may serve you as an investor.

AOL's Top Advisors' Corner for Investment Newsletters

America Online's approach is different from Prodigy's Wall Street Edge. AOL's selection is much smaller, with only 15 newsletters available. The digests appear to be written by the newsletter publishers themselves rather

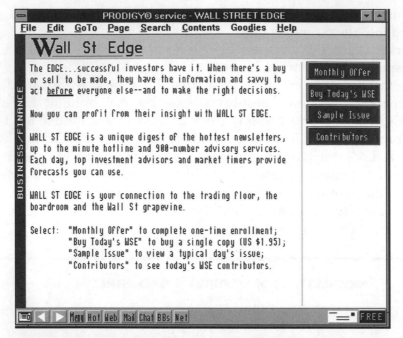

Figure 3.56   Prodigy's Wall Street Edge: 150 newsletters.

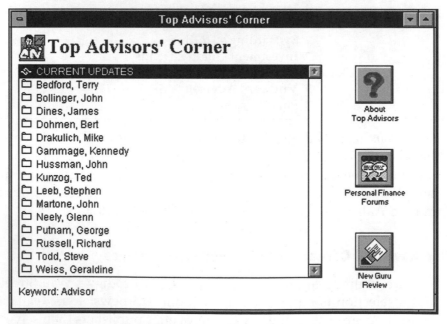

Figure 3.57   America Online: Top Advisors' Corner.

than digested by a staff of editors as the Market Data Corporation is doing for Prodigy. One letter on AOL had not been updated for six months. There are too few, with too little content, and many read more like ads than advice.

These digests are part of the basic fee services of AOL. There is no extra charge as with Wall Street Edge, and perhaps there should be (under the theory that you get what you pay for). There's a lot of potential here for AOL. In order to remain competitive, which is one of AOL's competitive strengths, expect them to restructure this section in the near future.

Meanwhile, the availability of *Investor's Business Daily*, Reuter's newswire, *Business Week*, the American Association of Individual Investor's forums and other services on AOL more than make up for the light selection of advisory newsletters.

CompuServe's Financial Advisory Newsletters

CompuServe has a database of more than 500 industry newsletters, with full-text files carried for five years. In addition, you can access more than 100 business publications from throughout the United States and Canada. Some of the specific newsletters included on CompuServe are:

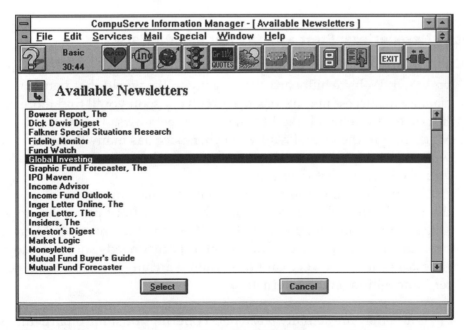

Figure 3.58   CompuServe's advisory newsletters.

❏ **IBM/Donoghue's Moneyletter**

❏ **Finch Investors Services' Bond Reader**

❏ **Otiva's IPO Maven**

❏ **Lynch Jones Ryan's IPO Aftermarket**

CompuServe is building its newsletter base. In addition, they are now using the high-tech Abode Acrobat software to give their reports a superior hard-copy appearance, with market information often transferred on high-quality tables, charts, and graphs. CompuServe is highly recommended, and even though CompuServe has relatively few newsletters by choice, they have such a great overall package of advisory information for the serious cyberspace investor.

Bottom line: The traditional newsletter has become less important than it was in the 1980s. Why? With the enormous growth of mutual funds, plus the development of so many new sophisticated analytical software packages for investors, investors have other resources and are themselves better decision makers. Moreover, with several new studies showing that a large majority of newsletters, as well as institutional fund managers, fail to beat the market averages, *the individual investor is being forced to rely on his or her own judgment, and less on outside advice* such as newsletters.

Financial Newsletters: Start with the Net's Meta-Lists

The Internet has very rapidly become the hot new place to hang out your very own Website billboard announcing to the world that you have a special key to success in the stock markets. Very soon you'll find more of these Internet newsletters linked to the major meta-lists. The reason is simple. Marketing in the virtual reality of cyberspace has many things in common with marketing in the real world. You need a location that will be seen and you need lots of customer traffic.

Fortunately, there are some interesting starting points if you're out there exploring cyberspace, surfing the Net for hot tips on the stock market. Yes, there are many newsletters other than the ones noted here. However, this is clearly one area of the Internet that needs some development. Investors should be very cautious when searching for substantial newsletter information on the Internet:

❏ Often they are actually *promotional* offerings pushing a particular stock, rather than independent publications written by unbiased experts.

MAJOR META-LISTS LINKED TO CYBERSPACE NEWSLETTERS

❏ The Yahoo meta-list has a subdirectory of 30 newsletters.
   http://www.yahoo.com/Business/newsletters
❏ Rich Financial Group (newsletter categories; downloadable).
   http://www.ino.com/nlindex.html
   • Global Markets
   • Foreign Exchange
   • Futures
   • Hedge
   • Interest Rates
   • Metals
   • Money Management
   • Mutual Fund
   • Options
   • Stocks
❏ NETworth's Website; The Capitalist lists 15 newsletters.
   http://networth.galt.com
   • Downing & Associates Technical Analysis
   • Equity Fund Outlook
   • Investment Horizons
   • Investment Research Reports
   • Morningstar 5-Star Investor
   • Mutual Fund Forecaster
   • Mutual Fund Timer
   • NeuroQuant Profiles
   • Paul Merriman's Fund Exchange
   • Sector Fund Newsletter
   • TICKtalk
   • The Muhlenkamp Memorandum
   • The Mutual Fund Letter
   • The Oberweis Report
   • The Turnaround Letter
❏ QuoteCom Website has a modest selection of newsletters links.
   http://www.quote.com/
   • NeuroQuant Profiles; predictions using new technologies
   • Paul C. Y. Huang's Future's Report
   • Predicto, Technical Analysis Report by Bob Moore
   • Market Beat, by Tom Petruno of the *Los Angeles Times*
   • Recommendations Update, digested from brokers' reports
❏ Wall Street Direct has an extensive newsletters subdirectory.
   http://www.cts.com/~wallst/
❏ Wall-Street-News monitors and digests 50 leading newsletters.
   http://wall-street-news.com/forecasts

❏ Many "newsletters" are often little more than *teaser ads*. After all, most of this material is free. Fortunately, many do offer free trial subscriptions to the real thing so you won't waste too much time or money.

❏ *Minimum content* in most cases, with little forecasting value. Can't blame them though. If they give away too much, nobody would buy their paid subscriptions.

❏ Also, many Web newsletters are *outdated*, several hadn't been updated for six months or more, obviously reflecting a disenchantment with the marketing potentials in cyberspace. Obviously, there is an opportunity for some enterprising publisher.

Bottom line: Keep your expectations to a minimum for now. In the future, you should expect to discover more quality newsletter information on the Internet, with the addition of more new services such as the Wall Street Edge and Benham's Market Monitor on NETworth's site. You'll also see future ventures attached to Microsoft's Network, or a commercial online service, or as part of some larger mutual fund or brokerage firm. In

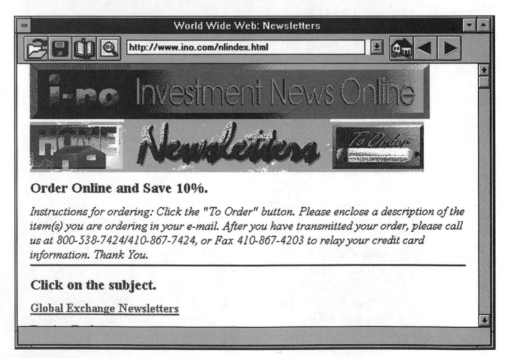

Figure 3.59   Investment News Online (I-NO) newsletters.

any case, these new services will probably be attached to some existing cyberspace location rather than free-floating like a disabled earth-orbiting satellite. In short, check back with your favorite meta-lists on a regular basis.

Internet Newsletters: Hot Stocks or Hot Air?

A number of the leading market forecasters do have their newsletters on the Internet. Usually the available material is substantially edited, often little more than extended headlines or mere teaser ads with no content. Hot Stocks is a notable exception, although it's more of an infomercial than a traditional newsletter, as you'll see.

Business Week ran a June 1995 cover story titled "Online Investing." They concluded that the area was a

> *new, unique, and potentially very powerful source of investor information and interaction . . . largely shunned by the established powers on Wall Street. The online world . . . is a world where small investors dominate, and where facts—not the Street's agenda—are paramount."* [The Hot Stocks Review Website was considered] *impressive . . . well-written, interesting, and free as the wind to anyone possessing a Web browser. But was it reliable?*

Hot Stocks Review aggressively and enthusiastically promotes risky OTC Canadian companies, not exactly your average retirement portfolio investments. Notably, the publisher even gets a "research and promotional fee" for them to be included on this Website. *Business Week* related a story of one investor who followed the advice of Hot Stocks Review and bought a stock that subsequently dropped. Undaunted, the investor *then created his own Website* to personally tout the stock. Folks, that's the kind of excitement and pioneering spirit being generated by today's cyberspace investing! Perhaps *Forbes* was right, cyberspace is truly like the California gold rush of a hundred years ago.

Bottom line: Hot Stocks Review appears to be more of a promoter's brochure than a truly independent adviser's newsletter, in spite of the publisher's claims of objectivity. But then, what the heck, many traditional newsletter writers typically have positions in the stocks they cover.

My advice to investors is to move cautiously, with due diligence. But definitely check this one out as an example of the emerging new electronic

Figure 3.60   Hot Stocks Review on the Net.

information. Even more important, every established newsletter writer should check out the Hot Stocks Review as a marketing prototype to see what gets attention and what sells on the Web. There's a lot more of this coming on the superhighway and it may be as much entertainment as information. Keep looking; you'll find them popping up on the key meta-lists.

Internet Newsletters: Where Is Rukeyser's Wall Street?

Louis Rukeyser's Wall Street was one of the first high-quality financial advisory newsletters to explore the potential of the new cyberspace publishing media. They joined the Electronic Newsstand's elite list of publications. They also have plans to locate the Rukeyser newsletter on another Website, possibly NETworth's Capitalist section, which may give them better access to the mutual fund investor. Other newsletter writers are expected to follow suit, searching for the best locations to generate an audience motivated to buy financial services and products.

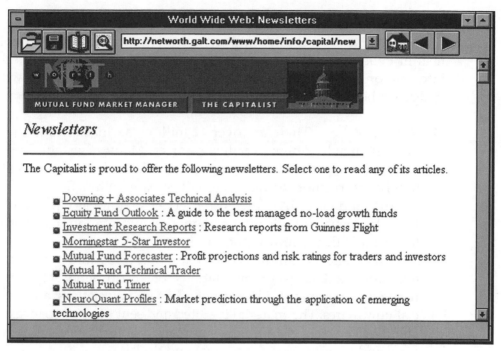

Figure 3.61 NETworth's Newsletters in the Capitalist.

Wall-Street-News Forecasts

The Wall-Street-News is another experiment in electronic publishing in cyberspace. This newsletter monitors about 50 other newsletters written by a select group of experts in four areas: technical analysis, cycles research, astro-economics, and quantitative analysis. Their methods include Elliott Wave and Gann theory, Fibonacci, astrophysics, and quant-neural nets. These newsletters are digested into four categories: bull/bear sentiment index, hot spots (timing and turning points), quotations by experts, and editorial commentary.

Originally offered as a free service by E-mail on the Internet, the mailing list rapidly became the single largest mailing list on Netcom's servers, and perhaps the largest financial newsletter on the Internet.

Still under development, Wall-Street-News is exploring ways to convert it into an income generator by aligning with a commercial online service, selling advertising, or selling subscriptions on the Internet. As with many other electronic publications in cyberspace, it is an experiment in journalism and an opportunity in publishing.

Newsletters: By Mail, Broadcast Fax, and 900-Number Hotlines

If all else fails and you can't find enough advice through the normal channels in cyberspace, here are a few alternative ways of getting the right information (or leads to it), at least until newsletters catch up with full-fledged cyberspace technology and get on the Internet:

❐ **Broadcast fax.**   There are over 12 million fax machines in operation, more than subscribers to online services. Many newsletter publishers continue using broadcast fax, a proven, reliable delivery system to send timely information to their subscriber base. Why? Because faxing is cheaper and faster than the postal service (yet not as cheap and fast as E-mail) when you're dealing with market information that is often useless if more than a few minutes or hours old.

An excellent example is *JAG Notes.* Every day they survey newsletters and hotline recommendations of institutional brokers, bank research departments, investment advisory newsletters, and the financial newswires. The material is edited and sent out by broadcast fax for about $40 a week. It's a timely summary of information being released from and to institutional investors and decision makers.

In a typical day an investor will see summaries from 30 or more research and advisory reports from companies such as Smith Barney, Lehman Brothers, Paine Webber, Bear Sterns, A.G. Edwards, Salomon Brothers, Dean Witter, and many more, plus the S&P MarketScope. And most of their recommendations are keyed to specific stock symbols for quick reference. As with most publications, you can sample *JAG Notes* free for three days. Check out their new Website.

❐ **900-number hotlines.**   Many newsletter publishers also have 900-number hotlines to capture an audience interested in the latest tips on shifts in the markets. They're usually updated at least once a day, often much more frequently. For example, there's the All-Star Traders Hotline with ten well-known advisers on a single 900-number hotline, each one a successful trader and writer, including Jake Bernstein, Walter Bressert, and Glenn Neely.

❐ **Mail-order catalogs.**   You can even go back to snail mail if all else really does fail. Contact the SEI organization in New York City. They are one of the largest suppliers of newsletter samples. For $69 you can get sample copies of SEI "all we have," about 250 financial advisory newsletters . . . that's right, 250. Only 37 cents a newsletter. What a deal. Every investor should try it once. And if you do it around the Christmas season you'll get copies of the annual forecast issues. SEI has been around for a few decades and is exploring a cyberspace presence in the near future.

Bottom line: It's unlikely that these alternative delivery systems will be quickly dropped by newsletter writers in the near future. They work. The 6- to 12-page printed newsletters, with hotline updates recorded in the confident voice of an expert, or faxed updates hot off the press are established modes of delivering timely investment advice . . . for now.

However, within a few years, cyberspace technology (especially interactivity and transaction payments) could well advance to a point where these alternative delivery systems are no longer cost-effective in the competitive, time-sensitive investment world.

Relatively speaking, newsletter publishers tend to charge a lot for their writings. For example, you can get a 100-page copy of *Money* magazine for $3.95 (4 cents a page) while an 8-page newsletter could easily cost you $20 a copy ($2.50 a page). And both may have some excellent information on

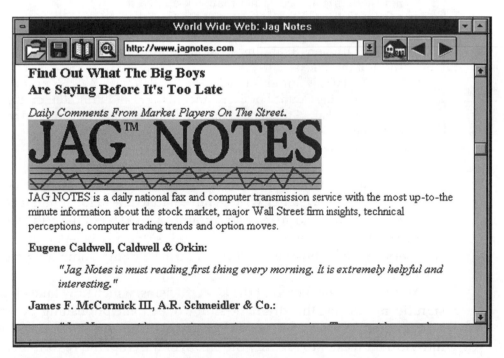

Figure 3.62 JAG Notes: market and securities recommendations.

how to invest your money. So far, the audience on the online services and the Internet (many of whom are merely looking for free information in cyberspace) hasn't quite warmed up to these high-priced items. Hopefully, that will change soon. And the Microsoft Network could very well accelerate this shift.

Financial Newsletters: Are They Worth the Price?

How valuable are financial newsletters to the investor—whether printed on paper or as electronic publications? Do newsletters really help investors make better, more profitable investment decisions?

RATING THE PERFORMANCE OF FINANCIAL NEWSLETTERS

❑ National Bureau of Economic Research released a 1995 survey of 237 investment newsletters published between 1980 and 1992. They concluded that less than 25 percent achieved returns higher than a buy-and-hold investor would with a passive portfolio. Moreover, most newsletters confused rather than helped investors.

❑ Mark Hulbert's highly respected *Hulbert Financial Digest* publishes a quarterly review of the performance of the major financial newsletters. Hulbert cautions that almost 90 percent of financial newsletters fall short of the indexes.

❑ Burton Malkiel, author of *A Random Walk Down Wall Street,* former member of the Council of Economic Advisers and Princeton professor, also noted that 65 to 70 percent of all mutual and pension fund managers fail to beat the market indexes over the long run.

Now that's a whole separate issue. Obviously the answer is yes to many investors. Newsletter writers have had to take a lot of harsh criticism for bad advice over the years, and certainly a good bit of the criticism is justified. Yet the fact is there are as many as 1,000 subscriber-paid newsletters still very much in business. So they must be doing something right—at least some of them.

You've probably heard of the key criticisms, which now take on greater significance during this dramatic shift to electronic publishing. Newsletter writers themselves admit to these criticisms. The key, of course, is for the individual investor to identify the cream of the crop, the 10 to 15 percent of the bunch whose newsletters are successful . . . that is, consistently make money for clients. Find a few select hotshots and stick with them. Or find a successful money manager to handle your portfolio, one who doesn't write newsletters, but instead is taking his or her own advice . . . and has a proven track record of making money in the markets.

Bottom line: Even when you discover an advisory letter you trust, remember, in the final analysis, *you and you alone* have to make the investment decision and "pull the trigger." It's *your* money. *Your* responsibility. *Your* portfolio. Keep the power.

THE HOT NEW CYBERSPACE INVESTMENT CLUBS

They're called a lot of names: *newsgroups, chat rooms, forums, roundtables, conferences,* and *bulletin boards.* You'll hear all of these terms in describing this unique cyberspace communication phenomenon that allows millions throughout the world to share their thoughts about areas of special interest, a kind of global town hall meeting, a cyberspace United Nations where

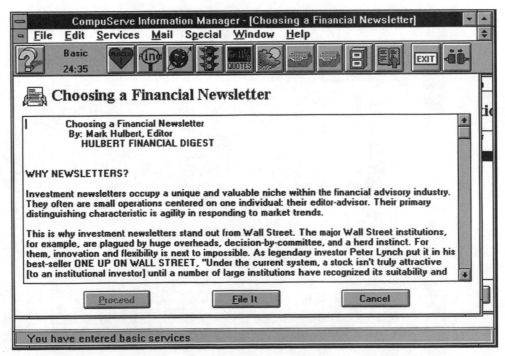

Figure 3.63   CompuServe: Mark Hulbert on choosing a newsletter.

anyone—from anywhere—can become a self-appointed ambassador and speak. It's an amazing communication opportunity.

Among the 5,000 groups on the Internet's Usenet newsgroup system, you'll find special groups on baroque and country music, paleoanthropology and Star Trek, fly fishing and jobs in Britain. The quality varies. Some are powerful clubs whose members are serious and active individuals dedicated to their topics.

However, others are the cyberspace equivalent of the midday television talk shows, allowing a participant to engage in virtual reality with a false personality rather than face the real world of people, things, and harsh reality. In the final analysis, these forums have won an enormous following internationally and are now an important link in cyberspace investing.

Special Usenet Newsgroups for Investors Only

These forums are an electronic version of your local investment club!

The Usenet newsgroups are the biggest system of electronic discussion groups in the world. It has been estimated that these 5,000 Usenet groups

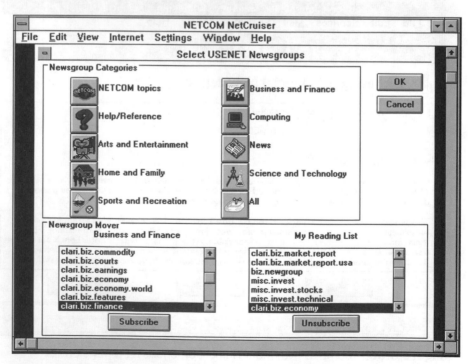

Figure 3.64   Internet Usenet newsgroups for investors.

link over 10 million people worldwide. Of the total number, however, there aren't more than a half dozen groups of primary interest to the investor, although you're likely to find another couple dozen of particular interest to your tastes on related business, financial, and news topics.

Most Web browsers will provide easy access to the Internet's many Usenet groups. They will also provide you with lists, or help you access lists, of other newsgroups. All you have to do to become a member of any one of these elite clubs is get up the guts to join. No entrance requirements. No extra dues. Not really much in the way of rules. And no special attire is required. So jump in, join one of the new elite clubs on Wall Street cyberspace. You are guaranteed to get something positive out of the experience.

USENET NEWSGROUPS FOR DISCUSSIONS ABOUT INVESTING

misc.invest	General discussion on investing
misc.invest.stocks	Major and secondary exchanges
misc.invest.funds	Mutual fund analysis and selection
misc.invest.futures	Index options, futures, derivatives
misc.invest.technical	Technical analysis for investors
misc.invest.canada	Investments north of the border
uk.finance	British financial dealings

Futures magazine recommends first reading the FAQS file for the misc.invest newsgroup located at: http://www.cis.ohio-state.edu/hypertext/faq/usenet/investment-faq/general/top.html. If you want to search a topic in these newsgroups, go to http://sift.stanford.edu.

Online Forums and Discussion Groups for Investors

All of the major online services have picked up the lead of the Usenet newsgroups. As a result you'll find similar forums or bulletin boards available for investors on CompuServe, America Online, and Prodigy.

Membership is limited to the subscribers of each particular online service. A CompuServe member wouldn't be caught dead on a Prodigy chat group (because he or she can't even get on one). This has advantages and disadvantages. Consequently, a CompuServe financial forum will have only CompuServe members sitting in on the discussion, sharing the shoptalk. As a result, it's likely you'll have a higher level of expertise sharing on CompuServe's electronic meetings than you'll hear on Prodigy, because of the profile of the typical CompuServe subscriber.

Some of the commercial online discussion groups get well over 1,000 entries daily. Many seem to have a strong orientation toward technical analysis, charting, and timing, probably because there is a feeling of urgency about the types of decisions made by investors who are into short-term market timing. As a rule they are always looking for more information on the next reversal point. So the discussion groups may get the spillover from their personal anxieties about particular trades.

Bottom line: If you're looking for an electronic meeting place and a place to discuss something special about investing, any one of these sites might suit you, although AOL has, by far, one the best collections of forums. The online forums can be extremely helpful, or time-consuming and dull; it's really up to you. Just remember to give a little, and you just might receive a lot.

With your investment decision making, in the final analysis, you and you alone must put your money on the line. Do not fall into the trap of letting one of these chat groups become a hideout, relying on them to make your decisions for you. Make very sure you have a method of investment analysis that works for you. Many successful investors never discuss their trades; they don't want to confuse their methods with all the noise from the market—rumors, tips, biases, and some news—noise that can draw them away from an otherwise proven method that works for them independently of the mob psychology of the market.

Club Rules: Read the FAQs and Observe Proper Netiquette

Emotions often run high with these discussion groups. You'd think that the absence of face-to-face human confrontation would add calm to a meeting, but it's actually the opposite. Emotions are often easily stirred on this supposedly neutral electronic media. So, while some investors swear by them, others swear at them. Seriously. There's also a healthy amount of honest, blunt commentary zipping across the wire at these discussions.

Basically they operate a bit like a community bulletin board where an investor can hang up a sign ("Anybody know why insiders are dumping my favorite stock?"). They're also like an investment club where a group of like-minded people can exchange information about a particular stock or sector of the market, or the value of new software, or the application of some esoteric analytic method.

In other words, you have to be on the inside of the game to really understand what's going on. Most chat groups may make no sense to the new member at first, but then American football doesn't look like cricket to most

INVESTMENT CLUBS ACTIVE ON THE ONLINE SERVICES

CompuServe

❏ Investor's Forum, stocks, mutual funds, personal finance, futures, taxes, etc.

❏ NAIC Forum, the National Association of Investment Clubs, a central electronic meeting place for NAIC's 140,000 members and 7,900 clubs.

❏ Consumer Forum, banking, credit and consumer issues.

America Online

❏ American Association of Individual Investors Online, one of the best all-round resources for investors.

❏ Morningstar Mutual Funds, hosted by the leaders in mutual fund research, analysis, and management.

❏ Investor's Network, a little of everything for the investor into basic fundamental portfolio analysis.

❏ Wall Street SOS Forum, hosted by an investment firm; market talk, selection of stocks and funds, etc.

❏ Decision Point Timing & Charts, technical analysis and charting, software and methods.

❏ Your Money, consumer issues, financial planning.

❏ Worth Online, portfolio management and more.

❏ Nightly Business Report, hosted by PBS, includes market discussion, stocks, mutuals, expert comments.

❏ The Motley Fool, actually a rather sophisticated discussion group run by two financial advisers with a sense of humor.

❏ Telescan Users group.

Prodigy

❏ Money Talk bulletin board, general discussion on stocks, bonds, futures, mutual funds.

soccer fans. So stick around a while; don't judge the value of these forums until you've taken the time to sit and listen to what's *really* going on.

Be forewarned, before you become a regular, take the time to read the FAQs (*frequently asked questions*) for the group you want to join. And then, if you decide to join, just "listen in" for a while before commenting. See what's going on before adding your two cents.

There are some drawbacks, however, that may try your patience while you're searching for a forum that fits your needs. Forums usually have no

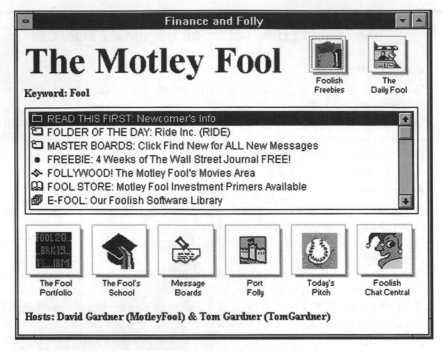

Figure 3.65   The Motley Fool: comedy club for investors.

membership requirements. Anyone with access and time can join. And most are not monitored, with minimal controls other than the collective anger of other members of the club.

Once you feel ready, you can get into the act. If you're reluctant to expose yourself and tell everyone what you're thinking, you can E-mail to just one other member who said something that sparked your interest. Soon you'll reach out and post a message for the reaction from the whole group. You can editorialize, advertise, and ask questions—about a special stock, analytical software, industry sector, government policy, you name it—as long as it fits into the subject matter of the group. Usenet groups are a must. Check out the major ones for investors. Join the fun—you might just get an education in the process.

The Commercialization of the Web's Usenet Newsgroups

One final thought. With the transfer of the Internet from academic/government control, several leading Internet watchers are now expressing concern that many of the newsgroups will become advertising vehicles, laden with classified ads. Certainly several of the new batch of books on Internet marketing strategies reinforce this trend, as they recommend that vendors post messages about their products on the Usenet newsgroups. It's a common recommendation from these new marketing organizations.

And certainly most of us have heard some of the horror stories about Internet marketing (e.g., the attorneys who blanketed the Internet groups to reach over 100,000 members). The new advertisers may be more subtle, but the recommendations are still being made, and the groups are often stuck with unwanted materials that are blatant ads rather than honest discussion.

Obviously these newsgroups are in transition, along with the entire Internet as it goes commercial. There's nothing bad about it, just different. This is a time of dramatic growth, with the introduction and testing of new ideas. Some will work, some won't. So please, let's reserve judgment. Many people read magazines for the advertisements and the special infor-

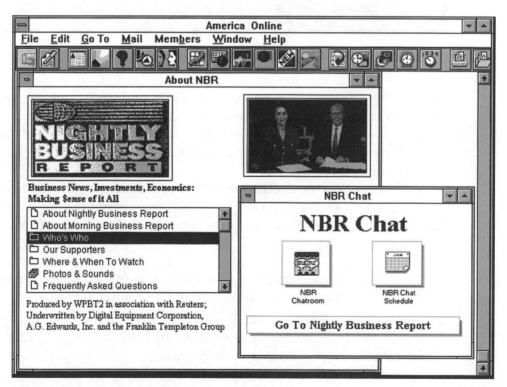

Figure 3.66 Nightly Business Report's forum.

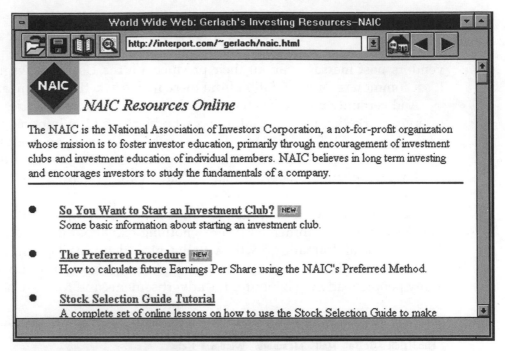

Figure 3.67   National Association of Investors Corporation.

mation they convey. Infomercials, though commercial, are becoming a widely accepted mixture of entertainment, education, and hype. Let's just hope that with the Usenet groups, advertisers will follow some of the basic rules of good advertising—inform and entertain—then we'll love it, buy it, and rush back for more.

Bottom line: As an interim suggestion, be extremely selective not only with the information you pick up on a newsgroup, but in your selection of the newsgroups you hang out with. Here are three guidelines you might consider:

1. *Monitored.*   If possible, use one that's monitored by an expert who gives some direction and control to the discussion topics.

2. *Serious professionals.*   Also, if you can, start and stick with a professional or specialized group, such AAII, NAIC, or a computer users' investment SIG (special interest group).

3. *Specialized.*   Select a forum that's focused on a particular subject, method, software, or technology. For example, technical analysis or

mutual funds, MetaStock or Telescan. Use them as an educational opportunity rather than a hot-tips hotline.

If you follow these guidelines and use common sense, the level of input to the group is liable to be sophisticated enough that the amateurs will be less vocal and the advice you do get will be more valuable. Remember, even the experts are wrong a majority of the time. So trust your own instincts.

DANGER AHEAD . . . INVEST WITH EXTREME CAUTION

The editor of the Money Column on GNN's Personal Finance Website, Bob Beaty, advises extra diligence when seeking advice on the newsgroups:

> I sometimes cruise the investment newsgroups as if they were singles bars under constant renovation. . . . I am sure newsgroups served a more useful purpose before the Big Bang (Internet style) occurred. . . .
>
> What is truly frightening is that the answers to posted questions, for the most part, lack any credibility, and can easily do more harm than good . . . one that stands out in my mind was an [investor] asking for guidance about investing $300 thousand for an elderly, disabled relative.
>
> Analysis . . . and common sense. There's the ticket to investment success. You're not going to find your fortune in a newsgroup on a bus-shelter wall. True success comes from your own gut feel, some raw data, and a favorable interest-rate environment. And patience . . .

The decision to invest is yours alone. . . . Trust your own instincts!

THE INTERNET . . . A "FORCE OF NATURE" TRIGGERING THE PARADIGM SHIFT ON WALL STREET CYBERSPACE

The rise of the Internet is, in Silicon Valley parlance, one of those paradigm shifts that come along every 15 years or so to flip the information technology industry on its ear. . . . The Internet's popularity is forcing powerhouses like AT&T, Hewlett-Packard, IBM, and, yes, Microsoft to rethink basic assumptions and business strategies, and to paddle furiously to catch the wave. Meanwhile, companies previously seen as niche players—workstation-maker Sun Microsystems, most notably, as well as its archival Silicon Graphics and database software supplier Oracle Systems—find themselves smack in the middle of the swiftly flowing new mainstream, largely because they have Internet expertise. . . .

Every computer Sun has ever shipped—more than 1.5 million of them—has included the hardware and the software needed to hook up to the Internet. Most of the machines are in networks that use the technology to link teams *within an organization*—automobile designers, Wall Street rocket scientists, software developers. Such networks have come to be called Intranets; they are separated from the public Internet by password security systems called firewalls. . . .

The Internet is already so big that it is almost a force of nature . . . the ultimate metamorphosis of the computer into a tool that satisfies mankind's urge to communicate better and more. Perhaps the most Gates or anyone can hope for is to add to its capabilities, rather than contain them.

(SOURCE: "Whose Internet Is It, Anyway?," Brent Schlender, *Fortune*, December 11, 1995.)

CHAPTER 4

Accessing Major Financial Market Data

UNITED STATES AND GLOBAL SECURITIES EXCHANGES

The major securities exchanges are also launching their big billboards out there along the new information superhighway . . . for every investor to see. And they're doing a credible job of it, with the Chicago Mercantile Exchange setting the pace. The specific securities and market indexes traded on these exchanges will be discussed in some of the following chapters. First, let's look at the exchanges themselves.

The Chicago Mercantile Exchange

The Chicago Mercantile Exchange was named "the top exchange in the world" by *Futures & Options World* in a 1994 survey. Nearly *$1 trillion* changes hands *daily* (versus $2.5 trillion *annually* on the NYSE), a total of 226 million contracts in 1994, almost half the total contracts traded by the U.S. futures industry. It's no surprise, then, that the Merc was one of the first major exchanges to launch onto the Web: They want to capture this new generation of cyberspace investors.

The Merc's Website is a wealth of information on the field of derivatives, commodities, options, and futures. Every cyberspace investor should

CHICAGO MERCANTILE EXCHANGE WEBSITE

- ☐ Daily settlements, futures, and options prices
  - Agriculture commodities (6)
  - Foreign currencies (13)
  - Interest rates (5)
  - Domestic and foreign stock indexes (6)
  - Special option offerings (9)
- ☐ CME volume and open interest
- ☐ Legislative and regulatory activities
- ☐ Financial futures: yen, peso, eurodollars
- ☐ Swaps and collateral depositories
- ☐ Rules of the exchange
- ☐ Financial safeguards
- ☐ Training classes, domestic and foreign
- ☐ History: news and photos archives
- ☐ A "What's New" file
- ☐ Glossary of terms for investors

Figure 4.1   Chicago Mercantile Exchange on the Net.

visit the Merc site at least once, even if your only interest is mutual funds. Through the Merc an investor has access to a considerable amount of material on a consistent basis, including closing prices for all the securities traded at the Merc. The Merc is obviously working hard to live up to its new recognition as the number one exchange in the world. Understandably, the Merc does not offer information on the other exchanges. What they do offer is quite extensive, and free.

American (AMEX) and Philadelphia Stock Exchanges

The Philadelphia Stock Exchange is the oldest in America and was also one of the first to come up on the Web. Both the Philadelphia and the American Stock Exchanges developed Websites ahead of the New York Stock Exchange. AMEX provides an interesting array of information, including news and a market summary of AMEX securities. They also post excellent information about AMEX contracts:

- ❏ Equity options
- ❏ Structured derivatives
  - – International indexes
  - – Domestic indexes
  - – Currency instruments
  - – Equity-linked term notes
- ❏ Index options and option families
- ❏ S&P depository receipts

Bottom line: Both exchanges offer excellent electronic brochures introducing investors to their respective exchanges. Worth bookmarking. Moreover, with all their lists of stocks, closing prices, and other company links, every investor is likely to discover something of value here, regardless of individual interests.

The Other Major U.S. Securities Exchanges

The Merc, AMEX, and Philadelphia Exchange Websites are excellent prototypes of what's to follow from the other exchanges. Most of the other major exchanges are following their leads, and are in various stages of

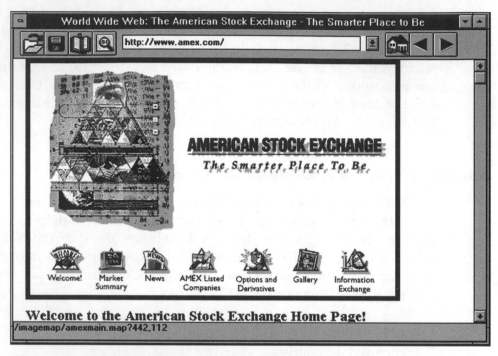

Figure 4.2   American Stock Exchange.

Figure 4.3   Philadelphia Stock Exchange.

development with their Websites, with many near completion at this time. These include:

NYSE	New York Stock Exchange
NYMEX/COMEX	New York Mercantile Exchange
NYFE	New York Futures Exchange
NASDAQ	Over-the-Counter Securities
CBOT	Chicago Board of Trade
CBOE	Chicago Board Options Exchange

In part, the presence of an exchange on its own Website is primarily a matter of competitive spirit and visibility rather than any *direct* attempt to sell and deliver essential information. For example, by the time the Merc freely provides all closing settlement prices at end of day, the same information has already been made available through hundreds of thousands of sources throughout the world, and communicated across the mass media.

In today's world of high-tech investing, the key is to have the information packaged in a format that can be readily analyzed by some special computer software. As a result, commercial data vendors, rather than the exchanges themselves, are the primary source of market information *to the investor*, because they can also help translate the raw data into useful information for analytical purposes.

The Chicago Board Options Exchange is coming on the Net with an innovative effort to include cross-references to market data on other exchanges, a departure from the existing pattern of restricting information to securities of just the host exchange. If CBOE succeeds, and that definitely is the likely next trend, then the door is open for free quotes to anyone, anytime, for all securities. The dynamics of this field are changing so rapidly, it's truly awesome.

Major International Securities Exchanges

Rich Financial Group's Website, Investment News Online (I-NO), has an extensive directory covering many of the international securities exchanges, complete with their telephone numbers. In traveling through cyberspace, we did run across several foreign exchanges with Websites. Surprisingly, at present there seem to be a few more foreign exchanges listed on the Internet than there are U.S. stock exchanges with Websites.

Other than the AMEX, CME, CBOT, and Philadelphia, the domestic exchanges appear to be moving slowly into cyberspace. Also, since there

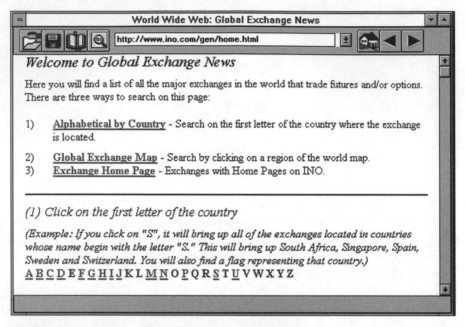

Figure 4.4   Global futures and options exchanges.

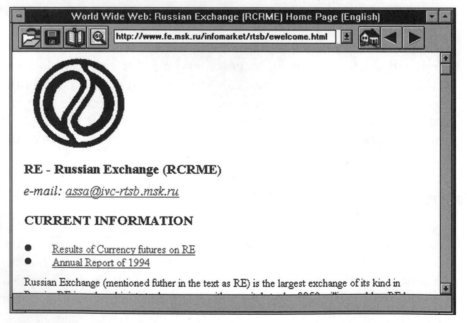

Figure 4.5   The Russian Exchange (RCRME).

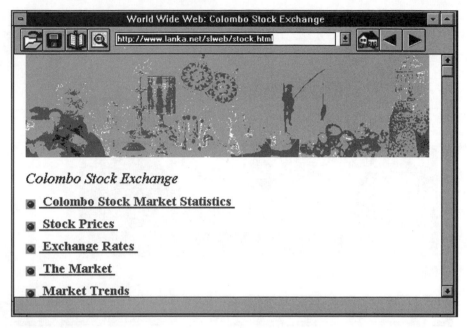

Figure 4.6   Colombo Stock Exchange in Sri Lanka.

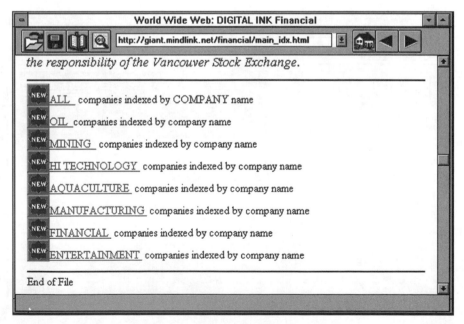

Figure 4.7   Vancouver Stock Exchange, Canada.

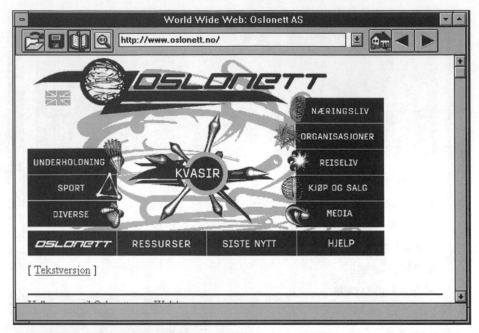

Figure 4.8   Oslo Stock Exchange, Norway.

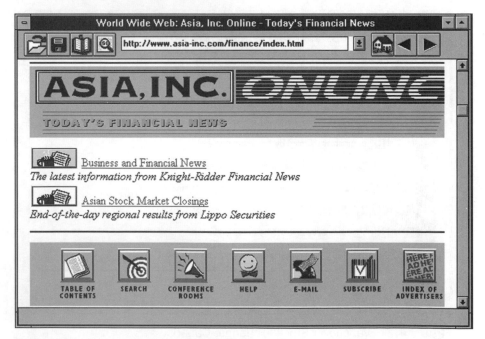

Figure 4.9   Asia, Inc. Online: financial markets.

are many Websites and countless commercial data vendors providing the essential stock and market quotes in cyberspace, up to this point it may not have been necessary for the exchanges themselves to be out there. Today it's different. In addition to the Rich Financial Group, FILL and the Yahoo meta-list also have links to several foreign stock exchanges, and can be expected to list more in the near future.

Securities Exchanges Versus Free Quotes on the Internet

According to our survey of the Internet, CME, AMEX, and Philadelphia Internet Websites are being followed by similar sites from the other major exchanges. If these three exchanges are any indication of what you can expect to come, it will take this form:

❑ *A billboard of general information.* Set up along the superhighway, telling investors about the merits of a particular exchange and its products traded; packed with general information about history, rules, terms, mini training courses, conferences, government regulations, and so forth.

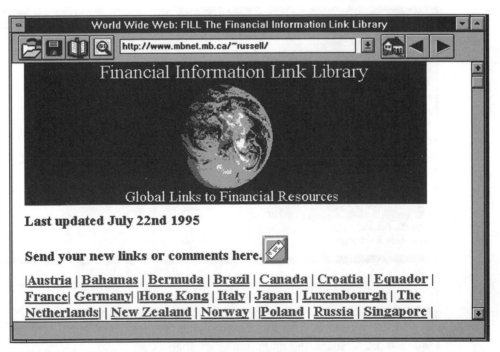

Figure 4.10 FILL: links to exchanges around the world.

❏ *Delayed and historical data.* End-of-day prices and volumes, with the data limited to securities traded on that exchange. The Chicago Board Options Exchange is attempting to go beyond this restriction, in which case all exchanges may have to make the same decision in order to be competitive, making at least closing-bell prices generally available in cyberspace.

Bottom line: If you want market quotes on a real-time or 15-minute-delayed basis, or even a few hours old—that is, data that can be used in making intraday trading decisions—you should expect to look somewhere other than the Internet for it, and expect to pay for it . . . from commercial vendors who buy raw data from the exchanges, whether from Quotecom or InterQuote, Reuters or Knight-Ridder.

The exchanges have been in the business of selling information to electronic data vendors for a long time, and they are not going to undercut their own base of income. So they're unlikely to start giving valuable data away free now merely because the Internet was originally based on a principle of the free exchange of knowledge.

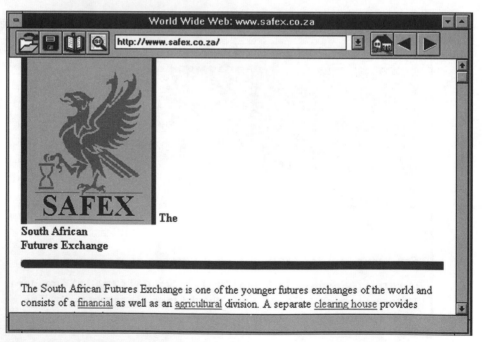

Figure 4.11 South African Futures Exchange.

INTERNATIONAL STOCK EXCHANGES LISTED ON I-NO

Australian Stock Exchange
Austrian Futures & Options Exchange
Belgium Futures & Options Exchange
Bolsa de Mercadorias & Futures (Brazil)
Budapest Commodity Exchange
European Options Exchange
Financial Termijnmarkt Amsterdam
Beijing Commodity Exchange
Copenhagen Stock Exchange
Deutsche Terminboerse
Finnish Options Exchange
Finnish Securities & Derivatives Exchange
Hong Kong Futures Exchange
Irish Futures & Options Exchange
Int'l Petroleum Exchange of London
Italian Stock Exchange
Kuala Lumpur Commodity Exchange
London Commodity Exchange
London Metal Exchange
London Securities & Derivatives Exchange
Marche a Terme Int'l de France
March des Options Negociables de Paris
Montreal Exchange
Manila Int'l Futures Exchange
New Zealand Futures & Options Exchange
Oslo Stock Exchange (Norway)
Santiago Exchange (Chile)
Singapore Int'l Monetary Exchange
South African Futures Exchange
Sydney Futures Exchange (Australia)
Tel Aviv Stock Exchange (Israel)
Tokyo Stock Exchange
Toronto Futures Exchange
Winnipeg Commodity Exchange
And other international exchanges

(SOURCE: Rich Financial Group Website, http://www.ino.com/chart.html.)

However, if things go as predicted, and all the major exchanges get on the Web with a Website, an investor may eventually be able to get free end-of-day information on all securities somewhere on the Web—a trend that may strengthen the role of the exchanges while further eroding the role of the brokerage industry as intermediaries between investors and the exchanges.

STOCK QUOTES AND MARKET INDEX REPORTS: BASIC DATA

Whether you are an investor, trader, broker, financial adviser, or money manager, you need basic information on price and volume. That's true whether you're looking at a particular stock or mutual fund, a sector of the market, an index of futures of options, or some broader market measures. You need price and volume data for Microsoft, Gold futures, or the S&P 500. Nothing happens in the investment world without this raw data. *Nothing*.

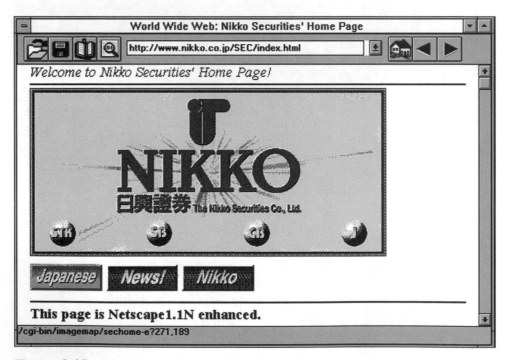

Figure 4.12   Japanese markets: Nikko Securities.

Cyberspace has a surprisingly large amount of free information available for today's new investor. And it's not necessarily true that you get only what you pay for. There's a lot of free information that is valuable . . . as well as a lot of costly resources that are, to say the least, overpriced in this new media.

Probably the single most important question with basic market and securities data is not *what* information you need, but *when* you need it:

❏ *Real time.* You're a day-trader or money manager, and minutes make a difference to you. A 15-minute delay takes you out of the game, spelling disaster. This is the highest-cost data. Plus you'll pay exchange fees. But you have the edge.

❏ *Delayed.* The vast majority of investors can make their investment decisions with quote information delayed 15 minutes, or even to closing. They are not full-time market professionals, and they are not entering and exiting the market several times a day, on a moment's notice. Rather, they have another business or profession that takes most of their time, but they have more than a passing interest in, and possibly an intense passion for, the market, not to mention an investment portfolio.

❏ *Historical.* You need long-term price and volume data to analyze and forecast future trends and patterns with individual securities, indexes, or the markets.

Where does all this data come from, and what do you do with it?

The answer to those questions are the subject of much of the rest of this book. Cyberspace is loaded with many vendors, many delivery systems, and emerging new technologies. We are going to examine several basic sources:

❏ *Internet Websites* and other sources
❏ *Commercial online services*, including CompuServe and others
❏ *Data vendors* feeding both institutional and individual investors
❏ *Other brokers*, including newswire services, software developers, etc.

In addition, data may be delivered by one of many communication delivery vehicles: telephone dial-ups via a modem, dedicated high-speed lines, cable channels, or wireless, through broadcast television, FM radio

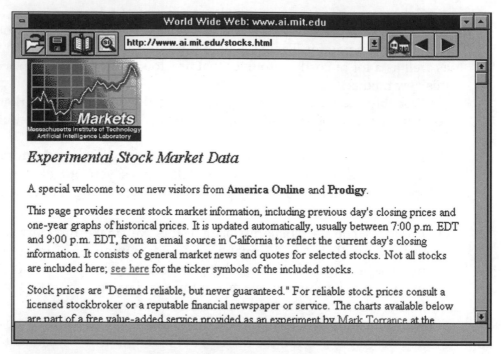

Figure 4.13   Quotes from MIT's Artificial Intelligence Lab.

antenna, and satellite dishes, or by CD-ROM disks. The actual method of delivery, however, is not as important as the timing. First, let's look at some starting points on the Internet's World Wide Web.

Internet: MIT's Experimental Stock Market Data

If all you really need is stock market data from the prior day's closing, and you're willing to tolerate longer delays on occasion, make your first stop the MIT's Experimental Stock Market Data site. For years the MIT site has been the best noncommercial Website for raw market data. It's managed by some very sharp grad students at Massachusetts Institute of Technology's Artificial Intelligence Laboratory. The title's a mouthful. The *Wall Street Journal* would have just called them "closing stock prices." The academic types must have decided they had to have an official/scientific-sounding label for the project to keep their nonprofit research status.

The MIT Website tells you that the closing prices are posted between 10:00 P.M. EDT and 1:00 A.M. However, the days we checked in, the quotes were a few days late. Still, the information is free, and there's a lot of it. Here's a list of what is available:

❐ *Stock quotes.* Open, high, low, close, and volume posted.

❐ *Mutual fund charts.* Check out your favorite funds.

❐ *Stock symbols.* Companies are sorted by ticker symbol.

❐ *Stock charts.* One-year price and volume charts.

❐ *Top stocks.* List of stocks most frequently graphed.

❐ *Historical data files.* How charts are structured, etc.

The MIT Website also has a subdirectory of links to meta-lists on the Internet's Web. The MIT links may not be as extensive as the other meta-lists recommended early; however, when it comes to stock quotes and volume, MIT is definitely a winner. Bookmark it.

Internet: Ohio State University's Financial Data Finder

Ohio State also has an excellent database for securities, with special emphasis on historical data. They have an incredibly good selection of links to Internet resources for investors. Take special note of the following historical databases:

❐ Weekly DJIA (1900–1989)

❐ Corporate debt issues (1983–1993)

❐ Treasury bond futures issues (1994–1995)

❐ Historical British stock prices (1700–1990)

❐ Historical interest rates (1700 to recent)

As you might expect, some of these databases are rather large. So be prepared for a long wait when you link to a specific database. For example, the 90 years of the DJIA is 2MB of information. But if you're looking for a slice of market history, here's a perfect place to start in cyberspace. In fact, Ohio State's site is one of the best Web starting points for everything the cyberspace investor needs.

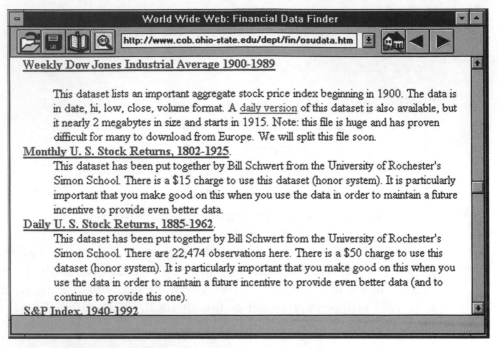

Figure 4.14   OSU's financial historical market data.

QuoteCom and Other Quote Sources on the New Web

In 1994 a new breed of commercial Websites began emerging alongside the government/academia ones already in cyberspace. You won't get unlimited, real-time access to the exchanges. Rather, many of these services are more like television infomercials. They give away some service—such as a limited number of free quotes or a free trial period—as a way of advertising other *paid-for* services, similar to advertising promotions in print publications. Several of these are worth your review.

QuoteCom was one of the early entrepreneurs to see the commercial potential of the Web. They offer anyone five quotes a day, free. All you have to do is register with QuoteCom. They have a search process to help you pick the right ticker symbols out of the database. Ticker symbol searches cover equities, indexes, commodities, options, and government securities. You have a choice of delivery systems for your quotes: by E-mail or on the Web. QuoteCom's basic quote service costs only $10 a month for a reasonably solid package, including:

❑ 100 quotes per day

❑ Automatic updates to your portfolio each day

❑ Portfolio alerts that pick up unusual movements

❑ End-of-day download of all 20,000 domestic symbols

❑ Selected company balance sheet information

❑ Newswire headlines

In addition, QuoteCom has a number of other very reasonable fee-based services: corporate charts, the S&P stock guide, S&P Corporate News, S&P MarketScope, bond quotes from Bear Sterns, both of the PR and Business wire services, financial newsletters, and even a weather service. For example, S&P's MarketScope, clearly one of the best sources of market news, would cost a trader almost $100 a month for the real-time version. QuoteCom is able to offer most of the same features on a delayed basis for about 20 percent of the real-time costs.

Bottom line: Log in. QuoteCom may well fit your needs. If the five free quotes don't do the trick, the cost of their other services is quite reasonable.

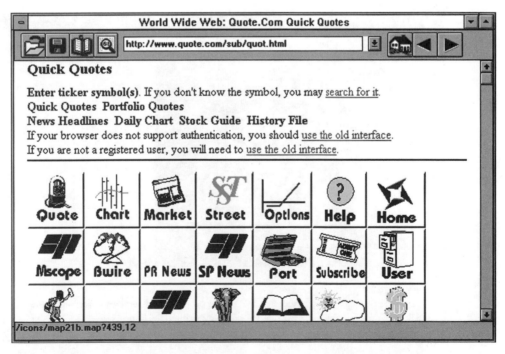

Figure 4.15 QuoteCom's Website and stock market quote system.

PC Quote: Leading Data Provider to Individuals and Institutions

PC Quote is one of the world's leading electronic providers of securities quotes and news. They are a Chicago-based global organization, highly regarded by individual investors as well as being a principal supplier to institutional investors, brokers, banks, pension funds, and money managers.

PC Quote claims that their "HyperFeed is the most accurate, most reliable, and most comprehensive digital data feed in the world" covering news, fundamental data, and prices on over 250,000 instruments traded on 145 exchanges in 55 countries. For many cyberspace investors and traders, PC Quote is the gateway to profits. Definitely log on and compare them to other leaders in the data delivery business.

PAWWS: More than Just a Few Free Quotes

PAWWS is short for Portfolio Accounting World Wide, a service from Security APL. PAWWS was one of the first on the Web and now gets over 2 mil-

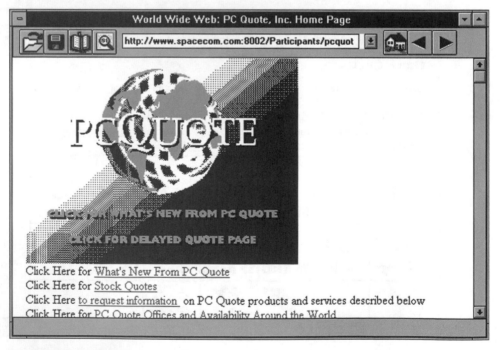

Figure 4.16   PC Quote: market news and stock quotes.

lion hits, or visitors, a week. Once registered, you may request a limited number of free quotes on a 15-minute-delay basis from DTN Wall Street's database. You can also link to the actual 15-minute-delayed charts of the NASDAQ Composite and S&P 500 Index. You can also get charts for one, five, and ten years and data for other indexes. In addition to the free quotes, the PAWWS Website has subscription services:

- Fundamental Data on 5,000 securities
- Quick Quote Server & Ticker Symbol Lookup
- Internet Financial Research Links to other Websites
- Market Analysis & Index Information
- DTN Wall Street News & Commentary Services
- Brokerage & Trading Services (Net Investor)
- Portfolio Management & Accounting

PAWWS also has an interesting investment contest. Both the PAWWS and the QuoteCom Websites are typical of the emerging new commercial

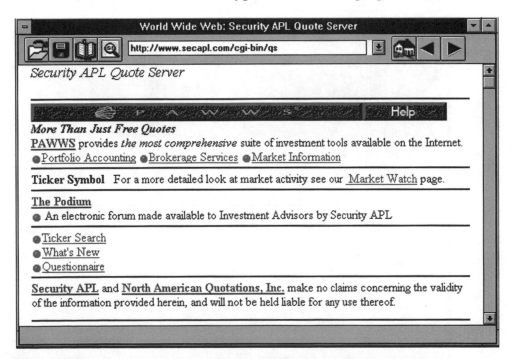

Figure 4.17 Quotes from PAWWS: Portfolio Accounting World Wide.

sites. While they are primarily advertising vehicles for various paid sub-scription services, they do offer valuable free information. And fortunately their paid services are reasonable. Besides, several free 15-minute-delayed quotes a day may be sufficient for many investors. And for others, the unlimited, end-of-day MIT service may be sufficient. If you have an exist-ing online commercial service, it most likely provides the same quotes available free on the Web, plus many more services . . . without having to log on to the Web.

NETworth: The Website for Mutual Funds Quotes

NETworth is always expanding and refining its Website, adding many fine resources for investors. For example, NETworth's Equities Center now offers free quotes, along with a wealth of other attractive information. Investors are encouraged to visit this emerging meta-list. You'll find such gems as the Benham Fund's weekly *Market Outlook,* Louis Rukeyser's *Wall Street* newsletter, and the Disclosure Database, among other information supplies. Definitely bookmark this site.

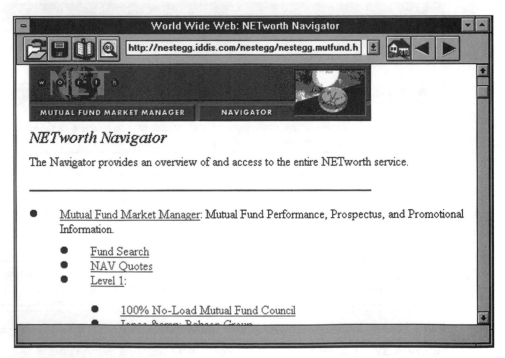

Figure 4.18 Mutual fund quotes: net asset value (NAV).

Holt's Stock Market Reports on the Internet

If you're surfing the Internet for a daily summary of the raw market information, Holt's Market Reports will deliver the essential data, covering these areas:

❐ Major Market Indexes and Averages

❐ Foreign Markets

❐ Issues Traded

❐ New Highs & Lows

❐ Foreign Currencies

❐ Gold & Interest Rates

❐ Most Active on NYSE, NASDAQ, and AMEX

Holt's Website may be short on visuals, but it is long on quality data. They also regularly post their Reports on Usenet groups. Depending on your particular needs, Holt's reliable service may well serve your needs.

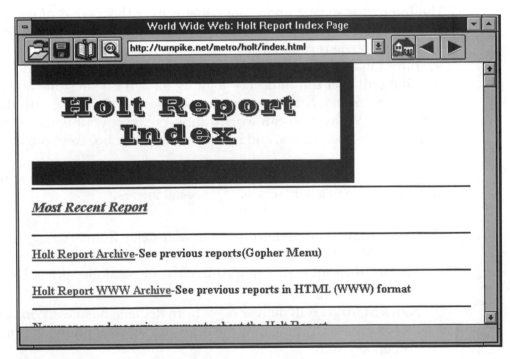

Figure 4.19 Holt Market Reports Website.

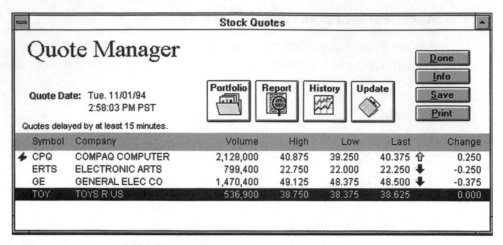

Figure 4.20   InfoManager's dial-up quote manager.

InfoManager: Central Data Manager for the Net

The Internet is so vast and chaotic that during this period of evolution it comes as no surprise to see an inventive new product or service designed to solve an obvious problem and minimize Websurfer frustrations.

InfoManager is a new product that may just save you the time of searching all over the Internet—logging on and off sites one at a time—for all the wonderful, free market quotes (and news) out there in cyberspace. With it you can work offline, organize your work, customize your Website bookmarks, and manage your portfolio, news retrieval, and E-mail.

For $20 a month, InfoManager delivers four basic services: quotes, news, E-mail, and a contacts list. Of special interest:

❑ **Quote Manager** delivers on a 15-minute delay from NYSE, AMEX, and NASDAQ. The information can be exported to a spreadsheet, or you can use their tools. It can also track your portfolio, price, P/E ratio, yield, dividend, etc.

❑ **News Manager** will deliver news from Reuters, Business Wire, and the PR Newswire, clipping only the news sections you profile. It can search also on keywords.

Bottom line: Another of the emerging new products designed to help investors use the Internet effectively. More will follow, but for now Info-Manager may just be an effective way to corral the wide, wide world Web. Call and get their info. See if InfoManager can help you simplify your cyberspace investing.

Internet's InterQuote: A Cost Comparison for Quotes

Considering all the alternatives, collecting raw data can be time-consuming, expensive, and confusing. What should you expect to pay if you're interested only in basic, raw data? There's a new provider on the Internet's Web with a simple pricing schedule and a first-class data service that can give you a clear picture of the costs. And if you still lack Web access, this is one service that may convince you to do it now, especially if you're a trader.

InterQuote can be accessed at their Website for real-time displays as well as the usual promotional material. They provide users with their *free* downloadable software package, which allows you to organize and manage up to six portfolios. Moreover, you can mix stocks, funds, and derivatives to customize your portfolios.

RAW QUOTE DATA (INTERQUOTES' MONTHLY CHARGES)	
Real-time interactive service	$82
Real-time WWW service	$47
Delayed interactive service	$20
Delayed WWW service	$10
End-of-day service	$ 5

InterQuote's real-time data costs include estimated exchange fees for NYSE, NASDAQ, and AMEX (about $12). All other exchanges are 15-minute delays. Plus InterQuote offers a 15-day free trial period.

Bottom line: InterQuote deserves special attention. For only $60 per month you can get the same *real-time* data you might pay four times as much for from other sources. And there's no setup charge. The software is free. Unlimited delayed quotes are $10 to $20 a month, a good price considering they supply the software, although you still have to transfer the data to your analytical software.

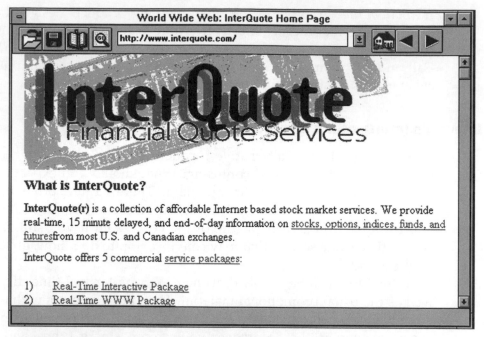

Figure 4.21   InterQuote's Website: a real-time ticker-tape.

Keep in mind, this is a relatively new Website. They are gradually improving their software to permit automatic interface with products such as MetaStock, Windows on Wall Street, Quicken, and other popular analytical software. They have yet to add historical data, although it's in the works. Hopefully, they'll add these improvements soon and find a customer base competing with more established quote vendors moving onto the Internet now.

Quotes from the Big-Three Commercial Online Services

If you're looking for 15-minute-delayed quotes, the online commercial services do a respectable job for you, and possibly better than the current Internet resources. Anyone getting a quote on the Internet is then left with that now-what feeling. The online services get you the quotes you want . . . plus, they have become a centralized mini war room of other tools, especially news and analysis, at a price competitive with Internet quote resources. They are an IntraNet, part investment club, part computer "special interest group," and part trading room. Let's look at what the big-three online services offer:

America Online

The basic AOL package provides a quote service, plus you get a package with many other services necessary for investment decisions. AOL has a search engine that allows you to check an alphabetic index of all companies listed on the NYSE, AMEX, NASDAQ, and the major indexes. You then get a 15-minute-delayed quote, which is usually only 15 minutes delayed:

❏ Yesterday's close

❏ Open, high, and low

❏ Volume

❏ 52-week high and low

❏ Yield and P/E ratio

In addition, you can input your investment portfolio and get a current update of its total value. More important, your basic AOL online service fee includes several other services: news from Reuters newswires and articles from the Investor's Business Daily, Business Week, Nightly Business

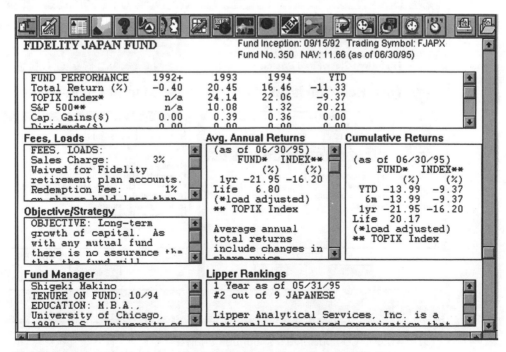

Figure 4.22 Stock and mutual fund quotes from America Online.

Report, ABC News, and access to a number of analytical tools, Hoover's Company Reports, forums, trading, investment games, and more—much more, but you get the point.

CompuServe

Quotes, quotes, and more. This database of the CompuServe online service is far and away the biggest and the best of the big-three online services: 12-year price histories on more than 100,000 stocks, bonds, and indexes, and 2,400 mutual funds from *Money* magazine.

CompuServe is also the most expensive of the big three to use. Every current quote you check on is a couple pennies, every historical quote a nickel. It keeps clicking away like the meter on a taxicab. It may even drive you to one of the Internet quote sources. But if you want a centralized source for all your investment information, CompuServe is the best of the big three.

Most likely you'll need more than the basic service, so you have to count on a bill much higher than the flat fee for the basic service. In a sense,

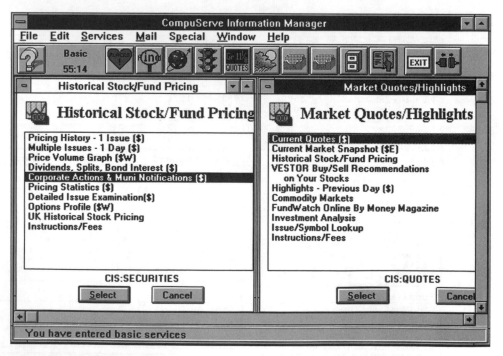

Figure 4.23 CompuServe's securities analyzer.

the meter is always running, with add-on hourly charges and individual fees for most investment data, plus a rate schedule that rivals the Federal Tax Code. You should assume that with every minute and every new request there's another click on the meter. Is it worth it? Well, a few million subscribers think so. Please look closely at this superior online service.

If you are a serious investor, the more you work with the Internet's discrete, isolated, unintegrated databases, the more you'll appreciate the importance of having an online service as a central focal point for your investment decision making. Sure, none of the big-three online services will provide you with the firepower of a thousand-dollar-a-month workstation from Dow Jones Telerate, Reuters, or Bloomberg, but they are often more useful than the odd collection of separate databases floating on the Internet right now.

For example, investors on CompuServe have at their fingertips many other data resources and analytical tools. Beyond simple market quotes on any one stock or mutual fund, you'll be able to access huge databases for company and news reports, economic surveys, advisory letters, credit reports, investment screening, portfolio games, trading, and many more services for you and your family on entertainment, sports, weather, etc.

Today's cyberspace investor is searching for a total-service package, everything wrapped into one. That's why StreetSmart, Telescan, and Reuters Money Network, as well as CompuServe, are so appealing.

Prodigy

With Prodigy's Quote Track service an investor can input a portfolio of stocks and follow it on a regular basis. Access it when you log on and check out your portfolio, including opportunities you're considering. You can also check individual quotes. Prodigy even "red flags" companies in the news, so you can jump over to Company News and find out exactly what is affecting your stocks.

In addition, Prodigy's Stock Hunter feature lets you screen through investment opportunities by various selected technical and fundamental criteria, such as P/E ratios, earnings, O'Neil's CANSLIM, and other benchmark tools. Plus Prodigy gives you access to economic news, Kiplinger's, and online brokerage. In August 1995, *Individual Investor* magazine, certainly one of the best of its kind, awarded Stock Hunter "the hands-down winner" as the "best stock-screening tool," so take another very close look at the Prodigy service.

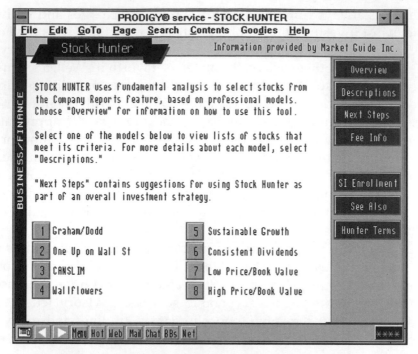

Figure 4.24   Prodigy's Stock Hunter: eight screening tools.

Competition Is Driving Down the Price of Quotes . . . to Zero

Buying quotes can become quite complicated and expensive. But the three main variables are (1) the number of quotes you need per day, (2) when you need them, and (3) the type of software you are using for analysis. However, it's very difficult to estimate and compare costs given the wide variations in anticipated usage and payment structures.

If you're on the Web, you can probably find one or more services with five free quotes to take care of you (five here, five there, it all adds up). Or better yet, find a service such as InterQuote, QuoteCom, or PC Quote to provide raw data (in the range of a mere $5 to $20 a month for delayed quotes). Or InterQuote can provide you with real-time quotes for $60 per month. And most online services can also service your delayed-quote needs for $10 to $20 a month.

If you need quotes in volume, or real-time data, or you need quotes to interface quickly and easily with your analytical software, then expect to pay more, at least $60 per month for delayed or end-of-day quotes. Dow

HOW VALUABLE ARE FIVE FREE QUOTES?

PC Quote is a Chicago Company that trades in investment information—real-time equity quotes, commodities, etc. They provide data to such notables as CompuServe, AOL, and Charles Schwab and Co., Inc. . . . To promote the service, PC Quote has hosted a World Wide Web page on Spacecom's server at http://www.spacecom.com/Participants/pcquote offering free stock quotes via the Web. A very simple screen form allows you to either look up the ticker symbol for a company, or get a 15-minute-delayed stock quote for it.

For the kind of serious investor PC Quote aims their Hyper-Feed at, this service would be of limited use. It's a bit slow, and sometimes doesn't work at all. . . . But the novelty of it might attract their attention. . . . The system seems to be attracting 2500 unique new visitors each day. . . . It is an excellent example of a company providing a limited free service as a means of attracting attention from the more serious potential customer they hope to attract.

(SOURCE: *BoardWatch*, July 1995.)

The solution? Until the exchanges themselves start giving them away free, *pay for quotes.* At a minimum, subscribe to a reliable vendor (e.g., CompuServe, Schwab, or the full service from PC Quote, InterQuote, or a similar service). Or trade up to someone such as Telescan, Signal, or even a leader such as S&P Comstock. After all, your portfolio has got to be worth at least ten bucks a month for the right information.

Jones News/Retrieval provides unlimited *off-hours* quotes (including historical quotes back ten years or more) plus their Market Monitor service and analytic tools for $60 a month. For unlimited real-time information you probably should expect to pay over $100 a month, possibly more like $200 to $250, after basic setup fees and including some analytics.

Bottom Line: Raw Data Versus Analytics and Instincts

The market for quotes is highly competitive . . . and will be even more competitive in the near term. Internet Websites, discount brokers, and even the exchanges are giving away quotes to keep you coming back their way.

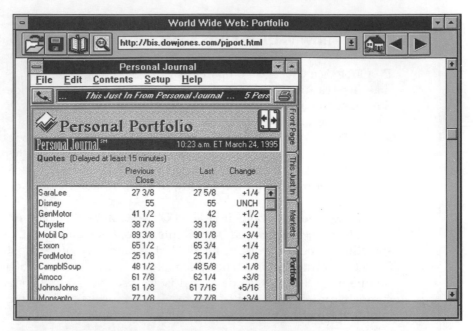

Figure 4.25   Quotes on Dow Jones' Personal Journal.

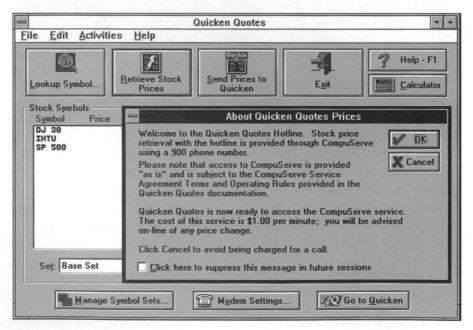

Figure 4.26   Quicken Quotes hotline into CompuServe.

And many news vendors are entering the retail market, online, on the Internet and from the major data services as they see the growing potential of the mass market of individual investors.

You can expect this competitive mass-market pressure to accelerate on the Internet, resulting in more favorable quote prices and other market data for the individual investor. In fact, we are heading for the day when the exchanges themselves are giving the data away free—not just closing prices but 15-minute-delayed data and possibly even real-time data—anything to stir up interest in trading *on their particular exchange* rather than on some competing exchange elsewhere around the world.

That's really what all this five-free-quotes fuss is about. It's a diversion, the leading edge of the trend to unlimited quotes. It's the tip of an iceberg that further exposes the fact that it is not the raw data—not even raw *real-time* data—that matters, *but what you do with it.* Your analytical tools plus your investment instincts turn raw data into information, intelligence, and wisdom.

BOTH WALL STREET AND BROADWAY ARE ON THE ROAD!

Recently *Forbes* ran an interesting article about the new Broadway. Reading it triggered some interesting parallels between what's happening to New York City's two most famous streets, Broadway and Wall Street, both of which are driven by high finance and high drama.

The article, titled "A Hundred Broadways Now," concluded that "Broadway is no longer a place." This new Broadway is a state of mind.

While Broadway is expanding into 100 regional theaters, Wall Street is also going on the road—the information superhighway—onto the Internet and IntraNets, the commercial online services and the vast new world of cyberspace.

Soon Wall Street will be playing in over 100 million "theaters" (computer monitors) worldwide. Like Broadway, Wall Street is no longer a place. Today's Wall Street is a state of mind in cyberspace, the ultimate exchange on a global stage.

CHAPTER **5**

Investment Research and Analysis

GOVERNMENT ECONOMIC AND MONETARY STATISTICS

The federal government generates an enormous volume of data about U.S. business and finance, economics, and monetary policies. Every investor should be aware of these resources, which can be accessed by anyone with a Web browser, often at no cost.

U.S. Census Bureau's Monthly Economic Indicators

The Commerce Department's Census Bureau makes available many government statistics—both current and historical—which are later published in the *Statistical Abstract of the United States.* If you want the *Abstract*, you can order it from the Census Bureau's Website. The Website includes many statistics, including population trends.

An investor should check out the specific file titled "Monthly Time Series—Economic Indicators." This file is updated monthly by the government, and in addition, they record the reported monthly statistics for several years, so you can see trends and patterns in the nation's economic health.

ECONOMIC INDEXES: MONTHLY TIME SERIES

Retail Trade
Wholesale Trade
Consumer Installment Credit
Building Permits & Housing Starts
New Home Sales
New Home Mortgage Rates
New Construction
Manufacturing
Index of Industrial Production
Foreign Trade
Money Supply (MP)
Consumer & Wholesale Price Indexes
Interest Rates
Civilian Labor Force & Unemployment
Index of Leading Economic Indicators
Personal Income
Gross Domestic Product

(SOURCE: Files at U.S. Census Bureau Website.)

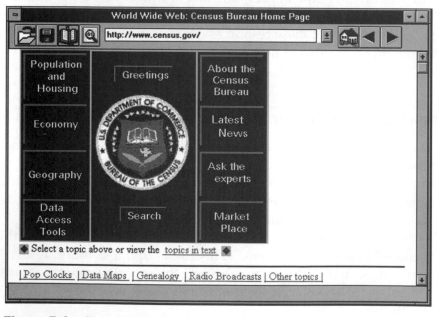

Figure 5.1   Department of Commerce's Bureau of Census.

University of Michigan's Economics Bulletin Board

If you're looking for statistics about the U.S. economy, head straight for the University of Michigan library, straight into the Economics Bulletin Board. You can access it from your Web browser through either EBB's Website or the Internet's Gopher search process.

Since the Internet grew up as a partnership between the federal government and our universities, it should be no surprise that the universities are a major vehicle for government statistics about our nation's economy and our monetary status.

The Economics Bulletin Board is an example of how well the Internet's network with university libraries functions. The U.S. Department of Commerce's Office of Business Analysis is the primary source of data for the EBB, pulling together economic information compiled by many government agencies.

With the downsizing of the federal government, it's possible that an enterprising commercial publisher or data vendor (e.g., Dow Jones, DBC Signal, CompuServe) may be called upon to deliver this data directly to

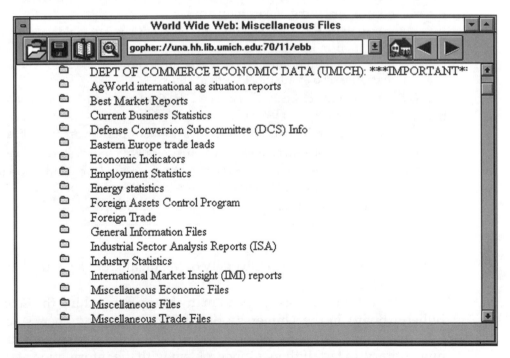

Figure 5.2 Economics Bulletin Board: University of Michigan.

ECONOMICS BULLETIN BOARD: UNIVERSITY OF MICHIGAN

Economic Indicators: The EBB's list of Leading, Lagging and Coincident Indicators was quite current when we accessed the file, only three weeks old. EBB's list includes many other specific economic indicators, such as housing starts, building permits, personal income, inventories, consumer prices, and various composite indexes.

Best Market Reports: The performance of various industry sectors was in a 75K file. If you're specifically interested in the high-tech companies, check out the subsections: computer software, computers and peripherals, telecommunications equipment, maybe even electric power. For example, in 1993, Japan was the leading 1993 importer of American computers at $45 billion. Germany was next with $27 billion.

Summaries of Current Economic Conditions: Most notable in this subdirectory was a recent report of the Commerce Department's chief economist. However, reports by Chairman Greenspan were outdated. Updating that file would take a search by a commercial source, such as Dow Jones News/Retrieval or Dialog.

Industrial Statistics: Every quarter the Department of Commerce posts reports analyzing 50 key industries.

Monetary Statistics: Here an investor will find current yields on federal, state, and municipal securities. These statistics are posted *daily* and include Fed fund rates, CD's, T-bills, and many more. Historical information is also available. Excellent source.

U.S. Treasury Auction Results: The U.S. Treasury posts information on every security sold by the government, short-term to long-term.

Regional Economic Statistics: Incomes by metropolitan areas (SMSA).

Energy Statistics: Oil, coal gas, etc., broken down by use, stocks, sector.

Foreign Trade: Import/export data, exchange rates (even some specialized reports on leads to new business in Eastern Europe!).

Employment Statistics: By state and metropolitan areas.

investors. But for now, the University of Michigan does a great job with the huge database.

An investor could easily spend many hours researching the Economics Bulletin Board in the University of Michigan's library. There's so much information, you actually feel like you're right there, walking through this huge library. In fact, if there's any problem with the information at the Economics Bulletin Board, it's simply that there's too much of a good thing, until you learn your way around it.

Bottom line: The Economics Bulletin Board is an excellent resource for today's investors. EBB may undergo some changes with the privatization of the Internet. A number of the other university-based meta-lists have gone after commercial support to continue providing these excellent services—for example, R.R. Donnelley with NYU's SEC/EDGAR database and Microsoft with Carnegie Mellon University's Lycos Internet search/ database.

In addition, the commercial online services (CompuServe, America Online, and Prodigy) and, more important, the highly competitive data vendors vying for the investor's business (Dow Jones, Reuters, Knight Ridder, DBC Signal, and others) are rapidly improving the quality and usability of economic information available to today's demanding investor. Meanwhile, EBB is a valuable resource available to the cyberspace investor.

VALIDITY OF GOVERNMENT STATISTICS AT UNIVERSITIES

1. **Information Overload?** The files are huge. The organization could be improved and an effective search engine added. Bookmark each specific subdirectory that fits your portfolio needs.

2. **Enough Analysis?** Raw data by itself is often essential. However, EBB could use more cross-referencing, analysis, and summaries.

3. **Not Current Enough?** There's some excellent historical data here. However, the investor who needs data in real time, or even by the end of day, must rely on commercial data vendors.

4. **The Right Data?** Probably the biggest problem is related to the validity of the data and indexes themselves. A 1995 *Business Week* cover story challenged the accuracy and adequacy of many government statistics, suggesting they tended to present a misleading picture of the state of the economy.

The problem is that the methods used by the government were okay in the 1950s but may not fit today's dynamic information-age economy. *Business Week* says that many economists agree that government statistics do not accurately measure inflation, unemployment, and productivity, for example. The Foundation for the Study of Cycles now publishes its own Index of Leading Economic Indicators for this very reason.

STAT-USA: Commerce Department's Economic Bulletin Board

The University of Michigan's site was developed in order to get information on the Internet, before the Web was even created. You may recall that their information is downloaded from U.S. government agencies, and then added to the Michigan database. The Economics Bulletin Board (EBB) itself is, in fact, maintained by the Department of Commerce from government databases. And, while the government agencies may have the information on a timely basis, there were often time lags in getting the information transferred and reloaded in the university's databanks (the sites are probably maintained by students).

The universities have been operating much as intermediaries or wholesalers for the federal government, often funded by the federal government's R&D division—the National Science Foundation—interested in experimenting and developing the Internet. In 1994 the NSF began cutting back on its funding to Michigan and other universities receiving funding for Internet sites.

Now that the Department of Commerce is promoting the Economics Bulletin Board directly on its own Website, we can expect to have access to

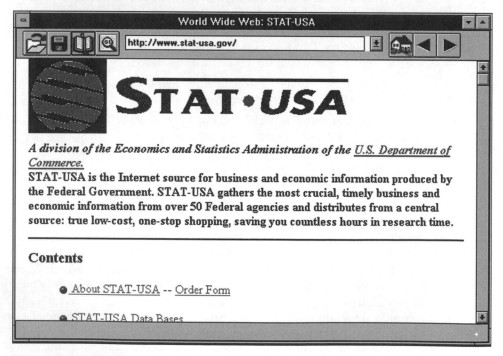

Figure 5.3   STAT-USA: U.S. Department of Commerce data.

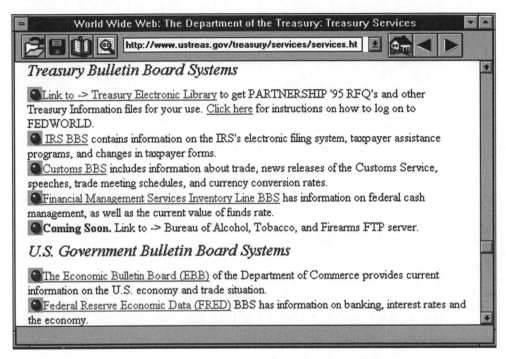

Figure 5.4   Web links: U.S. Treasury to other government BBSs.

information in a more reliable and timely manner. Note that the Department of Commerce does charge for some of its information, while the University of Michigan, which has been funded by other government programs, can be accessed for free. However, this arrangement is likely to change as the federal government continues to get greater control of the federal budget and the deficit.

Business Cycle Indicators: Software from Media Logic

If you want to stay current on economic trends and you're tired of the time-consuming search through a lot of Websites, Gophers, and dial-up services, check out Media Logic's *Business Cycles Indicators* software and data package.

Media Logic's data series covers the period from 1948 to the present, a total of 250 economic and business-cycle indicators from the Bureau of Economic Analysis' Survey of Current Business. The information is broken down into 13 general categories:

❒ Composite Indexes; Leading, Coincident & Lagging

❒ Labor Force, Employment & Unemployment

❒ Output, Production & Capacity Utilization

❒ Sale, Orders & Deliveries

❒ Fixed Capital Investment

❒ Prices; CPI, PPI, etc.

❒ Corporate Profits & Cash Flow

❒ Personal Income & Consumer Attitudes

❒ Saving: Government, Business & Personal

❒ Money, Credit, Interest Rates & Stock Prices

❒ National Defense

❒ Exports and Imports

❒ International Economic & Monetary Comparisons

Media Logic's statistics include leading economic indicators, money supply, price indexes, industrial production, inventories, consumer confi-

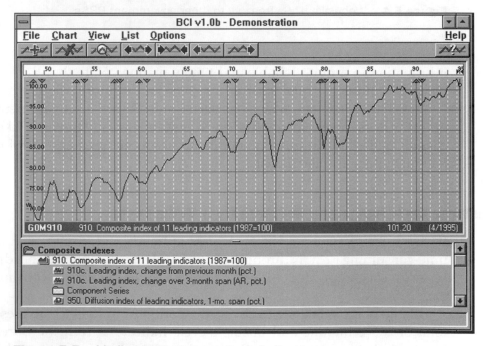

Figure 5.5 Media Logic: Business Cycle Indicators.

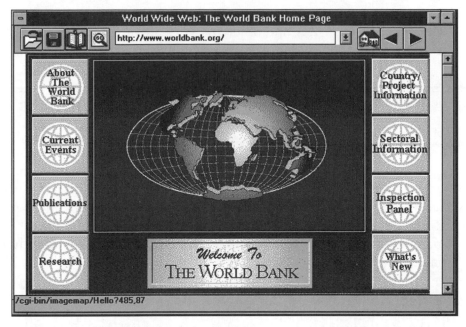

Figure 5.6 The World Bank: global Website.

Figure 5.7 FedWorld: gateway to government data.

dence, foreign trade, and more. Moreover, the data can be exported to MetaStock, Lotus 1-2-3, and other analytic software applications. The price is reasonable, about $130 for start-up, plus the cost of updates.

INDUSTRY SECTOR AND COMPANY ANALYSIS: FUNDAMENTALS

Many investors are naturally drawn to certain industrial sectors that they understand. Some are drawn to the agricultural commodities, or transportation, or biotech, or computer software. In structuring their portfolios, investors may research a particular sector, or screen for top performers according to some selection criteria. Or they may already know something about a specific company and want more information. There are now many excellent cyberspace resources to help you analyze individual companies and industry sectors.

Hoover's Reports: Profiles of Companies and Industries

Hoover's Reports are one of the best databases of American industry sectors. *Business Week* magazine said "you can't find more information on Corporate America in any other single source" when they reviewed their

---

OTHER INTERNET WEBSITES FOR GOVERNMENT STATISTICS

❏ **FedWorld** is another major gateway to many large government databases, and information of all kinds can be reached through the National Technical Information Service's FedWorld. (http://www.fedworld.gov)

❏ **FinanceNet** is federation of federal, state, and municipal governments. This group provides information on government assets, forums, mailing lists, training, asset sales opportunities, and maintains a meta-list of links to related organizations. (http://www.financenet.gov)

❏ **Commerce Business Daily,** the respected publisher of information on government contracts and related news, now has a Website. (http://cos.gdb.org/repos/cbd/cbd-intro.html)

❏ **The World Bank** has a powerful presence on the Internet. Their Website has several directories of information about the bank, the projects, and countries they're invested in, as well as research being done, publications, and press releases. (http://www.worldbank.org)

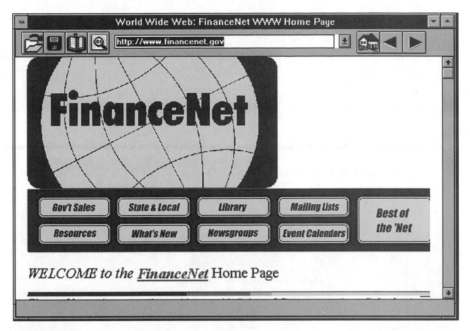

Figure 5.8   FinanceNet: government contacts plus.

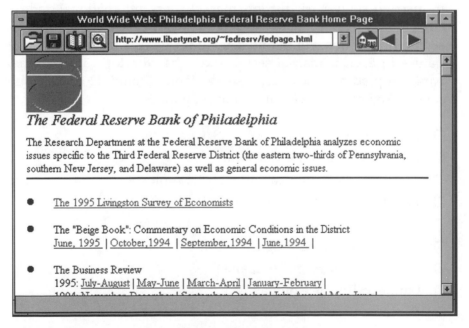

Figure 5.9   Federal Reserve Bank of Philadelphia.

Profiles of 500 Major Corporations. Hoover's is highly respected through-out the financial industry.

Hoover's can be found at many cyberspace outlets: on the Internet's Web, CompuServe, AOL, Lexis-Nexis, Bloomberg, and many other loca-tions. Hoover's Industry Profiles cover 7,800 companies in 196 separate industrial sectors under these eight major categories.

HOOVER'S LIST OF THE EIGHT MAJOR INDUSTRIAL SECTORS

Natural Resources & Energy
Construction & Related Materials
Industrial Materials & Components
Production & Manufacturing Equipment
The Consumer Industry
Transportation & Travel
Health Care
Finance/Business/Professional Services

A typical Hoover's Industry Profile will contain data on most recent industry revenues, production, market share, international trade patterns, current and five-year forecasts, and detailed descriptions of the industrial sector. In addition, you'll find several dozen lists ranking the largest com-panies in each industrial sector and subsector, top 25 law firms, top 50 banks, top ad agencies, etc. Also available through Hoover's Website are several key handbooks that profile companies.

- Master List of Major (7,800) U.S. Companies
- Profiles of 500 Major Corporations
- Master List of America's Top 2,500 Employers
- Handbook of Largest 160 World Businesses Outside U.S.
- Master List of America's Top 2,500 Employers
- Handbook of Emerging Companies
- Guide to Computer Companies
- Guide to Private Companies
- Business Best-Seller List
- The Essential Business Reference Library

Figure 5.10   Hoover's Reports on industry and companies.

Hoover's Website also features current news every week, the Top Ten Business Stories of the Week. Hoover also offers its catalog of stock guides, such as the 100 Best Stocks to Own, and quite a number of others focusing on the S&P 500, NASDAQ, and emerging stocks. And, on a lighter note that their America Online viewers are already aware of, Hoover's has a special Star Trek profile of Quark's Inc. Quark is the alien Ferengi owner of the restaurant and bar on *Star Trek/Deep Space Nine.* This comic relief is a welcome interlude amid all the dry business statistics.

OUTLINE OF A HOOVER'S COMPANY REPORT

Overview
History
Executives, salaries, etc.
Assets, sales, and income
Balance sheet and net incomes
Competition
Trends; earnings, P/E, dividends, book value,
   employees, stock prices, etc.

Bottom line: Hoover's Reports are a must for any investor going behind the scenes of Corporate America. Bookmark it. And while you're there, check out their bookstore if you need a copy of the *Statistical Abstract of the United States,* the *NASDAQ Fact Book,* handbooks of the computer industry, and hundreds of other publications. Hoover's Website is primarily an advertising vehicle at present, although that will likely change. The online locations—CompuServe, AOL, etc.—have more usable information and forms so you can quickly order reports online.

Dun & Bradstreet's Corporate and Industry Research

Dun & Bradstreet is one of the top business credit reporting agencies in the world and can certainly give investors another picture of a company that has captured their attention, especially a foreign corporation. The D&B database of corporations is exceptionally large, and it is constantly updated from more than 300 offices worldwide:

❐ 38 million companies worldwide

❐ 19.7 million companies in the United States

❐ 10 million North American companies

❐ 11.9 million executives of U.S.-based companies

❐ 1 million financial statements of privately held companies

D&B profiles companies in 838 industry sectors worldwide. Using the D&B search tool, Dun's Business Locator, you can screen through all databases using 34 selection criteria to target market opportunities. D&B can also sift through databases in 32 countries to uncover interlocking corporations: who owns whom.

Using their extensive database, they've developed profiles of typical industry financial statements. An investor can then match an individual company's balance sheet and income statements against industry norms for 14 key business ratios. The D&B Website includes some helpful information:

❐ Strategic business planning

❐ Predictably slow-paying companies

❐ How to research effectively

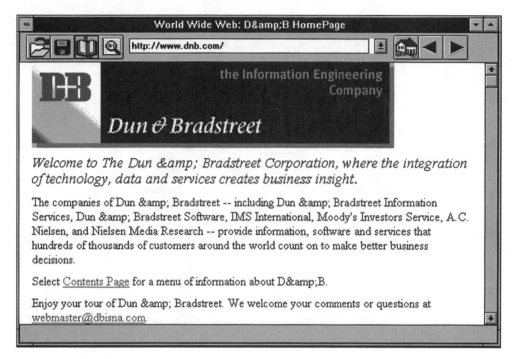

Figure 5.11 Dun & Bradstreet: industry and company research.

❐ Major businesses locator
❐ Tactical marketing targets
❐ How to manage vendors
❐ Marketing your business globally

The last item has statistics on the global regions with the fastest-growing GDPs, and some tips on how to export to those locations. This can be useful if you're doing in-depth research, looking to diversify your portfolio outside the United States. The Website also has several interesting graphs, such as the 10 Highest/Lowest Industry Profitability and Growth, and other criteria for analyzing industry sectors.

The Disclosure Database of Public Companies

The Disclosure Database is one of the primary commercial sources of legally required securities filings. Their database also has extensive *financial* as well as *legal* information about the 12,500 companies registered with

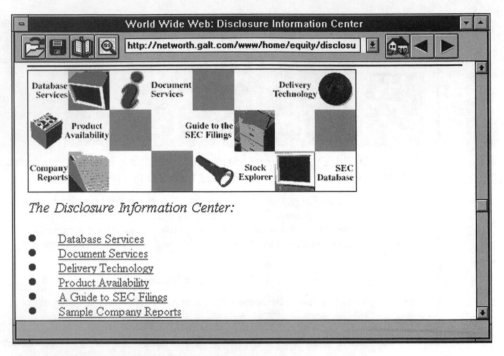

Figure 5.12   The Disclosure Database at NETworth.

the SEC. On their opening Website page they even call themselves, "your source for global public company information." The Disclosure team sells their information on securities filings through Dow Jones News/Retrieval, CompuServe, NETworth, Knight-Ridder's Dialog service, and other cyberspace locations. Disclosure's services are discussed in more detail in the next section on Securities Filings.

Value Line's Electronic Publishing: Value/Screen

Here's another good example of a traditional financial publisher responding to the challenge and opportunities of cyberspace. Every investor in the world has probably seen at least one of Value Line's advertisements, if not their publications themselves. Yes, they're pricey. Weekly updates are $2,000 annually, but you can get quarterly updates for $325 a year. Many investors swear by them.

Value Line provides over 50 fundamental and technical criteria on about 1,600 stocks, with software that permits screening based on 25 dif-

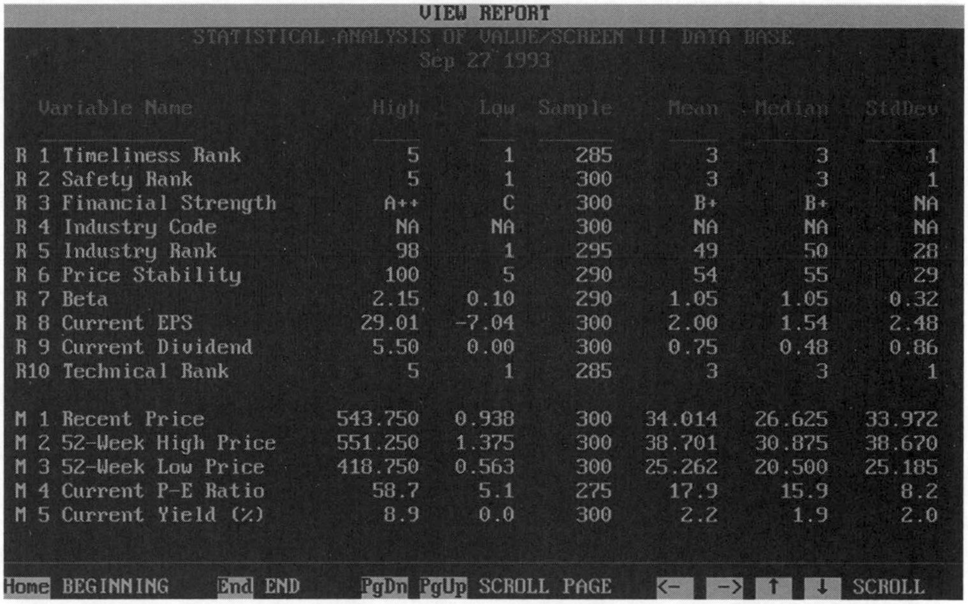

```
                          VIEW REPORT
              STATISTICAL ANALYSIS OF VALUE/SCREEN III DATA BASE
                            Sep 27 1993

  Variable Name              High     Low  Sample    Mean   Median   StdDev

R 1 Timeliness Rank             5       1     285       3        3        1
R 2 Safety Rank                 5       1     300       3        3        1
R 3 Financial Strength        A++       C     300      B+       B+       NA
R 4 Industry Code              NA      NA     300      NA       NA       NA
R 5 Industry Rank              98       1     295      49       50       28
R 6 Price Stability           100       5     290      54       55       29
R 7 Beta                     2.15    0.10     290    1.05     1.05     0.32
R 8 Current EPS             29.01   -7.04     300    2.00     1.54     2.48
R 9 Current Dividend         5.50    0.00     300    0.75     0.48     0.86
R10 Technical Rank              5       1     285       3        3        1

M 1 Recent Price          543.750   0.938     300  34.014   26.625   33.972
M 2 52-Week High Price    551.250   1.375     300  38.701   30.875   38.670
M 3 52-Week Low Price     418.750   0.563     300  25.262   20.500   25.185
M 4 Current P-E Ratio        58.7     5.1     275    17.9     15.9      8.2
M 5 Current Yield (%)         8.9     0.0     300     2.2      1.9      2.0

Home BEGINNING    End END    PgDn PgUp SCROLL PAGE   <- ■ -> ↑ ■ ↓ SCROLL
```

Figure 5.13   Value Line: Value/Screen online service.

ferent criteria, plus their own rating system. Data is downloadable into spreadsheet programs such as Lotus 1-2-3 and Excel.

Standard & Poor's: The Financial Industry's Standard

Many brokers, traders, and investors have used Standard & Poor's company research reports for decades and have come to rely on their comprehensiveness. Standard & Poor's Research Reports are thoroughly researched, objective, and unbiased assessments of the fundamental statistics of a company in a format convenient for investment analysis. The database is updated daily.

The S&P database has been one of the most respected in corporate America for over a hundred years. It is available for a fee through many commercial online dial-up services and Internet Websites. For about $400 a year an investor can access unlimited S&P research reports on 5,400 companies, including the S&P 500. In addition to the S&P company reports, 2,200 mutual fund reports are also available on a dial-up basis from Research Online, a San Francisco–based cyberspace research firm soon to go on the Net as www.researchmag.com.

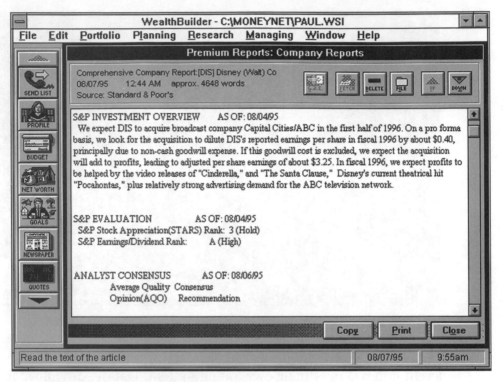

Figure 5.14   Standard & Poor's research reports.

Fundamental Research with Dow Jones News/Retrieval

Dow Jones is the pacesetter when it comes to basic research data on companies and industry sectors, so let's examine all that's available at DJN/R:

☐ **Tradeline.**   Dow tracks almost 150,000 domestic stocks, bonds, options, funds, and indexes, plus another 40,000 securities on 90 exchanges worldwide. Fundamental statistics about the companies and industry sectors are included along with newswire stories and quotes.

☐ **Company Reports.**   Profiles and histories of price, volume, earnings, dividends, financial statements, officers, new issues, and industry ratios, along with current market quotes.

☐ **Standard & Poor's.**   Business profiles from a database of 5,000 companies (dividends, earnings, products, markets, etc.).

☐ **WorldScope.**   Financial reports of 10,000 public and private foreign companies.

❑ **Zacks Corporate Earnings Reports.** Recent earnings and forecasts along with ratings from the investment analysts.

❑ **Disclosure.** Information filed with government agencies requiring registration for securities offerings.

❑ **Dun & Bradstreet.** Financial reports (credit histories and ratings).

❑ **Corporate Ownership Watch.** Insider trading alerts.

❑ **Media General Financial Services.** Performance statistics on companies in 50 industries, including price, volume, earnings, and a variety of financial ratios.

An investor interested in analyzing the fundamentals of a company or an industry sector will find that Dow Jones News/Retrieval has one of the most complete databases for company fundamentals. If your investor requirements aren't being meet by DJN/R, you may have to upgrade to a more powerful and expensive system, such as Dow Jones Telerate, Reuter's Instinet, or The Bloomberg.

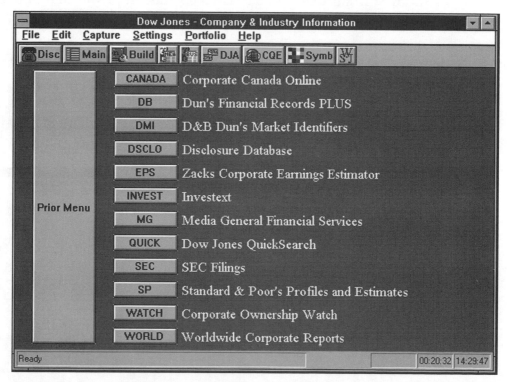

Figure 5.15 Dow Jones: company and industry information.

CompuServe's Company and Industry Sector Analyses

CompuServe, like Dow Jones News/Retrieval, is an online service specifically targeted at the investor and business executive. As a result, while there's some overlap between the two services, each has a considerable number of options to assist an investor in analyzing fundamentals:

❏ **Company Analyzer.** Profiles and histories of price, volume, earnings, dividends, financial statements, ratios, officers, and new issues, along with current quotes.

❏ **Standard & Poor's.** Business profiles from a database of 5,000 companies (dividends, earnings, products, markets, etc.).

❏ **Hoover's Company Profiles.** Full text of all databases, including assets, products, sales, employees, and other financial information.

❏ **TRW Business Profiles.** Covering 13 million companies; includes ownership, credit histories, liens, judgments, bankruptcies, and other government filings.

❏ **Dun & Bradstreet.** Database on 6.7 million private and public companies.

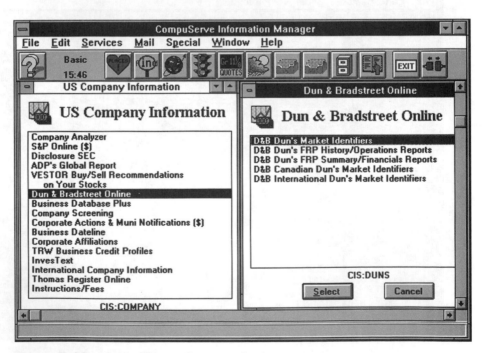

Figure 5.16 CompuServe: Company Analyzer menu.

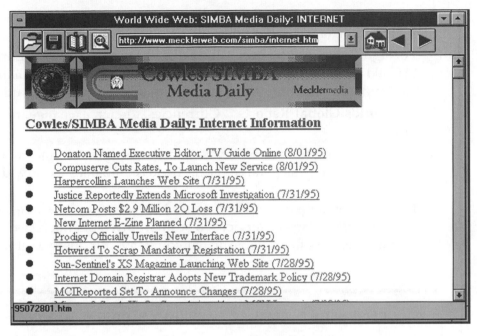

Figure 5.17 Cowles/SIMBA: analyzing the media sector.

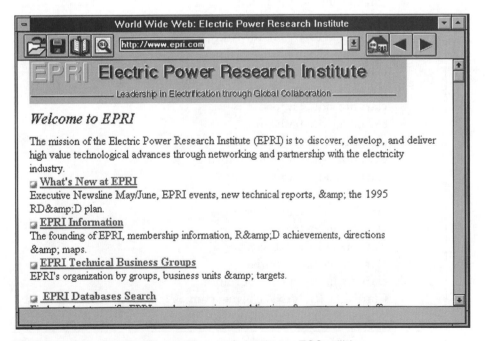

Figure 5.18 Electric Power Research Institute: 700 utilities.

❐ **Disclosure II.**   Information filed with government agencies requiring registration for securities offerings.

❐ **Foreign Company Reports.**   Including more than 2 million European, 350,000 Canadian, 400,000 United Kingdom, 100,000 Australian/New Zealand, plus German, Asian, and many other foreign companies.

❐ **Citibank's Global Reports.**   Currencies, foreign exchange, monetary policies.

❐ **InvesText.**   From over 50 investment advisory firms and more than 500 company newsletters, covering 10,000 companies worldwide.

Both the CompuServe and Dow Jones News/Retrieval services offer an impressive, wide range of services to support investors interested in analyzing the fundamentals of a particular company or industry sector.

CLARINET'S SPECIALIZED INDUSTRY SECTOR NEWSWIRES

clari.biz.industry.agriculture
clari.biz.industry.automotive
clari.biz.industry.aviation
clari.biz.industry.banking
clari.biz.industry.broadcasting
clari.biz.industry.construction
clari.biz.industry.dry_goods
clari.biz.industry.energy
clari.biz.industry.food
clari.biz.industry.health
clari.biz.industry.insurance
clari.biz.industry.manufacturing
clari.biz.industry.mining
clari.biz.industry.print-media
clari.biz.industry.real_estate
clari.biz.industry.retail
clari.biz.industry.services
clari.biz.industry.tourism
clari.biz.industry.transportation
ClariNet URL http://clarinet.com, is included with Netcom's
    Basic Services Package.

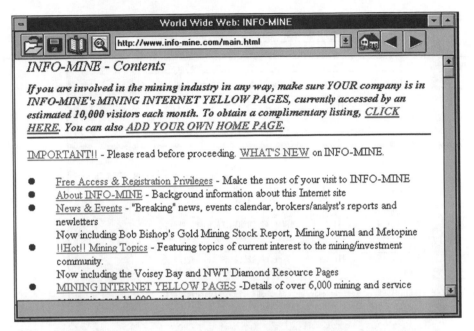

Figure 5.19 Info-Mine: yellow pages for the mining industry.

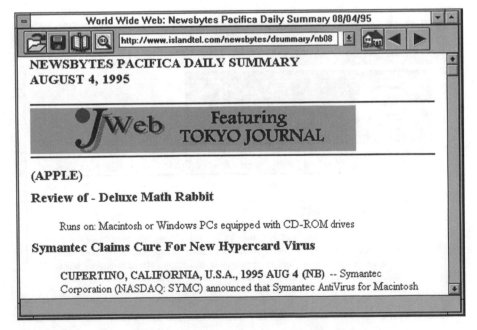

Figure 5.20 NewsBytes: technology and telecommunications.

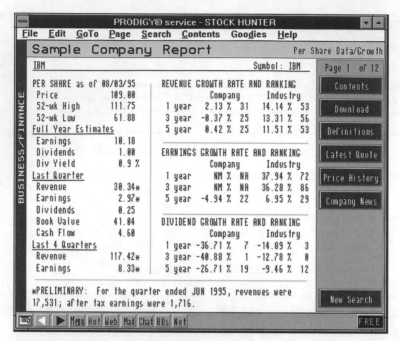

Figure 5.21   Company reports on Prodigy's Stock Hunter.

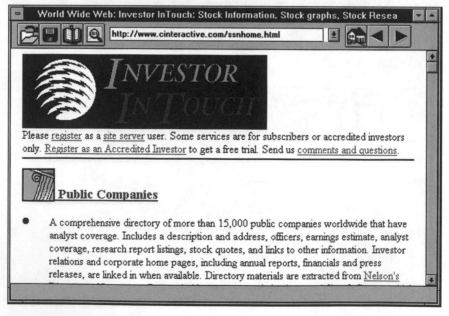

Figure 5.22   Investor in Touch: Nelson's Directory.

SECURITIES FILINGS: EDGAR, DISCLOSURE, AND THE SEC

Every investor doing fundamental research on a company knows that government securities filings and annual reports usually reveal facts that sales and promotional brochures ignore. The U.S. Securities and Exchange Commission and its state counterparts require full disclosure before permitting the sale and trading of securities on the exchanges or privately. Each year about 12,000 to 15,000 companies' major shareholders and officers file a total of 350,000 documents, creating an extensive database of new material.

Fortunately, electronic filing and retrieval is here today for many companies, which is making it easy for an investor to obtain most securities filings. In fact, most publicly held companies filing with the Securities and Exchange Commission will be required to file electronically by 1996.

There are at least four cyberspace resources working in the area of the electronic publication of registered securities filings: NYU/Stern School, Disclosure, Lexis-Nexis, and the Federal Filings newswire.

The EDGAR Project at New York University

The EDGAR project is located New York University's Stern School of Business. This government-funded project makes company filings available to any investor (i.e., the general public) through the EDGAR, the Electronic Data Gathering, Analysis & Retrieval project. Investors are encouraged to stop by and review the extent of information available at this resource:

- **Introduction to Electronic Securities Filings**
- **Guide to Corporate Filings,** form types described
- **R.R. Donnelley Library of SEC Materials**
- **Sample of Basic K-10 SEC Filing**
- **Phase-in Schedules Requiring Electronic Filings**
- **Master Indexes**
- **Archive Searches**

The EDGAR Website at NYU also has a search function that allows you to search on three parameters: company names, ticker symbol, and SIC classification. Some of these files are quite large, so you should be prepared for long download times. At the present, this information is purchased by

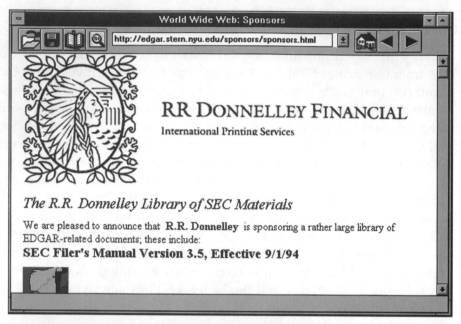

Figure 5.23   The Donnelley library at NYU/EDGAR.

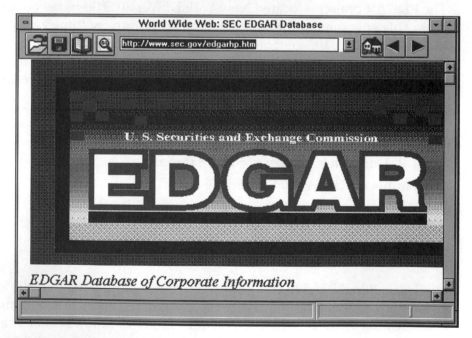

Figure 5.24   The new SEC EDGAR Website.

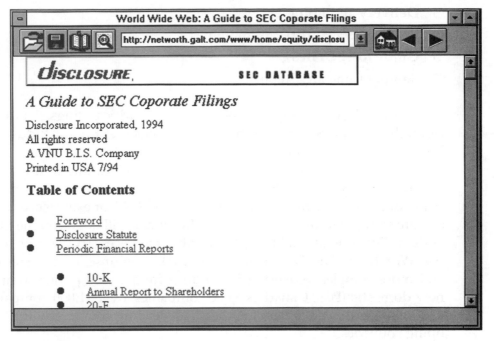

Figure 5.25   Disclosure Website: guide to SEC filings.

the EDGAR project from the SEC, the same as any other subscriber to the SEC database, and made available free to the public. The EDGAR is funded by advertisers and government grants, although the government funding is being restructured, which is likely to reduce the availability of free documents and also force them to go commercial. In fact, the SEC may soon take over the venture completely.

The Disclosure Organization Develops EdgarPlus

The Disclosure organization is one of the primary commercial sources of securities filings. Their database has the filings of 12,500 companies that have registered their securities with the SEC. In all, companies and their officers file over 350,000 documents with the SEC annually. Disclosure can be found at the NETworth Website's Equity Center, with the following information headlined:

❑ **Database Services**
❑ **Document Services**

❐ **Delivery Technologies**
❐ **Product Availability**
❐ **Guide to SEC Files**
❐ **Sample Company Report**

The Disclosure group also offers their securities filings data for sale through Dow Jones News/Retrieval, CompuServe, Knight-Ridder's Dialog service, and other cyberspace locations.

In 1995 the Disclosure organization took the EDGAR SEC filing system to a new level with EdgarPlus. With this new system they plan to overcome many of the shortcomings of the original EDGAR. For example, as the Disclosure staff points out, 40 percent of SEC filings will not be on the EDGAR system. Plus the raw data is often lacking the necessary formats for easy use. With EdgarPlus, Disclosure will be making your searches faster, easier, and more complete, covering SEC filings from 11,000 public companies, new domestic IPOs, Canada's 8,000 companies, over 11,000 companies in 40 foreign jurisdictions, and another 1,100 leading companies in 22 developing countries.

Lexis-Nexis and Required SEC Electronic Filings

The Lexis-Nexis organization has been a mainstay for legal research for a few decades and is your primary alternative to Disclosure. Lexis-Nexis has a contract with the Securities and Exchange Commission, assisting the SEC in reorganizing their electronic filing system. This procedure is expected to be fully operational by 1996. This information is then made available to the public, for a fee. Due to the size of these files, Lexis-Nexis and the SEC may eventually be forced to use CD-ROM technology as an alternative delivery system.

Dow Jones' Federal Filings Newswire

Cyberspace investors should also be reminded of the Dow Jones News/Retrieval's newswire, Federal Filings. This unique newswire helps investors access hard-to-find information. Federal Filings newswire includes *timely* reporting of securities registrations, plus mergers and acquisition documents, corporate insiders disclosures, bankruptcies, annual and quarterly reports, and major corporate events.

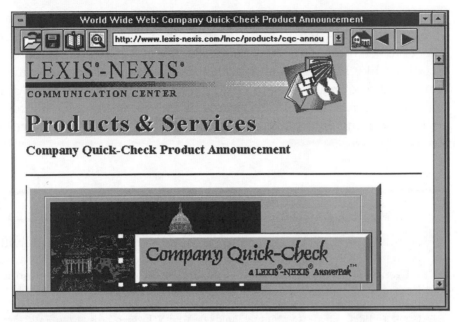

Figure 5.26   Lexis-Nexis databases for SEC filings.

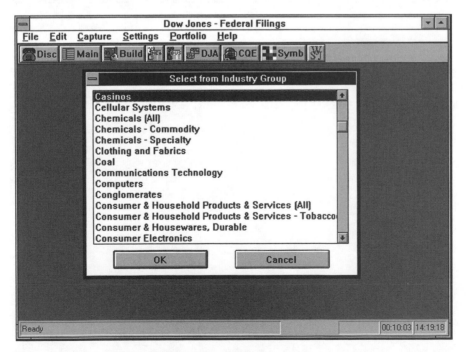

Figure 5.27   Federal Filings: Dow Jones newswire.

Bottom line: As government support continues to diminish, and the Internet ventures like EDGAR search for private backers, investors can expect to see the expansion of established, well-financed commercial organizations like Disclosure and Lexis-Nexis. They will become much more important resources on the Internet's Web. Meanwhile, the EDGAR project is fulfilling an important interim role in disseminating critical information to the evolving Internet community. For this it deserves a welcoming thanks.

MUTUAL FUNDS . . . THE PERFECT INVESTMENT VEHICLE

A mutual fund is the perfect investment. I don't just mean that mutual funds are the perfect investment for the '90s, or for people saving for retirement or college. I mean: A mutual fund is the perfect investment. Period.

(SOURCE: Bill Griffeth, "Let Mutual Funds Be Your Vehicle to Prosperity," in *10 Steps to Financial Prosperity,* Probius, 1994.)

CHAPTER 6

Alternative Securities for Online Investors

MUTUAL FUNDS: RESEARCH, ANALYSIS, AND SELECTION

Mutual funds are a driving force in the financial markets, an expression of major demographic and cultural change. In recent years, for example, the number of mutual funds has increased faster than the number of initial public offerings of equities. The trend toward risk diversification along with baby-boomers' retirement portfolios is fueling this interest in mutual fund investment. Their needs are reflected in the growth of the mutual funds themselves.

The largest, Fidelity Investments, is a family of 225 funds worth over $365 billion, 13 percent of the mutual fund industry. One of their funds, Fidelity Magellan, totals over $50 billion. On an average day this one family of funds trades nearly 29 million shares, *almost $1 billion or 7 percent of the average daily trading on the NYSE.* And the Fidelity Investments family is only one-eighth of the total assets of mutual fund industry.

Investors are beginning to see a wealth of new information on mutual funds in cyberspace. These include several major print resources that are now being electronically published and made available online, on disks and on the Internet.

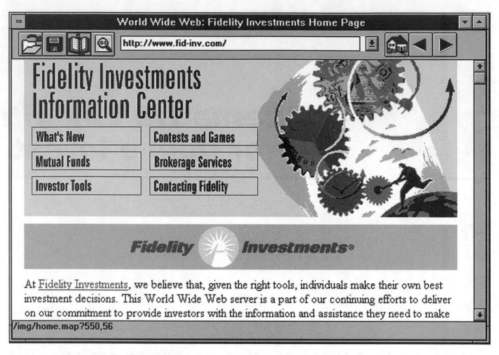

Figure 6.1   Fidelity Investments: mutual funds on the Web.

Morningstar Mutual Funds Research Services

The Morningstar mutual fund reports are the nation's leading source of information on mutual fund performance. They can be found at many cyberspace locations, including America Online, CompuServe, Telescan, and the Microsoft Network. You'll also find Morningstar on the Internet at NETworth's Website, along with many other useful services. They are also developing their own independent Website. Morningstar's America Online site is a first-class example.

Morningstar's Top 25 directory separates mutual funds into 20 categories, ranking them by performance. Each fund receives one to five stars, based on their risk, yield, and 30 other criteria. The Morningstar site is also designed so you can fine-tune your screening process by evaluating each category's Top 25 performers for the past 90 days, one year, three years, and their past five-year track records.

MORNINGSTAR MUTUAL FUND REPORTS

Top-performing funds by category:

❏ Top 25 Overall
❏ Top 25 Aggressive Funds
❏ Top 25 Growth Funds
❏ Top 25 Growth & Income Funds
❏ Top 25 Equity-Income Funds
❏ Top 25 Small Company Funds
❏ Top 25 World Stock Funds
❏ Top 25 Foreign Stock Funds
❏ Top 25 Europe Stock Funds
❏ Top 25 Pacific Stock Funds
❏ Top 25 Specialty—Unaligned
❏ Top 25 Specialty—Health
❏ Top 25 Specialty—Financial
❏ Top 25 Specialty—Natural Resources Funds
❏ Top 25 Specialty—Precious Metals
❏ Top 25 Specialty—Technology Funds
❏ Top 25 Specialty—Utilities Funds
❏ Top 25 Specialty—Asset Allocation Funds
❏ Top 25 Specialty—Balanced Funds
❏ Top 25 Specialty—Income Funds

You can also retrieve extensive information about each of the 5,000 funds in their database, as noted in the Morningstar Fund Profile.

MORNINGSTAR FUND PROFILE

❏ Profile of the fund
❏ Loading
❏ Yield per share
❏ Assets
❏ NAV quotes (net asset value)
❏ Top 10 holdings
❏ ROI (5 yr. and average)
❏ Management fees
❏ Family of funds
❏ Management salaries
❏ Investor contacts

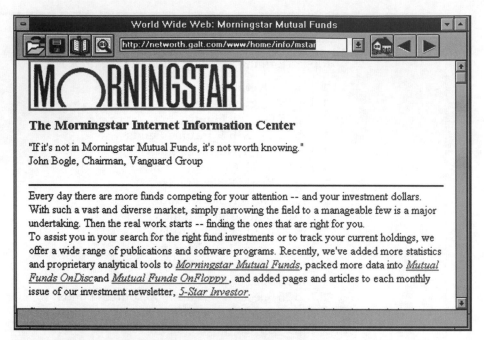

Figure 6.2   Morningstar Mutual Funds on the Web.

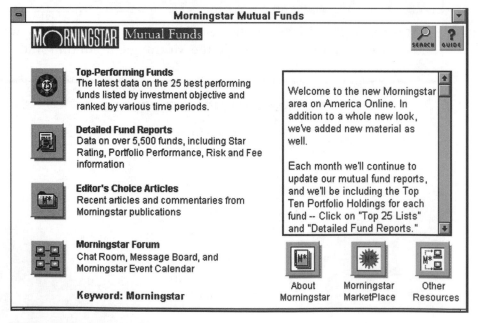

Figure 6.3   Morningstar Mutual Funds online.

If you don't see the information you want about mutual funds, you have a number of ways to get more information, all set up for quick access on AOL. You can bounce questions straight to the experts on the Morningstar team and get an answer directly from the horse's mouth.

You can also put your questions up on one of the 50 message boards, each of which is focused on many diverse topics of interest: load versus no-load, international funds, newsletters, timing, discussions of particular funds and families of funds, and any other obscure issue on your mind. There's also a "live chat room" where you can get real-time answers to burning questions. When it comes to mutual funds, if Morningstar doesn't know the answer, no one does.

Bottom line: Morningstar is a key source for reliable and comprehensive mutual fund information. Bookmark it on the Web. Morningstar is also located on the commercial online services.

NETworth's Website: Almost Everything on Mutual Funds

Morningstar is located on the NETworth Website as well as AOL. NETworth is an emerging new cyberspace resource for mutual fund information. The subtitle is a statement of their mission, "The Internet Resource for Individual Investors."

NETworth's opening screen even has an eye-catching display board with the S&P 500 Index topped with the header, "Mutual Fund Market Manager." They've staked their claim to mutual funds in cyberspace. Here's a sampling of the headings available to the investor:

❏ **Mutual Fund Market Manager**
   Search funds, performance, prospectus, and promotion
   NAV quotes free, updated daily on their NETnav
❏ Weekly **Experts' Forum,** focused topic with featured fund managers
❏ **NETworth's Equity Center**
   Stock Market Quotes, free to registrants
   Disclosure Database, complete company information
❏ NETworth **Market Outlook,** from the Benham Fund Managers
❏ NETworth **Internet Information** Center
   Morningstar Mutual Fund Services
   The Insider, an Internet directory, including links for information on stocks, bonds, quotes, company research, foreign exchange, newsletters, and much more

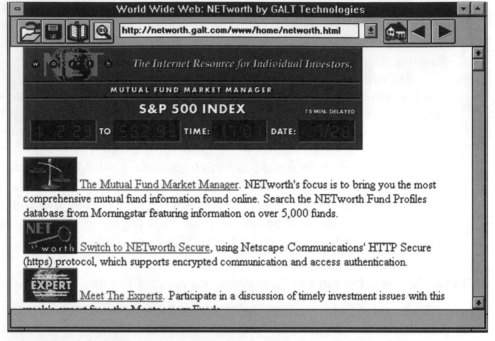

Figure 6.4   NETworth's mutual funds Website.

❐ **The Capitalist,** NETworth's own selection of newsletters
❐ **No-Load Mutual Fund Council,** 200 funds, Benham, Value Line, etc.
❐ **NETworth Insurance Network**

The Website combination of NETworth, Quicken, Disclosure, and Morningstar is awesome. The NETworth Website is definitely recommended as a five-star bookmark for cyberspace investors.

MIT's Artificial Intelligence Lab for Mutual Fund Data

There are some other important Internet Websites with mutual fund information. Another notable Website is the MIT Artificial Intelligence Laboratory Website (discussed previously in the Quotes section). They also have Experimental Mutual Fund Data, which provides data on certain funds in addition to the stock data discussed earlier. The information at MIT is supplied by the InterTrade group, which has a historical database of over 5,500 mutual funds.

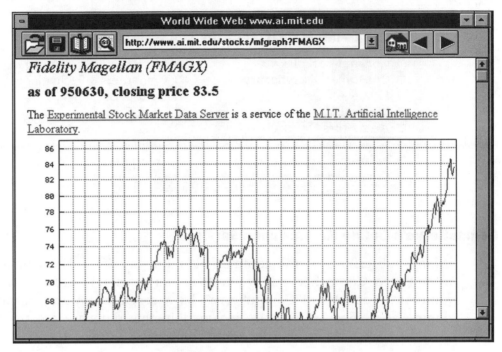

Figure 6.5 MIT's mutual fund charts and data.

The MIT Website makes information available on approximately 1,000 of the total number of funds. MIT posts the incoming data about every two weeks. InterTrade also sells detailed historic information on all 5,500 funds and the 9,000 stocks in its database. Their price schedule is also posted, and they will send you a free sample of a complete mutual fund report.

NYU/Stern School's EDGAR Project and Mutual Funds

In addition to the stock company filings, the EDGAR project also covers funds under their section Mutual Fund Sector Tracking. EDGAR uses the Zacks 16 industrial sector categories to track movement through quarterly filings by these funds.

This EDGAR database, with its legal emphasis, would be considered supplemental to financial information researched through other sources: the news, analysts' reports, quotes, charts, forecasts, and other inputs.

ZACKS INDUSTRIAL SECTORS CLASSIFICATION AT EDGAR

- ❏ Consumer Staples
- ❏ Consumer Discretionary
- ❏ Retail
- ❏ Medical
- ❏ Auto/Tires/Trucks
- ❏ Basic Metals
- ❏ Industrial Products
- ❏ Construction

- ❏ Multi-Sector Conglomerates
- ❏ Computers & Technology
- ❏ Aerospace
- ❏ Oil & Energy
- ❏ Finance
- ❏ Utilities
- ❏ Transportation
- ❏ Unclassified

CompuServe's Online Mutual Funds Services

Many subscribers of the commercial online services also own mutual funds, and CompuServe is where they can get solid information about mutual funds. One of CompuServe's basic services is *Money* magazine's FundWatch. The 2,000 funds included in this database are the major

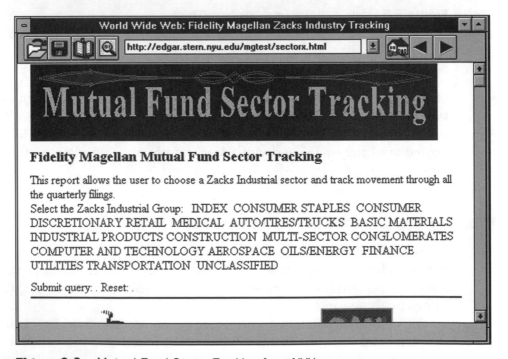

Figure 6.6 Mutual Fund Sector Tracking from NYU.

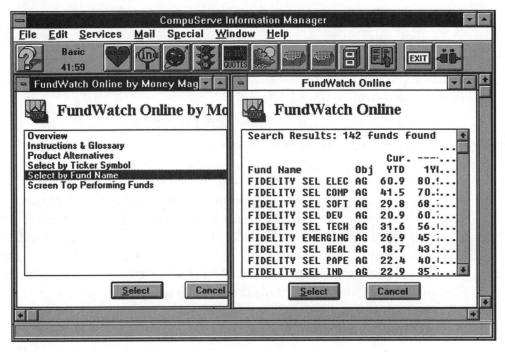

Figure 6.7 CompuServe's mutual funds resources.

mutual funds of interest to the investing community, and it is updated monthly.

CompuServe's database also includes about 150 international funds. You can set up your own performance criteria and screen through categories to create your own list of top performers. The information is quite detailed and includes major categories similar to Morningstar reports available on NETworth noted above.

America Online's Mutual Funds Services

America Online, of course, has Morningstar services available as a basic service to subscribers. In addition, both the Vanguard and the Fidelity mutual funds have excellent collections of information on AOL. Between these two families of mutual funds you would have a few hundred from which to choose, which is a major task in itself. And you can also check them out independently by using the Morningstar research and analysis. This competition between these two major families of funds on AOL is encouraging. Overall, with AOL you can:

❏   Take a short online course on mutual funds.

❏   Set your goals and portfolio strategy.

❏   Review profiles of funds and their performance.

❏   Access NAV quotes.

❏   Order prospectuses.

❏   Search funds according to selected criteria.

❏   Access fund libraries.

❏   Find a list of seminars in your state.

Vanguard even calls their educational section the Vanguard Mutual Fund Campus. They also make available a quarterly Market Overview that covers a lot of ground on financial, monetary, and economic trends. Generally speaking, the commercial online services do a solid job supplying mutual fund information and analytic resources to their subscribers. You can also find the major funds on the Internet.

The Calvert Group: Socially Responsible Mutual Funds

Here's one special group of mutual funds on the Internet "investing with vision," as their headline says. Calvert group has 29 funds with almost $5

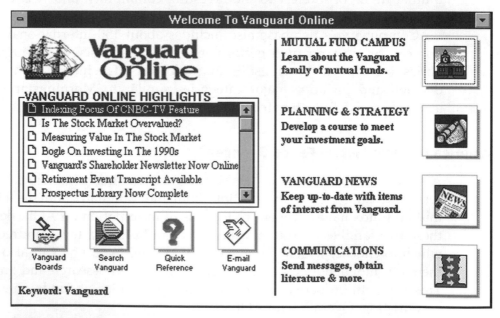

Figure 6.8   Vanguard mutual funds online.

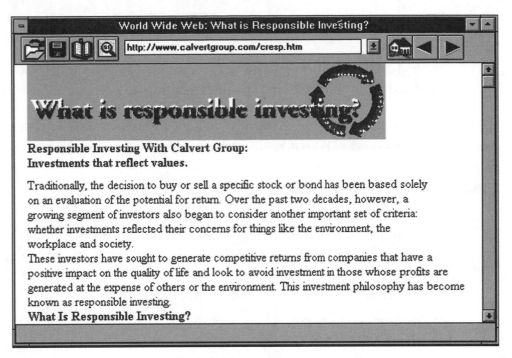

Figure 6.9   Calvert Funds: socially responsible.

billion under management. They're not only socially responsible, they're solid money managers. For general information, check into their Short Guide to Investing in Mutual Funds. You'll get the basics on setting objectives, risks, returns, and the types of funds available, stocks, bonds, and money markets.

Reuters and DJN/R: Competing for the Mutual Fund Investor

Technology has changed rapidly in the last decade. Expensive mainframes have given way to relatively cheap personal computers anyone can own and carry around in a briefcase. Analytic tools and databases once reserved for the larger institutional investors are now being mass-marketed to the individual investor with a small portfolio of stocks and mutual funds.

For example, market insiders know Reuters Instinet as a private global market, reserved for big institutional investors willing to pay top dollar, often well in excess of $1,000 a month per workstation for one of these high-powered Instinet terminals. Similarly, Telerate and Dow Jones News/Retrieval, once tools of the larger institutional players in the investment game, are also now expanding into the individual investors markets.

For example, the Dow Jones News/Retrieval service now offers a low-fee, off-hours, dial-up service to compete in this market for the smaller, individual investor.

This trend is good news for the cyberspace investor. Now they have the hardware, the software, and the data to compete effectively. Let's look at a couple of these new alternatives competing with the big-three commercial online services for the investor's dollars. Reuters especially is now going after this market with a vengeance.

Reuters Money Network: Mutual Funds and Much More

Awesome firepower for the cyberspace investor—that's the best way to accurately describe the Reuters Money Network and their WealthBuilder software. Their ads label RMN, "the fastest growing and least expensive online system available!" They have over 35,000 subscribers, and here's what they get with Reuters Money Network:

❑ **S&P Comstock Quotes** on a 15-minute delay on any stock traded on the NYSE, AMEX, and NASDAQ exchanges; no extra per-quote or prime-time fees, and no connection charges.

❑ **Standard & Poor's Research Database** of 5,000 stocks and 6,000 bonds, plus the tools to screen and chart securities according to any criteria you select.

❑ **Morningstar Mutual Funds Database** of 5,000 mutual funds, with 40 data points on each fund, including returns, risk, and fees, plus their five-star rating system.

❑ **Bank Rate Monitor** tracks CD and money market information from thousands of institutions nationwide, plus the Veribanc safety ratings.

❑ **Personalized News** covering companies, markets, and economies—filtered and clipped according to your selection criteria—from Dow Jones News Service, *Money* magazine, and Reuters Newswires, the largest global provider of news, including information from Reuters' network of connections with 200,000 brokers, traders, and portfolio managers around the world.

❑ **PC Financial Network,** one of America's largest online discount brokers gives you 24-hour-a-day trading controls and real-time trade validation, plus discount commissions. PC Financial is a subsidiary of Donaldson, Luftkin & Jenrette and the Equitable Life Assurance Society.

❏ **Round-the-Clock Data** covering Wall Street and global market information, giving the cyberspace investor an edge on the market with a
powerful arsenal of financial information, news, hard data, and the
analytic tools to make timely, intelligent investment decisions.

❏ **Investment Newsletters,** with Donoghue's Moneyletter, S&P Outlook,
Zacks Analyst Watch, Global Investing, Bond Fund Advisor, Oberweis
Report, etc.

All that investment firepower for a $50 setup fee and $24 a month. Some of
the services noted are extras, but the basic package is more than enough for
most investors. Combine Reuters Money Network with their WealthBuilder
software and you're in the big leagues with these additional features:

❏ **Personal Investment Profile**

❏ **Asset Allocation Model**

❏ **Net Worth of Your Portfolio**

❏ **Personal Budget Planning**

❏ **Retirement Planning, Goals & Strategies**

❏ **Timeline Forecasts of Your Portfolio**

❏ **Portfolio Management & Transactions**

Plus all this easily interfaces with the Reuters Money Network features—
quotes, news, and investment research. In addition, with their Alerts Manager routine, you'll be notified immediately when selected criteria are
triggered.

THE REUTERS MONEY NETWORK COMPARISON LIST

	Setup Cost	*Monthly Fees*
Reuters Money Network	$ 50	$ 25
Signal 4.0	$495	$ 80
DTN-Wall Street	$295	$ 61
Bonneville	$300	$183
Telemet America	$448	$ 62

(SOURCE: Reuters Money Network promotional materials.) Noticeably, CompuServe
and DJN/R were not on Reuters' list.

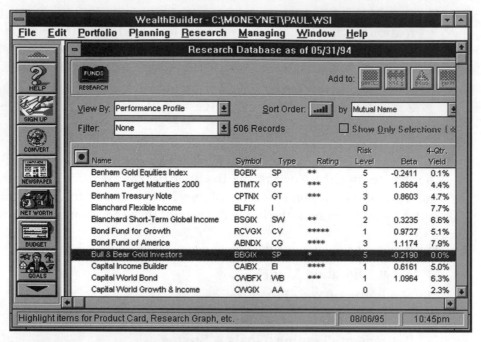

Figure 6.10   Reuters WealthBuilder for mutual funds.

If you're a Quicken fan, you can also get Reuter's Money Network for Quicken, although RMN quickly notes that you'll have more options and greater flexibility using their WealthBuilder version. *PC Computing* magazine compared RMN for Quicken to FundPro software from Manhattan Analytics and gave both a four-and-a-half star rating, also noting that FundPro was much more expensive at $400 for the software and was limited to mutual funds.

Bottom line: Reuters has come a long way from the expensive Instinet service for larger, established institutional investors to the Money Network and WealthBuilder services for the individual investor. There are some extra charges for special reports, but the basic package is quite inclusive so that you're not being nickel-and-dimed for every piece of information requested. This is a highly competitive alternative to all other products and must be given a five-star rating . . . check it out.

Dow Jones News/Retrieval: The Traditional Leader

Reuters' purchase of the Reality Online system along with WealthBuilder, an earlier product of *Money* magazine, was a smart strategic coup. This decision placed Reuters in position to move swiftly into the individual investors' market, and into direct competition with the Dow Jones News/Retrieval package of services. Ironically, the Reuters package is not only less expensive than the DJN/R Private Investors Edition, but it includes the Dow Jones newswire services. Moreover, quotes are 15-minute delayed versus DJN/R's off-hours usage.

DJN/R PRIVATE INVESTOR EDITION

Daily Quotes: mutual funds, stocks, bonds, treasury issues, options, money markets, etc.
Historical Quotes for one year
Dow Jones **Averages** from 1982
Daily **Mutual Fund Quotes**
Commodity Futures & Index quotes
Mutual Fund Performance Reports on 1,500
News Periodicals: 1,800 in full text, Barron's, *Wall Street Journal*, etc.
Top News Stories, financial, business, and investing
Clipping Service to scan and screen special interests
Newswires: all seven, including analysts reports
Insider Trading reports on 80,000 individuals
Wall Street Week, PBS transcripts
Media General research, 180 industries and 6,200 companies
Zacks Corporate Earnings Estimator (EPS) for 3,500
S&P online profiles on 4,700 companies
Innovest Technical Analysis Reports on 4,500 companies
Tools; fundamental and technical analysis; portfolio management

DJNews/Retrieval is an off-hours service for $30/month.

Nevertheless, the Dow Jones News/Retrieval has one of the most powerful total packages for the individual investor interested in mutual funds as well as stocks, bonds, and other securities. Every cyberspace investor is strongly encouraged to compare the Dow Jones system with Reuters to see which best fits your special investing and trading style. Either one could be an improvement over your current commercial online service, depending on the extent of your trading and the value of the other services offered.

With the Dow Jones News/Retrieval you get up to eight hours of non-prime-time usage. Their Tradeline service will increase the cost to $70 a month. Dow Jones' Price Schedule for the full News/Retrieval service offers a "volume discount program for customers with monthly usage over

$1,000," suggesting that the full DJN/R service may not be in line with the needs of the average individual investor seriously looking for alternatives to the Reuters Money Network.

Bottom line: Dow Jones is the Tiffany's of the investment information business, and their News/Retrieval is the gateway to their firepower. However, Dow Jones marketing and pricing structure currently does not make them *appear* competitive with the other major online services for investors—Reuters Money Network, CompuServe, and America Online—all of whom are aggressively marketing to the individual investor market.

The Dow Jones name is an American icon and certainly the best-known name on Wall Street, and it also appears to be the most expensive in the eyes of the individual investor, who perceives it to be more the tool of the institutional investor. Still, individual investors are strongly advised to compare the Dow Jones alternative. They are likely to restructure their approach to the individual investor market in the very near future in order to stay competitive and not miss this market.

THE INTERNET'S HOTTEST NEW WEBSITE FOR MUTUAL FUNDS

One of the leading Web and print resources for mutual fund news, research, and analysis is headed by Norman G. Fosback, editor in chief of *Mutual Funds* magazine. *Mutual Funds* has a circulation of 350,000. More important, their Website is already getting over 100,000 hits a day from the new cyberspace investors. Fosback's book, *Stock Market Logic* was originally published two decades ago. In addition to the magazine, Fosback has eight excellent publications on mutual funds and stocks:

- ❑ *Mutual Fund Forecaster*, profit projections and risk ratings
- ❑ *Mutual Fund Buyer's Guide*, an investment scoreboard
- ❑ *Fund Watch*, chart service featuring high-performance funds
- ❑ *Income Fund Outlook*, bond funds and money market funds
- ❑ *Mutual Fund Weekly*, combination of the four fund advisories
- ❑ *Market Logic*, full service on stock market and economy
- ❑ *Investor's Digest*, market advice from hundreds of services
- ❑ *The Insiders*, analysis and ratings of America's top investors
- ❑ *New Issues*, a guide to initial public offerings
- ❑ *Stock Market Weekly*, combination of the four stock advisories

Cyberspace investors visiting Fosback's Website are getting the benefit of all the research going into these publications. If you want more information, contact Fosback's Institute for Econometric Research located on the Web at http://www.mfmag.com, or call 800-442-9000.

You'll also find excellent reporting on mutual funds in other key periodicals. *Money* magazine and *Kiplinger's Personal Finance*, regularly cover the funds. In addition, *Smart Money, Forbes, Fortune, Inc., Worth, Business Week, Your Money,* and other top financial newspapers and magazines occasionally run special features on mutual funds.

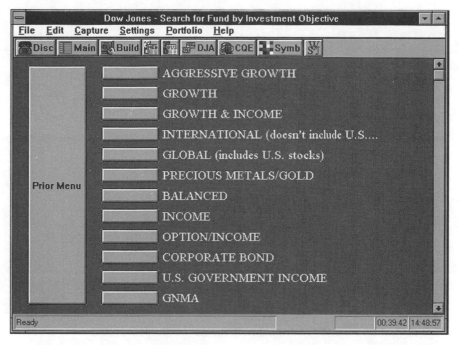

Figure 6.11   Dow Jones News/Retrieval's mutual funds.

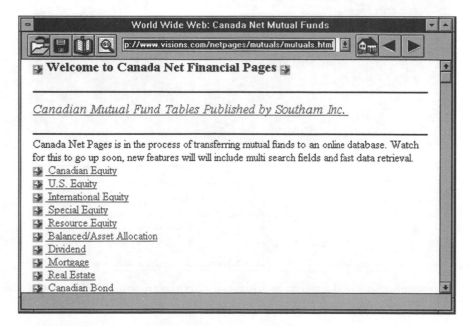

Figure 6.12   Canada Net: mutual funds Website.

Figure 6.13 Nest Egg Magazine's mutual fund information.

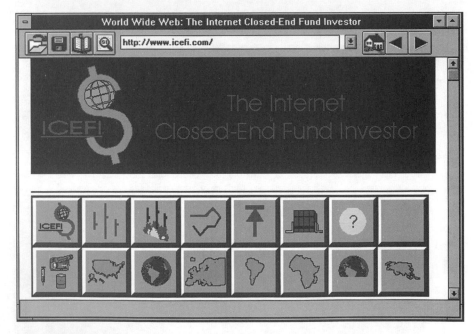

Figure 6.14 Internet Closed-End Mutual Fund Investor.

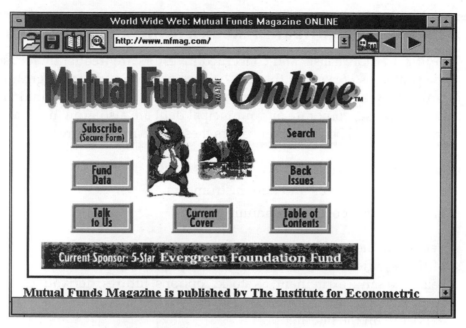

Figure 6.15   Norman Fosback's Mutual Funds Online.

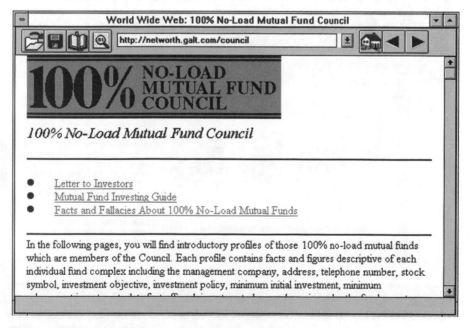

Figure 6.16   100% No-Load Mutual Fund Council.

FIXED-INCOME SECURITIES: TREASURY, MUNI, AND CORPORATE

Politicians, journalists and concerned investors are frequently focusing on the problems created by the U.S. balance of trade and the burgeoning federal debt. Our deficit spending pushes more and more bonds into the market. Likewise, corporate and municipal debt are also growing at alarming rates. The total bond market covers these three primary areas:

1. Federal government; U.S. Treasury issues
2. Corporate bonds and debt instruments
3. Tax-exempt or tax-free municipals

Yet, while the total bond market is perhaps 25 times greater than the value of the equities markets, the bond market just doesn't have the same pizzazz, the same excitement, as stocks, options, futures, derivatives, and precious metals. And that may be partially to blame for their current limited exposure on the Internet.

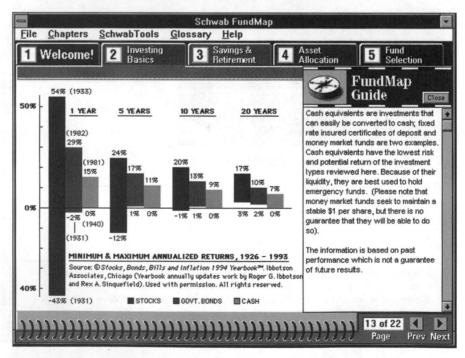

Figure 6.17   FundMap from Charles Schwab & Company.

"Bonds are boring," is a common remark. For many investors and analysts alike, bonds are like science documentaries on cable television compared to a science fiction thriller like *Star Trek*—that is, unless you're in need of immediate cash and you must liquidate bonds in your portfolio that have dropped in price as interest rates increased. Then bonds aren't so boring.

The fact is, bonds and other fixed-income securities are supposed to be boring. Bonds aren't supposed to stir up a lot of emotions. Bond investors want to go to sleep feeling secure—bored, if you will. Those feelings come with the certainty of knowing that the income promised will in fact be there when it's due. And while the value or price of the bond may fluctuate with interest rates over time, when the principal is due, it will, almost always, be paid back on time. Bonds may not have the guarantees of a CD or money market fund, but the returns are usually more attractive.

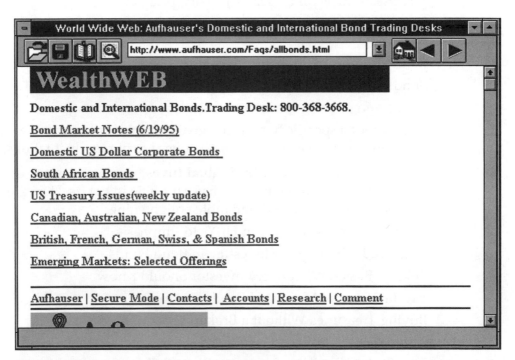

Figure 6.18 WealthWEB's domestic and global bonds.

America Online: Bond Mutual Funds

An investor who wants to discover what cyberspace has to offer about bonds might start with America Online. You can analyze, screen, and manage a modest portfolio at this one site. And while the emphasis in AOL is on bond mutual funds, it's an excellent opportunity to learn about the role of bonds in your portfolio.

America Online has extensive material about the two largest mutual funds families—Fidelity and Vanguard—both of which have billions of dollars in their bond funds. In addition, America Online also has the Morningstar Mutual Funds Reports and the American Association of Individual Investors database on bonds and bond mutual funds. If you aren't yet on AOL and you want a short course on the bond market, sign on to America Online and log in to Vanguard's site.

❏ **Vanguard Mutual Fund's Campus** is a solid starting point if you have questions about buying bonds or bond mutual funds. Start with the section, How to Select a Bond Fund:

The basics on income, yield, diversity, price, etc.

Three types of bonds; U.S. government, corporate, and tax-free municipals

Risks and rewards of bonds: income, yield, capital, and total return

Bond rating systems explained (e.g., How does a Baa differ from an Aaa?)

Bonds versus bond funds: maturities and tax advantages

Selection of a specific bond fund: goals, financial planning, taxes, fees, timing, commissions, expenses, tolerance of rate fluctuations, etc.

❏ **American Association of Individual Investors** also has some excellent articles that will round out your basic training in bonds. Here are ten of AAII's articles that you'll find quite enlightening:

Income Investors, Beware of Hi-Yield Emphasis

Rules and Warnings for Investing in Bond Funds

Beyond Basics, What Every Investor Should Know

Are Tax-Exempt Municipal Funds For You?

Buying Treasuries Without a Broker

General Bond Funds—Their Holdings

That Sinking Feeling: Unwanted Bond Calls

Taking Advantage of Diversity in the Bond Market

A Close-up Look at Closed-End Bond Funds

Trading Municipal Bonds: A Guide to the Marketplace

The American Association of Individual Investors is one of the best resources for investors in the world. Their publications cover many other aspects of investing, including bonds. The AAII deserves the highest of recommendations. Join it, and especially get a copy of their book on computerized investing.

❏ **Fidelity Mutual Funds** has all their income funds grouped together. After a definition of the difference between investing in bonds and a bond fund, you can look through Fidelity's portfolio of 37 bond funds in these five categories:

Government Bond Funds

Corporate Bond Funds

Global Bond Funds

Federal Tax-Free Bond Funds

State Tax-Free Bond Funds

Figure 6.19   Vanguard Mutual Fund Campus.

And, while you're at it, check out the rest of Fidelity's funds; as part of your education on bonds you should be aware of the alternatives in, for example, aggressive stocks and precious metals.

❐ **Morningstar Mutual Funds Reports** are also available on America Online. Here you can get the world's best rating system and independent analysis of bond funds and mutuals in general. And they will provide you with the latest quotes.

❐ **Forums & Bulletin Boards:** If you want the honest opinions of other investors, ask them to share with you their experience. Go to one of the many online chat rooms, post your question and check back later for the responses. You will be pleasantly surprised with the help you'll receive. However, use due diligence.

CompuServe's Bond Market Research Services

If you're a more advanced investor who needs more detailed information on bonds, you may want CompuServe or some other cyberspace resource.

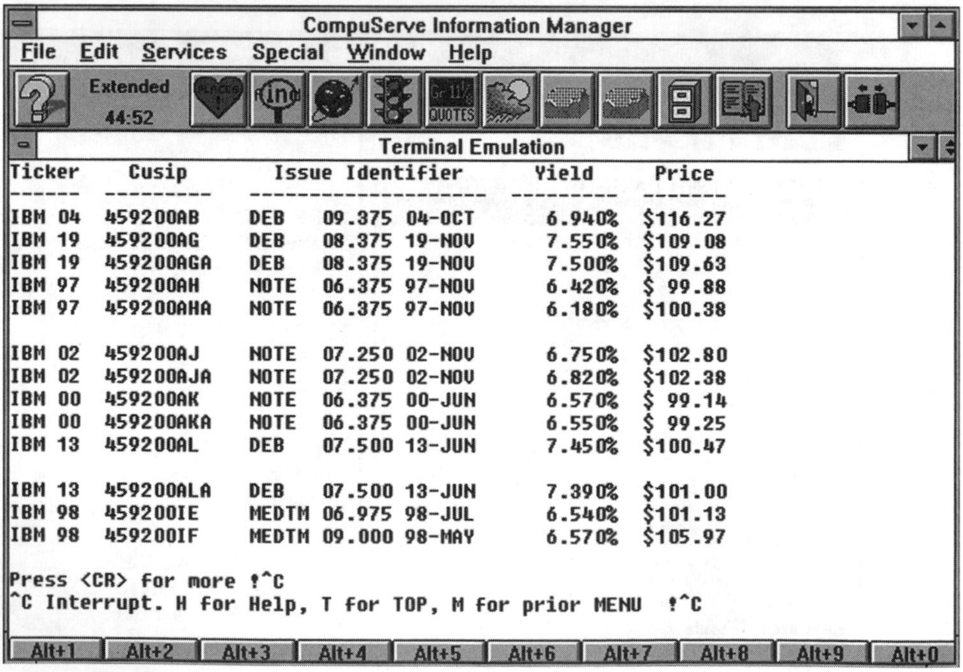

```
┌─┬──────────────────────────────────────────────────────────────┬───┐
│─│            CompuServe Information Manager                     │▼│▲│
├─┴──────────────────────────────────────────────────────────────┴───┤
│ File   Edit   Services   Special   Window   Help                    │
├─────────────────────────────────────────────────────────────────────┤
│  [?]  Extended  [icons...]                                          │
│        44:52                                                         │
├─┬──────────────────────────────────────────────────────────────┬───┤
│─│                   Terminal Emulation                          │▼│▲│
├─┴──────────────────────────────────────────────────────────────┴───┤
│Ticker    Cusip        Issue Identifier        Yield      Price      │
│------    ---------    --------------------    ---------  -------     │
│IBM 04    459200AB    DEB    09.375 04-OCT      6.940%    $116.27     │
│IBM 19    459200AG    DEB    08.375 19-NOV      7.550%    $109.08     │
│IBM 19    459200AGA   DEB    08.375 19-NOV      7.500%    $109.63     │
│IBM 97    459200AH    NOTE   06.375 97-NOV      6.420%    $ 99.88     │
│IBM 97    459200AHA   NOTE   06.375 97-NOV      6.180%    $100.38     │
│                                                                      │
│IBM 02    459200AJ    NOTE   07.250 02-NOV      6.750%    $102.80     │
│IBM 02    459200AJA   NOTE   07.250 02-NOV      6.820%    $102.38     │
│IBM 00    459200AK    NOTE   06.375 00-JUN      6.570%    $ 99.14     │
│IBM 00    459200AKA   NOTE   06.375 00-JUN      6.550%    $ 99.25     │
│IBM 13    459200AL    DEB    07.500 13-JUN      7.450%    $100.47     │
│                                                                      │
│IBM 13    459200ALA   DEB    07.500 13-JUN      7.390%    $101.00     │
│IBM 98    459200IE    MEDTM  06.975 98-JUL      6.540%    $101.13     │
│IBM 98    459200IF    MEDTM  09.000 98-MAY      6.570%    $105.97     │
│                                                                      │
│Press <CR> for more !^C                                              │
│^C Interrupt. H for Help, T for TOP, M for prior MENU  !^C           │
├─────────────────────────────────────────────────────────────────────┤
│ Alt+1 │ Alt+2 │ Alt+3 │ Alt+4 │ Alt+5 │ Alt+6 │ Alt+7 │ Alt+8 │ Alt+9 │ Alt+0 │
└─────────────────────────────────────────────────────────────────────┘
```

Figure 6.20   CompuServe's bond data resources.

Its approach to the bond market assumes that you're already familiar with the basics. If you're not, CompuServe does have a succinct beginner's file, called Bonds Made Easy. Beginner or old-salt, you'll find it in their library, a perfect refresher course.

CompuServe has the kind of straightforward approach to bonds that typically reflects the way most online customers and investors look at bonds—predictably boring. You simply log in to CompuServe's bond command, then type in the ticker symbol for the underlying common stock of the company. You'll get a complete list of all the available debt issues of the company. CompuServe's bond reports will show you the type of debt, coupon rate, maturity date, yield, and price, along with the credit ratings from Moody's and Standard & Poor's, the two major rating agencies.

Whether it's bonds or stocks, you'll want to use due diligence, doing some fundamental research about the company, its history, products, financials, officers, and so forth. So you'll want quotes on the underlying stock issues, and analysts reports on the company itself, in order to complete your research on the company as an investment opportunity.

The Web and the Bond Market: Limited Free Information

The Internet's World Wide Web has limited information on bonds. The Yahoo meta-list is one of the more likely locations for bond information; however, Yahoo has very few links specific to bonds, mainly U.S. Treasury bonds, minimal on corporate bonds or tax-exempt municipal bonds. In a recent check, Yahoo had 88 links for stocks and mutual funds and only two links to information on U.S. government bonds, but nothing on either corporate or tax-exempt bonds. However, more are coming on the Web soon.

❐ **U.S. Treasury bonds.** Yahoo does have a direct link to the Federal Reserve Bank's Quotes for U.S. Government Securities, located at the University of Michigan Website. The bond quotes are posted daily—including issue date, bid asked, change, and yield—for U.S. Treasury notes and bonds.

❐ **Newswire updates.** The second link from the Yahoo site was the ClariNet/Usenet newsgroup, clari.biz.market.misc, which is a subscription-based newswire from Associated Press covering the bond markets. It happens to be part of Netcom's basic services package and is a solid summary of the daily bond markets.

❏ **Quote-server Websites.** Websites that may have limited information about fixed-income securities are those offering quotes, such as Quote-Com, Security APL, InterQuote, and NETworth. The QuoteCom Website, for example, has a bond quotes' section covering U.S. Treasury securities only, with the following information:

Street Interest Rates

Bear Sterns Summary of Current Rates

Quotes & Analysis of Active Treasury Issues

Specific Government Bond Quotes

Given the competitive pressures on Websites offering financial information, it may be worth your while to surf the Internet for new sites offering quotes on bonds as well as stocks and mutual funds. For example, Morningstar covers bond funds at their NETworth Website and is a reliable resource for quality financial information.

Bottom line: It is unlikely that you'll uncover much *free* information on corporate and tax-free municipal bonds, primarily on the U.S. Treasury issues, which is public information anyway.

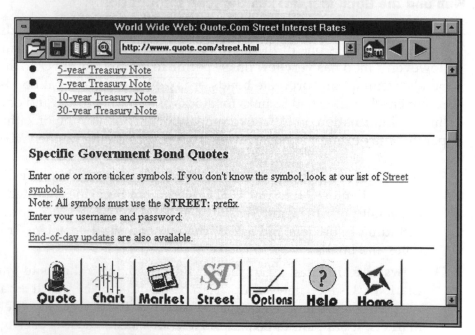

Figure 6.21 QuoteCom's Treasury bond data section.

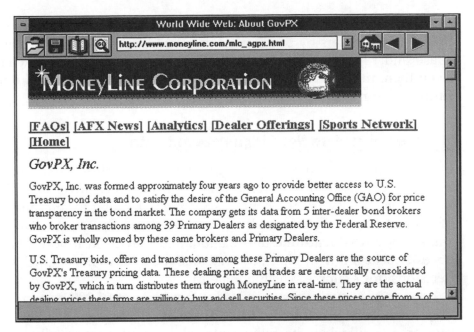

Figure 6.22   MoneyLine Corporation: government securities.

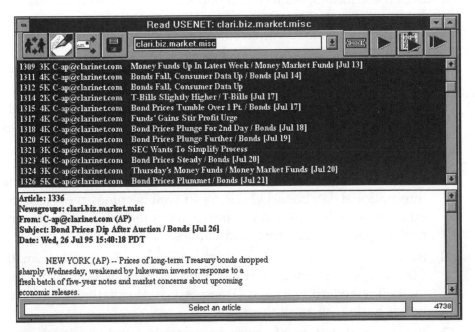

Figure 6.23   ClariNet's market news for bonds.

The information that is available in cyberspace is primarily for sale to professional traders by commercial data vendors reselling data they purchase and repackage from many domestic and international exchanges. Even then, investors are more likely to see information on bond options, futures, and mutual funds than the underlying securities themselves.

Professional Bond Traders Need High-Powered Data

Bond trading and investing is a game for the sophisticated individual investor, professional traders, and large institutional investors. The big institutional players in the bond market aren't looking for bits and pieces of free data from ten different Internet sites. They have too much money at stake. They need real-time information, and they need it now. They also need it packaged with high-powered analytic tools to make quick trading decisions (for example, The Bloomberg).

Bonds are usually denominated in amounts of $1,000 or more, while most stocks are priced under $100. There are fewer players in the $1,000-plus arena, and when the game is played, the trades are usually for much larger transactions than the individual stock investor normally trades. As a result of these factors, bond data is normally not as readily available free on the Internet or even the commercial online services. Here are several of the best routes that will lead you to complete bond information:

❑ Dow Jones News/Retrieval has the biggest database for securities—150,000 securities of all kinds, including bonds, stocks, options, index futures, and mutuals funds. If the security you want is traded, Dow Jones has it. That includes corporate, U.S. Treasuries, and tax-exempt munis. DJN/R also has the most comprehensive database on foreign stocks and bonds, with more than 25,000 securities traded on the 87 major exchanges throughout the world. Because of their extensive international database, DJN/R could well become an even more powerful force as the Internet minimizes all global barriers based on geography, time zones, culture, and politics.

❑ Reuters Money Network provides quotes and other information on 6,000 corporate bonds from the Standard & Poor's database, included in their standard package. There is no information on government bonds and tax-exempt securities.

❑ Professional traders, of course, are already familiar with the high-end services for the larger portfolio managers—Reuters (Instinet), Dow

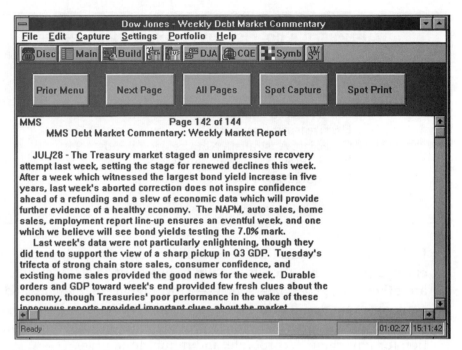

Figure 6.24   Dow Jones News: report on debt market.

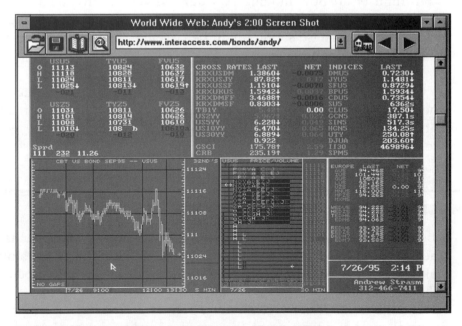

Figure 6.25   Aspen Graphics: market and bond data.

**AUFHAUSER & CO. DISCOUNT BROKER'S WEALTHWEB
BOND DIRECTORY**

Bond Market News
U.S. Dollar Corporate Bonds
South African Bonds
U.S. Treasury Issues
Canadian, Australian, New Zealand Bonds
British, French, German, Swiss & Spanish Bonds
Emerging Markets, Selected Offerings

(SOURCE: http:www.aufhauser.com/Faqs/allbonds.html.)

Jones Telerate, Knight-Ridder, and Bloomberg. They all install proprietary workstations, at costs usually in excess of $1,000 monthly. There
are other lower-cost data sources—DBC Signal, Bonneville, and Telescan, for example—for the individual trader, which will be discussed in
the next section. The better ones provide fixed-income bond information for government, corporate, and munis, for a price.

❏ Discount brokers such as Charles Schwab, Quick & Reilly, and
Aufhauser are now moving very aggressively to provide a wide variety of services to fit every possible customer need, including bond
information. These services will be covered in Chapter 8, which dis-
cusses discount brokers.

Generally, when it comes to information about fixed-income bonds,
whether government, corporate, or tax-exempt, you'll find that the information may not be as widely and freely available in cyberspace as a few
free stocks quotes. But the data is there somewhere, for a price.

COMMODITY FUTURES, OPTIONS, AND PRECIOUS METALS

If bonds are boring and you want some action, you've come to the right
place. Here is where fortunes are made . . . and lost. This is the stuff that
makes a George Soros and breaks a Barings Bank. And it happens with
lightning speed.

Thanks to modern telecommunications, we now have a single world
financial market operating at the speed of light. Hundreds of separate

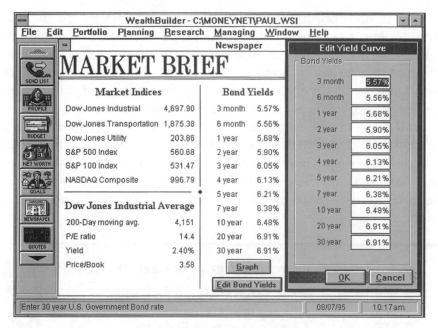

Figure 6.26 Reuters Money Network: bond market data.

exchanges and other financial networks operate as an integrated circuit, triggering virtually instant trades 24 hours a day anywhere around the globe. This is the real world of cyberspace investing, and trading of commodity futures fits in perfectly.

BARRON'S "WELCOME TO WONDERLAND"

The *nom du jour* for futures and options is "derivatives" (although this term really is broader and includes certain warrants and exotica). As that term implies, they are at least once removed from something real, such as gold or corn or Treasury bonds, and sometimes three or four times removed. While they have strong ties to the prices of whatever they are based on, they can and do move independently. That's because they are oriented toward future, not current, performance of their "underlying" markets. . . . There is nothing tangible about futures or options. . . . To the extent they exist at all, they are bits and bytes in computers somewhere . . . the futures market might be described as people selling what they don't have [5,000 bushels of corn or $100,000 of T-bonds] to people who don't want it anyhow.

(SOURCE: Douglas Sease and John Prestbo, "Welcome to Wonderland," *Barron's Guide to Making Investment Decisions*, Prentice Hall, 1994.)

In this nonstop, high-speed, high-tech, high-leveraged, high-anxiety environment, risks are often magnified exponentially. This environment makes risk management even more crucial. Here, many businesses and investors *need* to hedge against future fluctuations in the price of coffee or wheat, copper or silver, yen or dollars, while other institutions are in the business of providing that insurance for a reasonable fee.

And then on the other side of the equation, there's the speculative trader, waiting eagerly to bet against either side, chasing quick profits and an adrenaline rush. This arena is known to attract individuals interested in the quick buck and the thrill of the hunt, as well as established, conservative institutions. Serious investors are advised to move cautiously and very slowly.

IFCI'S LIST OF THE TOP 10 GLOBAL EXCHANGES

CBOE	Chicago Board of Options Exchange
CBOT	Chicago Board of Trade
CME	Chicago Mercantile Exchange
DTB	Deutsche Terminboese
LIFFE	London Int'l Financial Futures & Options Exchange
MATIF	Marche a Terme Int'l de France
MEFF	Renta Fija
SFE	Sydney Futures Exchange
SOFFEX	Swiss Options & Financial Futures Exchange
TOCOM	Tokyo Commodities Exchange

The derivative securities are becoming more and more popular. Conservative investors need to hedge against risk of losses and are willing to pay a modest premium for the protection. And the more aggressive traders are willing to take the gamble, in hopes of leveraging their money into sizable profits. Unfortunately, it often doesn't work.

In fact, insiders estimate that as many as 70 to 80 percent of all individual investors coming into this field will lose *all* their risk capital and leave within two years. Now those are rough odds if you're investing your retirement portfolio. At least Vegas offers good food, a floor show, and drinks around the pool before they take your money. If you're interested, and unfamiliar with this field, before you put up a nickel, read Jack Schwager's two *Market Wizard*'s books. Every business book store has these classics. His interviews with top traders will help you proceed with a more solid base.

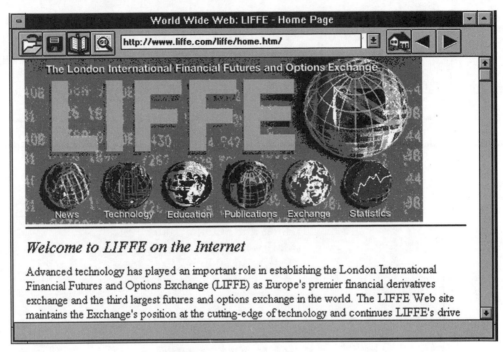

Figure 6.27 London International Financial Futures and Options Exchange.

World Wide Web: A Bright New Face for the Exchanges

If you're a cyberspace investor, the Yahoo meta-list is a logical starting point to look for information about these exotic securities, the red-hot derivatives. And due to the transition the Web is going through, you'll notice a major difference in quality between the smaller Websites and the larger institutional sites. For example, in linking to Yahoo's commodities and options Websites (about 10 percent of the total in their Marketing and Investments subdirectory), most of the smaller sites had old information that hadn't been updated in a couple months. Hardly useful to anyone trading in this dynamic field. A similar problem exists with certain university-based Websites staffed by students.

On the other hand, there were links to several larger institutions with visually attractive as well as informative Websites—in particular, the Chicago Mercantile Exchange (CME), the London International Financial Futures and Options Exchange (LIFFE), and the International Financial and Commodities Institute in Geneva, Switzerland (IFCI). The IFCI is of particular interest because it illustrates the quality of information beginning to emerge on the Internet's Web. In particular, their Futures & Contracts Database has links with information on contracts traded on ten of the top exchanges in the world, along with news, conferences, financial hot lists, and a directory of the addresses of all exchanges in the world.

AMERICAN STOCK EXCHANGE INDEX OPTIONS

International Indexes

☐ EuroTop 100 Index
☐ Japan Index
☐ Hong Kong Option Index
☐ Mexico Index
☐ AMEX/Israel Index

Broad-Based Indexes

☐ The Institutional Index
☐ Major Market Index
☐ S&P MidCap 400 Index
☐ Morgan Stanley Consumer Index
☐ Morgan Stanley Cyclical Index
☐ Flexible Exchange Index Options

Sector Indexes

☐ The Airline Index
☐ Biotechnology Index
☐ Computer Technology Index
☐ Natural Gas Index
☐ North American Telecommunications Index
☐ The Oil Index
☐ Pharmaceuticals Index
☐ Securities Broker/Dealers Index

On the way back from your trip to IFCI in Geneva, an investor should definitely stop off at the LIFFE Website in London. The London International Futures and Options Exchange trades over 100 million futures and options contracts a year. LIFFE's Website reflects a first-class operation, complete with sections on news, technology, education, publications, statistics, and links to other exchanges. Of course, when you return to the

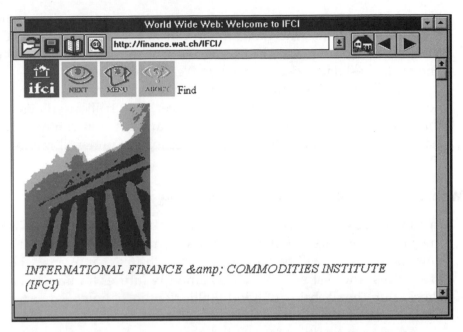

Figure 6.28 International Finance & Commodities Institute.

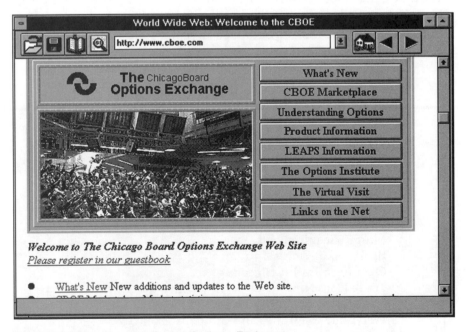

Figure 6.29 Chicago Board Options Exchange.

United States today, you can check on the American Stock Exchange for their latest updates. And then stop in Chicago and visit both the Chicago Mercantile Exchange and the Chicago Board Options Exchange, which has one of the best and most informative Websites on options.

The Chicago Mercantile Exchange is the biggest, with perhaps 225 million contracts traded annually, worth over $200 trillion—that's almost a *trillion dollars a day* traded on this one exchange. And if you're really interested, you can buy a seat on the exchange for just under $1 million.

The Web: A World Market for the New Brokerage Firms

In addition, expect to see many, many more discount brokerage firms coming into cyberspace. As they grasp the competitive opportunities of this new media, more will begin developing Websites that offer a whole array of services, and that will include commodity futures trading. In particular, check out the Website of Lind-Waldock, the nation's largest discount futures trader, reviewed in detail in Chapter 8.

Another interesting Website at this point is the one created by the Futures and Options Trading Group headquartered in Portland, Oregon. Their site has a lot of useful information, including their weekly *Trade Plans Newsletter* with a market overview and trades of the week for futures, options, and spreads. Cyberspace investors should definitely check this one out.

FUTURES AND OPTIONS TRADING GROUP WEBSITE

Closing Futures Prices, Major Contracts
Rules for Successful Futures Trading
Basics of Futures Trading
Basics of Options Trading
Futures & Options Contract Provisions
Margin Requirements
Brokerage Services
Opening a Trading Account
Trade Plans Newsletter; weekly with market overview, futures, options, and spread trades of the week, etc.
Web Links to Futures and Options Resources

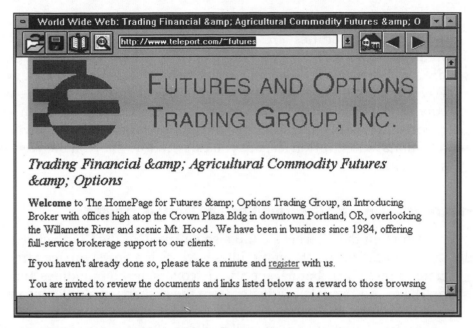

Figure 6.30   Futures and Options Trading Group.

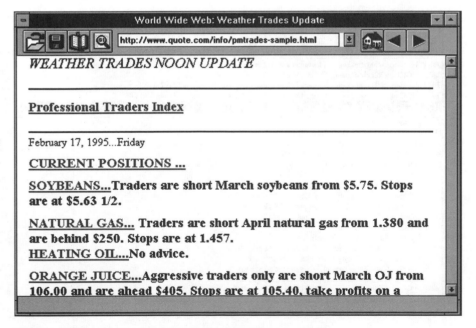

Figure 6.31   Freese-Notis: Professional Traders Index.

One more note on Websites covering commodities. Investors interested in commodities are always concerned about local and global weather patterns and how they'll impact agriculture commodities. Yahoo links to Freese-Notis Weather Service, which is also worth a glance. This Website is unique because it not only reports and forecasts the weather conditions, but makes *trading recommendations* based on these weather reports. Like many such sites, the most important information will cost an additional subscription fee, but you can window-shop on the Web for free, so check it out.

Usenet Newsgroups for Commodities and Futures Trading

Investors on the Internet should also be aware of the ClariNet Usenet service—clari.biz.market.commodities—which is a newswire feed from Associated Press. This channel specifically covers the commodities and futures markets, and the data originates from the exchanges. While this news service is a for-pay service, many Internet service providers include this newswire as part of their overall package of services, so in a sense they're free.

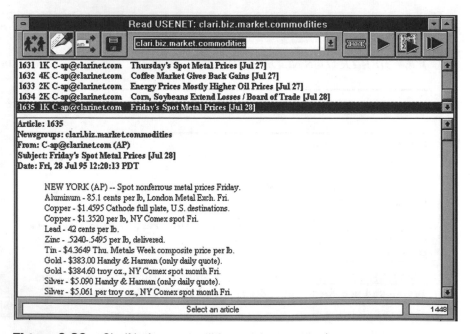

Figure 6.32   ClariNet's commodities markets newswire.

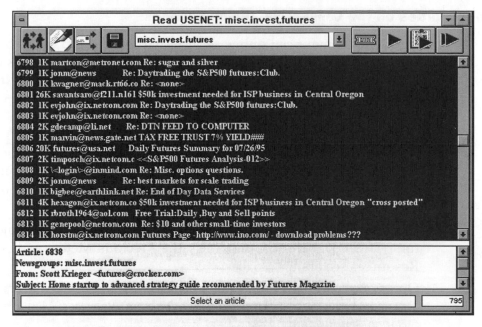

Figure 6.33 The Usenet newsgroup for futures traders.

In addition, investors interested in commodities have an opportunity to participate in the Usenet discussion group, misc.invest.futures, and discuss this hot topic with like-minded investors. Learn from their mistakes.

Bottom line: With the Internet's Web, if the current trends continue, the World Wide Web will very quickly become a major source of information on commodities, futures, and options. The large exchanges are gradually replacing the smaller, one-person Websites. In fact, investors should expect that all the major exchanges will soon have Websites offering considerable information about their particular securities. As this develops, investors should also expect to find better cross-links directly on the exchanges' Websites themselves, in addition to the meta-lists.

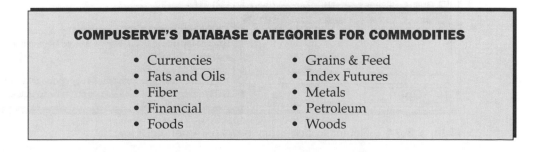

COMPUSERVE'S DATABASE CATEGORIES FOR COMMODITIES

- Currencies
- Fats and Oils
- Fiber
- Financial
- Foods
- Grains & Feed
- Index Futures
- Metals
- Petroleum
- Woods

Commodities on the Commercial Online Services

The profile of commercial online services' customers appears to be more oriented to risk reduction than risk taking, with heavy emphasis on the extensive mutual funds information at America Online. The extent of AOL's information on commodity futures is somewhat limited for trading purposes, but otherwise is solid coverage:

- ❏ Reuters Commodities newswire, covering cash and futures prices in the major markets: metals, agriculture, energy, grains, softs, and precious metals, covering key exchanges around the world. Reuters is always an excellent resource.

- ❏ Morningstar Reports has a list of the Top 25 funds in the major sectors. Two cover the commodities: the Precious Metals and Natural Resources sectors.

- ❏ Occasional coverage in *Investor's Business Daily*, *Business Week*, *Worth*, *Time*, and the newspapers, *Chicago Tribune*, *San Jose Mercury News*, *Orlando Sentinel*, etc.

Figure 6.34   Reuter's commodity news on America Online.

Figure 6.35 CompuServe's commodity futures menu.

Generally speaking, the AOL subscriber is not designed for the serious commodities trader or investor. However, AOL's coverage of this subject will help an investor keep tabs on general trends in the economy and the markets.

The CompuServe online service is obviously more in tune with the data and trading requirements of a typical commodity futures and options trader. CompuServe's MicroQuote II database includes symbols of contracts traded on a total of 14 exchanges. In their Financial group, for example, CompuServe covers prices on *all* major contracts: Treasuries, Eurodollars, CDs, mortgage-backed securities, and munis.

Obviously CompuServe's database for commodity quotes will save any trader and investor considerable time over searching out several Websites for free information. And time is critical to the serious commodities investor and trader. Closing prices are end-of-day trading, and ten years of historical information is also available—open, high, low, settle, volume, and open interest (puts/calls). CompuServe also offers expert analysis of the commodity markets on its News-A-Tron Market Reports and Agri-Commodities reports.

EXCHANGES FEEDING INTO COMPUSERVE'S DATABASE

Chicago Board of Trade
Chicago Mercantile Exchange
Chicago Rice & Cotton Exchange
Coffee, Sugar & Cocoa Exchange
Commodity Exchange New York
Commodity News Service
International Money Mart
Kansas City Board of Trade
MidAmerica Commodity Exchange
Minneapolis Grain Exchange
New York Cotton Exchange
New York Futures Exchange
New York Mercantile Exchange
Winnipeg Commodity Exchange

Cyberspace Is Old Hat to Professional Traders

The serious commodity futures and options traders aren't looking for a few free quotes from the Internet or even some delayed quotes from the online services. The truth is, information from those sources just isn't timely enough or extensive enough to do any *serious* trading . . . but if the majority of investors miss this point, the pros will have a decided trading edge.

In the next section we'll take a closer look at the high-powered cyberspace tools and data sources used by the power players in the investment and trading world. Meanwhile, here's a quick overview of the alternatives available for effective commodity futures and options as well as trading other securities, since the professionals need a wide perspective of the markets.

Special Online Services for Investors (under $100/month)

CompuServe's main competitor at this level is Dow Jones News/ Retrieval's Private Investor Edition. Reuters Money Network has opted out of this particular field, and has kept the costs of its service down, in part by avoiding the exotic world of futures and options in place of providing investors with top-notch tools for trading stocks and bonds.

Dow Jones News/Retrieval, on the other hand, delivers some data and tools for the investors and traders interested futures and options (although not enough for serious trading without paying for some extra services). DJN/R includes in their basic $30 package closing and historical futures quotes for 140 contracts from the major exchanges on off-hours (no day-trading here). And for twice the cost, an investor will get much more, including technical analysis tools, company reports, and a significantly larger database with *prime-time* delivery, including options.

Individual Professional Traders ($200–$1,000/month)

Many individual investors in this category may be full-time traders operating out of their dens or a small office. They may be retired individuals managing their portfolios. On the other hand, they may also have an active business or profession that occupies a good part of their time and spend only evenings, weekends, and off-hours tracking, trading, and investing in the markets.

Whatever the case, as we'll see in the next section, there are a large number of packages (data feeds and analytical tools) that are available in the range of $100 to $1,000 a month. These depend on your area of interest. A soybean farmer interested primarily in agricultural commodities may not need the same kind of firepower as the speculative day-trader using technical analysis and cycles research to track patterns in a hundred or more futures contracts.

Pick up any issue of *Investors Business Daily*, or browse through a recent copy of one of the two leading magazines in this field—*Futures* or *Technical Analysis of Stocks & Commodities*—and you'll see the advertisements of many of the competitors in this field. In particular, compare the offerings for Data Broadcasting Corporation, DTN Wall Street, Dial Data, Tick Data, Future Link, and IDD, to name a few.

If you're seriously interested in futures and options, *Futures* magazine has an annual *Guide to Computerized Trading* that's helpful, even though it's mainly a collection of paid ads. The single most comprehensive and objective list is the American Association of Individual Investors most recent *Guide to Computerized Investing*.

Institutional Investors/Traders ($1,000+/month)

These power players *invented* cyberspace investing. Long before the press started touting the Internet, institutional investors (international money center banks, large brokerage firms, foreign exchange currency traders, and pension and mutual fund managers) created their own cyberspace out

```
SYM: $INDU      VOL:  223M CHG:  +20.27     TIME: 12:48
LST:12119.67              HIGH:2148.12
                         LOW: 2112.20
                         PREV:2099.40
Detail Page: 1           Indices and Stocks        Collection: DEMO
  SYMBOL    T PRICE     CHANGE     PREV    VOL    HIGH        LOW      TIME X
# Indices (INDX)
$INDU        12119.67   +20.27    2099.40  223M  2148.12    2112.20    12:48
$TRAN       ↓ 879.48    +6.12      873.36         891.88     875.75   Jun14
$UTIL       ↓ 180.77    +1.42      179.35         182.79     179.82   Jun14
$ADV        ↓ 1006                                                    12:47
$DECL       ↑ 480                                                     12:47
$UCHG       ↑ 478                                                     12:47
$TVOL        223089K                      223M                        12:47

# Stocks (NYSE, AMEX, OTC)
IBM         ↓ 118 3/8   +1 3/8     117'0  2.30M  119 3/4    118 1/4   12:46 B
MMM         ↓ 64 1/8L   +1          63'1  840K   64 7/8     64 1/8    12:47 N
GE          ↑ 43 3/4    +0 3/8      43'3  2.40M  44 1/2     43 3/4    12:48 N
AAPL       N↓ 45 1/4    +0 1/4      45'0  2.40M  46         45        12:46 T
LSGA         c  0 1/8               0      0      0 1/8      0 1/8     12:47
EK         N↑ 44 3/4    +0 5/8      44'1  1.70M  45 1/4     44 3/4    12:46 N
1/2 +9/16   IBM JUL120C 2 3/8 +7/16   $INDU 2119.49  +20.09  BC M 41170 +320   IN XR
3-CENTS A SHR   DJ 10:33  [SNV] SYNOVUS FINCL BUYS BIRMINGHAM FEDL SAVINGS DEPOS
Tue 14 Jun 12:48:28          LIMITS  Limit Long         OK              N  6  1179
```

Figure 6.36   Data Broadcasting Corporation's Signal Service.

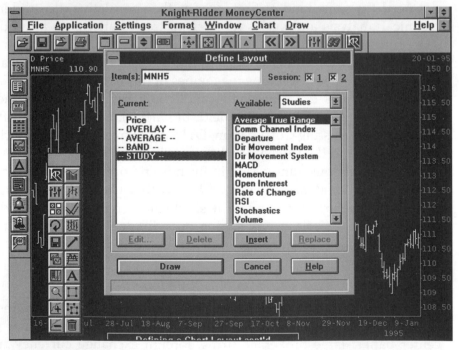

Figure 6.37   Knight-Ridder Financial's Money Center.

of necessity and have been working in it for many years. They are already networked to every exchange around the globe, with instant data, and instant analysis. They have invested heavily in the technology of the information superhighway—fiber-optic telecommunications, satellite downloads, sophisticated analytic programming, and massive databases.

When it comes to supplying cyberspace information and intelligence to the institutional investor, there are four key members of this elite strike force. Reuters Instinct, Dow Jones Telerate, and Knight-Ridder Financial are all in the $2 to $3 billion class, while Bloomberg, whose revenues are around $1 billion and growing, may actually have the best system. And when it comes to complete worldwide coverage of commodity futures and options, Knight-Ridder Financial is the recognized leader.

Knight-Ridder Financial: Cyberspace Leader in Commodities

If your main interest is the commodity futures and options, rather than the more traditional world of stocks, commodities, and mutual funds, then the Knight-Ridder Financial should be one of your first stops. The parent Knight-Ridder is the $2.5 billion news giant that owns, among its properties, 26 newspapers, including the *Philadelphia Inquirer,* the Dialog database of 330 million documents, and the prestigious Commodity Research Bureau. The CRB has been known for its work in the commodity information field since 1939 and is an often quoted and traded index. Knight-Ridder Financial is obviously a leader in this field.

Knight-Ridder's KR-Quote service is their lower-cost, end-of-day package you should first consider. Historical data is provided on a disk, and current data from KC-Quote is quickly downloaded, either automatically or manually, from Knight-Ridder's DataCenter bulletin-board system at the end of the trading day.

KNIGHT-RIDDER END-OF-DAY DATAKIT

❑ Final markets' end-of-day quotes for a year included
❑ Technical Analysis Software, either SuperCharts or MegaTech
❑ KR-Quote software used to quickly download and manage data
❑ Knight-Ridder Financial News Service one-year subscription included
❑ Datadisk, 10 years of historical data covering 40 markets.
All this for $55/month the first year; then news and quotes are about
   $75/month.

For the commodity futures and options trader, Knight-Ridder Financial's DataCenter is a highly competitive product. With it you get everything you need to become a smart trader. They offer a total package of historical and end-of-day prices, analytic software, and a newswire service targeted to your trading activities.

If you are a more aggressive investor and you're ready to move into *real-time* trading of commodity futures and options, Knight-Ridder Financial had a solid package of topflight services:

☐ **Commodities Center.**   KRF's basic real-time service supplying you with data all day, every day, from a one-year database. Receive 6,000 futures and options quotes on 25 quote pages, KRF News, weather maps, and charts with 13 technical indicators, RSI, stochastics, etc.

☐ **Money Center for Windows.**   A more sophisticated windows platform linking real-time data with Excel, search programs, drag-and-drop, and technical charting. The database covers a ten-year period.

☐ **Profit Center.**   KRF's most powerful data and technical analysis system. With this system you can display up to 24 screens at one time, create customized chart pages, quickly save/recall them, overlay charts, speed format, create hot keys, save and link trend lines for future analysis, projections, and forecasting.

KNIGHT-RIDDER FINANCIAL'S PROFIT CENTER—TECHNICAL STUDIES

Acceleration	Market Spectrum
A/D Oscillator	Momentum
ADX	MESA Studies
Average Balance Volume	Moving Averages
Bollinger Bands	Moving Average Momentum
Commodity Channel Index	Moving Average Oscillator
Cumulative Volume	On Balance Volume
Directional Movement Index	Parabolic
Directional Oscillator	Percent R
High/Low Oscillator	Relative Strength Index
Historical Volatility	Stochastics
Implied Volatility	Tick Volume
MACD	Varible Accum. Distribution
MACD Oscillator	Volume Accum. Oscillator
Market Profile	

Profit Center is a top-of-the-line system for the institutional investor. Each of these products is available in a wide range of computer platforms, including windows or text-only for a personal computer, and KRF will install their own proprietary terminals with software and support, if you prefer. And with the Profit Center, KRF offers access to a database of 256,000 financial instruments, including data on daily, weekly, and monthly histories.

Bottom line: Knight-Ridder Financial offers an excellent line of products for the commodity futures and options trading. They have a long-standing reputation, and can help the investor begin professional trading at their current-level needs and then help them move up to a more sophisticated system as the investor's activities increase.

FutureSource: Total Packages for Commodities Trading

The FutureSource organization is a solid competitor for Knight-Ridder Financial. FutureSource offers several basic products for traders and investors who are serious about the commodity futures and options business:

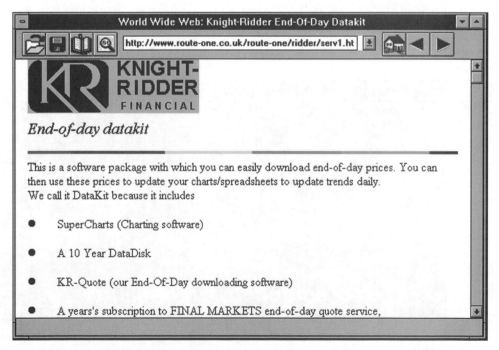

Figure 6.38   Knight-Ridder Financial's KR-Quote System.

❏ **FutureSource Quotes.** Real-time quotes from every U.S. exchange and the major foreign exchanges, reporting over 22,000 items, trade by trade.

❏ **FutureSource Analyst.** Powerful charting that allows the trader, in a few key strokes, to analyze market trends and patterns for successful trading.

❏ **FutureSource Technical.** State-of-the-art technical analysis system with more than 25 indicators, customized pages, spreadsheets, trend tools, and much more.

❏ **OptionSource.** Tracks and analyzes individual options.

FutureSource is a total system designed for individual traders, hedgers, brokers, and the corporate users who need real-time access to the global futures, options, and cash markets. With FutureSource you get data, charting, and analytics.

FutureLink and Futures World News for Traders

FutureLink says they're "today's best market information value" when it comes to position trading in futures. That may well be. Every ten minutes, FutureLink delivers a "snapshot," as they call it, of current prices and

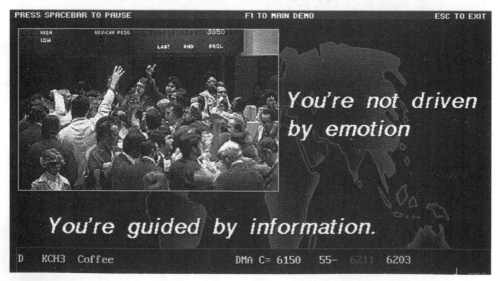

Figure 6.39 FutureSource: analytics for commodity futures.

Figure 6.40   FutureLink services and demo on the Web.

prices for all futures and options contracts trading on North American exchanges. All for under a $100 a month, with no phone charges. Delivery comes by satellite from Cedar Falls, Iowa, the center of American commodities.

In addition, the Futures World News service is included as part of their basic package. FWNews is one the best newswire services on commodity futures and options. It is also available through many data suppliers such as S&P ComStock, so it has got to be tops. Every cyberspace investor interested in commodities should contact Futures World News for a schedule of their daily reports covering the domestic and global markets. A first-class service. Another quality option for the cyberspace investor. Check it out.

Bottom Line: Futures and Options = Risk and Stress!

Most investors naturally shy away from high-risk futures and options trading. In fact, out of the 50 million investors who are shareholders of stocks, there are probably much less than 1 percent of them who are actively trading commodities futures and options. The portfolios of most

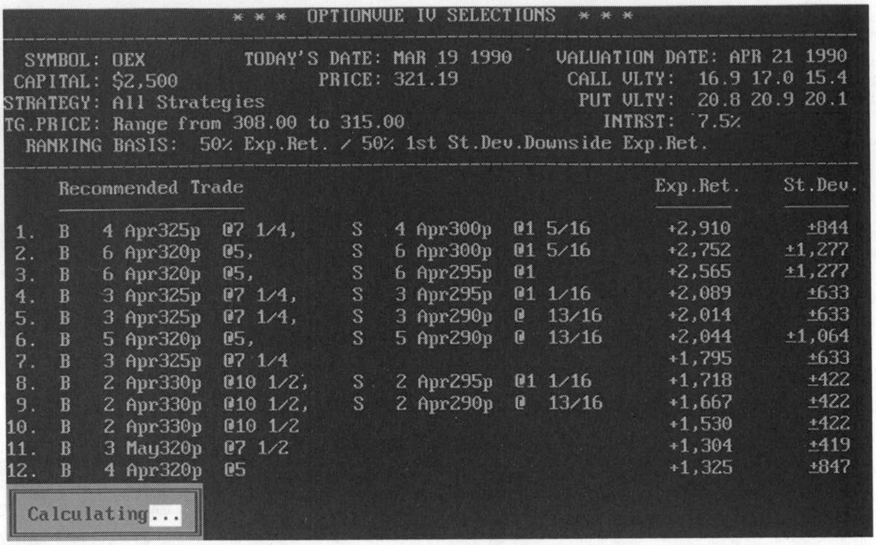

```
* * *  OPTIONVUE IV SELECTIONS  * * *

SYMBOL: OEX           TODAY'S DATE: MAR 19 1990    VALUATION DATE: APR 21 1990
CAPITAL: $2,500              PRICE: 321.19         CALL VLTY:  16.9 17.0 15.4
STRATEGY: All Strategies                           PUT VLTY:   20.8 20.9 20.1
TG.PRICE: Range from 308.00 to 315.00                INTRST:   7.5%
  RANKING BASIS:  50% Exp.Ret. / 50% 1st St.Dev.Downside Exp.Ret.

    Recommended Trade                                       Exp.Ret.    St.Dev.

 1.  B   4 Apr325p  @7 1/4,    S   4 Apr300p  @1 5/16       +2,910      ±844
 2.  B   6 Apr320p  @5,        S   6 Apr300p  @1 5/16       +2,752      ±1,277
 3.  B   6 Apr320p  @5,        S   6 Apr295p  @1            +2,565      ±1,277
 4.  B   3 Apr325p  @7 1/4,    S   3 Apr295p  @1 1/16       +2,089      ±633
 5.  B   3 Apr325p  @7 1/4,    S   3 Apr290p  @ 13/16       +2,014      ±633
 6.  B   5 Apr320p  @5,        S   5 Apr290p  @ 13/16       +2,044      ±1,064
 7.  B   3 Apr325p  @7 1/4                                  +1,795      ±633
 8.  B   2 Apr330p  @10 1/2,   S   2 Apr295p  @1 1/16       +1,718      ±422
 9.  B   2 Apr330p  @10 1/2,   S   2 Apr290p  @ 13/16       +1,667      ±422
10.  B   2 Apr330p  @10 1/2                                 +1,530      ±422
11.  B   3 May320p  @7 1/2                                  +1,304      ±419
12.  B   4 Apr320p  @5                                      +1,325      ±847

Calculating...
```

Figure 6.41   OptionVue IV software programming.

investors consist mainly of mutual funds, bonds, and stocks. The majority of individual investors who do venture into the exotic world of commodity futures and options, lured by the intense hype claiming huge returns in short periods, retreat empty-handed within a couple years, according to insiders in this business.

Bottom line: If you're one of the adventuresome cyberspace investors, you can easily find a relatively simple system to serve your needs. Often for less than $100 a month, the trader or investor has many choices, any one of which is likely to serve the special portfolio needs of most cyberspace commodity traders.

SHOULD YOU TRADE COMMODITY FUTURES AND OPTIONS?

Here's some sage advice from one successful trader.

Few novice traders can withstand the emotional pressure of watching a large chunk of their initial investment and/or previously hard-earned profits vanish in a short period. It is quite common for traders to stop trading after a series of losses, only to miss the one big winning trade that would have more than covered their losses. If you suspect that this may happen to you—"If you can't stand the heat," as the old saying goes—"then stay out of the kitchen." If you can't bear the thought of the misses, then don't trade futures.

(SOURCE: Jay Kaeppel, *Technical Analysis of Stocks & Commodities*, August 1995.)

* * * * * * *

And finally, in his book *One Up On Wall Street*, investment guru Peter Lynch also says,

I've never bought a future nor an option in my entire investing career, and I can't imagine buying one now. It's hard enough to make money in regular stocks without getting distracted by these side bets, which I'm told are nearly impossible to win unless you're a professional trader.

THE DISCIPLINE OF THE NEW MARKET WIZARD

Discipline was probably the most frequent word used by the exceptional traders that I interviewed. Often, it was mentioned in an almost apologetic tone. "I know you've heard this a million times before, but believe me it is really important."

There are two basic reasons why discipline is critical. First, it is a prerequisite for maintaining effective risk control. Second, you need discipline to apply your method without second-guessing and choosing which trades to take. . . .

Whether you win or lose, you are responsible for your own results. Even if you lost on your broker's tip, an advisory service recommendation, or a bad signal from the system you bought, you are responsible because you made the decision to listen and act. . . .

You need to do your own thinking . . . independence also means making your own trading decisions. Never listen to other opinions . . . even advice from a much better trader can lead to detrimental results.

(SOURCE: *The New Market Wizards*, Jack Schwager, Harper Business, 1994. Schwager's books are required reading for every cyberspace investor on the road to financial independence.)

CHAPTER 7

New Software for Real-Time Trading Systems

NEW TOTAL-SERVICE PACKAGES FOR CYBERSPACE INVESTORS

Cyberspace technology is one of the most exciting frontiers in the world. Full of exciting adventures. Back in the early 1980s we were on the launch-pad with Microsoft, Intel, and Compaq, plus cable television, cellular phones, and the fax machine. Today they remain part of the rapidly evolving cyberspace. The future of cyberspace lies hidden in its complexities, its unknowns, its richness of alternatives, and its wealth of opportunities. The Web's popularity caught many by surprise . . . expect even bigger surprises as cyberspace rapidly unfolds.

When it comes to resources for cyberspace investors, the area of technical analysis and data transmission systems is one of the most fluid, dynamic, competitive—and confusing—arenas in space! What you'll see in the next few chapters is an endless explosion of products and services that will make your head spin.

In fact, there is almost too much information on too many products and services. So much so that an investor can become overwhelmed even *before* beginning the equally overwhelming task of making the actual investment decisions. In short, even before you buy a stock or mutual fund, how do you pick the right sources for data and the right analytic tools to do your job well, with minimum risks and maximum returns in your portfolio?

A GLUT OF INTIMIDATING AND CONFUSING DATA

What's missing in this era of interactive television, multimedia computers, digital imaging, and free flow of information is a means of sorting out the glut of often intimidating and confusing data. No matter how accessible technology makes the markets to our customers and clients, the securities industry's strength has always been the collection, analysis, summary, and explanation of the sea of data, information, and facts in the marketplace.

(SOURCE: Marc E. Lackritz, Pres., SIA, *Wall Street & Technology*, July 1995.)

Actually, it's not as difficult as it may seem at first. When you look at software buying guides, such as the *Guide to Computerized Investing* published by the American Association of Individual Investors, with hundreds of alternatives, you might at first decide to follow the dart-throwing system occasionally discussed in the *Wall Street Journal* and other learned publications. Take a deep breath, walk around the block, and settle down. We'll make it easy for you.

Competition: The Investor's Search for a Total Package

A major part of the confusion comes from the fact that the competitive parties in this game are stepping over neat boundaries and out of their origi-

---

ROCKET SCIENTISTS VERSUS TRULY BRILLIANT STOCK-PICKERS

Suppose you could discern market trends, speed up time to see where trends were going, then make a bet on what you've discovered. That's how geeks in suits—known as rocket scientists—are raking it in now.

(SOURCE: Kevin Kelly, "Cracking Wall Street," *Wired*, July 1994.)

Will computers someday take the place of flesh-and-blood stock-pickers on Wall Street? At first, the very idea seems ludicrous. . . . But lately, scattered evidence has emerged suggesting that computers can be as good as human traders—if not better when it comes to buying and selling futures, unearthing arbitrage opportunities, calling market turns and constructing winning stock portfolios.

(SOURCE: Jonathan Laing, "New Brains," *Barron's*, February 27, 1995.)

---

nal niche markets. Today, many are offering more than one service, compatible links to related products, bundles of services, and total one-stop packages.

We'll go into this hyphenation and hybridization in detail in the following chapters. For now, here are some examples of the trends that cyberspace investors must wade through to decide which systems to buy in order to become a successful investor and trader:

❏ **Institutional vendors.**   Reuters used to provide just news, data, and analytic tools to the big banks and money managers with their Instinet system. Now they're selling software and data to the individual investor, too.

❏ **Discount brokers.**   Aufhauser, Schwab, and Quick & Reilly are no longer content with taking business away from full-service brokers; now you can go online and on the Web and get full-service from these brokers, including quotes, analytic software, and much more.

❏ **Traditional data feeds.**   Data Broadcasting, Data Transmission Network, and FutureLink were once primarily data delivery sources; now they not only give you a choice of satellite, radio, cable, and telephone connections, they also offer analytic tools, news, newsletters, interviews, and so forth.

❏ **Television networks.**   CNBC is making a major advance from just delivering a steady stream of programming news and analysis to also delivering newsletters, books, disks, and other forms of information to investors.

❏ **Newspaper publishers.**   Dow Jones was once the publisher of print news, which lead to a cyberspace network of news, data, and software, to the purchase of Telerate, to the creation of the Dow Jones News/Retrieval system that includes just about everything an investor needs. Knight-Ridder is another publisher expanding more and more into electronic publishing.

❏ **Online services.**   CompuServe and America Online are also hearing the drumbeat and feeling the heat of competition, as they add more and more content providers to the arsenal of services. And the Microsoft Network is coming on like a gigantic cyberspace shopping mall with many financial services.

❏ **The Internet.**   Fast emerging from being a secret tool of professors and government officials to a universal network available to anyone, with not only financial services, but also with telephone voice connections, music, and interactive video.

❏ **Private networks.**   Perhaps even more important than the Internet, from a strictly commercial standpoint, is the drive by many businesses and financial institutions to create their own private "Internets"—IntraNets—to serve their employees and customers. Many corporations already have their own communications and informations systems that tie together all aspects of their business and also link to other networks, local area networks (LANs), and wide area networks (WANs). Then there's Instinet and the Bloomberg. Expect more of these private networks, many more, upstaging the Internet.

❏ **Software developers.**   Equis, Omega, and Market Arts aren't satisfied with just selling you a box of disks and a manual. They know you have a problem and will supply you with all the connection support to download the quotes and data you need to score a profitable investment. They're constantly developing partnerships with firms such as Schwab, Zacks, and Hoover's. And Quicken is expanding.

❏ **Quants.**   Just when you thought you had a handle on all this technology, along come the quantitative analysts, firms such as Market Vision, Leading Market Technologies, and the other MBA finance types using econometric models and statistical regressions, armed with supercharged software. And they tell you that all the technical analysis methodology and its supporting software—their data integrators, analytical tools, and graphical software—may soon be as outdated as the Guttenberg press.

These quants already have total packages that are operational today. Their clients, the institutional investors, are already using these advanced systems. Some individual investors have even tapped into this part of the revolution. *You are next.*

Bottom line: In each of these examples, the lines between the original niche service of the provider and the current (and future) services are blurring . . . and expanding as they attempt to provide the one-stop services investors are demanding, like a regional shopping mall with all the necessary convenience and department stores under one roof.

In the next several sections, we'll be looking at the special products and services emerging from the leaders in each of the major categories. If one of your favorites is missing, the oversight is likely due to realistic space/time

ALTERNATIVES FOR DATA TRANSMISSION AND DELIVERY OF THE TOOLS OF ANALYSIS, TRADING, AND PORTFOLIO MANAGEMENT

Information Service Providers
Online services for individual investors
Institutional investor services
The Internet's World Wide Web

Personal Computer and Modem Manufacturers
Workstations
Portables

Wireless
Cellular phones
Quote and news reception
FM radio
Satellites
Paging systems

Telephone Connections
Modem dial-up
Modem dedicated lines
Broadcast fax distribution
Hotline 900-numbers

Television
Free broadcasting
Cable channel connections
Satellite channels

CD-ROMs and Disks
Historical databases

Internet
Internet text-only
Graphics and text
Interactive communications
Internet radio and music
Internet two-way telephones
Video programming

Bulletin Board Systems
Business support, technical and marketing
For-profit dial-up systems
Nonprofit, hobby and social

Software Developers
Technical analysts
Data vendors
Quants (quantitative analysts)

limitations, personal preference, or sheer oversight, rather than an objective survey of all products and services. Those covered are certainly not the only ones available, but they do appear to be on the leading edge of this exciting new Wall Street cyberspace.

REAL-TIME DATA DELIVERY SYSTEMS FOR INDIVIDUAL INVESTORS

Cyberspace investing is old news to the bulk of Wall Street's professional traders and institutional investors. They've been using electronic data transmission, analytic software, and electronic brokerage for over two decades, generating trading profits . . . *out there* in cyberspace. Now it's the individual investor's turn.

If you're going to pay $20 to $30 a month *or more* for quotes and some other services you find on the Internet or from one of the big-three commercial online services, then you should also be aware of what Wall Street's major money managers, investors, and traders have been doing in cyberspace for a long time.

While the commercial online services may seem to be a quantum leap up from the Internet resources for investors, the major data/analytic vendors may be yet another quantum jump up, in both quality and price, as you can see on the chart.

GENERAL COSTS OF CYBERSPACE DATA PACKAGES FOR INVESTORS

Telerate, Instinet, and The Bloomberg	$1,100–1,500/month
DTN Wall Street, Signal, Knight-Ridder	$250–750/month
Dial/Data, IDD, Telemet, CQG	$50–200/month
CompuServe, DJN/R, Reuters Money Network	$25–100/month
PAWWS, Quotecom, InterQuote	$10–20/month
Some Internet connections	Some free quotes

Since each of these data vendors may offer several levels of service plus add-ons, this comparison is obviously general, to give you some idea of the overall wide range of the costs involved in getting real-time, delayed, and historical costs.

Why should an investor pay 25 to 100 times more for the top-level services? There are several good reasons for paying top dollar: reliability, tech support, interfaces, and access to larger databases. Fortunately, today the

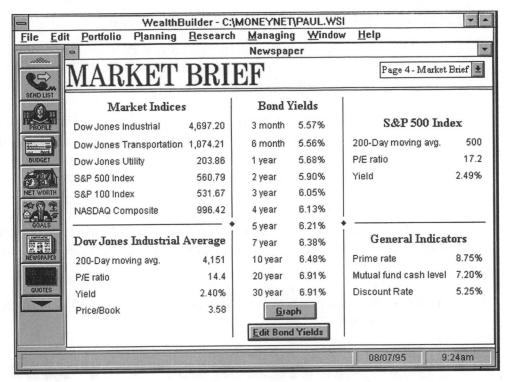

Figure 7.1   Reuters Money Network: Market Brief.

major information vendors—especially Dow Jones, Reuters, and Knight-Ridder—are going after the mass market, not just the institutional investor. They now see the individual investor as an untapped new market for their information businesses. This trend is tantamount to Rolls Royce or Ferarri designing a new model to compete with GM's lower-priced Saturn.

SIX REASONS TO PAY TOP DOLLAR FOR DATA SERVICES

Risk management: Too much at risk for institutional money managers.

Timeliness: Competitive edge on timely market-moving news.

Exchanges covered: Networked to massive databases.

High-tech analysis: Sophisticated, high-powered analytic tools.

Reliability: Technical support for analytic tools and data feed.

Total package: Prices plus analytic tools, news, and lots more.

Dow Jones News/Retrieval and Reuters Money Network

We already covered a couple examples of this powerful new trend in the Chapter 6 section on mutual funds. In recent years both Dow Jones Market Monitor and the Reuters Money Network were introduced as new products for the individual investor. Each is a multibillion-dollar company normally targeting the big institutional and corporate clients. Now both are targeting the individual investor . . . customers previously left exclusively to America Online, CompuServe, American Association of Individual Investors, and the discount brokers. And they're doing it with a much lower priced product.

The change in strategies is very much reflected in the advertisements of both the Reuters Money Network and Dow Jones Market Monitor, where each one of them aggressively identifies themselves as an *online* service. Their ads read:

❐ **Reuters Money Network:** "The fastest growing and least expensive *online* investment system available."

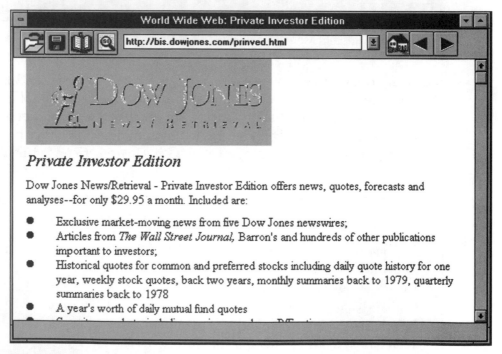

Figure 7.2   DJN/R's Private Investor Edition.

❏ **Dow Jones Market Monitor:** "Get the most comprehensive *online* service ever offered to private investors."

Moreover, their ads are run in the broad-based consumer magazines as well as investor publications. And the prices of both are competitive with the commercial online services, with Dow Jones Market Monitor only $30 per month and Reuters Money Network just $25 per month. And you'll recall that both offer a full range of company data and research tools, as well as the raw quote data.

They are clearly going after the new cyberspace investor, capitalizing on the popularity of AOL, CompuServe, and the Internet. Their market is the individual investor rather than the professional trader or institutional investor working with real-time data. However, both Reuters and DJN/R also offer much more expensive real-time services when the investor is ready to move up to more full-time trading activity.

S&P ComStock: The Leaders Rely on Standard & Poor's

S&P ComStock, a major real-time data provider is a wholly owned subsidiary of McGraw-Hill, the publisher of many business and financial books and periodicals, including *Business Week* magazine. Standard & Poor's has a history of 130 years' service to the financial community. S&P ComStock has many products for investors:

❏ **Quote Display:** Software 250,000 symbols on flexible, customized platform.

❏ **Digital Data Feed:** Compatible with over 60 third-party software packages.

❏ **OpenArc:** Windows system for quotes, news, charting, multitasking.

❏ **S&P MarketScope:** Business and financial news.

❏ Plus other information packages on equities, earnings, bonds, etc.

The basic raw data package for North American stocks, commodities, and options will run you almost $300 monthly, and another $90 if you order Market Scope and the news service. Dow Jones News Service and Futures World News would total another $50 and $75 a month on the à la carte purchase plan. So you see how easily and quickly an investor can get into the $500 a month range with just a few add-ons.

Figure 7.3   S&P ComStock at I-NO Website.

How good is S&P ComStock's information? Their list of strategic alliances—companies that rely on their data feeds—includes Aspen Research, Bull & Bear Financial, IDD Information Services, Instinet, Kapiti, Market Vision, OptionVue, Reuters, Townsend Analytics, TraderStation, and dozens of other respected leaders in the financial information business. For these market leaders, S&P Comstock means high quality, reliability, and timely data. Check them out.

Data Broadcasting Corporation: Signal and QuoTrek

One of the best real-time data services for the professional trader is Data Broadcasting Corporation, a spin-off company created when the Financial News Network was sold to CNBC-TV. DBC has about 30,000 subscribers using its Signal receiver system for real-time, delayed, or end-of-day information. Investors can pick the reception system that works best for them:

❏ **FM radio.**   Access to 90,000 issues. Windows platform lets you monitor your portfolio even when your PC is off. Displays every symbol. Compatible with 130 known technical analysis software packages.

❐ **Cable.** Connects to the same system that provides CNBC or C-SPAN, with access to every major U.S. and foreign exchange. Customize the unit to track information on the display of your computer using any major analytic software.

❐ **Satellite.** Many of the same features; ideal for traders following one market or a limited number of symbols, unit stores up to 800 symbols in memory.

❐ **SignalCard.** A real-time service designed for your laptop and traveling. *Star Trek* technology in a mobile unit the size of a credit card. Definitely check it out.

❐ **QuoTrek.** Another portable, handheld unit, perfect for the investor on the go, it travels anywhere, tracks your portfolio, accesses quotes, news, and market statistics.

Data Broadcasting's Signal service also includes news as part of the basic package—headlines and analysis from newswires, institutional research reports, and advisory newsletters. You can also purchase extra services, supplied by such organizations as Dow Jones News Service,

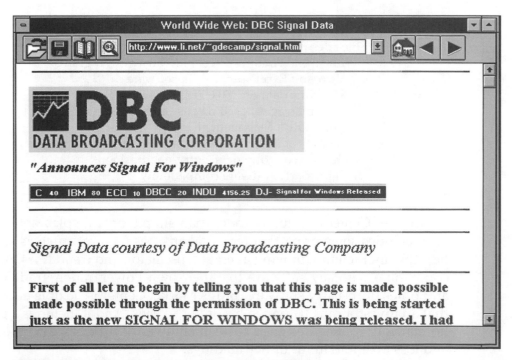

Figure 7.4 Data Broadcasting Corporation's Signal.

Option News Exchange, Futures World News, and others. DBC covers every U.S. and foreign market: national and regional stocks, commodity futures, stock and currency options, mutual funds, plus the indexes and market statistics.

BMI: Bonneville Market Information—First Class

BMI has a 20-year business history of reliability in delivering market data. In 1995, BMI/Bonneville Market Information was acquired by Data Broadcasting Corporation. And like DBC, data from BMI is broadcast over cable (via TBS Superstation), satellite, and FM radio frequencies in every major metropolitan area. With these three types of delivery systems, BMI is capable of blanketing the United States.

BMI's services include Market Center, their data management software used to display and chart your portfolio and symbols. Bonneville's system lets the investor access data on 150,000 securities, including stocks, bonds, futures, mutual funds, options, indexes, fixed income, FOREX, and market statistics, plus the weather.

BMI'S OPEN TRADING PLATFORM

Includes many features from . . .
Townsend Analytics, technical analysis programs
Microsoft Excel spreadsheet software
Real-time data on 150,000 securities
Alert messages based on customized triggers
Option Risk Management
News headlines from keyword searches and alerts
Trade accounting data, entry, and positions
Third-party software compatibility

Market Center is actually more than simple data display software. It also includes some important technical analysis features, such as stochastics, RSI, momentum, moving averages, oscillator, and trend lines. And it's compatible with key software like their own PowerTrader, TradeStation, and other third-party software. BMI's Market Center is flexible enough so that an investor can customize his or her screens. And it includes a portfolio manager routine designed to keep an investor up to date on the profit and loss positions in his or her holdings.

BMI also offers a number of add-on packages of intraday news for commodities and stocks. These include Dow Jones News, Futures World News, Fortucast Market Timing, BCOT Liquidity Data Bank, IPO Spotlight, S&P MarketScope, Zacks Earnings Estimates, Freese Notis Weather Reports, the Bullish Consensus, and other information to keep the cyberspace investor in the winning zone.

DTN Wall Street: "No Computer Needed!"

If you're interested in a low-budget operation, don't want to wait for end-of-day prices, and you can live with delayed quotes, try DTN Wall Street. They'll give you "all the quotes you need" from all major North American exchanges for less than $40 a month (plus a start-up fee of $300). No wonder DTN has 90,000 subscribers; it's a bargain to a lot of cyberspace investors.

Plus they supply all the equipment. You can operate it with your computer or as a stand-alone system. DTN's unit pulls in the data from satellite

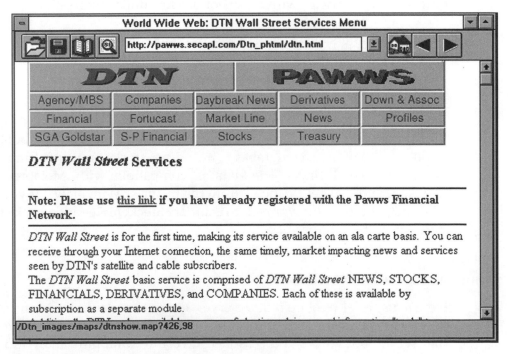

Figure 7.5 DTN Wall Street: Data Transmission Network.

or cable feeds 24 hours a day—over 20,000 stocks, bonds, mutual and money market funds, indexes, and futures contracts, plus news.

If you want real-time quotes, ask DTN about their DTNstant service: unlimited quotes from all major exchanges, historical data, charts, technical analysis, weather, and news from Futures World News. A solid service for $160 plus exchange fees.

One interesting side note: In a day and age when computer technology seems so essential, DTN's advertisements are surprising, touting the fact that "no computer is necessary" with DTN Wall Street. This reflects survey data from the American Association of Individual Investors. AAII says that a large percentage of their almost 200,000 members lack computers, so there definitely is still a market for this DTN's computerless data delivery technology . . . but for how long?

StockQuoter 2: Discount Competition for DBC and DTN

StockQuoter 2 is an aggressive competitor of the Data Broadcasting Corporation and Data Transmission Network. StockQuoter's ads directly compare all three services, with these bottom-line dollar figures:

- ❑ **StockQuoter:** No start-up costs and only $25 a month.
- ❑ **DBC Signal:** $249 start-up and $60 monthly.
- ❑ **DTN Wall Street:** $295 start-up and $46 monthly.

StockQuoter data comes from the S&P Comstock feed, just as it does for so many other vendors. You get instant quotes on your symbols, with 15,000 symbols in the database, including stocks, mutual funds, and money market listings. The data is compatible with MetaStock and Quicken, and you get the news from the Business Wire News. If you're on a budget, you owe it to yourself to compare StockQuoter and check current prices from the competition.

Tradeline Electronic Stock Guide

Here's a special Website that deserves a very close look. IDD Information Services has knocked themselves out here. They have great products that serve both novice and seasoned investor—data plus analytical tools. The IDD Tradeline Electronic Stock Guide is designed to interface with

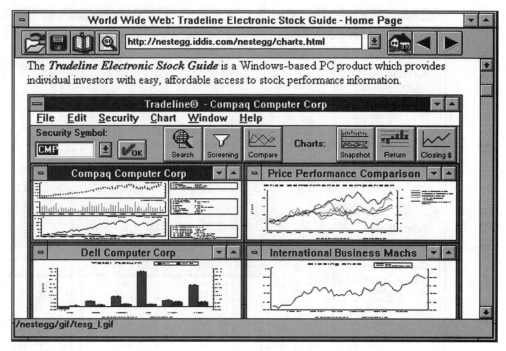

Figure 7.6   Tradeline Electronic Stock Guide.

Quicken. You can screen through a solid database of 7,000 securities to uncover opportunities. It's in a great graphical format that permits six stocks and indices on the same chart. And monthly updates come by disk for only $10 a month. Log in to the IDD Tradeline Website and find out for yourself how good this product really is.

Telemet America: A Leader in Radio Technology

Telemet America has sold over 25,000 quotation terminals and has the longest operating history of any service using radio technology, back to their 1979 beginnings. Their Windows-based Encore system allows you to include quotes, charts, news, and other Windows, all on the same screen. Telemet covers all the major markets and provides insider alerts for a basic fee in the neighborhood of $175 monthly.

Telemet is a leader in handheld portable systems. Their Pocket Quote Pro is an advanced, portable system that provides news alerts from Dow

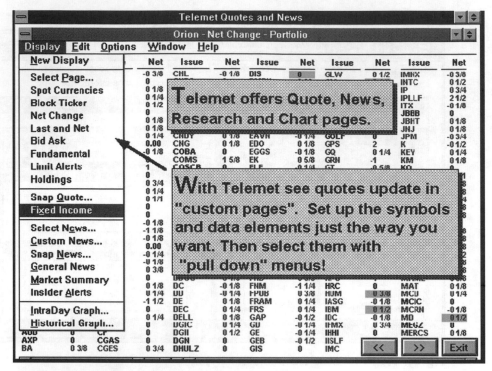

Figure 7.7   Telemet America: data by radio.

Jones and quotes from all exchanges from remote locations for the investor on the move. Telemet also provides an integrated portfolio management system, complete with analytic software designed for data management and easy transfer to charts and spreadsheets.

Dial/Data: Reliable Real-Time Data Delivery to Investors

Dial/Data is an institution among cyberspace investors, with thousands of individual and institutional investors relying on Dial/Data since 1972, they have become an industry standard for quote systems. They have a reputation for high-quality data, dependable service, and reasonable prices.

Many of the investment software vendors and online services regularly recommend Dial/Data along with their packages. You select and pay for only what you need. Definitely contact them for further information if you just want reliable quotes.

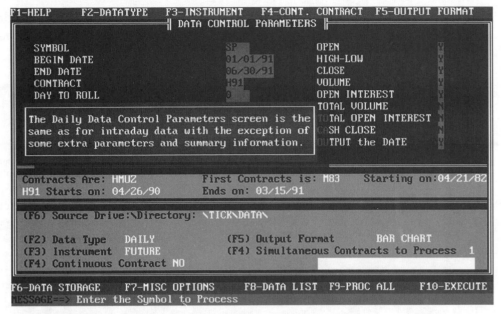

Figure 7.8 Tick Data's control parameters screen.

CD-ROM Technology: Historical Data and Telechart 2000

If you've ever tried to download a sizable file from an Internet location or from online sources, you know that downloading large amounts of historical data can be time-consuming and can take up hard-disk space. Unless you pay extra (a lot extra) to change from a standard analog telephone line to a ten-times faster ISDN (Integrated Switched Digital Network) system, you're stuck with long download times for large databases. Plus you're eating up large sectors of your hard drive. As a result, cyberspace data vendors are developing CD-ROM technology as an alternative, in order to solve both problems—information overload and limited bandwidth. As a result, you can work offline without connect charges.

The Worden Brothers TeleChart 2000 service is an excellent example of this trend. They offer the investor a massive historical database on a single CD-ROM disk for less than $30, plus updates for about $20 a month, depending on the data downloaded.

The TeleCharts 2000 database includes 8,400 stocks, 4,400 mutual funds, 250 indexes, major industrial groups, and internal statistics, complete with filters to screen for earnings, price, relative strength, volume, and capitalization. TeleChart 2000 is not just real-time data. In addition, you've got an inexpensive package that's compatible with many other software applications, including Windows on Wall Street.

HYBRID TECHNOLOGY: COMPUSERVE COMBINES ONLINE PLUS CD-ROM

CompuServe is the most aggressive about integrating CD-ROM. . . . One of the most sophisticated CompuServe hybrids is Managing Your Money, a new Windows CD-ROM version of H&R Block's financial management software. On the disk, advice from Andrew Tobias is cross-linked to corresponding online areas, such as *Money Magazine's* Fundwatch online . . . when you select the Update option, the link automatically logs on and downloads the data. . . .

Compuserve plans to add advanced update systems, messaging, polling and customized conferencing options . . . most observers see the convergence of CD-ROM and the online world as an interim phenomenon. . . . No matter what the outcome, it's clear we'll see many more intriguing hybrid experiments before broadband interactivity arrives.

(SOURCE: Domenic Stanberry, "Online/CD-ROM Connection," *NewMedia*, June 1995.)

Figure 7.9   TeleChart 2000: CD-ROM technology.

Expect to see a lot more use of CD-ROM technology. The new PC software and investor databases are demanding more and more hard-disk space, and many more of the newer PCs are coming equipped with CD-ROMs. In addition to TeleChart 2000, other large databases are available from Standard & Poor's, Moody's, Disclosure, and other major information suppliers. Software is also coming on CD-ROM, such as SuperCharts 3-CD charting software, which is in direct competition with the Equis MetaStock software. CompuServe also uses a CD-ROM for offline management, thus minimizing expensive online usage time.

Competition is heating up, so you can expect the data vendors to start distributing these disks free, or darn close to it. That way they'll hook the investor into coming back regularly for the paid updates. After all, this makes great marketing sense. The same marketing strategy worked for America Online in 1995 as they quadrupled their subscriber base by giving away disks and five free hours, anything to get new subscribers in the front door.

SOLVING THE TIME-CONSUMING PROBLEM OF COLLECTING QUOTES

Tired of scouring newspapers for security prices and typing them into your computer by hand? You need DownLoader . . . a software package so powerful yet so simple, it can collect a multitude of price quotes literally at the touch of a key. With it you can build your own database of stock, bond, commodity, future, index, option and mutual fund prices for use with MetaStock, the world's best-selling technical analysis software. . . . The DownLoader is unquestionably the most comprehensive data collection software available.

(SOURCE: MetaStock promotional brochure.)

Equis' DownLoader for Data Management

Here's an example of the comparative cost of basic data, and a solution to the problem of getting data easily and quickly interfaced with your analytic software. Equis International, the people who developed two of the more popular software packages used by serious investors—MetaStock and The Technician—also market a product called DownLoader for less than $100. Their descriptive brochure describes the data collection and interface problem DownLoader is trying to solve for the investor.

DownLoader may not be the most comprehensive data collection and management system. Nevertheless, the fact that Equis made a decision to create a product that interfaces with (and promotes) the "five popular data services" is instructive. Their list will give you other ideas of where to get basic market data and the price you should expect to pay for it (for the MetaStock system *or any other investment analysis system*).

The results of their survey were quite instructive. Some of these data sources—CompuServe, Dow Jones, and DBC Signal—also have their own stock analysis systems, which are competitive with the Equis products. The data vendor you decide to work with is, in effect, a subcontractor of raw data anyone can buy for resale.

COST COMPARISON OF FIVE POPULAR DATA FEEDS

Suggested for MetaStock and DownLoader
(from NYSE, NASDAQ, and AMEX exchanges)

DBC Signal (800-367-4670)
   Real-time setup $620 and $250/mo. unlimited quotes (FM)
   Delayed quotes are $340 setup and $60 per month.
Dial/Data (800-275-5544)
   Real-time; $190 setup and $183/month
   Delayed is $35 set-up and $15/month, plus two cents/quote/day.
Dow Jones (800-522-3567)
   With Dow Jones News/Retrieval at $29.95/month plus about 15 cents/
      quote
   Real time, add exchange fees; about $11/month for the three exchanges.
MarketScan (800-456-9190)
   End-of-day quotes only between 8 P.M. and 6 A.M.; $60 per month
CompuServe (800-848-8199)
   Basic CompuServe package is $9.95 plus a penny a quote/day

---

Each of these five popular data services was asked about the cost of buying the raw data. DBC Signal offered unlimited delayed quotes for $60 per month and a hefty setup charge. MarketScan offered closing quotes and off-hours service also for $60/month. Quotes through Dow Jones News/Retrevial were covered in a basic $30 monthly charge, plus a per quote charge of about 15 cents each. Add on exchange fees, or about $11 for NYSE, NASDAQ, and AMEX. Dial/Data has a $35 setup fee plus $15 per month and a two cents per quote per day fee. They also offer real-time quotes for $180 per month with a setup charge. CompuServe quotes come with the basic fee of $10 per month, plus a penny a quote.

NEW SOFTWARE FOR TECHNICAL ANALYSIS AND TRADING SYSTEMS

We have already reviewed the analytic software used by the institutional investors, from sources such as Reuters Instinet, Dow Jones Telerate, Knight-Ridder Financial, and Bloomberg. If they're all too rich for your blood, you can always go to the other end of the spectrum: Surf the Internet and download a lot of the free software and free quotes that are available. This may prove to be a very expensive decision.

New cyberspace investors will often run across directories of free software and shareware that's made available online and on the Internet. The *NetMoney* book group has compiled one of the best. However, you should naturally be skeptical and very cautious in this area. With freeware or

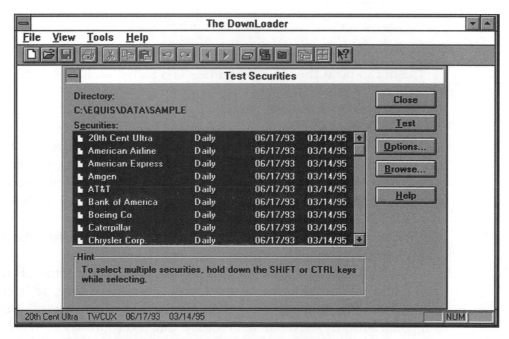

Figure 7.10 Equis DownLoader for data management.

shareware (which you are honor-bound to pay for if you like what you try) you can't be sure what's in (*or not in*) the software. How much has it been tested in the markets?

Also, "free" tech support can be spotty (and costly). Updates may be questionable. And there will probably be compatibility problems with your data sources and with other third-party software on your system. Then whom do you call? In other words, you may well be adding a major, unnecessary risk to your investing, one that may cost you dearly.

THE HIGH COST OF "FREE" SOFTWARE FOR INVESTORS

In August 1995 *Information Week* magazine polled its readers about the use of free software in the public domain. A whopping 83 percent said they used freeware or shareware on their personal systems. However, financial software was not outstanding among the free programs downloaded. The general policy of most businesses and their information systems managers is that you get what you pay for. Lack of support and low quality were given as the two biggest pitfalls. The potential risks outweigh the savings. Therefore, they do not use public domain software in business settings.

(SOURCE: John Foley, "Is Freeware Worth It?," *Information Week*, August 14, 1995.)

In short, spend the money on first-class software. It's not free, but it's less risky.

There are a number of excellent analytic packages with an initial price tag in the $200 to $400 range. Be forewarned: You may well wind up spending two to three times the base cost—$1,000 or more—before you finish buying all the add-ons and attend a seminar in order to get fully operational. And, of course, there's all the monthly data and news feeds, telephone connection charges, updates, and other paraphernalia. But you're more likely to get what you pay for, and you'll definitely have the incentive and firepower to generate many profitable trades and investments in order to recover your initial investment.

Although the software packages discussed here are some of the best available, they are only the tip of the cyberspace iceberg, as a cursory perusal of the AAII *Guide* or other software catalogs will reveal. With that as a constraint, let's look at some of the packages already in widespread use with today's cyberspace investors.

Figure 7.11   Telescan: a total package for investors.

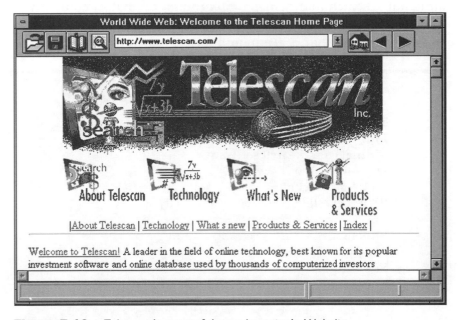

Figure 7.12   Telescan's powerful new investor's Website.

Telescan Analyzer: CyberSpace Analytical Powerhouse

Telescan is probably the leading provider of software to individual investors. Telescan's more than 100,000 subscribers sounds quite impressive compared to the alternatives being used by institutional investors. For example, Dow Jones Telerate has less than 100,000 terminals, and Bloomberg and Knight-Ridder together have perhaps 100,000 total systems in operation.

Granted, the institutional investors are paying more, often five to ten times more, and presumably getting more, so it's a bit like comparing apples to oranges. And there are many other differences. But the figures are nonetheless a strong endorsement, especially when you realize this is out-of-pocket cash for the individual investor versus an organizational expenditure.

Telescan is a powerful online total package for the investor. Telescan includes analytic software plus a database covering 80,000 North American stocks, bonds, mutual funds, options, and indexes. Moreover, Telescan database supplies the investor with more than 20 years of data that's updated every 15 minutes.

The Telescan software gives the cyberspace investor access to software programs for technical analysis charting, historical and current quotes, fundamental research and screening, earnings estimates, company research, market news, intraday trading patterns, and much more. Telescan's basic package costs less than $50 a month for unlimited off-hours usage.

TELESCAN'S CYBER-INVESTING KIT

Telescan software system and data for research and analysis
ProSearch stock search software
Mutual Fund Search software
Options Search software
MetaStock technical analysis software
S&P MarketScope for news and analysis
Zacks Earnings Estimates Service
StreetSmart, Charles Schwab's trading
Advisory Newsletters online
Seminars on cyber-investing
These services are offered for a subscription fee.

(SOURCE: Brown, *Cyber-Investing,* John Wiley & Sons, 1995.)

Then there are add-on charges, of course, for extras, which are actually essentials for the serious investor (e.g., Morningstar, Zacks, and S&P MarketScope news) all of which you would also pay extra for just about anywhere else, although, as with Reuters Money Network and Dow Jones News/Retrieval, the base price hardly tells the whole story. But, that's just a fact of life on Wall Street cyberspace, where there are very few free lunches.

Bottom line: The beauty of Telescan is that you're getting all you need for your investing in one package. It's a bit like ordering CompuServe without any of the entertainment, sports, family, and fun stuff. There's solid tech support, and if that's not enough, you can also find a Telescan discussion forum on America Online, or attend a Telescan seminar to get up to speed fast, or go to a Telescan workshop sponsored by a computer special interest group (SIG). With over 100,000 fellow Telescan users, you'll also find a lot of support on the Usenet groups.

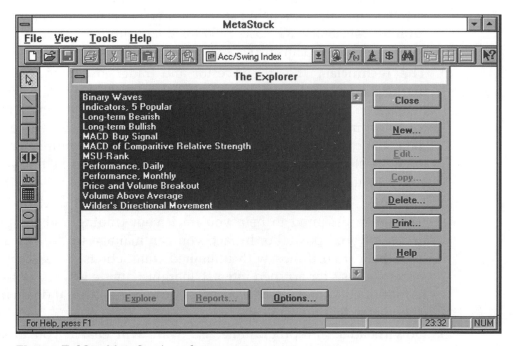

Figure 7.13 MetaStock: software system megapower.

Equis Research: MetaStock, DownLoader, and The Technician

Equis says "the world's best traders trust over $5 billion annually to Meta-Stock." If AAII's estimate of 30,000 MetaStock subscribers is accurate, that works out to about $150,000 for each MetaStock subscriber's portfolio. A rather strong endorsement, so they must be doing something right.

In fact, the data from more than 60 of the primary data providers are specifically programmed to input the MetaStock format. In other words, MetaStock is setting some kind of industry standard—they're that good. Every investor should start with the Equis catalog for complete details about their library of products. Here are some of the highlights:

- ❒ **MetaStock.** One of the premiere technical and fundamental software programs sold to individual investors. MetaStock charts price/volume trends and patterns using 75 preprogrammed technical indicators. In addition, using their math and statistical system, Indicator Builder, you can create your own customized criteria for technical screening.

    The flexible windows platform makes it easy to display as many as 50 charts simultaneously. A SmartCharts feature is used for storage and retrieval of often-used information. The Explorer feature lets you search your databases using specific criteria to screen buy/sell opportunities. MetaStock RT costs $350 for the off-hours system, while the real-time package runs $500.

- ❒ **The Technician.** For the investor and trader just interested in the market and the indexes (Dow Jones, Value Line, S&P 500, NYFE, etc.) here's a perfect package for you. This system has 200 technical indicators built in to test the market indexes. Backed with 15 years of daily data, you can analyze each index using momentum, sentiment, relative strength, stochastics, you name it, it's probably here, and if not, you can easily create your own technical indicators.

- ❒ **Portfolio Management.** Telescan's Pulse Portfolio Management package is designed to help you track your trading and the performance of your portfolio. In fact, you can manage up to 75 real and hypothetical portfolios with unlimited transactions. This accounting system adjusts for accrued interest, margins, dividends, and automatic reinvestments. International currencies can be handled and you have a calendar of trading activities.

- ❒ **DownLoader.** Preprogrammed software will enable you to access quotes fast from several of the major data suppliers, including Compu-

Serve, Dow Jones, and Telescan. This Windows format works in the background as you work other applications, collecting up to 63,000 securities in a single session.

DownLoader will also check the data's validity, permits easy copy-and-paste transfers into spreadsheets, and is even compatible with other similar software programs you may be using, such as Super-Charts and Windows on WallStreet. DownLoader minimizes the frustration of getting historical and end-of-day price quotes into your computer.

The Equis catalog also shows considerable compatibility between their products and other leaders in the investment community. For example, they also offer other cyberspace investor tools such as:

❐ Morningstar Reports
❐ Telescan Systems
❐ Reuters Money Network

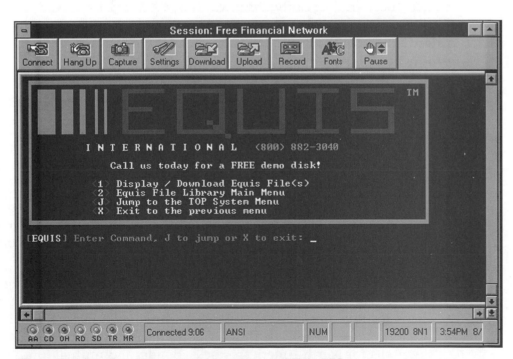

Figure 7.14 MetaStock demos and files on FFN's BBS.

❐ Quotel Historical Stock Database

❐ OptionVue IV, one of the most advanced options trading packages available

Equis also offers a collection of top-notch books by key analysts and traders—for example, Martin Pring's *Market Momentum,* John Murphy's *Technical Analysis of the Futures Markets,* Jack Schwager's *New Market Wizards,* Steven Achelis' *Technical Analysis from A to Z,* and many more.

Bottom line: The popular vote is in, and MetaStock receives a huge vote of confidence from where it counts: the individual investor. Anyone interested in technical analysis has to review and compare the Equis product line with all other alternatives.

Omega: Wall Street Analyst, SuperCharts, and TradeStation

Omega Research is another major power player in the field of analytic software for the cyberspace investor. In fact, their TradeStation real-time product won the *Technical Analysis of Stocks & Commodities* magazine readers' choice "Best Trading Software" award for 1993 and 1994. And that says a lot for a product that costs almost $2,000 up front. Omega offers lower-priced alternatives as well. Here are some of the features of their software products:

❐ **TradeStation.** This is Omega's top-of-the-line technical analysis software, distinguished by its advanced fifth-generation technology, software programming designed to parallel human thought processes. TradeStation has several unique features created to improve the trader's edge: an optimization system that allows you to discover and back-test successful trading settings; automatic scanning processes that constantly screen market data (intraday and overnight) using selected trading criteria and rules to uncover buy/sell opportunities, complete with audible screen alerts; over 150 built-in technical indicators and easy-to-read graphics.

❐ **SuperCharts.** This is Omega's software product competing with MetaStock and Windows on WallStreet, also with the Equis features for back-testing your trading system. It's reasonably priced at $250, and that even includes Dial/Data's CD-ROM 25-year database for 18,000 symbols for North American stocks, bonds, and mutual funds, plus a few years of futures contracts.

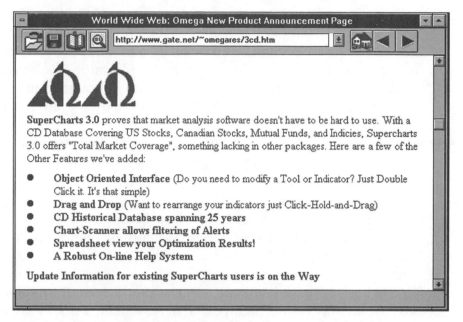

Figure 7.15   Omega's SuperCharts Website.

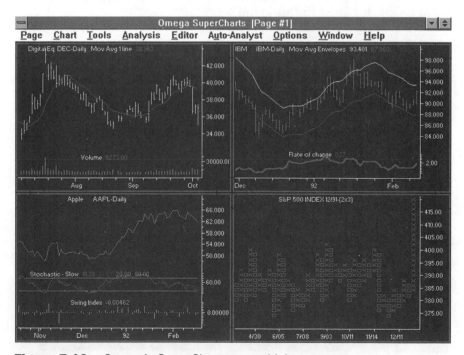

Figure 7.16   Omega's SuperCharts on multiple screens.

With over 15,000 subscribers, SuperCharts is certainly giving Meta-Stock a run for the money, in quality and performance. If you're in this market, ask them specifically for their comparison of the features in all three software packages, SuperCharts, Windows on WallStreet, and MetaStock: for charting, comparing technical indicators, fundamental research, data cost and compatibility, downloading, third-party software compatibility.

☐ **Wall Street Analyst.**   This is Omega's low-budget, Windows-based answer to TeleChart 2000 DOS software. Using Dial/Data's huge 25-year, 18,000-symbol database, you get state-of-the-art charting plus over 60 built-in technical and fundamental indicators, with the ability to interpret them. For about $50 to start up and $20 monthly for data updates, it's one of the most economical opportunities on the block. Plus there are no long download times; it's all on your CD-ROM.

Omega Research provides a full range of products for the independent investor, all the way from a high-powered, reasonably priced starter kit to mid-range software for the cyberspace investor getting serious about tracking his or her portfolio, to the semipro investor and/or professional trader. Call for their material and compare.

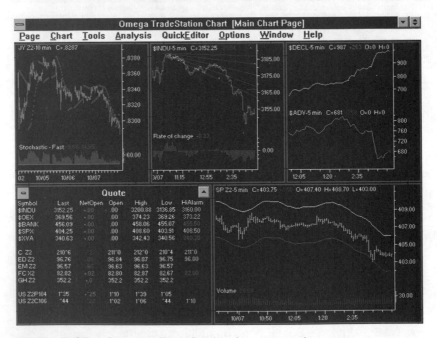

Figure 7.17   Omega's TradeStation for supertraders.

Windows on WallStreet from MarketArts

Windows on WallStreet is another complete technical analysis program designed for the cyberspace investor. WOW comes highly recommended. *PC Computing* magazine called it "Master of the Financial Universe." *Worth* magazine says it has the "best graphics we've seen." *Business Week* says WOW gives investors "the power of a Wall Street professional." And you know exactly whom they see as the competition. Windows on WallStreet directly compares itself with MetaStock and SuperCharts in its ads. Here are a few of its superfeatures:

❑ **SmartScan.** Quick search through large databases of securities and charts for price/volume changes, trading signals, and customized alerts. Save your favorite stocks in a portfolio; scanner then triggers automatic alerts.

❑ **System Tester.** An exclusive ranking system that pinpoints the best trading system for any security in seconds. Using System Tester you can create buy/sell signals and opportunities based on custom trading rules and historical data.

Figure 7.18   Windows on WallStreet from MarketArts.

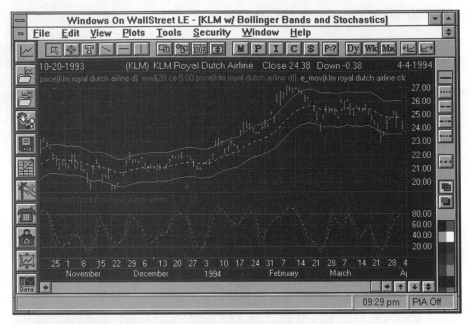

Figure 7.19   Windows on WallStreet: chart and indicators.

❏ **Personal Investment Assistant.** Automatically updates data and monitors your charts and portfolio, alerting you of changing market conditions that fit your preprogrammed trading criteria.

❏ **Quick Stock Picking Guide.** Compatible with all major data formats, Windows on WallStreet is designed to save the investor time with a flexible, easy-to-use system of selecting the right criteria as well as the right securities.

CNBC anchor Bill Griffeth says WOW is "incredibly easy to understand and operate. If you've been discouraged in the past by the complexity of other market analysis software packages, try this one." And we second the motion.

Aspen Research Group: Software for the Global Investor

Since 1985 Aspen has built an international reputation for great software. Today Aspen has over 25,000 satisfied real-time traders and investors in 17 countries. Aspen Graphics claims they are available "virtually anywhere in the world" and are compatible with S&P ComStock, DBC/Signal, Knight-

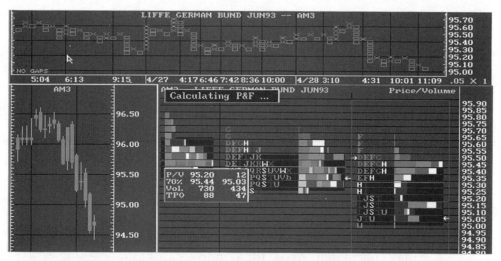

Figure 7.20 Aspen Graphics: high-performance analytics.

Ridder Financial, and the other leading delivery systems. This is real-time cyberspace investing on a global network. It's versatile enough to follow 1,000 to 100,000 symbols or more. And Aspen's unique design is flexible enough to serve a single trader, or a network of 300 users on a LAN, making it a perfect tool for a team of professional traders.

Aspen's software system is the equivalent of an Indy 500 formula racing car, with a high-performance database engine that automatically charts *every* tick on *every* symbol for *every* exchange. This instantaneous visual display is often the trader's edge in today's dynamic global markets, allowing investors to quickly apply built-in technical indicators, screening for opportunities.

Aspen's screens even look different: concise, uncluttered, and preformatted to permit ease of trading. Plus their system is designed with hot keys that permit rapid saving and retrieval of custom charts and data.

Aspen is competitive with other software products for cyberspace investors. For around $320 start-up costs and a similar monthly rental, you're in business. Definitely a major contender in this market.

Specialty Software Systems for Very Special Investors

There are so many other excellent systems available. Here are a few of the more specialized software packages that may interest you:

❒ **International Pacific Candlesticks.** Candlesticks have been a popular and effective technical analysis indicator for a long time. This method was first developed in the seventeenth century by the Japanese to track and analyze price movements in rice commodities. It has evolved in recent years to become an effective tool for technical analysis in commodities trading. Today, candlesticks techniques are used in conjunction with other timing tools, such as Elliott Wave, stochastics, RSI, and moving averages, to analyze and predict trends in the markets, equities, currencies, and other areas, as well as in commodities.

❒ **Manhattan Analytics.** For analytic software strictly designed for mutual funds by specialists who are not connected to a brokerage firm or mutual fund, call Manhattan Analytics in Manhattan Beach, California. Their FundPro 3.0 for Windows and Monocle software may serve your needs. *PC Computing* and *Technical Analysis of Stocks & Commodities* both give them high marks. Although *PC Computing* added that if you want to work with more than mutual funds, Reuters Money Network is more versatile and less expensive. AAII says Monocle is "the most complete mutual fund investing package out."

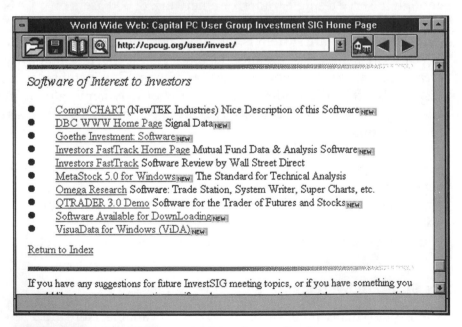

Figure 7.21 InvestSIG's computer software directory.

❏ **Recurrence IV.** The advertisements for AVCO Financial Corp's Recurrence IV say, "No other trading system can make this statement." Their claim is that in six years of trading, Recurrence IV has made an astronomical *851 percent annual return* trading Swiss francs. So why would anyone ever sell a product that successful?

AVCO Financial is an established institution, hopefully using this software to increase the value of their company stock as well as to offer it to independent traders. At $3,500, however, the Recurrence IV system may not be a competitive alternative for most individual investors.

❏ **Astro-Economics.** Many market timers are interested in astro-economics, the impact of planetary cycles on trends and turning points in the financial markets. Several market analysts have developed computer-based systems that incorporate astronomic and other cycles research, along with Gann and Elliott Wave theory, Fibonacci ratios, and a host of other technical indicators. These systems are used to time market indexes as well as specific stocks and securities.

SOFTWARE FOR ASTRO-ECONOMICS/TECHNICAL ANALYSIS

AstroAnalyst	Astrolabe, Inc.	(800) 843–6682
F.A.R. Trader's Software	M.M.A. Cycles Report	(810) 626–3034
Stock Market Program	AIR Software	(203) 232–6521

Bottom line: The number of software alternatives available to the cyberspace investor is huge and growing. This selection is just a glimpse of the tip of an enormous iceberg. If you want more details, please review our list of software directories at the end of this section, talk to experienced investors, and try several before you commit.

The Lowly Spreadsheet: Are We Going Back to Basics?

Do you really need all the sophisticated software (MetaStock, WOW, SuperCharts, etc.)? Or can you accomplish the same or even get better results with basic spreadsheet software such as MS-Excel, QuattroPro, and Lotus 1-2-3? Microsoft's Excel has over 5 million users, and QuattroPro another 2.5 million. All three have been basic business tools for well over a

WHY AN INDIVIDUAL INVESTOR PREFERS USING SPREADSHEETS

Investor and computer expert Harry Rood of InvestSIG, a special interest group of the Capital PC Users Group, made an interesting observation about this issue: The basic spreadsheet software

will do most things that the more sophisticated software will do, but you have to learn to use the @ functions and macros creatively.

You also have to know exactly what equations each type of analysis involves—unlike for example, MetaStock, which has many analytical techniques built in—with it, you don't have to know what it's doing. Just tell it RSI, for example, and up pops an RSI chart. That's one of the reasons why I prefer using spreadsheets—you have to learn what each type of technical analysis involves, and you get better understanding of them that way.

decade, successfully used in crunching large databases in search of historical trends and patterns.

MetaStock, Supercharts, and their competitors are basically spreadsheets, preformatted specifically for the investor, with the technical formulas preprogrammed into the software. They save you a lot of time, because the investor doesn't have to set up Excel or Lotus to receive your stock quotes or input your favorite technical indicators (RSI, moving averages, advance/declines, etc.).

Spreadsheets such as Excel, QuattroPro, and Lotus are used in many business applications other than Wall Street investment analyses. Overall, they have more than 10 million users, which may exceed by more than ten times the number of software systems specifically used by individual investors.

Harry Rood of InvestSIG prefers to use basic spreadsheets because it forces him as an investor to understand the formulas he's using, rather than mechanically applying something he doesn't fully understand. On the other hand, Stephen Wendel, President of StockPro Technologies, an investment adviser and computer expert, believes that "most investors don't want to waste time coding formulas when you can buy a package for a few hundred bucks." That's obviously why Equis, Omega, and MarketArts are so popular and successful among cyberspace investors.

New Software Battles: Spreadsheets, Chartists, and Quants

Another big reason for this renewed excitement about the new versions of the spreadsheet is the fact that today's institutional investors are jumping onto this bandwagon. Reuters, Bloomberg, Dow Jones, and Knight-Ridder are among the key players backing a new breed of quantitative software developers (*quants*) who eventually will be transferring more of their technology into the individual investor market. These quants are developing a new generation of flexible real-time data interfaces and analytic software capable of managing multiple data feeds easily.

These quants are helping end users sitting at workstations in the trading rooms of large investment institutions to tailor their own data/analytics/graphical/spreadsheet packages to suit their individual trading styles . . . *without* first having to convince the boss and some software technicians to write new programming codes and commands for the entire institution.

CAN THE LOWLY SPREADSHEET REPLACE METASTOCK?

Pity the lowly spreadsheet. The mainstay of the back-office bean counters, it gets about as much respect as a pocket protector. On Wall Street, however, Applix is sexing up the spreadsheet with "real-time" feeds. Its Applixware software enables traders and brokers to use up-to-the-second data in constructing the what-if scenarios they need to make on-the-fly decisions.

Sound too much like the half dozen wire services already running around your network? What makes Applixware unique is its flexibility. In addition to the real-time feeds that are at the program's heart, the product incorporates graphics software, E-mail, a spreadsheet, and a word processor. . . . With the big-name sales partners like Reuters and Bloomberg, Applixware is all the rage in many Wall Street firms.

Most don't want you to know who they are—they're so convinced that Applixware will give them a competitive advantage that the company is not allowed to identify them as customers. . . . Stiffer competition may come soon from Microsoft, which plans to make it easier to incorporate real-time feeds into Excel spreadsheets.

(SOURCE: Ronald Lieber, *Fortune*, July 10, 1995.)

Applix was one of the "25 Cool Companies" in *Fortune*'s Special Report on "Information Technology." Other companies included were, UUNET, Architext, Open Market, Netscape, On Ramp, Nexgen, @ Home and other new high-tech firms.

Granted, some of their technology is merely a more sophisticated level of data integration with basic "lowly" spreadsheet technology that has been around a while. But they are also going beyond, applying quantitative analysis as an alternative to technical analysis charting.

Some quants, such as Leading Market Technologies and Market Vision, have gone a quantum leap beyond merely adding souped-up graphics with multiple spreadsheets. Their computer platforms are the basis for applying sophisticated econometric models and statistical regressions to time series from multiple real-time data feeds.

THE INSTITUTIONAL QUANTS ARE NOW INVADING PC LAND

EXPO is a real-time graphical worksheet for the display, analysis, and management of financial market data. EXPO tracks real-time and historical data in a user-friendly, graphical environment. . . .

Leading Market Technologies' EXPO is the financial industry standard for quantitative analysis and display of financial market data. . . .

Now available to the Individual Investor. Until now, EXPO was only available to Global Market Traders—those equipped with UNIX Workstations, Vast Data Networks, and Hoardes of Capital to Trade. No Longer. EXPO is now available to *individual* licensing under Microsoft Windows.

(SOURCE: Leading Market Technologies ad in *Technical Analysis of Stocks and Commodities* and LMT's newsletter, *EXPO/MBA News*.)

As a result, the end user—the professional trader—now has available everything from new levels of flexibility and user-friendliness to multiple data and analytic tools, *plus* some remarkable new quantitative techniques not previously possible with earlier technologies, quantitative systems that are substantially different in theory and practice than the application of traditional technical analysis indicators.

Bottom line: Individual traders within large institutions are now *more* in control of their own destiny . . . a significant trend that parallels the new freedom of the individual investor on that Kansas farm using KR-Quote, Reuters Money Network, or Telescan and MetaStock.

These trends illustrate some of the leading-edge aspects of the overall revolution on Wall Street cyberspace. Here we see a flexible, intuitive, user-friendly technology that supports the uniqueness of the individual trader/investor working within the large institution. And, most probably, everything from this basic spreadsheet technology to the high-powered quanti-

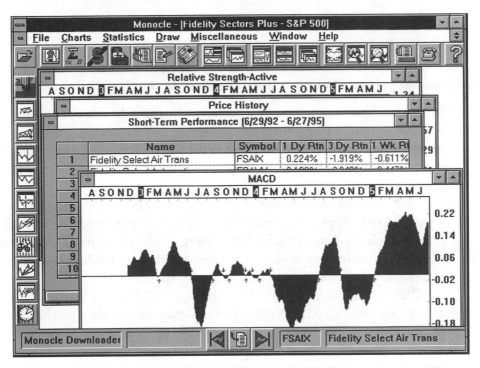

Figure 7.22 Manhattan Analytics' Monocle software.

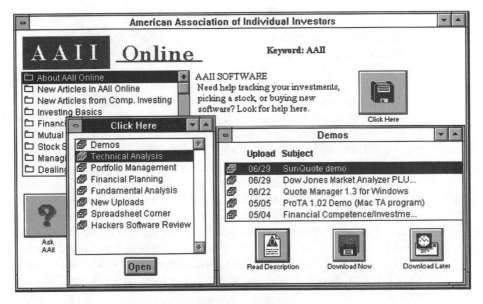

Figure 7.23 AAII's directory of investor software.

tative analytics will soon be developed and mass-marketed to the individual investor/trader.

Individual Investors: Profiting from the New Technologies

Keep your eyes open for names such as Leading Market Technologies and Market Vision, along with Open Market, A-T Financial, and Applix . . . if not to buy their software in the near future, then possibly as an investment in your portfolio, because their technologies are on the cutting edge of Wall Street cyberspace.

They are not only state of the art, they may be the emerging new industry standard. Applix, for example, is not only partnered with Wall Street giants such as Reuters and Bloomberg, they were recently selected by NASDAQ to develop a superpowered market-surveillance system on the exchange's Sun Microsystems' computer network.

Predictably, this advanced technology will become more widely available to the individual investor in the next couple years as the new 32-bit technology of Windows 95, the security of Internet commercial transac-

---

WILL QUANT SOFTWARE ALSO REPLACE TECHNICAL ANALYSIS!?

While the lowly spreadsheet may not replace MetaStock, it is possible that someday soon, *quantitative analysis* (econometrics, statistical correlations, regression analysis, etc.) itself may replace *technical analysis* as the analytic tool of choice for the *next* generation of traders.

The institutional clients of Leading Market Technologies, Market Vision, and their competitors often use *quantitative analysis* methods that are proving more powerful, more versatile, and more accurate than technical analysis and charting methods popular among today's individual traders.

Indeed, with the inability of many leading technical analysts to forecast the 1995 rally, and the concurrent successes of institutional quants (quantitative analysts), we may well be witnessing the *breakdown* of an entire system of thinking that has been the dominant theoretical model used by traders in analyzing the financial markets for many decades.

In other words, the paradigm shift underlying Wall Street Cyberspace may be much deeper and more comprehensive than is apparent on the surface.

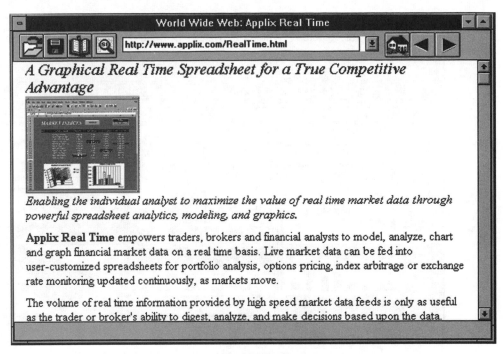

Figure 7.24 Applix real-time spreadsheet technology.

tions, and the competition that's driving down the price of basic data (quotes, news, etc.) all combine to provide these new software developers with the vehicles necessary to reach beyond the institutional investors and deep into the individual investor market.

**THE NEW HIGH-POWERED SOFTWARE DEVELOPERS—THE QUANTS
WITH GRAPHICAL PLATFORMS FOR DATA INTEGRATION,
ANALYTICS, NEWS, AND OTHER TOOLS**

Applix, Inc.	(508) 870–0300
A-T Financial Information, Inc.	(212) 608–3870
Leading Market Technologies, Inc.	(617) 494–4747
Market Vision Corporation	(212) 227–1610
Open Market	(617) 621–9500

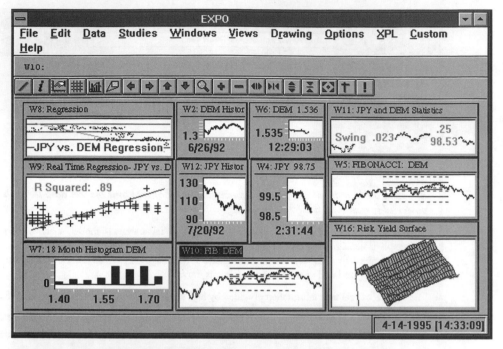

Figure 7.25 EXPO: leading market technologies platform.

Bottom Line with Investment Software: Go First Class

Meanwhile, MetaStock, SuperCharts, Windows on WallStreet, and their competitors are likely to remain the dominant analytic software of choice for cyberspace investors—at least the near term . . . until the new quant software developers start marketing less expensive products for the individual investor and his or her computer systems. Fortunately, that could be much sooner than we expect, since a number of these software geniuses are already marketing Windows-based products to individual investors.

Individual investors and traders spend a lot of time working with their investment and trading software. This is the guts of the command module for their cyber-spaceship, Wall Street profits. If it malfunctions, your ship (your investment portfolio) goes down in flames. So don't compromise, go first class.

Whatever you do, please take the time to compare software products, not just the superpopular ones such as MetaStock, SuperCharts, and Windows on WallStreet, but other systems discussed here. Discover for yourself the state of the art. Review products listed in the various printed guides from AAII and other publications. Perhaps more important, ask several *other* cyberspace investors you trust what actually has worked for them. Raise your questions on a Usenet newsgroup, an AOL forum, or a PC computer users' special interest group, for example.

RESOURCE DIRECTORIES FOR INDIVIDUAL INVESTORS

AAII's Guide to Computerized Trading	(312) 280–0170
Futures Magazine's Guide to Computerized Trading	(800) 635–3931
Technical Analysis of Stocks & Commodities, Bonus Issue	(800) 832–4642
Wall Street Software Digest	(619) 943–1936
Wall Street & Technology, Buyer's Guide	(800) 227–4675

You may well discover that the best system *for you* is *not* one of these more popular, highly advertised software packages. Let's face it, the initial cost of the software is peanuts compared to the mental aggravation of having a system that isn't quite suited to your special investment style and personality, not to mention the considerable risks to your portfolio. In fact, you may even discover that you don't need a fancy, sophisticated system for what you do.

Finally, remember the various total-package systems already discussed. Focus on finding a system that works as a whole unit, like a fine-tuned clock. Reuters Money Network, CompuServe, StreetSmart, Telescan, Dow Jones News/Retrieval, and America Online all have reasonably priced packages. They may not make you into a professional commodity futures day-trader, but they may well be more than adequate for most investment portfolios. And you'll sleep better at night without all the frustrations and anxieties inherent in active market tracking and day trading.

THE BEST LITTLE STOCK MARKET SCHOOL IN THE WORLD

You won't find it in a catalog of business schools. Nor will you find it in the training courses of any brokerage house. No, the very best place for you to begin a practical education that will make you piles of money in the market is right where you're sitting now—and that's probably in your own home.

You don't need an MBA, not even a bachelor's in economics or business, to become a reasonably successful independent investor. But you *do* need the modest weekly application of your own time, perhaps an hour or two a day, at least at first. And you will need to exercise a great deal of common sense.

I recommend the following eight steps for anyone who wants to graduate from rank amateur to market-savvy investor:

Step 1: *Read the financial pages of your local newspaper every day . . .*

Step 2: *Put your money on the line . . .*

Step 3: *Do even more financial reading of a national newspaper . . .*

Step 4: *Do still more reading of select magazines . . .*

Step 5: *Yes, more reading of key books on the market . . .*

Step 6: *Now you're ready to take a formal course somewhere . . .*

Step 7: *Consider subscribing to an investment advisory service . . .*

Step 8: *Take all advice with a grain of salt . . .*

The eight steps presented in this chapter are not a one-shot route to a "degree" that certifies you as a know-it-all. You're not supposed to do some reading, get some adivce, and then quit. No, the kind of "course" I'm talking about is an ongoing affair. Your education in investments should be a continuing, evolving process.

(SOURCE: *How to Be Your Own Stockbroker*, Charles Schwab, Dell, 1984. Buy this book now and read it while test-driving Schwab's FundMap and StreetSmart software. Take charge of your future and become a "reasonably successful independent investor.")

CHAPTER 8

New Electronic Brokers and Portfolio Management

ELECTRONIC TRADING AND DO-IT-YOURSELF BROKERAGE

Perhaps one of the most exciting developments for investors is the way the discount brokerage industry is moving into cyberspace competition. More than 20 retail brokers are already into electronic trading services, and more are entering the field. The brokerage industry estimates that we are rapidly approaching a million investors who trade electronically. Armed with this first-hand knowledge, they see the real commercial potentials and opportunities of trading online and on the Internet, and they're expecting much more expansion in the near future.

The Morgan Stanleys, Smith Barneys, and Merrill Lynches have been out there in cyberspace a long, long time. Back in the early 1970s, after the success of the Apollo Moonshot and well before Microsoft even existed, the big institutional investors moved into cyberspace with old IBM mainframes. By the late 1970s, more than a decade ahead of the individual investor, they had created their own cyberspace networks—the equivalent of a series of private, global, stock market exchanges.

Today's institutional investors have had enough lead time in cyberspace. Now it's the individual investor's turn, and the discount brokers are a perfect resource for them as one of their main links to cyberspace.

NEW CYBERSPACE INVESTORS BYPASSING BROKERAGE FIRMS

In the past if an individual investor wanted sound investment advice they simply called up their broker. Now, low-cost communications, the proliferation of PCs in the home, online research and quotes, an increasingly knowledgeable customer base, and the inevitable repeal of the Glass-Steagall Act make it easy to bypass the full-service intermediary.

Add to the brew an underlying distrust of brokers by individuals, and Wall Street's traditional brokerage services are facing a real challenge to their core retail business.

(SOURCE: Carrie Smith, "Running the Retail Race," *Wall Street & Technology*, July 1995.)

The information revolution has opened the competitive floodgates. The personal computer was the door-opener, followed by Microsoft's windows, and then the development of high-powered analytic software for investors and traders. Next the online services—especially CompuServe, Dow Jones, and America Online—began opening the eyes and minds of investors to the unlimited possibilities of networking, connecting, and communicating through the new world of cyberspace.

WHERE ARE ALL THE BIG FULL-SERVICE BROKERS?

So far, none of the full-service retail brokerage firms have launched their own firm-wide sites on the Web, nor will any of them utter a peep about what their plans might be.

Whether they want to or not, full-service firms are going to have to address the issue of cyberspace.... There's a concern that if brokerage firms send out their research online, people will take the advice and execute their trades via discount brokers, but [a survey] showed 57% said they were more likely to do business with a full-service broker if they could get the research online....

Above all else, though, the technology is awesome. That, in and of itself, will draw everyone in.

(SOURCE: Rosalyn Retkwa, "On & Off the Info Highway—Broker Automation," *Registered Representative* magazine, June 1995.)

Recently the Internet's World Wide Web exploded in space, and a new reality was born for the individual investor. Today they have all the firepower they need at their fingertips to compete effectively with the institutional investor . . . and the discount brokers sense that the revolution has started.

Imagine what this is going to do with the competition for discount commissions as the broker becomes no more than a nanosecond's contribution to the electronic trade that you (the investor) send to the "floor" (or rather, computer) of an exchange. Soon the telephone company will be doing more work for you than your broker!

PCFN: Investment Banker Turns Discount Broker

Personal Control Financial Network, PCFN, the largest discount broker, is a subsidiary of the prestigious Wall Street firm of Donaldson, Lufkin & Jenrette. Early in the development of the online networks, PC Financial Network joined Prodigy in providing brokerage services. PCFN is also on AOL and Reuters Money Network. They have executed 1 million trades and currently hold over $1 billion in customer assets for online investors.

SUBSCRIBERS TO THE ONLINE TRADING SERVICES

PCFN/Pershing	145,000
Charles Schwab	106,000
Fidelity (FOX)	40,000
Quick & Reilly	35,000
E*TRADE	30,000
AccuTrade	24,000
PC Line	20,000

(SOURCE: SIMBA Information, Inc. 1994 data summary: http://www.mecklermedia.com/simba/internet.htm.)

Trading is an easy procedure with PCFN. Once you have an account set up, input the symbol and the number of shares, specify whether it's a limit or market order and whether you have a cash or margin account, and zip . . . a short wait until confirmation. Before selecting PC Financial Network or any other broker, check and compare their commissions structure as well as their level of service.

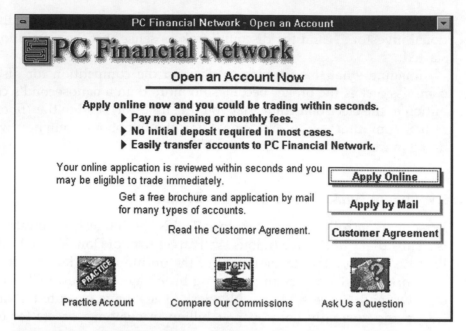

Figure 8.1   PCFN: PC Financial Network online.

Charles Schwab: Discount Broker Is Full Service Online

Schwab set the industry standard when they released StreetSmart on a windows platform. This investment software package is one of the best efforts so far from a discount broker. In fact, with their OneSource service, Schwab is rapidly becoming the best full-service discount electronic broker in cyberspace. And StreetSmart is a great name, suggesting a winner. With StreetSmart you'll get these features:

❏ Online trading and confirmation

❏ Transactions monitoring: trades, asset value, cash balances, interest, and dividends

❏ Real-time quotes with accounts (100 free per trade)

❏ Screening securities for opportunities based on your criteria for stocks, mutual funds, and other securities

❏ Mutual fund performance statistics

❏ Portfolio management, reports, and charts

❏ Discounts on commissions and third-party products

In addition, the third-party offers included in StreetSmart will tell you something about what Schwab believes the cyberspace investor will need to be a successful street-smart investor. Moreover, most of these are offered at a discount off stand-alone retail prices. Consider the following offerings:

- ❐ Reuters Money Network for a month
- ❐ Dow Jones New/Retrieval, one hour free
- ❐ S&P MarketScope, one hour free
- ❐ Company reports, a free one from S&P or Zacks

Of course, when you consider the real costs of a year on any one of these services, you will realize that the freebie is a *good deal for them.* But the real reason we mention these third-party services is not to push them on you, but to let you in on what one of the top Wall Street power players thinks is necessary *in addition* to the products they are offering to you.

By the way, Charles Schwab also has a software product for mutual funds investing, called FundMap Mutual Fund Selection software, free with all new accounts of $10,000 or more. In a simple step-by-step format, an

---

CHARLES R. SCHWAB: YOUR "ONE SOURCE" FOR MUTUAL FUNDS

With a blend of cutting-edge technology and old-fashioned sales and marketing, Schwab is once again radically altering how Americans of all incomes invest their money. . . .

He's struck gold again, this time with the exploding mutual fund business, a $2.5-trillion market, with 38 million individual investors and 5,600 stock, bond and money-market funds. . . .

In an adroit move to capture more of that business, Schwab developed a unique program in which people can use his firm to invest in 350 outside mutual funds with a single phone call and at no charge. . . .

It's an idea that seems astonishingly simple, yet one that required Schwab to invest heavily in complicated computer technology to link all the funds. . . .

The effort paid off. The program, Mutual Fund OneSource, and this year's bull market in stocks, are propelling Schwab's revenue and profit to record levels. . . . OneSource is also the latest building block in Schwab's bid to construct the one-stop financial supermarket.

(SOURCE: James Peltz, "Taking Stock of Schwab," *Los Angeles Times,* August 13, 1995.)

NEWSLETTERS OFFERED WITH A SCHWAB 500 ACCOUNT

Cabot's Mutal Fund Navigator	The Mutual Fund Stragest
Dick Davis Digest	**NoLoad Fund*X
Hussman Econometrics	OTC Insight
InvesTech Market Analyst	Peter Dag Portfolio Strategy &
InvesTech Mutual Fund Advisor	Management
Investors Intelligence	Switch Fund Timing
The Fund Exchange	Systems & Forecasts
The Mutual Fund Letter	The Zweig Forecast

investor can work through financial planning, calculate savings, define risk tolerance, set retirement goals, explore strategic alternatives, create criteria for screening funds, and then select the right investment opportunities.

Bottom line: Schwab is a pacesetter among discount brokers in cyberspace, and their StreetSmart and FundMap software prove that they will continue to be for some time to come. Moreover, Schwab, like many of the discount brokers, is beginning to look like one of those full-service brokers (e.g., Merrill Lynch), except that they are doing it in cyberspace. Check their Website. Call for more information. *Get street smart!*

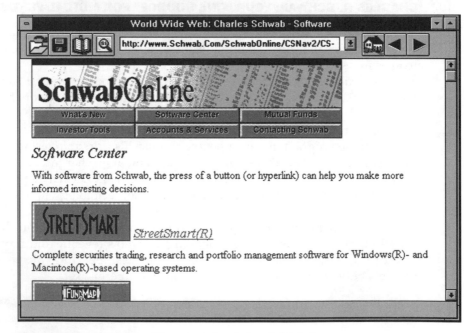

Figure 8.2   Get StreetSmart at the Schwab Website.

NEW SOFTWARE MAKES THE INVESTOR THEIR OWN BROKER

The Fidelity and Schwab brokerage houses have always attempted to be the full-service brokers, so the introduction of their on-line trading software was greatly anticipated. The main reason to buy software such as this seems to be the avoidance of any human contact in your investment process. With StreetSmart and FOX you can now screen a universe of stocks in the Dow Jones News/Retrieval gateway, retrieve a price history directly from Schwab or through Telescan on Fidelity, download a company summary report, get a real-time quote, and finally place your trade and receive a confirmation on-line.

This process has come full circle in that the full-service discount brokers have now made individual investors into a kind of broker for themselves. There's no need to call your friend the stockbroker and ask him what's hot today. You simply find it yourself. Some investors might enjoy this control; certainly an on-line broker gives you the option to ignore calls from your broker since you can place trades by yourself.

(SOURCE: Review by Paul Garverick, financial editor of the AAII online forum on AOL.)

Fidelity On-line Xpress: FOX Chasing Mutual Funds and Stocks

Fidelity is the largest family of mutual funds, commanding almost 10 percent of the daily trading on the New York Stock Exchange. So it's no surprise that they also have their own brokerage unit, Fidelity On-line Xpress (FOX). As with several of the discount brokers, you can find them online with AOL, for example. However, most of them are also developing rather sophisticated and polished Websites as stand-alones. FOX's brokerage software goes beyond simply helping you set up an electronic trade and includes:

❏ Investment software package (and a downloadable demo)
❏ Free real-time quotes, stocks, options, and mutual funds
❏ Fundamental company research
❏ Technical analysis
❏ Trade orders and execution
❏ Portfolio management

FOX and the other electronic brokers put you, the investor, in direct contact with Wall Street and the exchange floors. Download their software demo and try FOX while you compare products. There's a modest charge

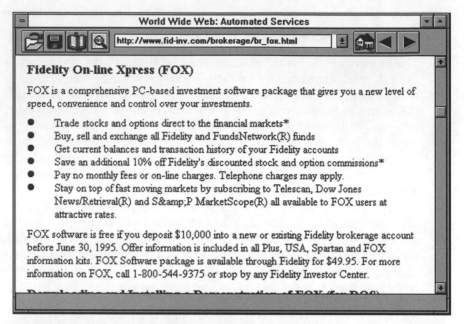

Figure 8.3   Fidelity On-line Xpress (FOX).

of $50 for FOX, but it may be just what you need, and you're getting an extra 10 percent off the commissions. Moreover, you won't need one of the online services to access most of these discount brokers. You can go direct, by dial-up, or catch them on the Internet and discover how easy it is to be your own broker.

Quick & Reilly: A New Breed of Broker

Quick & Reilly is another of the leading discount brokerage firms, with over 100 offices throughout America. You can reach their QuickWay Online Investment Service in cyberspace through CompuServe, Telescan, a touch-tone phone, and soon through other gateways. Their commissions are often as much as 30 percent below their main competition—Fidelity, Schwab, and Merrill Lynch. They don't mention E*TRADE in their comparisons, but Quick & Reilly does want to help individual investors get "the same information and trading capabilities as professional money managers." Here's what QuickWay offers:

❑ Quick online quotes, earnings, and P/E ratios
❑ Portfolio monitoring

❐ Timely market research

❐ Trading 24 hours a day by modem

❐ Secured electronic transactions

❐ OptionWatch for put/call traders

Quick & Reilly even says that "placing orders on QuickWay is no more difficult than using an automatic teller machine." Trades are simple through your PC, and if you need one, you have your own broker at the Quick & Reilly office. They even throw in a free checking account. You will probably also need Telescan and MetaStock, Signal and SuperCharts, or some other more sophisticated analytics package, but for no-frills discount trading, Quick & Reilly does keep it simple.

E*TRADE Securities: Global Coverage from Silicon Valley

One of the first electronic discount brokers online and on the Internet was E*TRADE, a brokerage firm physically located in Palo Alto, California, in Silicon Valley. Through the magic of cyberspace, an investor anywhere can reach and trade with these brokers, and take complete control of his or her own portfolio. You can reach them through the Internet, CompuServe, AOL, and other gateways. Their Website is organized with the following helpful information:

❐ E*TRADE's partners and strategies

❐ Stock quotes, stocks, mutuals, futures, etc.

❐ Trading procedures, stop orders, etc.

❐ TradeWeb links to other Websites

❐ Stock Game, no-risk test of skill

❐ Investor's Edge Newsletter

❐ Commissions structure

❐ How to open an account

Actually E*TRADE has a very informative Website. They also have some of the best prices. Cyberspace investors are encouraged to take the time to read through and compare E*TRADE's services to the other brokers surfacing online and on the Internet. Their Website is an education in detail on the operations of a highly automated electronic brokerage firm responding to needs of the cyberspace investor. Definitely check them out.

BROKERAGE COMMISSIONS COMPARED

Execution Price	Shares Sold		
	100 @ $40	1000 @ $21	5000 @ $20
E*TRADE-OTC	$ 20	$ 20	$ 20
E*TRADE-Listed	$ 25	$ 25	$ 25
AccuTrade	$ 48	$ 48	$ 150
Fidelity	$ 54	$147	$ 265
Schwab	$ 55	$146	$ 290
Merrill Lynch	$100	$384	$1097

(SOURCE: E*TRADE 1995 advertisement.)

AccuTrade Is Cruising the Financial Superhighway

AccuTrade is also very much at home in cyberspace. Their ads reflect both a strong appreciation of the impact of the information revolution, as well as the nature of the cyberspace investor's needs. In fact, one of AccuTrade's glitzy ads was headlined, "Cruise the Financial Services Super Highway."

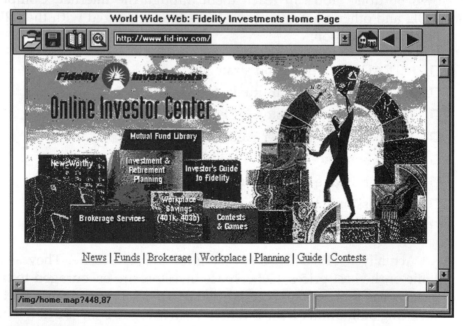

Figure 8.4   Fidelity Investments on the Net.

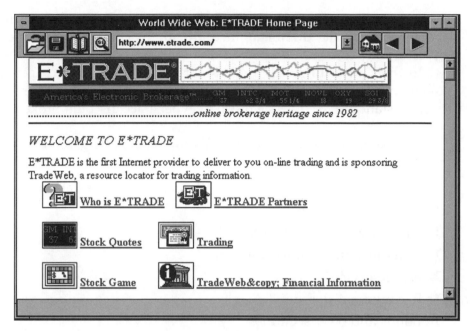

Figure 8.5 E*TRADE online discount brokerage.

And their ad in *Investor's Business Daily* reminds the investor: "You did the research. . . . You did the analysis. . . . You chose the stock. . . . Why did your broker get $346.17? This same trade done through AccuTrade would have saved you $298.17. . . . Start trading smart." Good questions every investor should ask. Smart ads. And that's a major thrust behind the development of the discount brokerage industry as a whole. On today's Wall Street, the investor has, in fact, become very savvy. That's why the discount brokerage business will continue growing.

And AccuTrade does offer a full line of services: unlimited access by modem, discount brokerage, funds with access to over 2,000 funds, no- or low-load funds, and insurance. Plus you can have real-time quotes for a nominal fee on their dial-up service.

WealthWEB: Aufhauser's Winning Website

Aufhauser & Company is another major discount broker that has taken advantage of this rapid trend toward electronic discount trading. *Fortune* and *Smart Money* magazines have already called this Website one of the best in cyberspace. Aufhauser, an SEC registered broker/dealer, calls their

Website, WealthWEB, which is a strong statement of their commitment to the Internet as the dominant medium for reaching the new electronic investors.

In their ads, Aufhauser asserts that this is "how the rich get richer." WealthWEB offers many of the same features that rapidly appear to be the coming standard for the new breed of cyberspace discount brokers:

- ❏ Access through the Web or an 800 number
- ❏ Round-the-clock trading
- ❏ Continuously updated quotes with major securities database
- ❏ Buy, sell, replace orders
- ❏ Automatic electronic confirmation
- ❏ Company and equities research
- ❏ News services
- ❏ Recommended issues
- ❏ Bonds and other securities
- ❏ Cash management

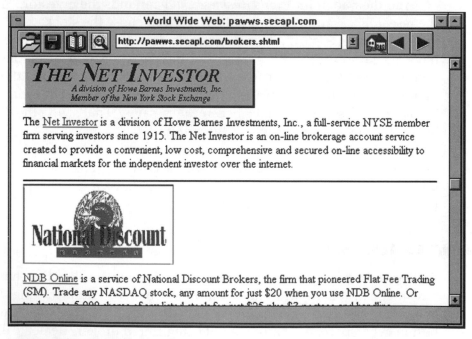

Figure 8.6   PAWWS: Net Investor and NDB Online.

Granted, some of the information on the WealthWEB site is quite naturally promotional; after all, they are brokers. And the data is not as inclusive as you'd get from Knight-Ridder, Reuters, or Dow Jones (for a price). But this Website is a pacesetter, with a lot of valuable free information. Therefore, you are strongly encouraged to check out Aufhauser's Wealth-WEB site, to see the kind of truly first-class efforts beginning to emerge in cyberspace.

Lombard's LIST: Unlike Any Online System You've Seen

LIST is another superquality new breed of electronic brokerage Websites, this one from the San Francisco–based firm of Lombard Institutional Brokerage. This one says it is "unlike any on-line system you've seen. It puts you in direct control. You get in-depth research, plus powerful graphing and analysis tools. Plus, you get real-time quotes and secure on-line trading. LIST is a quantum leap in on-line brokerage services." And it's free. Log on to the Lombard Investment Center and you'll find:

❐ **Trading Center,** all securities and secured transaction orders

❐ **Real-Time Quote Server,** with search procedures for symbols

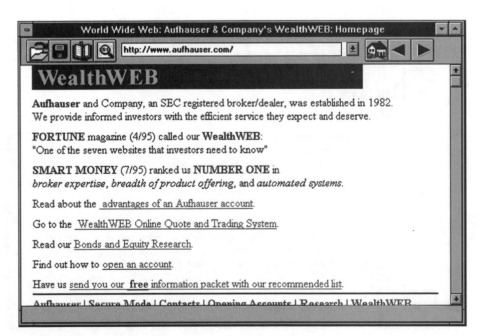

Figure 8.7 Aufhauser's WealthWEB and Web trading.

❑ **Research Tools,** both proprietary and on the Internet
❑ **Real-Time Graph Server,** to follow your favorite stocks
❑ **Portfolio Management,** to monitor trades, holdings, performance

Sure sounds more like a full-service retail brokerage firm, doesn't it! If the LIST sounds too good to be true, well, it's not quite a freebie equivalent to a Telescan and MetaStock combination, but once you try Lombard Investment Center you'll see again the great commitment discount brokerages are making to cyberspace and why you should start looking for new opportunities to help give you the investor's edge.

Lind-Waldock: The Nation's Largest Futures Discounter

Lind-Waldock is the nation's largest discount brokerage firm specializing in commodity futures. With their Lind On-Line service, you don't need any software or installation, just a modem to connect to their online system, *all in real time:*

❑ Fill reports, confirming order in real time
❑ Quotes according to your preset format

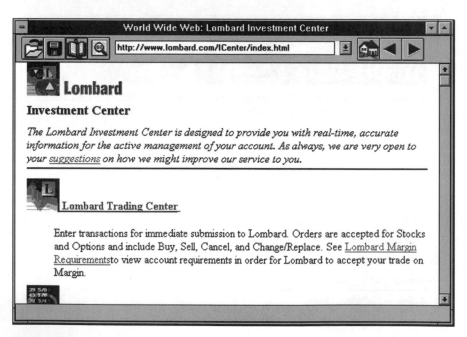

Figure 8.8   Lombard Internet Securities Trading.

❏ Portfolio information: real-time monitoring of order status, positions, balance

❏ Charting and technical analysis program

❏ Market news direct from New York City and Chicago trading floors

❏ Analysts reports and trading strategies

All this information is delivered to you in real time, right there on your monitor's screen, so you can follow along with the action. Of course, you must have a brokerage account with Lind-Waldock, as with most of the brokers. That's their incentive in providing all this free information to the investor. You must come aboard and trade in your account before they can make any commissions. Nevertheless, they're first class, whether you're a full-time futures trader or not, check them out. Discover what one of the leaders in the futures area is doing in cyberspace.

Bottom Line: Will AT&T, Sprint, and MCI Be Your Next Broker?

Electronic discount brokerage is rapidly becoming a fact of life for many of the new sophisticated cyberspace investors and traders. Indeed, for many of the new breed of investors and traders, the brokerage firm is an anachronism, nothing more than a necessary evil, a quick telephone connection on the way to the stock exchange, where the transaction is actually completed electronically.

The actual number of investors, traders, and electronic brokers is rising dramatically according to Forrester Research, a Cambridge, Massachusetts, firm that tracks these statistics. Meanwhile, connections to the World Wide Web are doubling *every four months,* and the expansion of the Microsoft Network will create more and more pressures in this competitive arena.

NO MORE PAPER CERTIFICATES? WHAT WILL BROKERS DO?

An SEC proposal to abolish paper certificates for retail investors is making waves in the brokerage industry. The plan would provide direct access to transfer agents and corporate issuers without the need for intermediaries . . . thereby invading Wall Street's brokerage houses' once exclusive domain.

(SOURCE: Daniel Strachman, "Certificate-less Trading Rocks the Industry," *Wall Street & Technology,* July 1995.)

These trends all add up to an exciting (and potentially dangerous) time for the American brokerage industry. How can a busy investor keep tabs on the volatile drama? One excellent resource is the AAII. Check with them occasionally for statistics comparing the commissions of brokerage firms. The new electronic brokers are becoming more and more prominent in every directory of Wall Street brokerage houses. And fasten your seat belts in front of your monitors. Get ready for the ride of your life . . . because the cyberspace investor is coming up the winner in this competitive scenario.

PORTFOLIO MANAGEMENT AND PERSONAL FINANCE SOFTWARE

Nearly 80 percent of the members of AAII using personal computers have portfolio management software to track their securities. Their popularity stems from the fact that record keeping for securities—costs, values, taxes, commissions, reinvestments, screening new opportunities, etc.—can be an enormously time-consuming job, hence the need to automate.

Many of today's software systems developed for portfolio management and personal finance are being bundled in with other investment

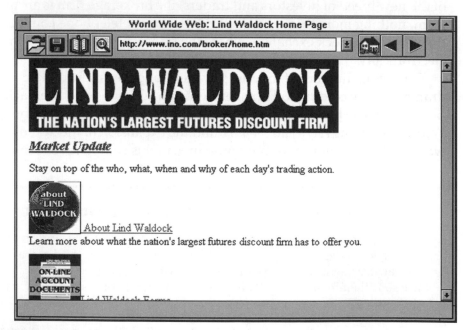

Figure 8.9   Lind-Waldock: discount futures brokerage.

software to create a total package for an investor. This may include other integrated programs for fundamental and technical analyses, securities screening, and trade execution.

Telescan's recommended Cyber-Investing Kit, for example, recommends that the investor buy Charles Schwab's StreetSmart software. In it is included a retirement planning and portfolio management program. In addition, an investor with a modest $10,000 account at Schwab will receive their complimentary FundMap software, another retirement planning and goal-setting program.

CompuServe has two portfolio management programs, Pulse and Quant IX. CompuServe also has two forums with software packages that may be useful, the Investors' Forum and the National Association of Investors Corporation forum. America Online provides portfolio planning systems through the mutual fund forums operated by Vanguard and Fidelity.

Let's look at a few of the more popular software programs aimed specifically at the portfolio management and personal finance market.

Home-Banking Revolution: Big Banks, Quicken, and Competition

First, you should be aware that the *pure* personal finance software market is about 10 million strong. Quicken has about 70 percent of the market with about 7 million users. Microsoft *Money* and the Computer Associates' *Simply Money* each have around a million copies. Each has some portfolio management capabilities. Quicken's lead is likely to increase substantially, as a consortium of major commercial banks and brokerage firms are now using Quicken software for online home-banking services.

Reuters Money Network even designed and markets one of its software packages specifically to work with Quicken, as an alternative to ROL's own WealthBuilders portfolio management/personal finance software. The stand-alone Quicken software costs $40 to $60, and its features include:

❏ Investment tracking module monitors all securities
❏ Portfolio performance graphs, reports, capital gains
❏ Quicken quotes and tradeline historical and current quotes
❏ Budget organization, bill paying, and check writing
❏ Tracks expenditures, bank accounts, and credit cards
❏ Record keeping of all profit/losses, cash flow, and taxes

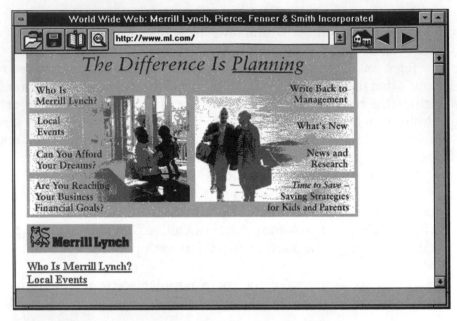

Figure 8.10   Merrill Lynch: the difference is planning.

❏ Retirement goals and planning and budgeting spreadsheets
❏ Customized reports to filter/screen alternatives

Millions of users already know that Quicken is a versatile, easy-to-use, and inexpensive program that works with Reuters Money Network and other investment software. Interested? Any investor can try Quicken for a month with a no-risk, money-back guarantee. Quicken is also working with the banking industry to develop home-banking software, which will put your PC online with your bank, with direct links to your accounts and a teller . . . helping you avoid those long lines in the bank. And their updated version of TurboTax software might just help you avoid the anxieties and pressures of filing taxes.

Home-Banking Competition: Computer Associates and Microsoft

Kiplinger's Simply Money and Microsoft's Money software programs are obviously Quicken's main competition for basic portfolio management and personal finance software, each with well over 1 million copies in use. Kiplinger's easy-to-use software is a powerful tool for the beginner and experienced investor alike. Each is an excellent software package.

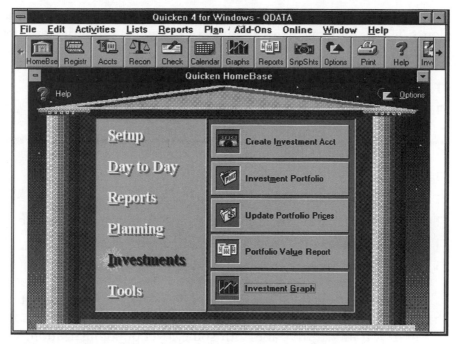

Figure 8.11   Quicken's portfolio management software.

However, as AAII's associate online editor Mark Fister notes in a review of Simply Money, "personal finance software tends to lack the level of power and detail that portfolio management software provides. Simply Money provides a set of features better than most personal finance software, but still not quite as good as the leading portfolio management software." So you'll probably need two separate systems, one for personal finance and one for portfolio management.

With Quicken's new banking connections, they are likely to become the industry standard for personal finance software. Nevertheless, explore the various alternatives for a month trial period before deciding. No matter what you choose, the home-banking revolution is likely to result in new products and services for you in a year or so. Microsoft is developing its own banking team, and Computer Associates will be close behind.

WealthBuilder from Reuters Money Network

Reuters Money Network offers WealthBuilder, which was originally developed by Time Warner's *Money* magazine. Reuters says there are "more than 150,000 success-minded people who are using WealthBuilder's powerful tools to meet their investment goals and gain financial independence." Their system carries an investor through a series of steps designed to achieve this goal:

- ❏ **Savings Strategy:** Resources for cash in/outflow.
- ❏ **TimeLine:** Strategic scenarios based on assets acquired.
- ❏ **Goal Setting:** Translates lifestyle goals into financial terms.
- ❏ **Personal Profile:** Based on risk tolerance and financial goals.
- ❏ **Budget Planning:** Designed to realize your financial goals.
- ❏ **Flexibility:** Ability to change plans to fit contingencies.
- ❏ **Asset Allocation:** Modeling to develop an optimum portfolio.
- ❏ **Portfolio Manager:** Track performance, with alerts.
- ❏ **Reuters Money Network:** Integrated for practical action.

WealthBuilder is excellent for new investors or anyone going through a major transition who needs the discipline of reassessing your financial goals. If you are an investor with some level of sophistication, you may

Figure 8.12   Personal FinanCenter.

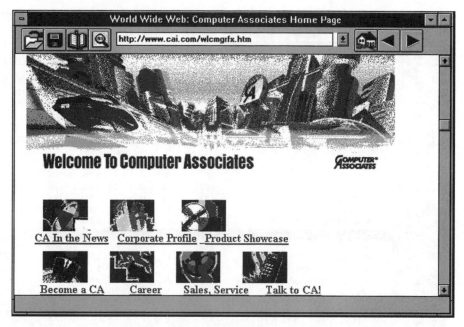

Figure 8.13 C/A's Website: Kiplinger's Simple Money.

have already moved past this planning stage and simply want to get on to the more exciting portfolio management decisions that you'll make with the superpowerful Reuters Money Network. Nevertheless, even an advanced investor will get something of a necessary review out of the WealthBuilder planning process.

TechServe's CAPTOOL: The Professional Choice

TechServe's CAPTOOL software is a sophisticated portfolio management program designed to the demanding specifications of professional money managers and independent financial advisers. TechServe has a wide range of products priced from $30 to $1,000, including software for competition with Quicken and Kiplinger's Simply Money, and superaccounting systems for businesses and multiple-client accounting. The CAPTOOL portfolio management system packs a lot of punch:

❏ Supports all security and transactions types, including stocks, options, munis, annuities, reinvestments, zero coupons, splits, mergers, etc.

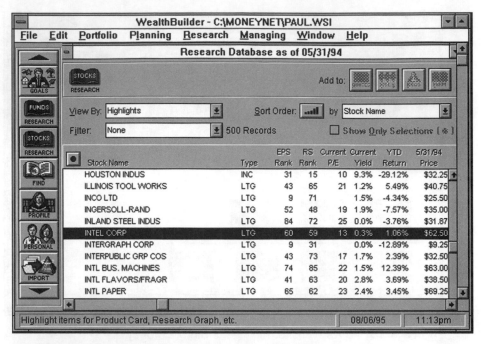

Figure 8.14   WealthBuilder on Reuters Money Network.

☐ Download pricing data from CompuServe, Dial/Data, and other vendors.

☐ Track taxable cost basis and compute estimated taxes.

☐ Fundamental and technical analysis programs.

☐ Evaluate portfolio's securities and returns.

☐ Generate multiple reports with easy-to-understand graphics.

The CAPTOOL portfolio management is a thoroughly professional software package with a user-friendly design. There are over 10,000 users of the CAPTOOL software system. Originally developed for financial advisers and money managers, their individual investor edition is an excellent working tool in conjunction with transactions-based imports from Schwab, Fidelity, and other stock brokers and mutual fund dealers.

Bottom Line on Portfolio Management Software

Cyberspace investors need software programs that work together as a whole system, with maximum efficiency, low cost, minimum hassle, and solid investments controls. Data and news downloading, stock screening, online brokerage, portfolio management, personal finance banking . . . in the best of all worlds, the cyberspace investor has to make it all work together, and the information vendors know this.

The cyberspace institutional investor already has this kind of control with Reuters Instinet, Dow Jones Telerate, Knight-Ridder Profit Center, and The Bloomberg.

PORTFOLIO MANAGEMENT AND PERSONAL FINANCE SOFTWARE

CAPTOOL	Techserve	(800) 826–8082
Fidelity Online Xpress	Fidelity Investments	(800) 544–0246
Managing Your Money	Meca Software, Inc.	(800) 537–9993
Market Manager	Dow Jones News/Retrieval	(800) 815–5100
MS-Money	Microsoft	(800) 426–9400
Pulse Portfolio Mgt.	Equis International	(800) 882–3040
Quant IX and Pulse	CompuServe	(800) 848–8990
Quicken	Intuit	(800) 964–1040
Kiplinger's Simply Money	Computer Associates	(800) 225–5224
StreetSmart	Charles Schwab	(800) 334–4455
Telescan Portfolio Mgr.	Telescan, Inc.	(800) 324–8246

Now the individual investor market is being served. Quicken, Reuters Money Network, and Quicken's bank consortium are there. Telescan is bundled up with Dial/Data, MetaStock, Schwab, and Quicken. And, lest we forget, CompuServe and Dow Jones News/Retrieval have been providing investors with total packages for a couple decades—with Quicken clones.

The online home-banking link is a major part of the information revolution. Personal finance and portfolio management software such as Quicken, Money, Simply Money, and WealthBuilder, coupled with the growing trend toward online discount brokerage, will accelerate the cyberspace investors' ability to compete on an equal footing with the major institutional investors, banks, brokers, and other money managers . . . and do everything right from the privacy of their home.

A Sanwa banker participating in the Quicken home banking consortium predicted that "the change in banking over the next 5 years will surpass the changes over the last 25 years." In other words, the day is rapidly approaching when you as an individual investor will have both total con-

---

FINANCIAL-PLANNING PHOBIA? DR. QUICKEN HAS THE CURE

If you're one of the many people who have lingering phobias about finances and computers, Quicken Financial Planner may relieve you of both these fears. From Intuit, the maker of the popular Quicken home-budgeting program, the Financial Planner provides generous help screens, tutorials from noted financial columnist Jane Bryant Quinn, and colorful charts and graphs to demystify the whole process. And while some programs on the market give only a lump-sum estimate of how much your defined goals are going to cost and how much savings you'll have, Quicken provides a detailed grid showing year-by-year projections of your expected income, cash flow and expenses.

(SOURCE: Amy Dunkin, "Set Yourself Free From Financial-Planning Phobia," *Business Week*, May 29, 1995.)

---

trol of your own bank deposits, and the ability to instantly move your money in and out of trading positions as if you are a member of any exchange, anywhere in the world. And it's coming very soon.

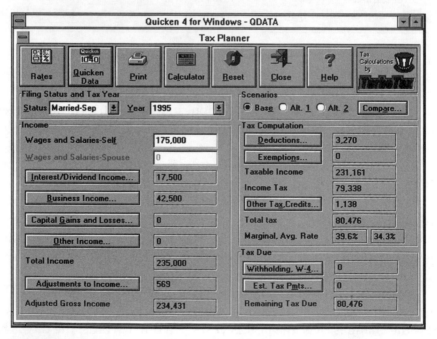

Figure 8.15   Quicken: Tax Planner and Turbo Tax.

CHAPTER 9

Alternative Information Systems for Cyberspace Investors

FINANCIAL TELEVISION AND RADIO BROADCASTING

Most individuals who are into serious investing have a study or a corner of a den set aside for their research, analysis, and trading. It may contain a workstation, computers, monitors, printer, file cabinets, a small library of books, magazines, newsletters, and newpapers . . . and a television set with cable and/or satellite hookups to one or more of the main sources for financial, market, business, and economic news.

A mini war room, you might call it, with television being an interesting combination of two media at once, text-based graphics and also voice-based commentary. In fact, many cyberspace investors just *listen* to their set as they would a radio. Others primarily want to *see* the data.

In addition to the basic data, the sound bites and the headlines, business and financial television programming adds a steady stream of experts analyzing the news and providing summaries of market data.

The real heroes here are the emerging new breed of on-air anchors, reporters, producers, and business television staffers who sift through tons of incoming information for you. These pros check the newswires, interviews, commentaries, market data, securities quotes, and rumors in order to give the investor top-quality information for investment decision mak-

> ## THE EXPANDING IMPORTANCE OF FINANCIAL TELEVISION
>
> In less than 20 years, financial television news has become an important resource for many cyberspace investors. So important that one viewer surprised me recently when he said that he *taped all eight hours of programming on the local financial/business channel every day* so that he'd miss nothing. Moreover, he often replayed segments previously seen, as well as running important segments missed when he was away from the television set. That's one powerful vote for the value of television to cyberspace investors. And there are many others like him.
>
> Similarly, many institutional investors such as large brokerage firms, banks, and trading-room and money managers have television monitors on all the time. They're all looking for that *edge*—some special insight or early warning alerting them to hot news items before they become common knowledge.

ing, in a *timely* manner. Often financial television is one of the *primary* resources for a cyberspace investor.

CNBC: National Television for Cyberspace Investors

The premiere *national* business and financial channel is CNBC, which merged with the Financial News Network in 1991. I have a special affinity for CNBC and their anchors. Back in the early 1980s, before CNBC went on air, I had the good fortune of joining its predecessor, FNN. Today CNBC has over 56 million subscribers on 4,000 cable systems.

Although it seems like such a short time ago, those were the early pioneering days of cable television. The networks were chuckling at Ted Turner's CNN. We glimpsed the new MTV in the employees' lounge on breaks. It was a rough time for FNN to hit the market for an initial public offering (IPO), with the Dow dipping below 750. But the challenge and the pioneering spirit was there. Like others, I left the newspaper business for television news.

The core of most television and radio news programming is a cycle of topics that repeat every hour. CNN developed it well. And CNBC has elevated this format to a sophisticated broadcasting art, as have the regional financial news broadcasters.

The cyberspace investor can rely on this schedule for eight straight hours throughout the trading day. The programming rhythm is almost as important as the content. And for many investors who aren't active day-traders, looking for trends and patterns to gauge moves into and out of the markets, there's the final Market Wrap at the close of the trading day, summarizing all the relevant news of the day.

In addition, CNBC opens with a half-hour summary of the Asian markets, then features a two-hour *World Business* segment before the trading day opens. Later, they have several hours of business and financial programming after the Market Wrap in the evening. In several more hours of programming, CNBC provides interviews and analysis, talks with corporate heads, commentary by gurus and money managers, tips on managing your portfolio, panels on major trends, and more.

CNBC'S "MONEY WHEEL" (HOURLY FORMAT)

:00 Top New Stories in business and finance
:03 Scoreboards of all major indexes
:04 Wall Street Report from AMEX
:12 Newsmakers and the analysts
:20 Market Watch, indexes in graphic format
:21 Market Insiders
:30 Top News Stories
:33 Scoreboards, timely reporting on indexes
:43 Credit Markets, stocks, global, governments
:50 Market Watch, the indexes
:51 Winners & Losers, movers of the day
:52 Futures/Commodities Analysis
Plus the ticker tape rolls on the screen.

In addition, CNBC offers many other services to the cyberspace investor:

❒ CNBC anchors host seminars and conferences in various cities.

❒ Fax service is available for historical price charts, S&P company and industry reports, Micropal Mutual Fund Charts, and Vickers Insider Trading Reports.

❒ CNBC InSight, a monthly financial newsletter, furnishes in-depth information.

❒ A 900 number is provided for stock quotes and the latest corporate earnings estimates.

Figure 9.1 New CNBC-TV Website: First in talk and business.

❏ And Dan Dorfman contributes news-breaking reports on what's really moving markets.

Recently CNBC took some bold new steps: CNBC-Asia began broadcasting from Hong Kong, and they also created a new CNBC online service, complete with news, quotes, portfolio management, and other investor services. *Smart Money* magazine was right when it called CNBC the leader in financial television.

Today, however, CNBC's position is being challenged. CNN is starting a financial network that could eventually threaten CNBC, and the regionals will be soon moving onto the global Web. Expect some exciting competition in the new world of financial television.

Regional Television: KWHY-TV in Los Angeles

The regional television channels are also a wealth of timely financial and business information for the investor operating from a cyberspace war room. Most notable:

❏ KWHY-TV Channel 22 covers the Los Angeles metropolitan region via cable and broadcast networks.

❏ Chicago's WCIU-TV Channel 26 covers the Midwest with special emphasis of the commodities, futures, and options markets.

EXCHANGES COVERED ON KWHY-TV LOS ANGELES

New York Stock Exchange
American Stock Exchange
NASDAQ Over The Counter
Chicago Board of Trade
Chicago Mercantile Exchange
New York Coffee, Sugar and Cocoa Exchange
New York Cotton Exchange
New York Mercantile Exchange
New York Futures Exchange
Kansas City Board of Trade
New York Commodity Exchange

The format of the Los Angeles station (as well as the Chicago station) is actually quite inventive and informative. With several street-smart and knowledgeable anchors, KWHY-TV interviews almost 100 experts throughout the programming week, including many successful money managers and newsletter publishers. Parenthetically, the newsletters published by all these experts would cost an investor over $20,000 annually . . . while the cyberspace investor watching KWHY is getting it for free.

Moreover, every 15 minutes KWHY-TV displays the major indexes, future prices, most actives, interest rates, bond, currency and commodity prices, technical indicators, and more. And throughout the market day, the ticker tape is rolling across the bottom of the screen, with the NYSE, AMEX, and NASDAQ trades.

Along with the rolling tape at the bottom of the television screen, KWHY has one important feature not on CNBC. Market At-A-Glance includes continual updates of the major indexes: Dow S&P 500, AMEX, NASDAQ, Value Line, CRB, Gold, New York Composite, Utilities, Transports, plus the technical ratios such as the tick, arms, volume, advance/declines, and other benchmarks. All day, every trading day. And the advertisements and infomercials are surprisingly instructive with their free offers and tips. This is the new Wall Street cyberspace at work for the investor.

MARKET EXPERTS INTERVIEWED WEEKLY ON KWHY-TV

StockMarket Cycles, Peter Eliades
High-Tech Growth Forecaster, Robert Morrow
Crawford Perspectives, Arch Crawford
Dow Theory Forecasts, Chuck Carlson
Union Bank of Switzerland, Steve Jury
Foundation for the Study of Cycles, Richard Mogey
Todd Market Timer, Stephen Todd
Commodity Insight, Jerry Welch
Money & Capital Market Monitor, Robert Parks
The Global Market Strategist, Dan Ascani
Fixed-Income Management Group, Robert Craven
Granville Market Letter, Joe Granville
WaveWatch, Elliott Wave Institute, Glenn Neely
American Heritage Fund, Heiko Thieme
The Dines Letter, James Dines
Investors Intelligence, Michael Burke
S&P Industry Reports, Sam Stovall
CycleWatch Newsletter, Walter Bressert
Medical Technology Newsletter, Jim McCamant
Merrill Lynch Options Strategist, Eric Matson
California Technology Stockletter, Michael Murphy
Plus another 50 or more experts every week

The Los Angeles channel is really quite remarkable in its ability to deliver so much varied, high-quality, global as well as national content to investors in California. Their Market Wrap is first class and their daily half-hour Market Buzz in-depth interview and audience call-in segment is a winner. Generally, their editorial content deserves broader exposure ... and the Internet may well be the vehicle as it improves its delivery capabilities in the very near future.

In fact, we would expect that investors will see much more of these regional television stations and their content providers online and on the Internet in the near future. As these stations fully grasp the potential of the cyberspace communication media, and as the technology develops to permit full delivery of television on the Net, they will begin searching for ways to tap into these global audiences with the incredible databases at their disposal.

Figure 9.2 PBS's Nightly Business Report.

Television Networks Moving into Cyberspace

In addition to the high-quality programming coming through the cyberspace broadcast, satellite, and cable channels, investors can also tap into information about several resources through the online services:

❑ **Nightly Business Report** has several features on America Online.

❑ **National Public Radio** transcripts are available through the Lexis-Nexis and Dialog databases.

❑ **CNN Online** is a CompuServe feature. You can search for and order transcripts, check out upcoming programming, participate in discussion forums about hot news, and attend CNN-sponsored online conferences featuring global newsmakers, market experts, and CNN staffers.

❑ **ABC News** is also on America Online; however, at present ABC News primary coverage is general news, with limited business coverage.

❑ **CBS** also has a new Website, but little news, investment or otherwise—only programming schedules that you might find in a TV guide or your newspaper.

❏ **NBC** has a special news-on-demand video service without anchors. Their clients, mainly institutional investors, get full news coverage of critical events not otherwise available; for example, Fed chairman testimony and security analysts presentations. Think of it as a financially oriented C-Span, direct into your computer, although at three grand a month it's probably a bit too pricey for the average investor.

There are some important resources for financial and investment information here. Hopefully many of them will eventually reach out for more exposure in cyberspace, whether online or on the Internet. At present, however, the major networks have not adapted to this new media as well as the print publishers. Apparently they already have too much competition from the cable industry, and thus may be missing some important cyberspace opportunities.

Radio Also Delivers Investment News

In general, radio is of lesser importance as an investor *news* broadcasting vehicle. For example, a local channel such as the Money Channel in Riverside is available to Los Angeles residents in a limited area, but it has seri-

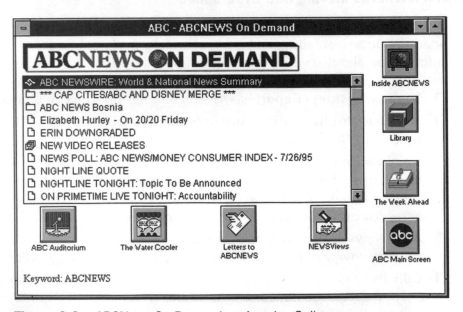

Figure 9.3   ABCNews On Demand on America Online.

ous competition from KWHY-TV with its much larger base of content providers. One exception, of course, is the Bloomberg Business News, which is now expanding in the New York metropolitan area while also providing some of its programming internationally. Dow Jones considers Bloomberg a serious enough threat that it is now tooling up its own station.

Radio's primary role for the cyberspace investor is in the transmission and delivery of text-based market information, as we have also seen. Data Broadcasting Company's Signal and QuoTrek systems, Telemet America, and others have used FM radio delivery systems for decades.

Bottom Line: Local Television Going Worldwide

Many investors rely quite heavily on television for a major part of their business and financial information. For them, television reporting has become an integral part of their cyberspace informational network:

❐ *Quotes.* Television taps into the major exchanges, reporting index and securities quotes on a 15-minute delay throughout the trading day.

❐ *News.* Television is linked into the major business and financial newswires—Reuters, Knight-Ridder, Dow Jones, and Bloomberg— with breaking news stories.

❐ *Analysis.* Through interviews, panels, and forums, television presents the views of experts from many camps, fundamental and technical, monetary and economic, bulls and bears, money managers, authors, advisers, academics, and government officials.

CNBC is a definite leader here, with KWHY-TV a solid regional contender in California and station WCIU in the Midwest. CNBC especially is showing signs of becoming a true cyberspace information provider, with an Asian branch as well as the use of other delivery systems, such as their new online service, 900 numbers, and fax delivery of information, in addition to newsletters, seminars, and conferences. In the near term—as the information revolution kicks into high gear in the next few years— investors can expect some exciting new developments from television stations as they deliver business and financial information.

Bottom line: Both CNBC-TV and KWHY-TV have become content providers for the new Microsoft Network, looking ahead a couple years to new technologies that will permit audio and video transmission on the World Wide Web, while also offering a service that is unique to the new media.

When television can be broadcast on the Web, so-called local channels will be as easily picked up in Singapore and Zurich as in Los Angeles and Chicago, without the need for satellites and affiliates, making them not only national but global broadcasters. In addition to challenging CNBC's dominant national position, this trend could be a boon to cyberspace investors throughout the world, providing a wealth of new financial information resources to a huge global audience.

BULLETIN BOARD SYSTEMS FOR INVESTORS

Bulletin board systems (BBSs) are no more than local dial-up versions of their bigger cousins, America Online, Prodigy, Netcom, EarthLink, and others. Although there are 22 million users and almost 100,000 BBSs according to the industry's leading magazine, *BoardWatch*, many BBSs are the cyberspace equivalent of your neighborhood singles bar, personals columns, and adult entertainment stores.

What's available for the cyberspace investor?

The prestigious American Association of Individual Investors recently listed a mere 22 BBSs in America with financial and business as their focus, down from about 60 not too many years ago. There's a list of the other financial BBSs in the appendix of AAII's *Guide to Computerized Investing*. Apparently BBSs have limited use for investors, mainly because of all the other alternatives in cyberspace.

Bulletin board systems were knocked off course by the sudden popularity of the Internet's Wide World Web, as were the commercial online service companies. The Web's easy and inexpensive access and its interactive and colorful graphic format make it superior to the older, text-based systems used by the bulletin board systems. BBSs will continue as local chat groups, and as a way for corporations to provide customer support. But when it comes to financial services, the BBS may be phasing out as a major player in cyberspace.

The following two BBSs illustrate the dramatic changes occurring in cyberspace. The AAII was a pioneer in this exploration, creating its BBS way back in 1983. In 1994 they also joined the America Online service as one of their local forums. However, in 1995 AAII phased out their 12-year experiment with the BBS in favor of a new Web site to arrive in 1996. The other BBS we'll examine is the Free Financial Network (FFN) in the New York City area, another pioneer.

In many ways, the different strategies AAII and FFN have employed in cyberspace offer strong clues as to why and how the Internet's Web could eventually replace investor-focused BBSs altogether . . . or, if they adapt quickly, give them a whole new lease on life.

American Association of Individual Investors

Every individual investor will eventually be led to the American Association of Individual Investors (AAII). The investment needs, resources, and strategies of the *individual* investor are different from the *institutional* investor. And this nonprofit organization, the AAII, is certainly one of the top support systems a cyberspace investor will ever find, with almost everything you need for investing your own portfolio.

SELECTED LIST OF AAII SERVICES THROUGH AOL

❏ **Books, newsletters, and reports.** Including basic references, portfolio strategies, and home study courses, and the more esoteric topics for the advanced investor.

❏ **Software for investors.** AAII has one of the most complete research databases on available software for investors. Systematic and complete comparisons of all database vendors as well as analytic software.

❏ **Seminars and conferences.** Over 50 sponsored each year.

❏ **Local chapter support.** Over 60 active chapters in major cities.

❏ **Directory of other BBSs.** List of 20 other BBS for investors.

❏ **Quotes.** Members get quotes through a dial-in service.

❏ **Discounts.** Member discounts on software purchases and books.

❏ **Credit card.** You can even get a no-annual-fee credit card.

Bottom line: An AAII membership is a must for the individual investor, and reasonable at $49 per year. Be especially sure to order their *Guide to Computerized Investing* for your library. And keep your eyes on cyberspace—AAII will be on the Web soon with a killer app Website. Thank God, because the AOL online location is too restricting for such an important resource as this. AAII should be available to investors anytime, anywhere in cyberspace!

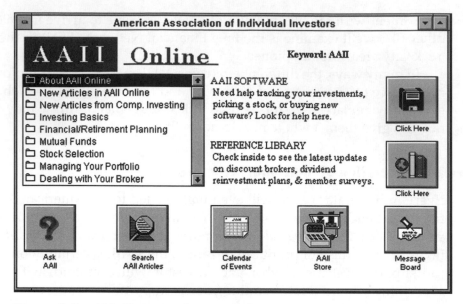

Figure 9.4 AAII discussion forum on AOL.

FinComm and the Free Financial Network

The Free Financial Network bulletin board bills itself as "the world's largest financial BBS." FFN went online in 1987, the year of the Crash. It's an impressive operation. Granted, it is not totally "free." But it does offer some excellent free services. You pay for dial-up phone connections for many services.

INVESTOR'S SERVICES ON THE FREE FINANCIAL NETWORK BBS

- ❐ ProQuote. Plug in the symbol for your favorite stocks or index.
- ❐ Market news and financial wrap-ups.
- ❐ Reports on mutual funds, high-tech industries, and other sectors.
- ❐ Most actives: Advance/Decline, etc.
- ❐ Electronic mail and online time.
- ❐ Investment forums and database libraries.
- ❐ Computer software from major software vendors such as MetaStock. You can even download demos of many popular brands.
- ❐ Newsletters, including the Wall Street Software Digest.

You definitely need to check out the Free Financial Network to see what it offers. It may well serve your needs, especially if you live in the New York City metro area, where it's physically located. And please compare its services to the many others now available to you in cyberspace.

FFN and its partner, FinComm, have so much to offer the investor. However, its traditional BBS format may be too limiting for today's highly competitive environment. Here are some examples of the major drawbacks of many BBSs:

☐ *Text-based BBS.* Back in 1987 (which today must be seen as the dinosaur age in cyberspace development) the content offered by FFN seemed fresh and exciting. However, today, with the power of the Internet's Web graphics, FFN seems more like a stodgy, historic relic. The system is frustratingly slow, locked into a dull, unfriendly, non-windows format.

☐ *Long-distance charges.* Except for a New York City residence, you are probably in for an expensive long-distance call to access FFN, which certainly makes it anything but a free service compared to the much lower costs of an Internet connection with local access numbers.

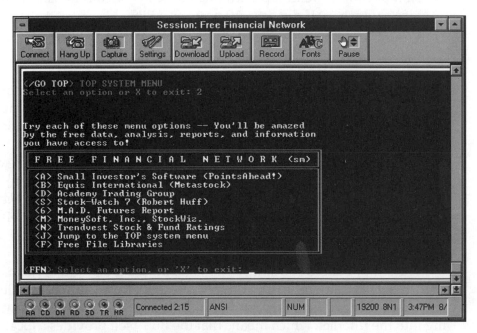

Figure 9.5 FFN: the Free Financial Network BBS.

❏ *Internet competition.* FFN (no more than Microsoft) could not have guessed the rapid growth of the Internet's World Wide Web since mid-1994. Today's Internet Web now offers so many free financial services that FFN's free services may no longer be truly free or competitive.

All this is forcing the Free Financial Network and its BBS competitors to take drastic steps in order to compete effectively in cyberspace. The decline in the number of investor BBSs noted by AAII attests that this may be a losing battle, which is unfortunate.

The BBS of the Future: Strategic Demands and Alternatives

The "world's largest financial BBS" (and for that matter the entire BBS industry) is being forced to redefine its strategic role in cyberspace. Here are some strategic alternatives being considered by financial BBSs such as FFN to meet the competition:

❏ *New interfaces.* Offer an Internet Web-style graphics browser (and fortunately many BBSs are now providing Internet access).

❏ *Joint ventures.* Team up with one of the major commercial online services, which AAII did after 10 years as a BBS.

❏ *Website creations.* Create their own Website, similar to AAII's next move, a strategic detooling.

Without major changes, financial BBSs like FFN are likely to remain, at best, an interesting local BBS . . . with a declining audience that's out having fun surfing around the Web—on another server—looking for more exciting, free information!

Bottom line: AAII and FFN are taking quite different paths in the drama unfolding in cyberspace. Expect major changes in the near future as the BBSs adjust to conditions . . . as the *Internet is suddenly shrinking the entire globe into one single, powerful "bulletin board"*—the Wide World Web—that is accessible through easy-to-use graphical interfaces and local access numbers.

The savvy editors of *Boardwatch* magazine see their industry expanding with new BBSs, more services, more subscribers, and more profits. The main reasons for this redefinition of BBSs is that in fact they are now hooking into the Internet, which means that the BBS itself provides a local access connection (at local access prices), graphical displays, and personalized

Figure 9.6   *Boardwatch* magazine's Website.

service, overcoming many of the earlier drawbacks. So the Internet may, in the near future, reverse the decline in the number of financial services BBSs . . . and the Web, rather than destroying the BBS, may, paradoxically, be their savior.

Creating a Marketing and Tech-Support BBS for Your Business

In his book, *Creating Successful Bulletin Board Systems*, Alan Bryant describes three basic types of BBSs—hobbyist, entrepreneurial, and business BBSs.

The Free Financial Network is an entrepreneurial board, a for-profit operation providing dial-up services for a per-unit fee. The AAII BBS is more like a business board. It is a support system for the 175,000 members of the association, providing them with news articles, software reviews, product data and comparisons, technical support, marketing for books and periodical subscriptions, forums, schedule of seminars, and other services.

Although the financial-services/entrepreneurial BBS is being replaced by the larger commercial online services and the Internet, a cyberspace investor may still want to get his or her business organization online some-

---

KEY BOOKS ON BULLETIN BOARD SYSTEMS (BBS)

❑ *Bulletin Board Systems for Business,* Lamont Wood, John Wiley & Sons, 1992
❑ *BBS Secrets,* Ray Werner, IDG Books, 1995
❑ *Creating Successful Bulletin Board Systems,* Alan Bryant, Addison-Wesley, 1994
❑ *How to Successfully Run a BBS for Profit,* S. Carol Allen and Cary Harwin, Aaron-Stone, 1993

Leading BBS Software Developers and Suppliers

PCBoard, Clark Development	(800) 356–1686
Major BBS, Galacticomm	(800) 328–1128
MindWire, Durand	(805) 961–8700
TBBS, eSoft	(303) 699–6565
Wildcat! Mustang Software	(800) 999–9619

---

how, as a specialized mini-CompuServe. If so, it may well be more cost-effective to maintain a BBS on a low-cost 386 coprocessor in your own home or office than to maintain a high-end Website. For business support, tech services, and sales, the BBS may be just the right solution, so don't ignore it in spite of the trend suggested by FFN and AAII. Under the right circumstances, the BBS is definitely an alternative to a Website.

If you are interested in creating your own BBS, Galacticomm has some excellent new Windows software worth examining. Call and ask about their Worldgroup package. Other competitors such as Mustang, TBBS, and PCBoard are frequent advertisers in industry magazines such as *Board-watch* and *BBS,* both excellent monthlies.

If you are a business owner interested in having your own BBS, but without the headaches of owning and maintaining it yourself, try one of the service bureaus. For a fee, they will provide all the hardware, software, and technical support necessary. One service bureau is the Business BBS in Los Angeles. You'll find others periodically listed in *Boardwatch, BBS,* and other industry magazines.

Bottom Line: Federal Policies Are Commercializing BBSs

We have already seen another example of this trend on the Internet, with the U.S. Department of Commerce's Economic Bulletin Board (EBB). For years federal government statistics were available on their dial-up EBB

Figure 9.7   Galacticomm's Website.

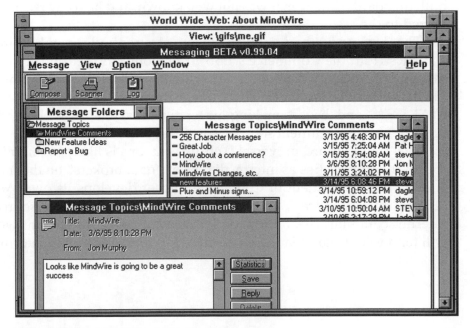

Figure 9.8   MindWire on Durand's Website.

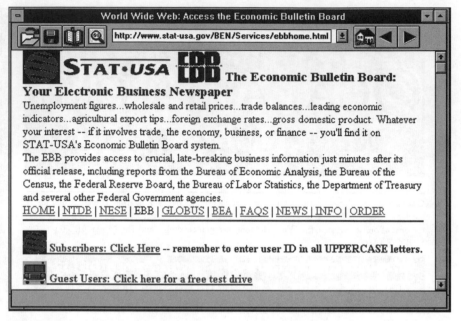

Figure 9.9   STAT-USA: federal government statistics.

bulletin board. However, it was not well known, and has only recently connected to the Web.

The University of Michigan began electronically republishing the statistics from the Commerce's EBB in text-only format on the Internet. Michigan was funded by grants from the National Science Foundation. Then, in 1995 the Commerce Department created its own Internet Website, STAT-USA, and began making its statistics available without delays directly from government sources, some free and some for a fee.

This trend toward universal Website creations is likely to diminish the role of the universities as intermediaries or "data brokers" on the Internet. And as the Department of Commerce further develops its own Website, offering more services and timely statistics direct from the source, the Internet community—and especially the Wall Street investment world—will tend to rely more on these resources for *timely*, first-hand information.

CHAPTER 10

Other Resources for Investors

This book is a combination of several themes and many resources. It is a cyberspace road map for investors, a set of yellow pages to the Internet, a meta-list for the World Wide Web, and a bibliography for a new era of electronic investing—a synthesis of the revolutionary forces creating cyberspace Wall Street.

In this chapter we'll complete our network description by pointing you to several other important resources that should be helpful for cyberspace investing. These will be covered under the following six general headings, with references:

1. **The New Mental Game: Cyberspace Psychological Coaching**
2. **The Winning Edge: Investment Games and Simulations**
3. **Marketing Yourself: Successful Selling in Cyberspace**
4. **Transactions: E-Cash, Firewalls, Hackers, and Scams**
5. **Cyberspace Dictionaries of Investment Terms**
6. **Catalogs, Books, Periodicals, and Software**

Many of these topics are covered in more detail elsewhere. You are encouraged to follow up on resources—both print publications and Websites—cited in this book.

THE NEW MENTAL GAME: CYBERSPACE PSYCHOLOGICAL COACHING

Investment decisions are tough to make for many investors because the decision brings up a lot of feelings regarding ego and personal self-worth.

Futures magazine ran a cover story called "Mind Games" a couple years ago. The lead-in to this excellent article says, "Many traders are turning to psychological 'coaches,' eager to find an edge on the unknown they can control—their own behavior."

FIVE PSYCHOLOGICAL BELIEFS OF SUCCESSFUL TRADERS

1. Trading is a game.
2. They've won the game before they start.
3. Money is *not* important.
4. It is okay to lose in the markets.
5. Mental rehearsal is important for success.

(SOURCE: Van Tharp, "The Psychology of Trading," in *Market Wizards*, Jack Schwager, HarperBusiness, 1993.)

In addition, *Futures* noted that one major portfolio manager, Bruce Frasier of Pring Turner Capital Management Group, was convinced that mental state is everything in today's trading environment, "I used to say trading was 80% technical analysis and 20% mental. Today I say it's 80% mental. . . . Biases in trading relate back to biases in our personal lives. For example, taking a loss is tied to self-worth."

As the investment world becomes more and more global, immediate, and round-the-clock, and as the availability of data and sophisticated analytic software becomes equally universal, this trend will increase. As the playing field is leveled by the new technologies—and it surely will be—the *mental game will become the whole game*. In the future, the investor's state of mind will be the key to the winner's edge, the difference between success and failure.

There are no computerized psychology programs, tests, or Websites for investors yet, but there are several books you can read on the subject. There are also several specialists noted in *Futures* magazine who are familiar with coaching investors and traders on how to control their behavior and create the right mental state for successful trading.

Many traders and investors try to avoid facing the possibility that their emotions (or mental state) may cause poor performance: for example, hesitating when they should "pull the trigger" and buy, or hanging on to a losing trade too long instead of cutting their losses. But like it or not, your emotions run the show. Suppressing them never works for long.

Every investor and trader should become familiar with the resources in this field. If your performance falls off, you might want to read one of the books, see one of the coaches, or take one of their courses. The best athletes and musicians need coaches to help maintain the winner's edge, and so do investors and traders.

THE WINNING EDGE: INVESTMENT GAMES AND SIMULATIONS

In spite of the label, investment *games*, these contests or simulations are often anything but games to the players. Whether it's Monopoly or an investment game, most players take it very serious. Nobody, let alone an investor, really wants to be a loser. It's an "ego thing."

Aside from the emotional issues, there's also a very important educational factor here. This is a great way to develop trading skills, without risking a quarter-million-dollar portfolio. And there are many opportunities to play with a larger portfolio than you already have, or are willing to risk. If you're interested, here's how you can test your trading wings:

❐ **E*TRADE Internet Stock Market Game.** Here's a free one on the Internet. Log on to their Website and register. E*TRADE is so generous, they're going to bankroll you with $100,000 in a trading account every month (in a hypothetical account, of course). The top ten winners are posted daily, using your stage name. And the rest get anonymity, thank

---

BOOKS ON THE MENTAL STATE OF CYBERSPACE INVESTORS

❐ *The Disciplined Trader, Developing Winning Attitudes*, Mark Douglas, New York Institute of Finance, 1990.
❐ *The Inner Game of Trading*, Howard Abell and Bob Koppel, Probus, 1994.
❐ *Investment Psychology Explained*, Martin Pring, John Wiley, 1993.
❐ *The New Market Wizards*, Jack Schwager, HarperBusiness, 1994.
❐ Books sales: Investment News Online, http://www.ino.com

God. There are two games, one called "The Stock Game" and the other is "Stocks & Options." Pick your weapons.

Play by E*TRADE's rules and you'll learn something, even if it's just not to make the same mistake twice. You may even win one of their cash prizes. In fact, these E*TRADE games are serious business, run by one of the best electronic discount brokers. This is a great service to the investment community, and they deserve a round of applause. You can also play with E*TRADE on AOL and CompuServe.

❐ **PAWWS Portfolio Management Challenge.**   Security APL, the backers of the PAWWS Website, are one-upping E*TRADE. They'll give you $200,000 of funny money to play games with them. Kidding aside, here's another opportunity to create and trade a hypothetical portfolio in a contest pitting you against anyone in the known Internet world. There are prizes for the top ten, and you'll get posted for everyone to see if you're in the top rankings. That should be an incentive to play seriously.

❐ **StockNet.** Here's an interesting competitive alternative for the cyberspace investor. The students of the National University of Singapore have created and manage a dead-serious stock market game for

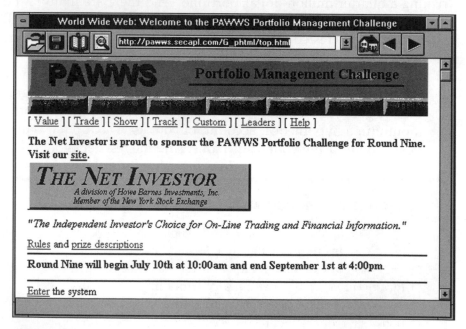

Figure 10.1   Portfolio Management Challenge from PAWWS.

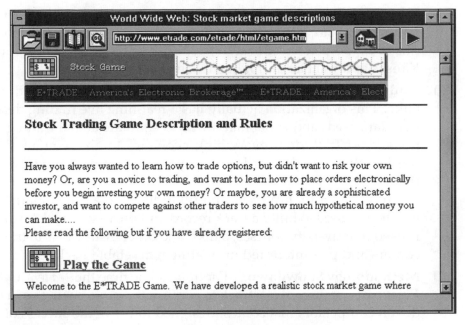

Figure 10.2   E*TRADE's stock game: $100,000 stake.

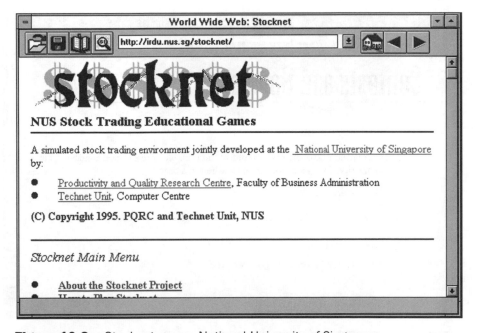

Figure 10.3   Stocknet game: National University of Singapore.

educational purposes. If you're willing to play during the trading hours of the Stock Exchange of Singapore, using "live" data from SES, this may be perfect education, especially if you're an insomniac in Kansas and want an all-night challenge and education.

❑ **AudiTrack.**   This one's for professionals and tough-minded novices alike. This organization actually has a real-time live trading desk with live data feeds and brokerage firms to simulate actual trading conditions. AudiTrack does everything necessary to give you an objective third-party verified record of how you are trading a model or hypothetical portfolio.

You'll get actual callbacks on fill orders and all the monthly statements you need to build a track record and prove it's "real." AudiTrack is used in university courses, banks, and other institutions to train newcomers and pros interested in creating marketable track records.

❑ **Methodology Showdown.**   For quite some time the *Traders' Catalog & Resource Guide* used AudiTrack to confirm the performances of a couple dozen competitors in a contest designed to prove the success of different methodologies used in trading in identical market conditions.

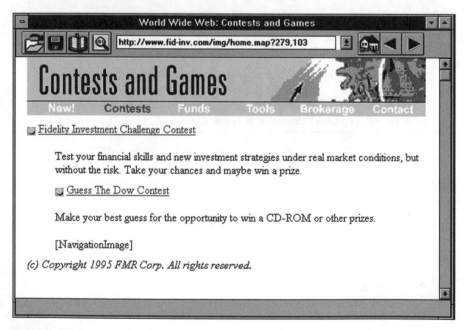

Figure 10.4   Fidelity's Contests and Games.

Market timers use Gann theory, Elliott Wave, Candlesticks, McClellan Oscillator, Fibonacci Ratios, Cycles Research, and so forth. One of the top players attracted enough press as a result of this contest that he was asked to manage an offshore portfolio. What's missing in this contest? The buy-and-hold investors, the Peter Lynches and the Warren Buffetts, successful fundamentalists who dismiss the technicians and scoff at market timing as darn near impossible.

Of course you can always set up a hypothetical portfolio in Quicken, AOL, or MetaStock. And there are other market games and simulations available at Egghead and CompUSA discount software centers, and more are likely to come online and on the Internet as marketing gimmicks. Look around; these alternatives are available now if you're shy of capital but ready to play the Wall Street game, convinced you've got the winner's edge.

MARKETING YOURSELF: SUCCESSFUL SELLING IN CYBERSPACE

Everybody's getting into the act; why not your organization? *So why not you!* You can set up your own basic Website up for less than a $500 initial outlay and perhaps $50 a month to the server to stay on their files. Maintenance just depends on the amount of time you want to spend. If you keep it simple and shop around a little, you can get it cheaper. And if you do it yourself . . . well, we did one for a total cash outlay of $195 to the Internet provider and about $70 for the software from Brooklyn North Software located in Nova Scotia. It's a great editor. Today, Netscape and Microsoft will practically give the software to you.

Sure, if you're a big corporation and you have to impress the shareholders, you'll dump $25,000 to $50,000 on design, staff, and equipment. Double that to start up, and annual expenditures of at least that much are not uncommon. But it's not necessary for a basic do-it-yourself site. As with many new ventures, huge sums are being wasted exploring this new territory.

ActivMedia, an Internet media and market research company, conducted a survey of 1,600 Internet sites in 1995. About 40 percent responded. And although the mean age of the respondent sites was only seven months, 21 percent reported sales in excess of $10,000 and 3 percent reported more than $100,000 from the Internet. When you consider that the

World Wide Web was virtually unknown until the middle of 1994, these are truly amazing figures.

SEARCH FOR NEW FINANCING ON THE WEB

Do you need financing for your expansion? One Internet expert chose the WebCrawler, Yahoo, and InfoSeek search engines to search for information on venture capital resources. WebCrawler came up with a list of 223, and the list was neatly alphabetized. Yahoo's list returned organized into categories to help you manage your search. According to the author, the InfoSeek search was shorter and more focused. "InfoSeek also offers a commercial version that will search and retrieve articles from a growing list of databases."

(SOURCE: Michael Robin, "Surfing for Financing on the Web," *MicroTimes*, July 24, 1995.)

In fact, there are a lot of advantages to doing business or publishing on the Internet. For example, try sending out a print mailing of 200 newsletters. The direct cost is 50 cents per unit: a total of $100 for postage, printing, and stuffing. Compare that to an E-mailing we did to a list of 3,500 subscribers, where E-mailing was *included* as part of your Internet provider's basic $17.50 monthly charge. Unit costs dropped by a factor of 100, from $.50 per letter to about $.005 per E-mail message. Plus no printing costs, no postage, minimum production time, and instant delivery. The economics are mind-boggling.

If you decide to advertise on someone else's Webpage, be wary of their claims of Web traffic "hitting" their site as a justification to charge you a large monthly fee to be on their "super-cybermall" or whatever they choose to call it. The *Wall Street Journal* reported that the number of hits by one-time newbies and other Websurfers may be 5 to 25 times as many as the number of repeat or frequent users.

Fortunately, there are several rating agencies that are now emerging to keep the Websites honest. Neilsen, of TV-ratings fame, a subsidiary of Dun & Bradstreet, has been investigating the field, while a number of savvy Internet start-up companies are already testing systems to rank popularity independently. New names such as Internet Profiles, WebTrack, and Digital Planet NetCount are leading competitors, and likely joint venture partners of larger firms like Neilsen. In any event, ask for some independent clarification; otherwise you may be on a site that's mainly a curiosity to col-

ALTERNATIVES: CREATING A MARKETING PRESENCE ON THE WEB

1. Rent space on a cybermall.
2. Rent Space on an Internet server, but have your "storefront" a separate stand-alone store, not a part of the cybermall.
3. Set up your own Web server, but have it maintained and housed by third-party specialists.
4. Set up your own Web server and have your organization operate and maintain it.

Costs: Options 1 and 2 range from $10 to several hundred dollars monthly. Options 3 and 4 cost $3,000 to $10,000 or more to set up and a few hundred to more than $1,000 a month for monthly staff and maintenance.

HOW TO ADVERTISE YOUR NEW INTERNET WEBSITE

1. Send an announcement to Internet's net-happenings.
2. Announce on topical mailing lists and Usenet newsgroups.
3. Get links on meta-lists and other servers (co-op advertising).
4. Use traditional advertising media with URL and E-mail addresses.

(SOURCE: Vince Gelormine, *Internet Marketing BlackBook,* special book bonus in *Success* magazine; to order call (800) 848–0334.)

lege kids accessing from a freenet. And for marketing research on the Internet, check out Forrester Research in Cambridge, Massachusetts.

A year ago *Forbes* magazine reviewed Internet mania and concluded the excitement reminded them of the California gold rush of the last century. The people who made the real money back then were the railroads, the hotels, and the hookers. The *service* industries were reaping the gold, rather than the prospectors. There's more than a grain of truth in this analogy. As the Internet's Web connections double every four months, it's the

REFERENCES FOR MARKETING ON THE INTERNET

How to Advertise on the Internet, M. Strangelove (SII, 1994)
Internet Advertising FAQs, M. Strangelove (mstrange@fonorola.net)
Internet Marketing BlackBook, V. Gelormine (Success, 1995)
Launching a Business on the Web, Cook & Sellers (Que, 1995)
Marketing on the Internet, Ellsworth (John Wiley & Sons, 1995)

Netscapes, Netcoms, America Onlines, and CompuServes that are expanding. Like the railroads of the nineteenth century, they are carrying dazed Internet gold prospectors to the promised land . . . for a fee.

TRANSACTIONS: E-CASH, FIREWALLS, HACKERS, AND SCAMS

"Doing business in cyberspace sounds like a great deal—low overhead, no real estate, no traffic. But how are you going to get paid? Or pay for what you buy?" *Business Week* was asking the right questions in their Special Report on cyber-money in February 1995. The per-transaction cost of secure systems is currently high. More important, the data is insecure and fraud is a big danger.

The electronic payment issue has often been cited as one of the major reasons the Internet has been slow to expand commercially, holding back the major corporations and banks from moving ahead faster.

And as always, the problem is also the "big opportunity." Microsoft certainly saw the potential upside in electronic banking when they went after Intuit and Quicken. Now Microsoft is developing its own Smart-

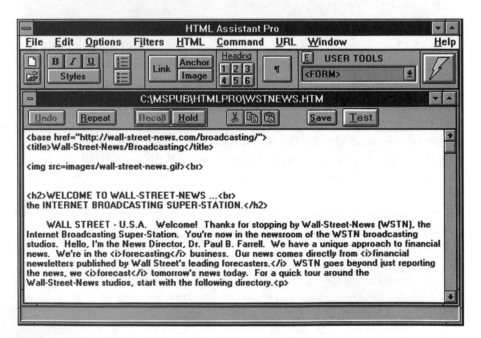

Figure 10.5   HTML Assistant Pro Webpage editor.

Cards, credit cards embedded in a microchip. *Business Week* raised an important point: "This could be bad news for banks. What if the phone companies offered their own brand of E-money?" Well, maybe with credit card interest rates so high the banks need a little healthy competition.

THE FUTURE OF MONEY . . . THE NEW WORLD OF E-CASH

The Opportunities
❏ More convenient and flexible than traditional money
❏ Potentially cheaper than checks with paper records
❏ Greater consumer privacy than traditional credit cards

Some Big Problems
❏ Potential competition, existing banking, and monetary systems
❏ Money stored on a PC hard drive less secure than in a bank
❏ Class distinctions separating those who have no computers

Worst-Case Scenarios
❏ Money laundering and tax evasion through offshore transfers
❏ Counterfeiters creating own personal mints of E-cash
❏ Potential for new criminal hackers to break into E-cash systems

(SOURCE: Adapted from "The Future of Money," *Business Week* cover story, June 12, 1995.)

There are an estimated 4 to 5 million investors online and on the Internet. And virtually every Internet traveler today who connects with the Usenet newsgroups for investors knows that the number of outright ads is increasing. Many newsgroups should now be called "adgroups." And most of these ads sound too good to be true.

For example, *Online Access* magazine reported a Texas State Securities Board investigation where an Austin retiree sent $10,000 to a man who identified himself as a skilled money manager on one of the bulletin boards. And as the number of Webpages increases, we're also seeing more and more stuff bordering on offerings of new investments and investor services. "Hot Tips!" "Unbelievable Returns!" "Once in a Lifetime!" Deals too good to be true. . . . hype. The *Wall Street Journal* offered these tips for avoiding online stock hustlers:

1. Don't use newsgroups, forums, and bulletin boards for stock-buying tips.

2. Beware of headings with big forecasts, exclamation marks, and the word *hot*.

3. Be particularly cautious with low-priced and penny stocks, diamonds, etc.

4. Ask if someone connected with the company wrote it, or if they paid for it.

Many of these "ads" are posted for locations outside the United States, making it more difficult for the SEC to control. So the potential for criminal fraud as well as outright theft of assets is high in cyberspace.

HOW AN INVESTOR CAN AVOID BECOMING A CYBER-SCAM VICTIM

❏ Don't expect to get rich quick . . .
❏ Don't assume your online or Internet service polices bulletin boards . . .
❏ Don't buy thinly traded, little-known stocks strictly from online hype . . .
❏ Don't act on the advice of anybody who hides his or her identity . . .
❏ Don't get suckered into claims of insider information and other hot tips . . .
❏ Don't assume promoters have checked facts just because they say they did . . .
❏ Don't forget to investigate for conflicts of interest . . .
❏ Do confirm that the promoter and the securities are registered . . .

(SOURCE: Adapted from David Noack, "Online Investment Scams," *Online Access*, November 1994.)

Your position as a consumer is also vulnerable to fraud. Fortunately, there are some institutional forces working in favor of the cyberspace investor. For example, the issues of fraud are different for the consumer than for the merchants and the banks. Although investors who give out their bank account numbers may not have the same protection as the credit card buyer who is liable only for a maximum of $50 on a credit card fraud, there is the larger question of fraudulent use of other records. But these issues are common to all of today's computer databases. With records at insurers, telephone companies, the department of motor vehicles, and so on, our privacy is easily invaded today.

FIREWALLS AND THE PROBLEM OF SECURITY ON THE NET

Firewalls are important, as there's always going to be marauders out there on the Net. We wouldn't be connected to the Net without a firewall, because our internal network is so important to our business. We don't want every hacker in the world just wandering around our network.

(SOURCE: Bill Joy, "The Future of the Internet," in *Information Week* magazine's July 1995 cover story. Joy is an Internet pioneer and cofounder of Sun Microsystems.)

The banks and the merchants, however, have more at stake, as do businesses worried about corporate cyber-espionage and cyber-terrorism. These financial giants are exposed to gigantic frauds. They are exposed to massive cyber-theft of customer and cardholder account records and deposits, with little protection. The development of secure systems to protect businesses, banks, and corporations will protect the individual consumer as well.

Where is all this headed? There's so much at stake that you can be absolutely sure the American banking industry, the federal banking regulations, and the U.S. Securities and Exchange Commission will be working to control the flow of money in cyberspace. They've already been controlling electronic financial transactions for decades, and they'll keep control of E-cash too. For example, the SEC and state agencies are creating special divisions to handle cyber-fraud. Legislation is coming. Let's face it, there's already a substantial amount of electronic business going online and on the Internet. We find ways to buy books, pay for online services, or send cash when necessary. Where there's a will there's a way.

Bottom line: Electronic currency, E-money or E-cash, is not a myth—it's already here. And with it commerce on the Internet is exploding exponen-

---

LEADING CONTENDERS IN THE E-MONEY GAME

❑ CyberCash working with Wells Fargo Bank
❑ Microsoft and Visa in a joint venture
❑ Mondex, a British banking venture for E-cash
❑ Netscape, encryptions for MasterCard, B/A, and MCI
❑ DigiCash, a Dutch software start-up

(SOURCE: *Business Week*, February 27, 1995.)

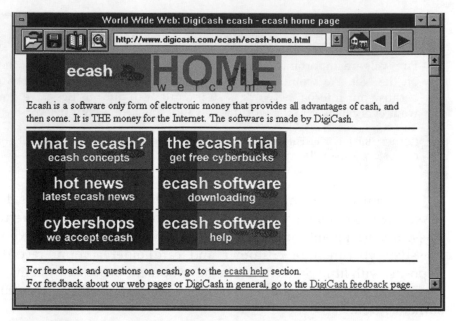

Figure 10.6　Digicash's Website for electronic money.

tially, along with anything to do with business, financing, and investing. As the bugs are worked out, the Internet may well replace shopping malls, banks, and brokerage companies . . . or at least force a restructuring of every business and every organization that has anything to do with money and investing.

CYBERSPACE DICTIONARIES OF INVESTMENT TERMS

One of the more complete dictionaries, or "glossary" as they call it, was prepared by the *Traders' Catalog & Resource Guide,* one of the leading publications for investors and traders. *TC&RGuide* added this dictionary of terms to their Website, The Money Mentor. Another futures-oriented list of terms is on the Chicago Mercantile Exchange Website. The Capital PC Users Group SIG also has a wealth of material that should explain just about anything you don't understand about investments.

For a slant more toward mutual funds, try the NETworth site and its competitors. In addition, the America Online service has some excellent dictionaries of investment terms. The Fidelity Mutual Funds section has an

Figure 10.7 Financial Technology at Wat.ch, Switzerland.

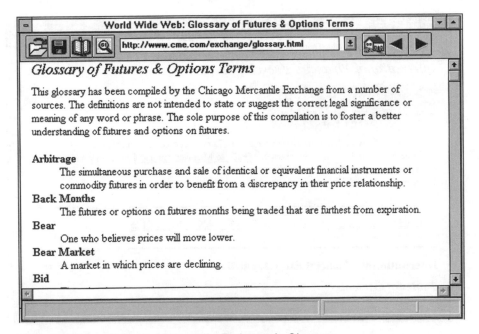

Figure 10.8 Chicago Mercantile Exchange's Glossary.

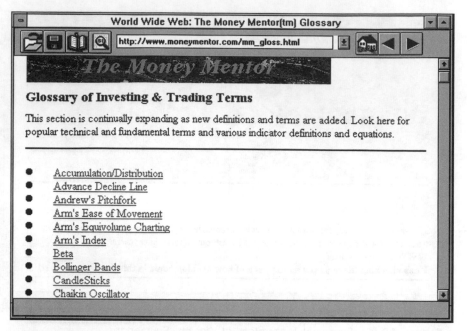

Figure 10.9   The Money Mentor's Glossary of Terms.

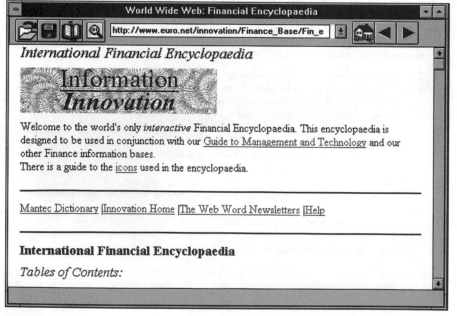

Figure 10.10   Innovation's International Financial Encyclopaedia.

Investment FAQs directory titled Investment Terms and Principles. And Vanguard's Mutual Fund Campus is a whole course on investing and finance.

When it comes to straightforward objective definitions of terms, in detail, with articles and references, go directly to the American Association of Individual Investors' material on AOL and their new Website. AAII's contribution online and in cyberspace is unsurpassed. What they offer is practically a university MBA course in investing. Their new Website should match this super effort and make their materials and experience universally available to investors all over the world. Similarly, a computer user group such as the Capital PC User Group SIG offers a wealth of definitional information on their Website. Visit them regularly.

CATALOGS, BOOKS, PERIODICALS, AND SOFTWARE

If you want to purchase books, newsletters, and software there are some key locations where you can view whole catalogs online, on the Web, and even send for printed catalogs. Almost every major meta-list already mentioned includes a list of available products, services, books, periodicals, and some software. And certain of them deserve one more special note of recognition:

- ❑ American Association of Individual Investors, on AOL and Internet
- ❑ *Futures* magazine; Web location at Investment News Online
- ❑ *Technical Analysis of Stocks & Commodities* magazine and Website
- ❑ InvestSIG Capital PC Users SIG Website for references
- ❑ *Traders' Catalog & Resource Guide*'s Website, Money Mentor

It's unlikely that electronic news publishing and Website catalogs will completely replace the printed word very soon. Someday, perhaps in the next century, we may come close, but not right away. Software is making the transition already, as more and more software is downloaded without disks, or loaded on huge-megabyte CD-ROMs. But in the interim—at least for the next decade—you can expect to continue using printed books and catalogs.

Investing on the Net: Your Key to Financial Independence

Headlines from two major financial magazines grabbed my attention as we were going to press. Together, their message suggests a tense battle coming between the Wall Street's old guard, the Merrill Lynches and Smith Barneys, and a new generation of revolutionaries led by the Charles Schwabs and Leslie Quicks. This battle is destined to transform Wall Street.

> Gravity Pulls Wall Street into the Net. . . . Financial services firms are salivating at the idea of being able to do business over the Internet.
>
> (SOURCE: Dean Tomasula, *Wall Street & Technology*, October 1995.)
>
> Discount Brokers: More Information, Better Technology, Power Surge in Discount Brokerage.
>
> (SOURCE: Willard C. Rappleye Jr., Vice Chairman, *Financial World*, October 10, 1995.)

While the big Wall Street firms are huddled at the starting gate, the discount brokers have been racing around the cyberspace track. Thanks to favorable economic and market conditions, discount brokers have been riding the explosive growth of the Internet for some time.

The success of the discount brokers is now a call to battle, forcing the big institutions to fight back, to prepare a major counteroffensive. Although they're reacting a bit late, this battle is triggering a major revolution in the financial world. On the surface, the contest is between the big institutional investors and the discount brokers—but only on the surface.

The Power Is Shifting from Institutions to Individual Investors

The new rules of the game are not being set by the big Wall Street institutional investors—the investment bankers, brokerage houses, and mutual funds. Nor by the major exchanges. Nor even by the discount brokers. In fact, they're all just *reacting* to larger economic and technological forces.

At one level, the new individual investor is controlling the rules of the game. New technologies and the information revolution are transforming Wall Street. And this paradigm shift is reallocating financial power.

This new world of cyberspace investing is a perfect example of John Naisbitt's prediction that "the new source of power is not money in the hands of a few, but knowledge in the hands of many."

The new technologies are shifting financial power into the "hands of many" . . . to the newly empowered individual investor. More and more, individuals, not institutions, are calling the shots. Why? Because, the individual investor now has the technological firepower to compete on equal terms with the big-time institutional investors.

The Whole Internet Is Your Computer

Recently *Internet World* magazine explored the technological revolution with George Gilder, a well-known cyberspace futurist and author of ten books, including *Telecosm.*

Gilder notes that "a fundamental change is taking place in the computer industry: The functions that were once on your CD-ROM and hard drive are now on the network, and that is an immense transformation. . . . Now *the whole Internet is becoming the computer*," expanding on the long-held conviction of Scott McNealy, founder and CEO of Sun Microsystems, that *"the network is the computer."*

In this new arena, we have a level playing field. The advantage large Wall Street institutions had with their privately held, high-powered technologies is rapidly fading. Individual investors are no longer outgunned, limited by the power of their own personal computer. Today's individual investor has direct access to all the computing power and information everywhere on the Internet.

The Net is your computer.

This is the ultimate in financial leverage and technological synergism—an awesome, empowering reality. And it is this new power in the hands of the individual investor that is creating the revolution and transformation of Wall Street.

The Net Is Your Key to Financial Independence

At another level, cyberspace and the Net have a mind of their own, beyond institutions, beyond individuals. Carl Jung called this invisible force the *collective unconscious,* a higher power wired into both your individual DNA and the intelligence guiding the universe. Some call it God or the Tao. We do know for certain that with every new technological advance anywhere in this vast system, the leading edge is transferring more and more power to the individuals linked to this massive network.

In *Global Paradox,* John Naisbitt quotes a story told by telecommunications leader, Randall L. Tobias, the former vice chairman of AT&T:

> *A theologian asked the most powerful supercomputer, "Is there a God?" The computer said it lacked the processing power to know. It asked to be connected to all the other supercomputers in the world. Still, it was not enough power. So the computer was hooked up to all the mainframes in the world, and then all the minicomputers, and to all the personal computers. And eventually it was connected to all the computers in cars, microwaves, VCRs, digital watches, and so on. The theologian asked for the final time, "Is there a God?" And the computer replied: "There is now!"*

While AT&T has some obvious reasons for seeing divine power in the global telecommunications network, there is an extremely positive message in the combined wisdom of Tobias, Gilder, and McNealy.

Whether your god is economics and technology, or spiritual and transcendent, it is both exhilarating and profoundly reassuring to know that your personal computer can leverage this massive, powerful, global network: the Net. And with that power at your fingertips, you have a perfect opportunity to take control of your destiny.

The Net is your key to financial independence.

Index

AAII:
  and bond market, 240–241
  and electronic trading, 330
  glossary of terms, 373
  Guide to Computerized Investing, 39, 53, 349
  meta-lists, 54–55
  services offered, 349
Accessing large databases, 106–119
Accessing market data, 157–187
AccuTrade, 324–325
Active investor, 31
ActivMedia, 363–364
Advertising:
  in cyberspace, 363–366
  on newsgroups, 152–155
Aliweb, 115
Alternative investment securities, 219–269
America Online:
  and bond market, 240–242
  commodity futures, 259
  investment clubs, 151
  investors' services, 6–8
  mututal fund reports, 227–228
  newsletters, 135–137
  newspapers online, 66, 70–71
  newsstands, 125
  quotes, 181–182
American Association of Individual Investors
  (*see* AAII)
American Stock Exchange, 159
  index options, 252
AMEX (*see* Amercian Stock Exchange)

Analytics:
  government data sources, 189–198
  industry data sources, 198–212
  securities filings, 213–218
AOL (*see* America Online)
Applixware, 307
Architext, 116
Artificial Intelligence Laboratory, 49
  mutual fund reports, 224–225
Aspen Graphics, 302–303
Associated Press (AP) newswires, 95–96, 102–103
Astro-economics, 305
AT&T/Ziff-Davis, 9
AudiTrack, 362
Aufhauser & Company:
  bond directory, 248
  and electronic trading, 325–327
AVCO Financial Corporation, 305

Backup protection, 30
BBS (*see* Bulletin board systems)
Big three commercial online services, 1–9
  (*See also* America Online; CompuServe; Prodigy)
Big three online services' browsers, 34–35
Bloomberg, 21–24
  investors' services, 22–23
  newswire services, 101
Bloomberg Business News, 101
BMI, 282–283
Bond market, 238–248
Bonds:
  professional trader information, 246–248

Bonneville Market Information (*see* BMI)
Bookmarking, 61–62
"Broadcasting superstation" (*see* Wall-Street-News)
Brokers online, 315–338
    cost comparisons, 324
    do-it-yourself, 315–317
Browsers, 32–38
Bryant, Alan, 353
Bulletin board systems, 348–356
    drawbacks of, 351–352
    federal policies regarding, 354–356
    as investment clubs, 147–156
    resources for, 354
Business Cycles Indicators, 195–198

Calvert Group:
    mutual fund reports, 228–229
Candlesticks techniques, 304
CANSLIM formula, 70
Capital PC User Group (*see* CPCUG)
CAPTOOL, 335–336
Carnegie Mellon, 49
Catalogs online, sources for, 373
CD-ROM technology, 287–289
CERN, 116
Charles Schwab (*see* Schwab)
Chat rooms, 147–155
Chicago Board Options Exchange, 161
Chicago Board of Trade, 161
Chicago Mercantile Exchange, 157–159
ClariNet:
    newswire addresses, 210
    newswire services, 102–103
Clipping services and digests, 81–95
CNBC television, 340–342
Commerce Business Daily, 198
Commerce Department:
    BBS policies, 354–356
    Economic Bulletin Board (EBB), 194–195
    economic indicators, 189
Commercial online services, 1–11
    commodity futures, 258–260
    keyword searches, 109–110
    newsgroups, 149–150
    newsstands, 125–126
    quotes, 180–184
Commodity futures, 248–269
Commodity Research Bureau, 263
Company analysis statistics, 198–212
CompuServe, 3–6
    and bond market, 242–243
    and CD-ROM, 288–289
    and commodity futures, 259

ENS, 81
industry analysis statistics, 208–210
mutual fund reports, 226–227
newsletters, 137–138
newspapers online, 66
newsstands, 125
online database, 4
quotes, 182–183
securities exchanges listing, 260
Website, 5
Computer hardware/software for investors, 27–40
ComStock (*see* S&P ComStock)
Conferencing online, 147–156
Cornell Law School, 49
Corporate bonds, 238–248
Costs of cyberspace investing, 29, 260–263
CPUG:
    glossary of terms, 370–373
    meta-lists, 52–53
CRB (*see* Commodity Research Bureau)
Creating Successful Bulletin Board Systems, 353
Currency, electronic, 366–370
CustomClip, 15
Cyber-scams, 366–370
Cyberspace:
    market size, 2
    power players, 11–27
Cyberzines (*see* Zines)

D&B (*see* Dun & Bradstreet)
Data, stock market, 168–187
    (*See also* Data delivery systems)
Data Broadcasting Corporation, 280–282
Data delivery systems, 276–291
    and CD-ROM, 287–289
    cost comparisons of, 276, 290
Data Transmission Network (*see* DTN)
Databases, accessing, 106–119
DataStar, 107–108
Day-trader, 31
DBC (*see* Data Broadcasting Corporation)
Definitions of investment terms, 370–373
Delphi, 9–11
Derivatives, 248–269
Dial/Data, 286
Dialog search tool, 106–108
Dictionaries of investment terms, 370–373
Digests and clipping services, 81–95
Direct dialing, 45, 63
Directories for individual investors, 313
Disclosure:
    Database, 203–204
    and EdgarPlus, 215–216

Discount brokers versus old guard, 375–377
DJN/R:
    financial news, 74–75
    industry sector data, 206–207
    for mutual funds, 229–230, 232–235
    newspapers online, 78–81
    overview, 15–16
    Private Investor Edition, 233
    (*See also* Dow Jones)
Donaldson, Lufkin & Jenrette, 317
Dow Jones, 13–17
    bond reports, 246
    and data delivery, 278–279
    Market Monitor, 15, 74–75
    mutual fund reports, 232
    News/Retrieval (*see* DJN/R)
    newsstands, 126–127
    newswire services, 96–98
    Personal Journal, 71–74
    and securities filings, 216–218
    Telerate, 15
Dow Jones News/Retrieval, 15, 78–81, 232–235
    (*See also* DJN/R; Dow Jones)
DownLoader:
    and data delivery, 296–297
    and data management, 289–291
DowVision, 15
DTN, 283–284
Dun & Bradstreet, 202–203

E-cash, 366–370
E-money, 366–370
E-news, 120–121
E*TRADE:
    online brokerage, 323–324
    online games, 359–360
EBB (*see* Economics Bulletin Board)
Economic indicators:
    government, 189–198
    industry sector, 198–212
    and the SEC, 213–218
Economics Bulletin Board, 191–193, 354–356
EDGAR project:
    meta-lists, 49–50
    mutual fund reports, 225–226
    securities filings, 213–216
Editor & Publisher magazine, 68
EINet, 115
Electronic Data Gathering, Analysis & Retrieval
    project (*see* EDGAR)
Electronic newsstand (*see* E-news)
Electronic trading, 315–338
ENS (*see* Executive news services)

Equis:
    books for investors, 298
    and data delivery, 295–298
    Downloader, 289–291, 296
    MetaStock, 296–298
    Technician, 296
European meta-list, 56–57
Excel spreadsheets, 305–306
Exchanges (*see* Securities exchanges)
Executive news services, 81–95
EXPO, 308

FAQs, 150–152
Farcast news digest service, 88–89
Fax for newsletters, 144–146
Federal filings, 98
Federal policies regarding BBSs, 354–356
FedWorld, 198
FFN, 350–352
Fidelity Investments, 219–220
    and electronic trading, 321–322
    mutual funds, 241–242
    On-line Xpress (*see* FOX)
Filo, David, and Yahoo, 44–46
FinanceNet, 116, 198
Financial news online, 65–156
    executive news services, 81–95
    investment clubs, 147–155
    magazines, 119–133
    newsletters, 133–147
    newspapers, 65–81
    newswires, 95–105
    search tools, 106–119
Financial Times of London, 69–70
FinComm, 350–352
FINWeb, 46–48
    investors' services, 51
Firewalls, 366–370
Fixed-income securities, 238–248
Foreign newswires, 103–105
Forrester Research, 329, 365
Forums, 147–155
Fosback, Norman, 234
FOX, 321–322
Fraud online, 366–370
Free Financial Network (*see* FFN)
Free stuff:
    bond market information, 243–246
    electronic brokerage, 327–329
    FFN BBS, 350–352
    games, 359–360
    market data, 170–176, 179, 184–187
    news online, 89–90, 94, 141–142

Free stuff (*continued*):
  securities filings from EDGAR, 213–215
  software, 291–292
Free Stuff from CompuServe, 4
Freese-Notis, 255–256
Frequently asked questions (*see* FAQs)
FundWatch, 4, 226–227
Future of cyberspace investing, 352–353,
  375–377
FutureLink, 266–267
Futures (*see* Commodity futures)
*Futures Magazine's Annual Guide to Computerized
  Trading*, 39
Futures and Options Trading Group, 254
Futures World News, 267
FutureSource, 265–266

Galacticomm, 354
Games/simulations for investors, 359–363
General Electric, 9
GEnie, 9–11
Gilder, George, 376
Global Network Navigator (GNN), 55–56
Global Research Library, 61
Glossaries of investment terms, 370–373
GNN (*see* Global Network Navigator)
Government statistics, 189–198
Graphical user interfaces (GUIs), 37
Guide to Computerized Investing:
  for futures and options, 261
  for software guidelines, 272

H&R Block, 5
Handbooks, company profile, 200
Hardware for cyberspace investing, 27–30
Heads Up ENS, 82
Holt's Market Reports, 177
Home banking, 331–333
Hoover's Reports, 198–202
Hot Java, 38
Hot Stocks newsletter, 141–142
How to Make Money in Stocks, 70
Hulbert Financial Digest, 146

IDD Information Services, 284–285
IFCI, 251–252
Individual investors versus institutions, 24–27,
  375–377
Industry sector statistics, 198–212
InfoExpress, 86–88
InfoManager:
  data manager, 178–179
  executive news service, 86–88

InfoSeek, 114
I-NO, 161, 167
Instinet, 18
Institute for Econometric Research, 234
Institutional investor:
  defined, 31
Integrated Switched Digital Network (*see* ISDN)
Interchange, 9–11
International Financial and Commodities Insti-
  tute (*see* IFCI)
International newspapers, 67–70
International newswire services, 103–105
International Pacific Candlesticks, 304
International securities exchanges, 161–165,
  167
Internet:
  free news services, 89–90, 94
  impact on Wall Street, 156
  keyword searches, 110–111
  mutual funds Website, 234
  search engines, 112–119
  versus Microsoft Network, 1–3
Internet address directories, 63
Internet Broadcasting Super-Station
  (*see* Wall-Street-News)
InterQuote, 179–180
IntraNets, 27, 156
Investment clubs online, 147–155
Investment News Online (*see* I-NO)
Investment-professional magazines, 129–130
Investment research/analysis, 189–218
Investment securities, alternative, 219–269
Investor's Business Daily, 70–71
InvestSIG, 52–53
ISDN, 287

JAG Notes, 144–145

Keyword searches, 109–111
Kiplinger's Simply Money:
  portfolio management software, 332–333
KISS, 127
Knight-Ridder, 19–21
  commodity futures, 263–265
  investors' services, 20
  Mercury Center, 77–78
  Money Center, 20
  News, 98–100
  newswire services, 98–100
  Profit Center, 264–265
  search tools, 106–108
KRF (see Knight-Ridder)
KWHY-TV, 342–344

Lexis-Nexis:
  newsstands, 126–127
  search tools, 108–109
  and securities filings, 216–217
Library:
  investor's global resource, 41–63
  for cyberspace investing, 39–40
LIFFE, 251–252
Lind-Waldock, 328–329
LIST, 327–328
Lombard, 327–328
London International Financial Futures and
    Options Exchange (*see* LIFFE)
Los Angeles TimesLink, 76–77
Lotus spreadsheets, 305–306
Lycos, 49, 113–114

Magazines in cyberspace, 119–133
  computer/technology-oriented, 129–130
  for professional investors, 128–129
Mail-order newsletters, 144–146
Manhattan Analytics, 304
Market Center, 282–283
Market data, accessing, 157–187
Market data sources, 168–187
Market Monitor, 74–75
Market Wizard, 250
MarketArts, 301–302
Marketing in cyberspace, 363–366
MarketScope news service, 104
McNealy, Scott, 376–377
Media Logic, 195–198
MediaInfo Interactive, 67–68
Merc (*see* Chicago Mercantile Exchange)
Mercury Center, 77–78
Meta-lists, 41–63
  commercial, 52–61
  create your own, 61–62
  and newsletters, 138–141
  university-based, 42–51
MetaStock, 296
Methodology Showdown, 362–363
MicroQuote, 4
Microsoft:
  portfolio management software, 332–333
Microsoft Network, 1–3
MIT, 49
  Artificial Intelligence Laboratory, 170–171
  Experimental Stock Market Data, 170–171
  mutual fund reports, 224–225
Money on the Internet, 366–370
Money Mentor, 57
Moore's law and Internet growth, 46

Morningstar mutual fund reports, 220–223
Morningstar Reports:
  mutual funds and commodities, 258
Motley Fool, 8, 152
Multidatabase newspaper searches, 78–80
Municipal bonds, 238–248
Munis (*see* Municipal bonds)
Murdoch's News Corporation, 9
Mutual Funds, 219–237
  free quotes Website, 176
Mutual Funds magazine, 234

Naisbitt, John, 377
National Science Foundation, 194
National University of Singapore, 360–361
NCSA, 56
Neilsen, 364
Netcom's NetCruiser, 33–34
Netiquette, 152–154
NetMoney, 291
Netscape, 114–115
Netscape's Navigator, 32–33
NETworth:
  free quotes, 176
  mutual fund reports, 223–224
  periodicals, 122
New York Times online, 75–76
New York University, 49–50
  EDGAR project, 213–216
  mutual fund reports, 225–226
News (*see* Financial news online)
News Manager, 178
NewsAgent, 85
NewsFlash, 83–84
Newsgroups:
  cautions, 152–155
  etiquette, 150–152
  as investment clubs, 147–150
Newsletters online, 133–147
  alternative delivery, 144–146
  Schwab, 320
  searching for, 138–141
NewsNet, 82–85
NewsPage, 85
Newspapers online, 65–81
Newsroom, The, 89–90
Newswire services, 95–105
900-number newsletters, 144–146
NSF (*see* National Science Foundation)

Ohio State University, 49–50
  databases, 171–172
Omega Research, 298–300

O'Neil, William, 70
Online brokerage:
   providers, 315–330
   software, 330–338
Online financial news (*see* Financial news online)
Online services:
   numbers of subscribers, 10
   ratings of, 364
Online trading (*see* Online brokerage)
O'Reilly & Associates, 55

Passive investor, 31
Pathfinder, 122–124
PAWWS:
   free quotes, 174–176
   games, 360
PC Quote, 174
PC World:
   rating of online services, 10
PCFN, 317–318
Personal Control Financial Network
   (*see* PCFN)
Personal Journal, 14–15, 71–74
Philadelphia Stock Exchange, 159
Phone numbers:
   astro-economics software, 305
   BBS software, 354
   data-feed companies, 290
   publications, basic, 39
   resource directories, 313
   software developers, 311
   software providers, 337
Portfolio Accounting World Wide (*see* PAWWS)
Portfolio management online, 315–338
   discount brokers, 317–330
   do-it-yourself, 315–317
   software, 330–338
Private Investor Edition (*see* DJN/R)
Prodigy, 7–9
   ENS, 82
   Investment Center, 9
   investment clubs, 151
   newsletters, 134–135
   newspapers online, 66
   newsstands, 125
   quotes, 183–184
Professional bond trader information, 246–248
Professional investor magazines, 129–130
Profound search system, 85–86
ProSearch, 117–118
Psychology of investing, 357–359

Quantitative analysis (*see* Quants)
Quants, 307–311
QuattroPro spreadsheets, 305–306
Quick & Reilly, 322–323
Quicken, 331–333, 338
QuickWay, 322–323
Quote Manager, 178
QuoteCom, 172–173
Quotes, cost comparison for, 179–180
QuoTrek, 280–281

Radio for investors, 346–347
Recurrence IV, 305
References:
   computer-related investing, 39, 313
   for cyberspace investing, 39–40
   glossaries of investment terms, 370–373
   marketing on the Internet, 365
Research:
   investment, 189–218
   tools, 106–119
Resources:
   BBSs, 348–356
   for books, catalogs, periodicals, software, 373
   for computerized investing, 39, 313
   directories for individual investors, 313
   games/simulations for investors, 359–363
   glossaries of investment terms, 370–373
   marketing in cyberspace, 363–366
   psychology of investing, 357–359
   TV and radio, 339–348
Reuters, 17–19
   bond reports, 246
   commodities, 258
   and data delivery, 278–279
   Money Network, 230–232
   mutual fund reports, 229–232
   newsstands, 126–127
   newswire services, 100
Rich Financial Group, 56, 161
RMN, 230–232
   (*See also* Reuters)
Road Map to the World Wide Web, 42
Roundtables, 147–155
Rukeyser, Louis, 142

S&P (*see* Standard & Poor's)
S&P ComStock, 279–280
S&P's MarketScope, 104
San Jose Mercury News, 77–78
Scams on the Internet, 366–370

Schwab, 318–321
Schwager, Jack, 250
Search tools, 106–119
SEC:
    and EDGAR, 213–216
    and fraud online, 369
    news and federal filings, 98
Securities, alternative investment, 219–269
    commodity futures, options, precious metals,
        248–269
    fixed-income, 238–248
    mutual funds, 219–238
Securities exchanges, 157–168
    top 10 global, 250
Security and the Internet, 366–370
SEI, 144–145
Selling in cyberspace, 363–366
SIC classification, 213
Signal for Windows, 280–281
Silicon Valley, 77–78
Simply Money, 332–333
Simulations for investors, 359–363
Software:
    for cyberspace investing, 30–40
    data delivery systems, 276–291
    developers, 310–313
    investment, 271–313
    new technologies, 310–312
    overview, 272–276
    for portfolio management, 330–338
    providers' phone numbers list, 337
    specialty systems for traders, 303–305
    for technical analysis and trading, 291–313
    total-service packages, 271–276
Spiders, 119
Spreadsheet software, 305–310
Standard & Poor's, 205
    and data delivery, 279–280
Stanford University, 44, 46
Starter kit for cyberspace investing, 27–40
STAT-USA, 194–195, 356
Statistical Abstract of the United States, 189
    and Hoover's Reports, 202
Statistics:
    government, 189–198
    industry sector, 198–212
Stern School (*see* EDGAR project; New York
    University)
Stock Hunter, 183–184
Stock market data, 168–187
Stock market searches, 117–119

StockNet, 360–362
StockQuoter, 284
StreetSmart, 318–320
SuperCharts, 298–300
Superpowers of cyberspace investing, 1–40

Technical analysis software, 291–313
Technical Analysis of Stocks & Commodities,
    Annual Bonus Issue, 39
TechServe, 335–336
TeleChart 2000, 287–288
Telecommunications companies in
    cyberspace, 11
Telemet America, 285–286
Telescan, 293–295
Telescan's ProSearch, 117–119
Television for investors, 339–348
Theft on the Internet, 366–370
Time Warner's Pathfinder, 122–124
TimesLink, 76–77
Tobias, Randall, 377
Top Advisors' Corner, 135–137
Tradeline, 15
Tradeline Electronic Stock Guide, 284–285
Trader's Catalog & Resource Guide, 39
    directory of resources, 57
    glossary of investment terminology, 370
    Website, 59
TradeStation, 298
Traditional institutions versus discount brokers,
    375–377
Transactions on the Internet, 366–370
Treasury issues, 238–248
TV in cyberspace, 339–348

United Press International (UPI) newswires, 95–96
University of Michigan, 49
    Economics Bulletin Board, 191–193
University of Texas and FINWeb, 46–48
University of Virginia, 49
University-based Websites, 42–51
URL addresses:
    Aufhauser bond directory, 248
    ClariNet, 210
    free news services, 94
    for government statistics, 198
    Institute for Econometric Research, 234
    for newsletter information, 139
U.S. Census Bureau, 189
Usenet newsgroups, 148–149
    for commodities and futures, 256–257

Value Line, 204
Vanguard, 227–228
  Mutual Fund Campus, 240–241
Venture capital in cyberspace, 364

Wall Street Analyst, 300
Wall Street Directory, 57, 59
Wall Street Edge, 134–135
Wall Street Journal's Personal Journal, 14–15, 71–74
Wall-Street-News, 58–61
  and forecasting, 143
Wall Street & Technology's Buyer's Guide, 39
WCIU-TV, 343
WealthBuilder, 231–232
  portfolio management software, 333–335
WealthWEB, 325–327
Weather reports online, 256
Web browsers (*see* Browsers)
WebCrawler, 112–113

Webmaster, Innovation Information, 56–57
Windows on WallStreet, 301–302
Wire services (*see* Newswire services)
Worden Brothers, 287–288
World Bank, 198
World Wide Web:
  and bond market, 243–246
  for commodities, futures, options, 251–258
World Wide Web Worm, 115
WOW (*see* Windows on WallStreet)

Yahoo, 42–45
  Newsroom, 89–90
Yang, Jerry, and Yahoo, 44–46
Yellow pages, defined, 42
  (*See also* Meta-lists)

Zacks industry classifications, 226
Zines, 119–133